973   History

The Colonial Spirit of 1776

DATE DUE

DEMCO

JOYCE
SPIKE
LOVE & BEST WISHES
ADRIENNE - Elway
4 - 15 - 80

FROM A WATERCOLOR PAINTING BY KAY SMITH

*The Old State House in Boston, Massachusetts is one of the most historic buildings
in America. It dates back to 1713 and survived a disastrous fire in about 1753,
which gutted the interior but left the walls intact. In this building and its square,
the drama of American history unfolded as the years passed. The city grew; the colony
became embroiled in war and, ultimately, a part of the United States of America.
Here, in the open square, stood a cage for the display of those who had dared to violate
the Sabbath. Here were the stocks, the pillory, and the whipping post—all parts of
seventeenth and eighteenth century life. The Boston Massacre occurred in this square
on March 5, 1770.*

FROM A WATERCOLOR PAINTING BY KAY SMITH

*One of the finest examples of Georgian architecture in America, the Miles Brewton House
in Charleston, South Carolina, was built in 1769 by Ezra White, an English architect and builder,
for Miles Brewton, a wealthy Charleston businessman. It was selected as headquarters by
British military leaders Sir Henry Clinton and Lords Rawdon and Cornwallis during the
British occupation of Charleston in the Revolutionary War. In the Civil War it was occupied
by Union Generals Hatch and Meade. During the British occupation one of the officers carved
a profile of the head of his commanding officer, Sir Henry Clinton, on one of the marble mantels,
as well as the outline of a full rigged ship, probably using a diamond ring, though some say
it was done with the point of a bayonet. These romantic markings are still visible. There are
extensive grounds and outbuildings in addition to the impressive main structure.*

The People of the Revolution

THE COLONIAL SPIRIT OF '76

—Sketch by Kay Smith

End sheet art of Monticello, Thomas Jefferson's beloved plantation home.
—Watercolor painting by Kay Smith

Monticello, near Charlottesville, Virginia, is more peculiarly the achievement of the brain and hand of one man than any home ever built. As a young man, Thomas Jefferson selected the site for his dream home on the summit of land he had inherited, 867 feet above sea level. He called it Monticello, Italian for "little mountain." He was architect and builder of this masterpiece which was under construction for forty years between 1768 and 1809. The bricks were made and the timber hewn on the property. Even the nails and hardware were made on the site under his direction. He once wrote, "All my wishes end where I hope my days end, at Monticello." He brought his wife here after their marriage January 1, 1772, and she lived only ten years, bearing him six children in that time, only two of whom survived childhood. Jefferson passed away here on July 4, 1826, fifty years after the Declaration of Independence. He and his family are buried on the property in the family lot.

George Washington's study in the Ford Mansion at Morristown, New Jersey —From a wash sketch by Kay Smith
(A watercolor painting of the exterior of this headquarters appears opposite page 160)

The People of the Revolution

THE COLONIAL SPIRIT OF '76

The Lives of Members
of the Continental Congresses
and Other Prominent Men and Women
of the Period

by
DAVID C. WHITNEY

Featuring water-color paintings and sketches by
KAY SMITH

EDITED BY THOMAS C. JONES

Assistant to the editor
HARRIET B. HELMER

J. G. Ferguson Publishing Company / Chicago

BOUND IN HANDCRAFTED MISSION LEATHER BY BROWN & BIGELOW, ST. PAUL, MINNESOTA

INTRODUCTION & ACKNOWLEDGMENTS

As the Bicentennial anniversary of the American Revolution approaches, the words and actions of a few of the dominant figures of that period will be reviewed and repeated many times, but the deeds of lesser known heroes and heroines will continue to be largely ignored. It is to the memory of many of these forgotten leaders and legends that this book is dedicated.

The impression generally prevails that the Bicentennial refers to that glorious occasion of July 4, 1776, the official signing of the Declaration of Independence. Yet in truth the whole period from 1774 to 1789 marked events that deserve to be celebrated as the 200th anniversary of each arrives on the calendar.

In May 1774, Paul Revere of Boston arrived in Philadelphia with the general idea that a convention of the colonies be called. In this manner the impetus for a Continental Congress began, resulting in the first Congress, which met in Carpenters' Hall, Philadelphia, beginning September 5, 1774. The Royalists warned the Carpenters' Company that their hall might be confiscated and that "their necks might be inconveniently lengthened." The Carpenters patriotically voted to allow the meeting of the delegates despite the threats.

"Such an assembly as never before came together"

At the first meeting, the members, "conscious of the impending perils of the movement, resolved that all their deliberations should be kept inviolably secret." John Adams described the delegates in these words:

It is such an assembly as never before came together on a sudden, in any part of the world; here are fortunes, ability, learning, eloquence, acuteness equal to any I ever met with in my life. Here is a diversity of religions, impossible to unite on one line of conduct.

The momentum generated by this first Continental Congress continued through the Declaration of Independence and the prosecution of the war.

The complete listing of the rosters of the Continental Congress is unique among books dealing with the colonial period. More unusual, yet, are the biographies of these remarkable men and women who were risking their fortunes and the "inconvenience of having their necks lengthened."

David Whitney has written essays about customs in the colonies without attempting to explore in depth the life style at all levels of the social strata. Indeed, much of what seems now a romantic way of life in a simple manner was in fact struggle for existence, with very few frills. The ingenuity that it took to carve out a home and provide for a family was certainly much greater then than now. Yet, the lives of the leaders of the period reflect great activity, a deep sense of responsibility, a strong desire for personal accomplishment.

All of the color illustrations in this volume are reproductions of watercolor paintings and sketches by Kay Smith, the talented and respected Chicago artist who also illustrated *The Pictorial History of the American Revolution* by Rupert Furneaux. Each of the subjects was painted at the scene, which gives an authenticity and fidelity that can be achieved only by direct interpretation. The use of watercolor as a medium imparts a liveliness and style that project the viewer to the period and mood of the subject in a manner that cannot be accomplished with even the finest, most imaginative photography. The black and white sketches and washes further add to the interpretation of the colonial period in a manner not possible with even the most vivid description.

Five hundred separate biographies

The five hundred separate biographies tell in simple terms the brief stories of the highlights of the successes and failures of Americans who, for one reason or another, were prominent in the period of the Revolution. It is interesting to note that the average life span of these people comes to sixty-five years, which is somewhat surprising considering the medical advances made since then, which have increased the average span by only five years.

There are many unusual facets of information about these people that are revealed in the brief sketches offered by David Whitney. Abigail Adams was the only woman to have been a wife of a President and the mother of a President. Ethan Allen stormed the gate at Fort Ticonderoga demanding that it surrender "in the name of the great Jehovah and the Continental Congress."

William Campbell led the militia in the attack on King's Mountain with the words "Shout like hell and fight like devils." Charles Carroll of Carrollton, the only Roman Catholic signer, was the last surviving signer of the Declaration of Independence, dying at the age of ninety-five, November 14, 1832. Jonathan Dayton was the youngest signer of the Constitution at the age of twenty-six. Benjamin Franklin was the oldest signer of the Constitution at the age of eighty-one.

Mordecai Gist was so imbued with the spirit of the time that he named his sons Independence and States Rights. Benjamin

(Pictured at left) The left half of the bronze door on the House of Representatives wing of the United States Capitol depicting events in the formation of the nation. The right half of the doorway is shown on page 8.

Harrison, a signer of the Declaration of Independence, was the father of President William Henry Harrison and the great-grandfather of President Benjamin Harrison. John Paul Jones, commanding the sloop *Ranger*, received from the French the first salute ever given to the American flag by a foreign warship. Pierre L'Enfant, designer of the District of Columbia, died in poverty while petitioning Congress to pay him his commission for his city plan.

James Madison was the last surviving signer of the Constitution, passing away June 28, 1836. Daniel Morgan, a cousin of Daniel Boone, survived 500 lashes across his back and an Indian bullet that knocked out his teeth, and was awarded one of the eight medals of honor. He accumulated one quarter million acres of land in West Virginia where he died in 1802. At the Constitutional Convention, James Wilson was so concerned that the basic power of the government should rest with the people that he asked the questions: "Can we forget for whom we are forming a government? Is it for *men* or for the imaginary beings called *States*?"

       *   *   *

As the years of the Bicentennial period roll by, it is worthy of noting a chronology of some of the important events of the Revolutionary period.

Sept. 5, 1774	Meeting of the first Continental Congress
April 19, 1775	The Battles of Lexington and Concord
May 10, 1775	Fort Ticonderoga was captured by Ethan Allen and company
June 15, 1775	George Washington was elected Commander in Chief
June 17, 1775	The Battle of Bunker Hill
July 4, 1776	The Declaration of Independence, Philadelphia
Sept. 22, 1776	Nathan Hale executed as a spy at New York
Oct. 28, 1776	The Battle of White Plains, New York
Dec. 26, 1776	The Battle of Trenton
Jan. 3, 1777	The Battle of Princeton
July 7, 1777	The Battle of Hubbardton, Vermont
Aug. 16, 1777	The Battle of Bennington
Sept. 11, 1777	The Battle of Brandywine
Oct. 7-17, 1777	The Battle of Saratoga—Burgoyne surrendered
Nov. 16-20, 1777	British captured Forts Mifflin and Mercer
Dec. 18, 1777	The American Army went to Valley Forge for the winter
June 18, 1778	The American army broke camp at Valley Forge
June 28, 1778	The Battle of Monmouth
July 4, 1778	George Rogers Clark captured Kaskaskia
Aug. 29-31, 1778	The Battle of Rhode Island
January, 1779	George Rogers Clark captured Vincennes
Mar. 3, 1779	Battle of Briar Creek, Georgia
July 16, 1779	The Battle of Stony Point
Sept. 23-Oct. 9, 1779	The Siege of Savannah
December 1779	The army wintered at Morristown, New Jersey
April 10-May 12, 1780	The Siege of Charleston, South Carolina

Any work of this size involves teamwork, substantial investment ot time, money, and talent, and a sincere desire to produce a volume worthy of the important subject — the 200th anniversary of the founding of the United States of America.

We, are indeed grateful for a magnificent team effort — first of all, to David C. Whitney, the author, who produced a voluminous and fascinating manuscript in time to meet the publisher's commitments.

Certainly, Kay Smith, whose brilliant paintings of historic locations make the story of the colonial period more vivid and entertaining, deserves the high critical approval that has greeted her work wherever shown. The reproductions of her paintings and her numerous black and white sketches help to capture the colonial spirit.

Harriet Helmer has devotedly handled all phases of editorial and production assistance under great pressure. As for the actual design and production, Al Josephson of Photopress has been dedicated and brilliant. Others at Photopress Inc. — including Don Vendl, John Lauer and Edward Chalifoux, Jr. — have made the project run smoothly, with quality, on schedule. We are grateful to Jim Fox and the American Can Company — Composition Division for their efficient and excellent service and to Jim Stewart and the Engdahl Company for their patient and enthusiastic cooperation.

The Print and Photo Division of the Library of Congress rendered splendid service and assistance throughout this extensive production program and we acknowledge with gratitude the valued suggestions of the many individuals working in that section.

The most important ingredient in any creative work is the incentive, and this was provided by the management of Brown & Bigelow, St. Paul, Minnesota, for whom the first limited number of copies of this book were produced.

Thomas C. Jones, Editor

CONTENTS

Tea chest

A list of some of the more prominent men and women of the Colonial Period whose biographies are included along with almost four hundred other important but less well known participants in that important period in American history —alphabetically arranged by their surnames.

PAINTINGS AND SKETCHES IN COLOR

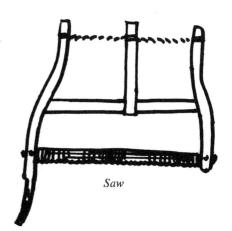

Saw

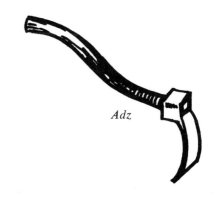

Adz

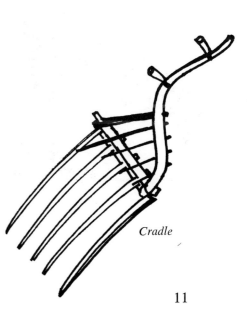

Cradle

(continued)

Well sweep

—From an engraving by A.H. Ritchie

"The Colonial Spirit of '76"

Patrick Henry addressing the House of Burgesses in Williamsburg, Virginia, nine days after he had taken his seat for the first time, when he concluded his speech supporting resolutions condemning the Stamp Act with the words, "If this be treason, make the most of it."

—From an engraving by Alf Jones

14 AMERICAN REVOLUTION

WHAT WAS THE AMERICAN REVOLUTION?

EDITOR'S NOTE: *In 1816 Hezekiah Niles of Baltimore, editor and publisher of a magazine, the Weekly Register, printed an appeal to participants in the American Revolution and their descendants to send him reminiscences and documents. Expressing the hope that readers would catch a "spark from the altar of '76," Niles published the letters and documents that he received in his magazine and then gathered many of them in a book called "Principles and Acts of the Revolution" that he published in 1822. Among the treasure trove of materials that Niles received was the following letter from former President John Adams written to Niles in 1818, expressing in fiery terms his own personal recollections and sentiments concerning the Revolution. Subheads have been added for the convenience of the reader.*

The American Revolution was not a common Event. Its Effects and Consequences have already been Awful over a great Part of the Globe. And when and where are they to cease?

But what do We mean by the American Revolution? Do we mean the American War? The Revolution was effected before the War commenced. The Revolution was in the Minds and Hearts of the People. A Change in their Religious Sentiments of their Duties and Obligations. While the King and all in Authority under him were believed to govern, in justice and Mercy according to the Laws and Constitutions derived to them from the God of Nature and transmitted to them by their Ancestors, they thought themselves bound to pray for the King and Queen and all the Royal Family, and all the Authority under them, as Ministers ordained of God for their good. But when they saw those Powers renouncing all the Principles of Authority, and bent upon the destruction of all the Securities of their Lives, Liberties and Properties, they thought it their Duty to pray for the Continental Congress and all the thirteen State Congresses, &c.

There might be, and there were, others who thought less about Religion and Conscience, but had certain habitual Sentiments of Allegiance and Loyalty derived from the Education; but believing Allegiance and Protection to be reciprocal, when Protection was withdrawn, they thought Allegiance was dissolved.

Another Alteration was common to all. The People of America had been educated in an habitual Affection for Eng-

James Otis, the firebrand from Massachusetts, protesting the Writs of Assistance. —From a painting by S.W. Wood

land as their Mother Country; and while they thought her a kind and tender Parent (erroneously enough, however, for she never was such a Mother,) no Affection could be more sincere. But when they found her a cruel Beldam, willing, like Lady Macbeth, to "dash their Brains out," it is no Wonder if their filial Affections ceased and were changed into Indignation and horror.

This radical Change in the Principles, Opinions, Sentiments and Affections of the People was the real American Revolution.

How thirteen clocks were made to strike together

By what means, this great and important Alteration in the religious, moral, political and social Character of the People of thirteen Colonies, all distinct, unconnected and independent of each other, was begun, pursued and accomplished, it is surely interesting to Humanity to investigate, and perpetuate to Posterity.

To this End it is greatly to be desired that Young Gentlemen of Letters in all the States, especially in the thirteen Original States, would undertake the laborious, but certainly interesting and amusing Task of searching and collecting all the

The Old South Meeting House—also known as the Old South Church where Benjamin Franklin was baptized in 1706—was the largest meeting hall in Boston. Many protest meetings were held here, including the one immediately preceding the Boston Tea Party. During the Siege of Boston this became a riding school for British cavalry. The carved pews were removed, and one is known to have been made into a hog sty.

This New England colonial farm was reconstructed at Sturbridge Village in Massachusetts, where it and other typical features of colonial life can be observed by the public. It is an authentic working farm, with the animals, tools, and utensils that were a part of daily life in the colonies two hundred years ago. This scene, painted by Kay Smith at the peak of the glorious autumn season, captures the vivid coloring and natural harmony of nature on the farm that are a part of our heritage. With the harvest at its peak, the New England farm family had work for everyone from dawn until dusk. It was a healthful, satisfying, independent life that developed sturdy, responsible, patriotic citizens.

Records, Pamphlets, Newspapers and even hand-Bills, which in any Way contributed to change the Temper and Views of The People and compose them into an independent Nation.

The Colonies had grown up under Constitutions of Government so different, there was so great a Variety of Religions, they were composed of so many Nations, their Customs, Manners and Habits had so little resemblance, and their Intercourse had been so rare and their Knowledge of each other so imperfect, that to unite them in the same Principles in Theory and the same System of Action was certainly a very difficult Enterprize. The compleat accomplishment of it, in so short a time and by such simple means, was perhaps a singular Example in the History of Mankind. Thirteen Clocks were made to strike together; a perfection of Mechanism which no Artist had ever before effected.

In this Research, the Glorioroles of Individual Gentlemen and of separate States is of little Consequence. The *Means and the Measures* are the proper Objects of Investigation. These may be of Use to Posterity, not only in this Nation, but in South America, and all other Countries. They may teach Mankind that Revolutions are no Trifles; that they ought never to be undertaken rashly; nor without deliberate Consideration and sober Reflection; nor without a solid, immutable, eternal foundation of Justice and Humanity; nor without a People possessed of Intelligence, Fortitude and Integrity sufficient to carry them with Steadiness, Patience, and Perseverance, through all the Vicissitudes of fortune, the fiery Tryals and melancholy Disasters they may have to encounter.

The importance of principles and feelings

The Town of Boston early instituted an annual Oration on the fourth of July, in commemoration of the Principles and Feelings which contributed to produce the Revolution. Many of those Orations I have heard, and all that I could obtain I have read. Much Ingenuity and Eloquence appears upon every Subject, except those Principles and Feelings. That of my honest and amiable Neighbour, Josiah Quincy, appeared to me the most directly to the purpose of the Institution. Those Principles and Feelings ought to be traced back for Two hundred Years, and sought in the history of the Country from the first Plantations in America. Nor should the Principles and Feelings of the English and Scotch towards the Colonies, through that whole Period ever be forgotten. The perpetual discordance between British Principles and Feelings and those of America, the next Year after the Suppression of the French Power in America, came to a Crisis and produced an Explosion.

The period of the great awakening

It was not till after the Annihilation of the French Dominion in America that any British Ministry had dared to gratify their own Wishes, and the desire of the Nation, by projecting a formal Plan for raising a national Revenue from America by Parliamentary Taxation. The first great Manifestation of this design was by the Order to carry into strict Execution those Acts of Parliament which were well known by the Appellation of the Acts of Trade, which had lain a dead Letter, unexecuted for half a Century, and some of them I believe for nearly a whole one.

This produced, in 1760 and 1761, *An Awakening and a Revival* of American Principles and Feelings, with an Enthusiasm which went on increasing till in 1775 it burst out in open Violence, Hostility and Fury.

The Characters, the most conspicuous, the most ardent and influential, in this Revival, from 1760 to 1766, were—First and Foremost, before all, and above all, *James Otis;* next to him was *Oxenbridge Thatcher;* next to him *Samuel Adams;* next to him *John Hancock;* then Dr. Mayhew, then Dr. Cooper and his Brother. Of Mr. Hancock's Life, Character, generous Nature, great disinterested Sacrifices, and important Services, if I had forces, I should be glad to write a Volume. But this I hope will be done by some younger and abler hand. . . .

Tarring and feathering a British tax collector in Boston in January 1774. —From an engraving

LIFE IN THE AMERICAN COLONIES

EDITOR'S NOTE: *Describing the conditions of government and ways of life in the American colonies that led almost inevitably to the American Revolution, this chapter provides a backdrop for clearer understanding of the lives of the American patriots that follow. The chapter is adapted from Woodrow Wilson's five-volume "The History of the American People," which was published in 1901, before he had any other claim to fame than as a historian.*

The statesmen of both France and England accepted the same theory about the use colonies should be put to—the doctrine and practice everywhere accepted in their day. Colonies were to be used to enrich the countries which possessed them. They should send their characteristic native products to the country which had established them, and for the most part to her alone, and should take her manufactures in exchange; trade nowhere else to her disadvantage; and do and make nothing which could bring them into competition with her merchants and manufacturers. It was provoking enough to the English colonists in America to have, in many a petty matter, to evade the exacting Navigation Acts, which restricted their trade and obliged them to buy manufactured goods at prices fixed by the English merchants.

The colonists were both cramped and irritated that they were forbidden to manufacture now this and now that, though the material lay at their very doors, because English manufacturers wished their competition shut out. Restriction was added to restriction. In 1706, naval stores and rice, which the Carolinas were learning to produce to their increasing profit, were added to the list of products which must be sent to England only; and in 1722 copper and furs. In 1732 the manufacture of beaver hats was forbidden, and in 1750 the maintenance of iron furnaces or slit mills. But there was always an effort made at reciprocal advantage. Though the colonies were forbidden to manufacture their iron ores, their bar and pig iron was admitted into England free of duty, and Swedish iron, which might have undersold it, was held off by a heavy tariff, to the manifest advantage of Maryland and Virginia. Though the rice of the Carolinas for a time got admission to market only through the English middlemen, their naval stores were exported under a heavy bounty; and in 1730, when the restriction laid on the rice trade pinched too shrewdly, it was re-

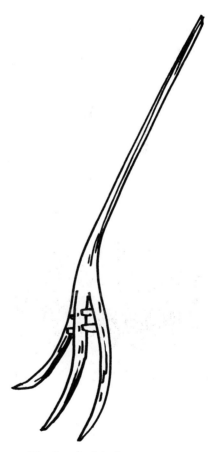

Wooden pitch fork

moved with regard to Portugal, the chief European market open to it. Parliament had generally an eye to building up the trade of the colonies as well as to controlling it.

Colonists learned to wink at British restrictions

The home government, moreover, though it diligently imposed restrictions, was by no means as diligent in enforcing them. An ill-advised statute of 1733 laid prohibitory duties on the importation of sugar, molasses, and rum out of the French West Indies, in the hope that the sales of sugar and molasses in the islands owned by England might be increased. To enforce the act would have been to hazard the utter commercial ruin of New England. Out of the cheap molasses of the French islands she made the rum which was a chief source of her wealth—the rum with which she bought slaves for Maryland, Virginia, and the Carolinas, and paid her balances to the English merchants. But no serious attempt was made to enforce it. Customs officers and merchants agreed in ignoring it, and officers of the crown shut their eyes to the trade which it forbade. Smuggling upon that long coast was a simple matter, and even at the chief ports only a little circumspection was needed about cargoes out of the Indies.

Moreover, the men who governed in England contented themselves with general restrictions and did not go on to manage the very lives of the colonists in the colonies themselves. That was what the French did. They built their colonies up by royal order; sent emigrants out as they sent troops, at the King's expense and by the King's direction; could get only men to go, for the most part, and therefore sent very few women or families. For the English there was nothing of the sort, after the first. Rich men or great mercantile companies might help emigrants with money or supplies or free gifts of land in order to fill up the colonies which the crown had given them the right to establish and govern; but only those went out who volunteered. Emigrants went, moreover, in families, after the first years were passed and the colonies fairly started, if not at the very outset of the enterprise—in associated groups, congregations, and small volunteer communities. When they reached the appointed place of settlement they were left to shift for themselves, as they had expected, exactly as they would have been at home; and they insisted upon having the same rights and freedom they would have had there. They were making homes, without assistance or favor, and for their own use and benefit.

Colonial legislatures were free of controls

Bake kettle

It was inevitable in the circumstances that their colonial governments should be like themselves, homemade and free from control in the management of what chiefly concerned their own lives. They were just as hard to supervise and regulate when the settlements were small as when they grew large

EDMUND BURKE Esq.

Edmund Burke, member of the House of Commons, who opposed the Stamp Act and other severe measures toward America in favor of a more moderate course.

British ships at anchor were sometimes used as prisons to hold colonials captured in combat.

—From a wood engraving by P. Meeder

22   LIFE IN THE COLONIES

and populous—a little harder, indeed, because the colonists were the more anxious then about how the new life they were beginning was to go, and the less sure of their power or influence to resist the efforts of the crown to manage and interfere with them. By the time the French war came there was no mistaking the fact that the English colonies had grown to miniature states, proud, hard-fibred, independent in temper, practised in affairs. They had, as Edmund Burke said, "formed within themselves, either by royal instruction or royal charter, assemblies so exceedingly resembling a parliament, in all their forms, functions, and powers, that it was impossible they should not imbibe some opinion of a similar authority." At first, no doubt, their assemblies had been intended to be little more than the managing bodies of corporations. "But nothing in progression can rest on its original plan. We may as well think of rocking a grown man in the cradle of an infant. Therefore, as the colonies prospered and increased to a numerous and mighty people, spreading over a very great tract of the globe, it was natural that they should attribute to assemblies so respectable in their formal constitution some part of the dignity of the great nations which they represented." They "made acts of all sorts and in all cases whatsoever. They levied money upon regular grants to the crown, following all the rules and principles of a parliament, to which they approached every day more and more nearly." And Burke saw how inevitable, as well as how natural, the whole growth had been. "Things could not be otherwise," he said; "English colonies must be had on these terms, or not had at all."

Making a birch broom.
—Sketch by Kay Smith

Colonies controlled their own purse strings

They had used their governments for their own purposes, and rather like independent states than like dependent communities. In every colony the chief point of conflict between governor and assembly, whether in the proprietary or in the crown colonies, had always been connected with the subject of salaries. Again and again, governors had been instructed to insist upon an adequate income, charged permanently upon some regular source of public revenue; but again and again, as often as made, their demand had been refused. They could get only annual grants, which kept all officers of the crown dependent upon the people's assemblies for maintenance while in office. There had long been signs that the ministers of the King and the proprietors at home were tired of the contest, and meant, for the mere sake of peace, to let the colonial assemblies alone, to rule, as Parliament ruled, by keeping control of the moneys spent upon their own governments.

New England's daring seamen and developing industry

There was, too, more and more money in the colonies as the years went by. New England, where, except in the rich valley of the Connecticut, the soil yielded little beyond the bare nec-

essaries of life, led the rest of the colonies in the variety of her industries. Though parliamentary statutes forbade the making of woollen goods or hats or steel for export, the colonists were free to make anything they might need for use or sale within a single colony or in their own homes; and the thrifty New England farmers and villagers made most of their own furniture, tools, and household utensils, while their women or the village weavers wove the linen and woollen stuffs of which their clothes were made. They lived upon their own resources as no other colonists did. And their trade kept six hundred vessels busy plying to and fro, to English and foreign ports. Almost every sea-coast hamlet was a port and maintained its little fleet. A thousand vessels, big and little, went every year to the fisheries, or up and down the coasts carrying the trade between colony and colony. A great many of these vessels the colonists had built themselves, out of the splendid timber

View of Boston, Massachusetts from the road leading to Dorchester, sketched about 1776.

which stood almost everywhere at hand in their forests; and everyone knew, who knew anything at all about New England, that her seamen were as daring, shrewd, and hardy as those bred in past generations in the Devonshire ports of old England. Their boats flocked by the hundreds every year to the misty, perilous banks of Newfoundland, where the cod were to be caught. They beat up and down the long seas in search of the whale all the way from "the frozen recesses of Hudson's Bay and Davis's Straits" to the coasts of Africa and Brazil, far in the south. "Neither the perseverance of Holland, nor the activity of France, nor the dexterous and firm sagacity of English enterprise," exclaimed Burke, "ever carried this most perilous mode of hardy industry to the extent to which it has been pushed by this recent people—a people who are still, as it were, but in the gristle, and not yet hardened into the bone of manhood."

Sauce pan

Dining at a colonial inn was a festive occasion, and indeed is today at any one of the restored inns at Williamsburg, Virginia.
—Sketch by Kay Smith

Massachusetts had been known, while peace held and men breathed freely, between Queen Anne's and King George's wars, to complete one hundred and fifty ships in a single year, every town upon the coast and even little villages far within the rivers launching vessels from busy shipyards. Ship building became New England's chief industry; and in 1724 the master builders of the Thames prayed Parliament for protection against the competition of the colonies. The annual catch of whale and cod by the New Englanders was worth two hundred and fifty thousand pounds sterling; and, besides fish and fish-oil, they even shipped their fine timber, and not a little hay and grain, across the sea or to the other colonies. Everywhere in America the forests yielded splendid timber, as his Majesty's ministers well knew; for they sent into the northern forests of pine and had the tallest, straightest trees there marked with the royal arms, as a notice that they were reserved to be used as masts for his Majesty's warships—as if the King had a right to take what he would.

The colonies grew richer and richer

"New England improved much faster than Virginia," Colonel William Byrd admitted; and yet Virginia had her own rich trade, of which tobacco was the chief staple; and all the colonies busied themselves as they could, and visibly grew richer year by year. The middle colonies were scarcely less industrious than those of the bleaker north, and prospered even more readily with their kindlier climate and their richer soil. Pennsylvania, with her two hundred and twenty thousand colonists, with her thrifty mixture of Germans, Quakers, Scots, and Scots-Irishmen, needed a fleet of four hundred sail to carry each season's spare produce from the docks at Philadelphia; and New York had her separate fleet of close upon two hundred sail.

England depended upon the colonies for much of the naval stores, of the potash, and of the pearlash which she needed every year. Mines of iron and of copper had been opened both in the middle colonies and in the south. The colonists made their own brick for building, and their own paper and glass, as well as their own coarse stuffs for clothing, and many of their own hats of beaverskin. Substantial houses and fine, sightly streets sprang up in the towns which stood at the seaports; and in the country spacious country seats, solidly built, roomy, full of the simpler comforts of gentlefolk. The ships which took hides and fish and provisions to the West Indies brought sugar and molasses and wine and many a delicacy back upon their return, and the colonists ate and drank and bore themselves like other well-to-do citizens the world over. They were eager always to know what the London fashions were; there was as much etiquette to be observed upon quiet plantations in Virginia as in English drawing rooms. It was, indeed, touched with a certain beauty of its own, because of the pro-

Minstrel at Christmastime at Campbell's Tavern at Williamsburg, Virginia.
—Sketch by Kay Smith

27

vincial simplicity and frank neighborliness which went along with it; but it was grave and punctilious, and intended to be like London manners. There was as much formality and gaiety "in the season" at Williamsburg, Virginia's village capital, as in Philadelphia, the biggest, wealthiest, most stately town in the colonies.

The colonies learned to become self-sufficient

There were many ways in which the colonies finished and filled out their lives which showed that they regarded themselves as, in a sense, independent communities and meant to provide for themselves everything they needed for their life alone on a separate continent. They had no thought of actually breaking away from their allegiance to the home government over sea; but no man could possibly overlook the three thousand miles of water that stretched between England and America. At that immense distance they were obliged in great measure to look out for themselves and contrive their own ways of sustenance and development, and their own way of culture.

Before the French war began, two more colleges, in addition to Harvard in Massachusetts and William and Mary in Virginia, had been established to provide the higher sort of training for youths who were to enter the learned professions. Besides Yale, the College of New Jersey had been founded. At first set up in 1746 as a collegiate school, at Elizabethtown, it was in 1756 given a permanent home and built up into a notable training place for youth at Princeton. In 1754, the year George Washington attacked the French in the western forests, King's College (later Columbia University) was added to the growing list, in New York, by royal charter. Ten years later (1764), upon the very morrow of the signing of peace in the French and Indian War, certain public-spirited men of the Baptist communion followed suit in Rhode Island by founding the school which was afterwards to be called Brown University. Here were six colleges for this new English nation at the west of the Atlantic. Many wealthy colonists, particularly in the far south, continued to send their sons to the old country to take their learning from the immemorial sources at Oxford and Cambridge; but more and more the colonies provided learning for themselves.

A growing feeling of common interests

Their growing and expanding life, moreover, developed in them the sense of neighborhood to one another, the consciousness of common interests, and the feeling that they ought in many things to cooperate. In 1754, while the first sharp note of war was ringing from the Alleghenies, a conference with the Six Nations of Indians was held at Albany, which, besides dealing with the redmen, and binding them once more to be friends and allies of the English against the French, consid-

A hand carved chest used for storing valuable papers and the family Bible.

The alcove bed was quite characteristic of the colonial homes even in such large and impressive estates as Monticello.
—Sketch by Kay Smith

ered nothing less than a plan of union for the colonies. This was the fourth time that the representatives of several colonies at once had come together at Albany to confer with the Iroquois. The first conference had taken place there in 1689, the year King William's War began. Albany lay nearest the country of the Iroquois. It was necessary when war was afoot to make sure that the redskins should side with the English, and not with the French; and that was now for the fourth time, in 1754, more critically important than ever. The home government had directed that the conference be held, before they knew what George Washington had done. It was the ministers in London, too, who had directed that a plan of union be considered, in order that the colonies might act in concert in the coming struggle with the French, and if possible even under a single government. Seven colonies were represented at the conference. Twenty-five delegates were there to take part in the business; and there was no difficulty about securing their almost unanimous assent to a plan of union. They adopted the plan which Benjamin Franklin, one of Pennsylvania's delegates had drawn up as he made the long journey from Philadelphia.

The plan of union Franklin suggested at Albany was that the colonies should submit to have their common interests cared for by a congress of delegates chosen by their several assemblies, and a "president-general" appointed and paid by the crown; giving to the congress a considerable power of actual law-making and to the president-general the right to veto its acts, subject to the approval of the ministers at home. To all the delegates at Albany except those from Connecticut the plan seemed suitable and excellent; but the ministers at home rejected it because they thought it gave too much power to the proposed congress, and the colonial assemblies rejected it because they thought it gave too much power to the president-general. Franklin said that the fact that neither the assemblies nor the King's ministers liked the plan made him suspect that it must be, after all, an excellent halfway measure, the "true medium" between extremes, effecting a particularly fair and equal distribution of power.

Then the French and Indian War came and made many things plain. The colonies did not cooperate. They contributed troops, watched their own frontiers as they could against the redskins, and freely spent both blood and money in the great struggle; but when it was all over, and the French dominion swept from the continent, it was plain that it had not been the power of the colonies but the power of England and the genius of the great Pitt that had won in the critical contest. France could send few reinforcements to Canada because England's ships commanded the sea. The stout Canadians had had to stand out for themselves unaided, with such troops as were already in the colony. In 1759, the year Wolfe took Quebec, there were more soldiers in the English colonies threatening the St. Lawrence than there were men capable of bearing arms in all Canada—and quite half of them were regulars, not provincials.

Pitt saw to it that enough troops and supplies were sent to America to insure success, and that men capable of victory and of efficient management even in the forested wilderness were put in command of affairs in the field. He did not depend upon the colonies to do what he knew they had no plan or organization for doing, but set himself to redress the balance of power in Europe by decisive victories which should make England indisputable mistress of America. "No man ever entered Mr. Pitt's closet who did not find himself braver when he came out than when he went in," said a soldier who had held conference with him and served him; and it was his statesmanship and his use of English arms that had made England's dominion complete and England's colonies safe in America.

First Attempt to tax the colonies

English fleets and armies had not been sent to America, however, and equipped for warfare there, sustained in war

An early view of the north battery in Boston harbor.

The south battery of Boston harbor with the British flag showing prominently in the foreground.

season and out of it, without enormous expense; and that expense, which had set the colonies free to live without dread of danger or of confinement at any border, England had borne. Colonial governors, viewing affairs as representatives of the government at home, had again and again urged the ministers in London to tax the colonies, by act of Parliament, for means to pay for frontier forts, armies of defense, and all the business of imperial administration in America. But the ministers had hitherto known something of the temper of the colonists in such matters and had been too wise to attempt anything of the kind.

Now that the French were driven out, it was more useless than ever to argue the point. The chief and most obvious reason for feeling dependent upon the mother country was gone. Awe of the British was gone, too. The provincial levies raised in the colonies had fought alongside the King's troops in all

A cartoon of the day showing Bostonians in the act of tarring and feathering a tax collector

—From a lithograph by H.R. Robinson

the movements of the war, and had found themselves not a whit less undaunted under fire, not a whit less able to stand and fight, not a whit less needed in victory.

It was the worst possible time the home government could have chosen in which to change its policy of concession towards the colonies and begin to tax and govern them by act of

FROM A WATERCOLOR PAINTING BY KAY SMITH

*The Senate House at Kingston, New York, was built about 1676 by Colonel Wessel Ten Broeck,
who came to America from Westphalia. After the adoption of the first state constitution the first Senate
of New York met here in 1777 until the burning of Kingston by the British, October 16, 1777.*

This restored grist mill, oak dam, and stone manor house of Philipsburg Manor on the Pocantico River in North Tarrytown, New York, is an authentic re-creation of early Dutch-American life. It is a reflection of the early eighteenth century when the Hudson River Valley still carried the heavy influence of its Dutch heritage. This was originally the country home of a man who began as a carpenter and ended by owning a third of Westchester County. Frederick Philipse, who built this property, worked for Peter Stuyvesant and gradually acquired property and shipping interests. By 1664, when the British seized New Amsterdam, he was indeed a man of means. He swore allegiance to the British crown and kept buying land. Upon his death he had an estate that extended from the northern tip of Manhattan to the village of Croton-on-Hudson, one of the largest landholdings in the colonies. The estate, consisting of 200 square miles, over 90,000 acres with manor houses and productive land for foodstuffs, timber, quarried stone, and access to the Hudson River, was broken up after the American Revolution because the owner, Frederick Philipse III, supported the British. He died in Chester, England, on April 30, 1785. In the ensuing years the property was sold at auction and divided many times. In 1916 it was purchased by Elsie Janis, the "sweetheart of the A.E.F." in World War I. In 1937 a bank foreclosed on the property. Public spirited citizens with John D. Rockefeller, Jr., established the organization to save and restore Philipsburg Mill and Manor. Thus one can see today this charming bit of eighteenth century life in the midst of twentieth century suburbia.

FROM A WATERCOLOR PAINTING BY KAY SMITH

FROM A WATERCOLOR PAINTING BY KAY SMITH

*These sturdy stone houses on Huguenot Street in New Paltz, New York, are said to constitute
the oldest street in the United States with its original houses. The house on the right
was built in 1712 by Abraham Hasbrouck, a Dutch patentee landholder, once a soldier in
the British army, and a friend of early Governor Andros, the English administrator
of the colony. On the left is the Hugo Freer house, built in 1681 with the south portion
being added by Johannes Low in 1735.*

Parliament; and yet that was exactly what the ministers determined to do. In March, 1764, therefore, upon the introduction of the annual budget in Parliament, Prime Minister George Grenville introduced a bill, which was passed, laying fresh and more effective taxes on wines, sugar, and molasses imported into the colonies, tightening and extending the old Navigation Acts, and still further restraining manufactures. At the same time he announced that he would, the next year, propose a moderate direct tax upon the colonies in the form of an act requiring revenue stamps to be used on the principal sorts of documents employed in America in legal and mercantile business.

Grenville had no desire to irritate the Americans. He thought they might protest; he never dreamed they would disobey. He was, no doubt, surprised when he learned how hot their protests were; and when his Stamp Act the next year became law, their anger and flat defiance must have seemed to him mere wanton rebellion. He introduced the Stamp Act with his budget of 1765. The Commons gave only a single sitting to the discussion of its principles; passed it almost without opposition; and by March 22 it was law.

Like a spark dropped on tinder

The Stamp Act operated in America like a spark dropped on tinder. First dismay, then anger, then riot and open defiance showed what the colonists thought and meant to do. The act was not to go into operation until November 1, 1765; but long before the first of November it was evident that it would not go into effect at all. There was instant protest from the colonial assemblies as soon as it was known that the act was passed; and the assembly of Massachusetts proposed that a congress of delegates from the several colonies be held in October, before the act went into effect, to decide what should be done to serve their common interest in the critical matter.

The agitations and tumults of that eventful summer were not soon forgotten. In August, Boston witnessed an outbreak such as she had never witnessed before. Andrew Oliver, who had been appointed distributer of the stamps there, was burned in effigy; the house in which it was thought the stamps were to be stored was torn down; Oliver's residence was broken into and many of its furnishings were destroyed. He hastily resigned his obnoxious office. Mobs then plundered the house of the deputy registrar of the court of admiralty, destroying his private papers and records and files of the court—because the new acts of trade and taxation gave new powers to that court. The house of the comptroller of customs was sacked. Thomas Hutchinson, the lieutenant-governor of the colony, found himself obliged, on the night of the twenty-sixth, to flee for his life; and returned when order was restored to find his home stripped of everything it contained, including nine hundred pounds sterling in money, and manuscripts and

A tailor
—Sketch by Kay Smith

33

books which he had been thirty years collecting. Only the walls and floors of the house remained.

There was tumult everywhere, but in most places the mobs contented themselves with burning the stamp agents in effigy and frightening them into the instant relinquishment of their offices. Not until the autumn came, and the day for the application of the act, did they show a serious temper again. Then New York also saw a house sacked and its furnishings used to feed a bonfire. The people insisted upon having the stamps handed over to their own city officers; and when more came they seized and burned them. At Philadelphia many Quakers and Church of England men, and some Baptists, acted as if they would have obeyed the act; but the mobs saw to it that they should not have the chance. The stamp distributer was compelled to resign, and there was no one from whom stamps could be obtained. Stamp distributers who would not resign found it best to seek safety in flight. There was no one in all the colonies, north or south, who had authority to distribute the hated pieces of stamped paper which the ministers had expected would so conveniently yield them a modest revenue for their colonial expenses.

England's Parliament gives in

It was singular and significant how immediately and how easily the colonies drew together to meet the common danger and express a common purpose. Early in October, the congress which Massachusetts had asked for came together at New York, the delegates of nine colonies attending. It drew up and sent over sea a statement of the right of the colonies to tax and govern themselves—as loyal to the King, but not as subject to Parliament—which arrested the attention of the world. Grenville and his colleagues were just then, by a fortunate turn of politics at home, most opportunely obliged to resign, and gave place to the moderate Whigs who followed Lord Rockingham (July 1765), and who thought the protests of the colonies not unreasonable. On the eighteenth of March 1766, accordingly, the Stamp Act was repealed—within a year of its enactment. It was at the same time declared, however, by special declaratory act, that Parliament had sovereign right to tax the colonies, and legislate for them, if it pleased. It was out of grace and good policy, the ministers declared, that the tax was withdrawn: a concession, not of right, but of good feeling: and everybody knew that it was done as much because the London merchants were frightened by the resolution of the American merchants to take no cargoes under the tax as because the colonies had declined to submit. But the results were none the less salutary. The rejoicings in America were as boisterous and as universal as had been the tempest of resentment.

The colonists were accustomed to actual representation, had for a century or more been dealt with by means of it, and

Citizens of Williamsburg voice their grievances to the representatives of the crown.

were not willing now to reverse their history and become, instead of veritable states, merely detached and dependent pieces of England. This was the fire of principle which the Stamp Act kindled. And, once kindled, it burned with an increasing flame. Within ten years it had been blown to the full blaze of revolution.

We the Ladys
of Edenton do
hereby Solemnly
Engage not to Conform
to that Pernicious Custom
of Drinking Tea, or that we the
aforesaid Ladys will not promote ye wear
of any Manufacture from England
untill such time that all Acts
which tend to Enslave this our
Native Country shall be Repealed

The society of patriotic ladies at Edenton, North Carolina —From a mezzotint by Philip Dawe

TRAVEL AND COMMUNICATIONS BETWEEN THE COLONIES

Before and during the American Revolution travel and communications between the colonies was no faster than a horse. It took weeks and sometimes months for news to travel from one end of the colonies to the other. Few persons ventured more than a few miles from their own homes throughout their entire lives. Consequently, they knew little of life in any other colony than the one in which they lived. Even the best educated and wisest of the leaders of the American Revolution were homebodies for the most part until the crisis with England made more travel and communications necessary.

A New England schoolmarm travels to New York

In the early 1700s forty-year-old Sarah Kemble Knight, a New England schoolmistress, journeyed from Boston to New York with nine days of hard riding on horseback. Her diary, first published more than a hundred years later, vividly recounts the hardships and humor of the trip. Following are exerpts from her diary, published as *The Journal of Madam Knight:*

Starting the Journey, October 2, 1704, Monday. About three o'clock afternoon, I began my journey from Boston to New Haven; being about two hundred mile. My kinsman, Captain Robert Luist, waited on me as far as Dedham, where I was to meet the western post.

I visited the Reverend M. Belcher, the minister of the town, and tarried there till evening, in hopes the post would come along. But he not coming, I resolved to go to Billings; where he used to lodge, being twelve miles farther. But being ignorant of the way, Madam Belcher, seeing no persuasions of her good spouse's or hers could prevail with me to lodge there that night, very kindly went with me to the tavern, where I hoped to get my guide, and desired the hostess to inquire of her guests whether any of them would go with me. I told her no, I would not be accessory to such extortion.

"Then John shan't go," says she; "no, indeed, shan't he;" and held forth at that rate such a long time that I began to fear I was got among the quaking tribe, believing not a limber-tongued sister among them could outdo Madam Hostess.

Upon this, to my no small surprise, son John arose, and gravely demanded what I would give him to go with me.

*A coach belonging
to the Chew family
of Germantown, Pennsylvania*

A sketch of colonial activities in the Boston vicinity in the year 1766 —From an etching by Veridicus and Junius

"Give you?" says I. "Are you John?" "Yes," says he, "for want of a better;" and behold! this John looked as old as my host, and perhaps had been a man in the last century. "Well, Mr. John," says I, "make your demands." "Why, half a piece of eight and a dram," says John. I agreed, and gave him a dram (now) in hand to bind the bargain.

My hostess catechized John for going so cheap, saying his poor wife would break her heart. . . .

When we had ridden about an hour, we came into a thick swamp, which by reason of a great fog, very much startled me, it being now very dark. But nothing dismayed John: he had encountered a thousand and a thousand such swamps, having a universal knowledge in the woods, and readily answered all my inquiries, which were not a few.

In about an hour, or something more, after we left the swamp, we came to Billings', where I was to lodge. My guide dismounted and very complacently helped me down and showed the door, signing to me with his hand to go in; which I gladly did—but had not gone many steps into the room, ere I was interrogated by a young lady I understood afterwards was the eldest daughter of the family, with these, or words to this purpose; viz., "Law for me! What in the world brings you here at this time of night? I never see a woman on the road so dreadful late in all the days of my versal life. Who are you? Where are you going? I'm scared out of my wits!"—with much more of the same kind.

I stood aghast, preparing to reply, when in comes my guide—to him Madam turned, roaring out: "Lawful heart, John, is it you? How de do! Where in the world are you going with this woman? Who is she?"

John made no answer, but sat down in the corner, fumbled out his black junk, and saluted that instead of Deb; she then turned again to me and fell anew into her silly questions, without asking me to sit down.

I told her she treated me very rudely, and I did not think it my duty to answer her unmannerly questions. But to get rid of them, I told her I came there to have the post's company with me tomorrow on my journey, etc. Miss stared awhile, drew a chair, bade me sit, and then ran up stairs and put on two or three rings (or else I had not seen them before), and returning, set herself just before me, showing me the way to Reading, that I might see her ornaments, perhaps to gain the more respect. But her granam's new rung sow, had it appeared, would have affected me as much. I paid honest John with money and dram according to contract, and dismissed him, and prayed Miss to show me where I must lodge.

She conducted me to a parlor in a little back lean-to, which was almost filled with the bedstead, which was so high that I was forced to climb on a chair to get up to the wretched bed that lay on it; on which having stretched my tired limbs, and laid my head on a sad-colored pillow, I began to think on the transactions of the past day.

Riding by Post to Narragansett, October 3, 1704, Tuesday. About eight in the morning, I with the post proceeded forward without observing anything remarkable; and about two, afternoon, arrived at the post's second stage, where the western post met him and exchanged letters. Here, having called for something to eat, the woman brought in a twisted thing like a cable, but something whiter; and, laying in on the board, tugged for life to bring it into a capacity to spread; which having with great pains accomplished, she served in a dish of pork and cabbage, I suppose the remains of dinner. The sauce was of deep purple, which I thought was boiled in her dye kettle; the bread was Indian, and everything on the table service agreeable to these. I being hungry, got a little down; but my stomach was soon cloyed, and what cabbage I swallowed served me for a cud the whole day after.

Ox slide

Having here discharged the ordinary for self and guide (as I understood was the custom), about three afternoon went on with my third guide. . . .

Being come to Mr. Haven's, I was very civilly received and courteously entertained, in a clean, comfortable house; and the good woman was very active in helping off my riding clothes, and then asked what I would eat. I told her I had some chocolate, if she would prepare it; which with the help of some milk, and a little clean brass kettle, she soon effected to my satisfaction.

I then betook me to my apartment—a little room parted from the kitchen by a single board partition—where, after I had noted the occurrences of the past day, I went to bed, which, though pretty hard, was yet neat and handsome.

But I could get no sleep, because of the clamor of some of the town topers in the next room, who were entered into a strong debate concerning the signification of the name of their country, viz. Narragansett. One said it was named so by the Indians, because there grew a brier there, of a prodigious height and bigness, the like hardly ever known, called by the Indians *narragansett;* and quoted an Indian of so barbarous a name for his author, that I could not write it. His antagonist replied no—it was from a spring it had its name, which he well knew where it was, which was exteme cold in summer, and as hot as could be imagined in the winter, which was much resorted to by the natives, and by them called *narragansett* (hot and cold), and that was the originial notice, which he uttered with such a roaring voice and thundering of their place's name—with a thousand impertinences not worth blows with the fist of wickedness on the table—that it pierced my very head.

I heartily fretted, and wished them tongue-tied; but with as little success as a friend of mine once, who was (as she said) kept a whole night awake, on a journey, by a country lieutenant and a sergeant, ensign, and a deacon, contriving how to bring a triangle into a square. They kept calling for t'other gill, which, while they were swallowing, was some intermission; but, presently, like oil to fire, increased the flame. I set my candle on a chest by the bedside, and sitting up, fell to my old way of composing my resentments, in the following manner:

I ask thy aid, O potent Rum!
To charm these wrangling topers dumb.
Thou hast their giddy brains possest—
The man confounded with the beast—
And I, poor I, can get no rest.
Intoxicate them with thy fumes:
O still their tongues till morning comes!

And I know not but my wishes took effect; for the dispute soon ended with t'other dram; and so good night!

Pushing on to Kingston, Rhode Island, October 4, 1704, Wednesday. About four in the morning we set out for Kingston with a French doctor in our company. He and the post put on very furiously, so that I could not keep up with them, only as now and then they would stop till they saw me. This road was poorly furnished with accommodations for travelers, so that we were forced to ride twenty-two miles by the post's account, but nearer thirty by mine, before we could feed so much as our horses, which I exceedingly complained of.

But the post encouraged me, by saying we should be well accommodated anon at Mr. Devil's a few miles farther. But I questioned whether we ought to go to the devil to be helped out of affliction. However, like the rest of deluded souls that post to the infernal den, we made all possible speed to this devil's habitation; where alighting, in full assurance of good accommodations, we were going in.

But meeting his two daughters, as I supposed twins—they so nearly resembled each other, both in features and habit, and looked as old as the devil himself, and quite as ugly—we desired entertainment, but could hardly get a word out of them, till with our importunity, telling them our necessity, etc., they called the old sophister, who was as sparing of his words as his daughters had been, and "no," or "none," were the replies he made us to our demands. He differed only in this from the old fellow in t'other country; he let us depart.

Thus leaving this habitation of cruelty, we went forward; and arriving at an ordinary about two miles farther, found tolerable accommodation. But our hostess, being a pretty full-mouthed old creature, entertained our fellow traveler, the French doctor, with innumerable complaints of her bodily infirmities; and whispered to him so loud that all the house had as full a hearing as he: which was very diverting to the compa-

A Randolph coach
—Sketch by Kay Smith

The birthplace of Ethan Allen in Litchfield, Connecticut

ny (of which there were a great many), as one might see by their sneering. But poor weary I slipped out to enter my mind in my journal, and left my great landlady with her talkative guests to themselves.

Crossing the Ferry to New London, Connecticut, October 5, 1704, Thursday. About three in the afternoon, I set forward with neighbor Polly and Jemima, a girl about eighteen years old, who he said he had been sent to fetch out of the Narragansetts, and that they had ridden thirty miles that day, on a sorry lead jade, with only a bag under her for a pillion, which the poor girl often complained was very uneasy.

About seven that evening we came to New London ferry; here, by reason of a very high wind, we met with great difficulty in getting over—the boat tossed exceedingly, and our horses capered at a very surprising rate, and set us all in a fright, especially poor Jemima, who desired her father to say "So, Jack" to the jade, to make her stand. But the careless parent taking no notice of her repeated desires, she roared out in a passionate manner: "Pray sooth, father; are you deaf: Say 'So, Jack' to the jade, I tell you." The dutiful parent obeys, saying "So, Jack; so, Jack," as gravely as if he'd been to saying catechize after young Miss, who with her fright looked of all colors in the rainbow.

Being safely arrived at the house of Mrs. Prentice's in New London, I treated neighbor Polly and daughter for their diverting company, and bade them farewell; and between nine and ten at night waited on the Reverend Mr. Gurdon Saltonstall, minister of the town, who kindly invited me to stay that night at his house, where I was very handsomely and plentifully treated and lodged; and made good the great character I had before heard concerning him, viz., that he was the most affable, courteous, generous, and best of men.

Near Disaster at a Connecticut Bridge, October 6, 1704, Friday. I got up very early, in order to hire somebody to go with me to New Haven, being in great perplexity at the thoughts of proceeding alone; which my most hospitable entertainer observing, himself went and soon returned with a young gentleman of the town, whom he could confide in to go with me. . . .

The roads all along this way are very bad, encumbered with rocks and mountanous passages, which were very disagreea-

The siege of Rhode Island on August 24, 1778

A 1670 weathervane

ble to my tired carcass; but we went on with a moderate pace which made the journey more pleasant. But after about eight miles riding, in going over a bridge under which the river ran very swift, my horse stumbled and very narrowly 'scaped falling over into the water, which extremely frightened me. But through God's goodness I met with no harm, and mounting again, in about half a mile's riding, came to an ordinary, was well entertained by a woman of about seventy and vantage, but of as sound intellectuals as one of seventeen.

Description of the People of Connecticut, October 7, 1704, Saturday. About two o'clock afternoon we arrived at New Haven, where I was received with all possible prospects and civility. Here I discharged Mr. Wheeler with a reward to his satisfaction, and took some time to rest after so long and toilsome a journey; and informed myself of the manners and customs of the place, and at the same time employed myself in the affair I went there upon.

They are governed by the same laws as we in Boston (or little differing), throughout this whole colony of Connecticut, and much the same way of church government, and many of them good, sociable people, and I hope religious too: but a little too much independent in their principles, and, as I have been told, were formerly in their zeal very rigid in their administrations towards such as their laws made offenders, even to a harmless kiss or innocent merriment among young people, whipping being a frequent and counted an easy punishment, about which, as other crimes, the judges were absolute in their sentences.

Their diversions in this part of the country are on lecture days and training days mostly; on the former there is riding from town to town. And on training days the youth divert themselves by shooting at the target, as they call it (but it very much resembles a pillory), where he that hits nearest the white has some yards of red ribbon presented him, which being tied to his hatband, the two ends streaming down his back, he is led away in triumph with great applause, as the winner of the Olympic games.

They generally marry very young: the males oftener, as I am told, under twenty than above: they generally make public weddings, and have a way something singular (as they say) in some of them, viz., just before joining hands the bridegroom quits the place. He is soon followed by the bridesmen, and, as it were, dragged back to duty — being the reverse to the former practice among us, to steal mistress bride.

And they generally lived very well and comfortably in their families. But too indulgent (especially the farmers) to their slaves: suffering too great familiarity from them, permitting them to sit at the table and eat with them (as they say, to save time) . . .

Being at a merchant's house, in comes a tall country fellow, with his cheeks full of tobacco; for they seldom loose their

Beekman Arms Inn, Rhinebeck, New York, dates back to the early eighteenth century and in much the same manner as then continues to serve the public in the atmosphere of the 1700s with the conveniences of today.

A mulberry phaeton
—Sketch by Kay Smith

cut, but keep chewing and spitting as long as their eyes are open. He advanced to the middle of the room, made an awkward nod, and spitting a large deal of aromatic tincture, he gave a scrape with his shovel-like shoe, leaving a small shovelful of dirt on the floor, made a full stop, hugging his own pretty body with his hands under his arms, stood staring around him, like a cat let out of a basket. At last, like the creature Balaam rode on, he opened his mouth and said, "Have you any ribinen for hatbands to sell, I pray?" The ribbon is brought and opened. Bumpkin Simpers cries, "It's confounded gay, I vow;" and beckoning to the door, in comes Joan Tawdry, dropping about fifty curtsies, and stands by him; he shows her the ribbon. "Law, you," says she, "it's right gent, do you take it, 'tis dreadful pretty." They generally stand after they come in a great while speechless, and sometimes don't say a word till they are asked what they want, which I impute to the awe they stand in of the merchants, who they are constantly almost indebted to, and must take what they bring without liberty to choose for themselves; but they serve them as well, making the merchants stay long enough for their pay.

Journeying on to New York, December 6, 1704, Wednesday. Being by this time well recruited and rested after my journey, my business lying unfinished by some concerns at New York depending thereupon, my kinsman, Mr. Thomas Trowbridge, of New Haven, must needs take a journey there before it could be accomplished; I resolved to go there in company with him and a man of the town whom I engaged to wait on me there.

Accordingly, December 6th, we set out from New Haven, and about eleven same morning came to Stratford ferry; which crossing, about two miles on the other side fed our horses and would have eat a morsel ourselves, but the pumpkin and Indian mixed bread had such an aspect, and the barelegged punch so awkward or rather awful a sound, that we left both, and proceeded forward, and about seven at night came to Fairfield, where we met with good entertainment and lodged.

The Tavern in Rye, New York, December 7, 1704, Thursday. Early next morning we set forward to Norrowalk, from its half-Indian name "North-walk," where about twelve at noon we arrived, and had a dinner of fried venison, very savory. . . .

From hence we hastened towards Rye, walking and leading our horses near a mile together, up a prodigious high hill; and so riding till about nine at night, and there arrived and took up our lodgings at an ordinary, which a French family kept.

Here being very hungry, I desired a fricassee, which the Frenchman, undertaking, managed so contrary to my notion of cookery, that I hastened to bed supperless; and being shown the way up a pair of stairs which had such a narrow passage that I had almost stopped by the bulk of my body, but arriving at my apartment found it to be a little lean-to chamber,

Pennsylvania stove

Pennsylvania German blacksmiths and wheelwrights began building these Conestoga wagons around 1730 and by 1750 they had produced over seven thousand units. The rugged construction enabled settlers to travel very rough terrain in safety if not in comfort. —Sketch by Kay Smith

furnished among other rubbish with a high bed and a low one, a long table, a bench, and a bottomless chair.

Little Miss went to scratch up my kennel, which rustled as if she had been in the barn among the husks, and suppose such was the contents of the ticking. Nevertheless, being exceedingly weary, down I laid my poor carcass (never more tired), and found my covering as scanty as my bed was hard.

Anon I heard another rustling noise in the room—called to know the matter—little Miss said she was making a bed for the men; who, when they were in bed, complained their legs lay out of it by reason of its shortness. My poor bones complained bitterly, not being used to such lodgings, and so did the man who was with us; and poor I made but one groan, which was from the time I went to bed to the time I rose, which was about three in the morning, sitting up by the fire till light.

The Final Lap to New York City, December 8, 1704, Friday. Having discharged our ordinary—which was as dear as if we had had far better fare—we took our leave of Monsieur and about seven in the morning came to New Rochelle, a

Mrs. William Cushing
—From a painting by James Sharples

William Cushing, associate justice
—From an engraving by C.I. Parkyns

French town, where we had a good breakfast. And on the strength of that about an hour before sunset got to York.
— *The Journals of Madam Knight*

John Adams describes his journey to the Continental Congress

Seventy years after Madam Knight made her hard-riding horseback trip, John Adams made the same journey to New York by carriage and then on to Philadelphia. It took him and his companions eleven days to get to New York. As a delegate to Congress, he was feted and feasted all along the journey. But, having never traveled outside the Boston area before, he was as intrigued as was Mrs. Knight with the differences of the people of the other colonies. Following are exerpts from his *Diary* about the trip.

Leaving Boston, August 10, 1774, Wednesday. The committee for the Congress took their departure from Boston, from Mr. Cushing's house, and rode to Coolidge's, where they dined in company with a large number of gentlemen, who went out and prepared an entertainment for them at that place. A most kindly and affectionate meeting we had, and about four in the afternoon we took our leave of them, amidst the kind wishes and fervent prayers of every man in the company for our health and success. This scene was truly affecting, beyond all description affecting. I lodged at Colonel Buck's.

Traveling to New Haven, August 16, 1774, Tuesday. At four we made for New Haven. Seven miles out of town, at a tavern, we met a great number of carriages and of horsemen who had come out to meet us. The sheriff of the county, and constable of the town, and the justices of peace, were in the train. As we were coming, we met others to the amount of I know not what number, but a very great one. As we came into the town, all the bells in town were set to ringing, and the people, men, women, and children, were crowding at the doors and windows as if it was to see a coronation. At nine o'clock the cannon were fired, about a dozen guns, I think.

These expressions of respect to us are intended as demonstrations of the sympathy of this people with the Massachusetts Bay and its capital, and to show their expectations from the Congress, and their determination to carry into execution whatever shall be agreed upon. No governor of a province nor general of an army was ever treated with so much ceremony and assiduity as we have been throughout the whole colony of Connecticut hitherto, but especially all the way from Hartford to New Haven inclusively.

Arrival in New York City, August 20, 1774, Saturday. We breakfasted at Day's, and arrived in the city of New York at ten o'clock, at Hull's, a tavern, the sign the Bunch of Grapes. We rode by several very elegant country seats before we came to the city. This city will be a subject of much speculation to me.

The Lamb Tavern in Boston dated back to 1746 and served for many years as a hospitable stop for travelers and Boston citizens.

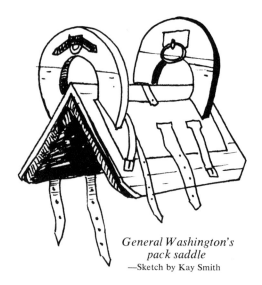

General Washington's pack saddle
—Sketch by Kay Smith

The streets of this town are vastly more regular and elegant than those of Boston, and the houses are more grand, as well as neat. They are almost all painted, brick buildings and all. In our walks they showed us the house of Mr. William Smith, one of their Council, and the famous lawyer, Mr. Thomas Smith, etc., Mr. Rivington's store, etc.

Breakfast with the New York Delegates, August 22, 1774, Monday. This morning we took Mr. McDougall into our coach and rode three miles out of town to Mr. Morin Scott's to breakfast—a very pleasant ride. Mr. Scott has an elegant seat there, with Hudson's River just behind his house and a rural prospect all around him. Mr. Scott, his lady and daughter, and her husband, Mr. Litchfield, were dressed to receive us. We sat in a fine airy entry till called into a front room to breakfast. A more elegant breakfast I never saw—rich place, a very large silver coffeepot, a very large silver teapot, napkins of the very finest materials, toast, and bread, and butter in great perfection. After breakfast a plate of beautiful peaches, another of pears, and another of plums, and a muskmelon were placed on the table.

Mr. Scott, Mr. William Smith, and Mr. William Livingston are the triumvirate who figured away in younger life against the Church of England, who wrote the *Independent Reflector,* the *Watch Tower,* and other papers. They are all of them children of Yale College. Scott and Livingston are said to be lazy; Smith improves every moment of his time. Livingston is lately removed into New Jersey and is one of the delegates for that province.

Views about New Yorkers, August 23, 1774, Tuesday. The way we have been in, of breakfasting, dining, drinking coffee, etc., about the city, is very disagreeable on some accounts. Although it introduces us to the acquaintance of many respectable people here, yet it hinders us from seeing the college, the churches, the printers' offices and booksellers' shops, and many other things which we should choose to see.

With all the opulence and splendor of this city, there is very little good breeding to be found. We have been treated with an assiduous respect, but I have not seen one real gentleman, one well-bred man, since I came to town. At their entertainments there is no conversation that is agreeable; there is no modesty, no attention to one another. They talk very loud, very fast, and all together. If they ask you a question, before you can utter three words of your answer, they will break out upon you again, and talk away.

Arriving in Philadelphia, August 29, 1774, Monday. We crossed the ferry over Delaware River to the province of Pennsylvania. . . . After dinner we stopped at Frankfort, about five miles out of town. A number of carriages and gentlemen came out of Philadelphia to meet us—Mr. Thomas Mifflin, Mr. Kean, of the lower counties, one of their delegates, Mr. Rutledge of Carolina, and a number of gentlemen from Philadelphia, Mr. Folsom and Mr. Sullivan, the New Hampshire delegates. We were introduced to all these gentlemen, and most cordially welcomed to Philadelphia. We then rode into town, and dirty, dusty, and fatigued as we were, we could not resist the importunity to go to the tavern, the most genteel one in America. Here we had a fresh welcome to the city of Philadelphia, and after some time spent in conversation, a curtain was drawn, and in the other half of the chamber a supper appeared as elegant as ever was laid upon a table. About eleven o'clock we retired.

First News of George Washington, August 31, 1774, Wednesday. Made a visit to Governor Ward of Rhode Island at his lodgings. There we were introduced to several gentlemen. Mr. Dickinson, the farmer, of Pennsylvania, came in his coach with four beautiful horses to Mr. Ward's lodgings to see us. He was introduced to us, and very politely said he was exceedingly glad to have the pleasure of seeing these gentlemen; made some inquiry after the health of his brother and sister, who are now in Boston; gave us some account of his late ill health and his present gout. This was the first time of his getting out. Mr. Dickinson has been subject to hectic complaints. He is a shadow, tall, but slender as a reed, pale as ashes; one would think at first sight that he could not live a month, yet upon a more attentive inspection, he looks as if the springs of life were strong enough to last many years.

The approach to the back entrance of Mount Vernon as it appeared in 1786. —From a painting by C.W. Peale

John Dickinson, American farmer and patriot

We dined with Mr. Lynch, his lady and daughter, at their lodgings, Mrs. McKenzie's; and a very agreeable dinner and afternoon we had, notwithstanding the violent heat. We were all vastly pleased with Mr. Lynch. He is a solid, firm, judicious man. He told us that Colonel Washington made the most eloquent speech at the Virginia Convention that ever was made. Says he, "I will raise one thousand men, subsist them at my own expense, and march myself at their head for the relief of Boston."

—from the Diary of John Adams

COLLEGE LIFE
BEFORE THE REVOLUTION

T here were seven colleges in the colonies: Harvard, Yale, Brown, Pennsylvania, William and Mary, Princeton, and King's College (now Columbia). Many of the leaders of the Revolution attended these colleges, although some were educated in England, and some, like George Washington, had little formal education.

What college life in those days was like is best described by the following letter written on November 30, 1770, by twenty-two-year-old Philip Vickers Fithian to his father from Princeton. Among his classmates at the time were Aaron Burr, who would become the third Vice President of the United States, and Henry "Light Horse Harry" Lee, who would win fame as a cavalry leader in the Revolution.

Harvard College—Holden Chapel, Hollis Hall, Stoughton Hall, and Massachusetts Hall (from left to right)

The original building of the University of Pennsylvania, founded in 1756
—From a painting by Lakeman

*Protestant Episcopal Academy,
in Philadelphia, 1790*

Very Dear Father.

Altho' I am very busy seeing I began to study three Weeks later than the rest of our Class, yet I think it my Duty to give you Notice of my Admission to this flourishing Seminary of Learning, which is another grand Step towards the Summit of my Wishes; and I shall also mention as many of the Customs, as my short Acquaintance with the College & Students will allow me. . . .

Mr. Hunter and myself were admitted into the junior-Class on the twenty-second day of November, after a previous Examination by the president, Tutors, & some residing Graduates; which was about three Weeks after the College-Orders began.

The Rules by which the Scholars & Students are directed, are, in my Opinion, exceedingly well formed to check & restrain the vicious, & to assist the studious, & to countenance & encourage the virtuous.

Every Student must rise in the Morning, at farthest by half an hour, that everyone may have time to dress, at the end of which it rings again, & Prayrs begin; and lest any should plead that he did not hear the Bell, the Servant who rings, goes to every Door & beats till he wakens the Boys, which leaves them without Excuse.

There are Bill-keepers in each Class, appointed generally by the President, or in his absence by one of the Tutors, who take Notice, & set down those who are absent from Morning or evening Prayrs, & once every week present their Bill to the Doctor, or one of the Tutors, who call each delinquent, & demand their Excuse, which if it is thought sufficient is accepted. If not, they are fined, or privately admonished, & if the same person is found frequently guilty, without good reason, he receives public Admonition in the Hall of Contempt of Authority.

After morning Prayrs, we can, now in the Winter, study an hour by candle Light every Morning.

We breakfast at eight; from Eight to nine, is time of our own, to play, or exercise.

The oldest schoolhouse in America—in St. Augustine, Florida —Sketch by Kay Smith

At nine the Bell rings for Recitation, after which we study till one, when the Bell rings for Dinner. We dine all in the same Room, at three Tables, & so we breakfast and sup.

After dinner till three we have Liberty to go out at Pleasure. From three till five we study, when the Bell rings for Study; and a Tutor goes through the College, to see that every Student is in his own Room; if he finds that any are absent, or more in any Room than belongs there, he notes them down, & the day following calls them to an Account.

King's College —now known as Columbia University

After nine any may go to bed, but to go before is reproachful.

No Student is allowed, on any pretence, Sickness only excepted, to be absent on Sunday, from public Worship. We have two Sermons every Sabbath: one at eleven in the morning, in the Church; & the other at three in the Afternoon, in the College Hall. I am indeed much pleased with Dr. Witherspoon & think his Sermons almost inimitable.

We rise on Sabbath mornings & have Prayrs as usual.

There is a Society that meets every Sabbath Evening at six o Clock, for religious Worship; this is a voluntary Society made up of any who belong to the College, & choose to attend.

The Exercises in this Society go in the alphabetical Order of those who are willing to perform. They sing a Psalm & pray, after which a Tutor reads a Sermon & dismisses them.

About seven the supper Bell rings, immediately after which, each Class meets separately in Rooms belonging to one of the Seniors; & the Juniors by themselves meet in a Room belonging to one of themselves; & in like manner do the inferior Classes. And one in each Class, as his Name comes in alphabetical Order, gives out a Psalm to be sung, & prays; after which they disperse, and retire to their respective Rooms. . . .

There are upwards of an hundred now in the College including the grammar Scholars. The present Senior Class consists of ten: the *Junior* of twenty-eight: the *Sophomore* of twenty-five: and the *Freshman* of eighteen. In the School there are twenty-five.

I am, through divine goodness, very well, & more reconciled to rising in the Morning so early than at first. . . .

From, Sir, your dutiful Son.

A VISIT
TO PEALE'S MUSEUM

Charles Willson Peale —From a mezzotint by St. Memin

Charles Willson Peale, a saddle-maker who turned portrait painter and painted many of the Revolutionary War leaders, founded a museum in Philadelphia that became a leading tourist attraction. On a trip to Philadelphia in 1787, Manasseh Cutler of Hamilton, Massachusetts, visited Peale's museum and described it as follows in his *Journal.*

Immediately after dinner, we called on Mr. Peale, to see his collection of paintings and natural curiosities. We were conducted into a room by a boy, who told us that Mr. Peale would wait on us in a minute or two. He desired us, however, to walk into the room where the curiosities were, and showed us a long narrow entry which led into the room. I observed, through a glass window at my right hand, a gentleman close to me, standing with a pencil in one hand, and a small sheet of

Charles Willson Peale, distinguished painter of the colonial period, was deeply interested in the study of natural history, and to share his interest with the public he opened this first museum in Philadelphia in 1794. He made application to the Legislature of Pennsylvania for the use of the State House (Independence Hall) and in 1802 the second floor was granted to him and he placed his portrait gallery of distinguished people, painted chiefly by himself and his son Rembrandt, there, along with some other artifacts for public view. In 1805 his ambition for an academy to promote the fine arts was at last realized when a group of influential citizens formed an association which in 1806 was chartered "The Pennsylvania Academy of Fine Arts." Peale lived long enough to enjoy many of the Academy functions and contributed to seventeen of the annual Academy exhibitions.

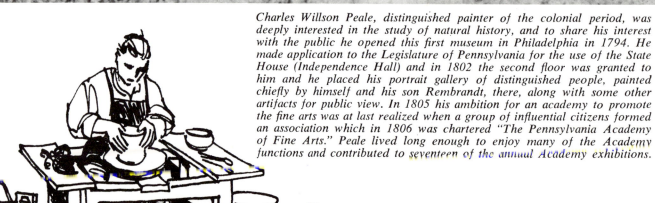

A potter plying his trade
—Sketch by Kay Smith

ivory in the other, and his eyes directed to the opposite side of the room, as though he was taking some object on his ivory sheet. Dr. Clarkson did not see this man until he stepped into the room, but instantly turned about and came back, saying, "Mr. Peale is very busy, taking the picture of something with his pencil. We will step back into the other room and wait till he is at leisure."

We returned through the entry, but as we entered the room we came from, we met Mr. Peale coming to us. The Doctor started back in astonishment, and cried out, "Mr. Peale, how is it possible you should get out of the other room to meet us here?" Mr. Peale smiled. "I have not been in the other room," says he, "for some time." "No!" says Clarkson, "Did not I see you there this moment, with your pencil and ivory?" "Why, do you think you did?" says Peale. "Do I think I did? Yes," says the Doctor, "I saw you there if I ever saw you in my life." "Well," says Peale, "let us go and see."

When we returned, we found the man standing as before. My astonishment was now nearly equal to that of Dr. Clarkson; for, although I knew what I saw, yet I beheld two men, so perfectly alike that I could not discern the minutest difference. One of them, indeed, had no motion, but he appeared to me to be as *absolutely* alive as the other, and I could hardly help wondering that he did not smile or take a part in the conversation.

This was a piece of waxwork which Mr. Peale had just finished, in which he had taken himself. So admirable a performance must have done great honor to his *genius* if it had been that of any other person, but I think it is much more extraordinary that he should be able so perfectly to take himself. To what perfection is this art capable of being carried! By this method, our particular friends and ancestors might be preserved in perfect likeness to the latest generation. We seem to be able in some degree to disappoint the ravages of time, and prevent mortality itself, the common lot of man, from concealing from us in its dreary retreats our dearest connections.

This room is constructed in a very singular manner, for the purpose of Exhibitions, where various scenery in paintings is exhibited in a manner that has a most astonishing effect. It is very long but not very wide, has no windows, nor floor over it, but is open up to the roof, which is two or three stories, and from above the light is admitted in greater or less quantities at pleasure. The walls of the room are covered with paintings, both portrait and historic. One particular part is assigned to the portraits of the principal American characters who appeared on the stage during the late revolution, either in the councils or armies of their country. The drapery was excellent, and the likenesses of all of whom I had any personal knowledge were well taken. I fancied myself introduced to all the General Officers that had been in the field during the war, whether dead or alive, for I think he had every one, and to

Sauce pan

most of the members of Congress and other distinguished characters. To grace his collection, he had a number of the most distinguished clergymen in the middle and southern states who had, in some way or other, been active in the revolution. In other parts were a number of fine historic pieces, executed in a masterly manner. At the upper end of the room, General Washington, at full length and nearly as large as life, was placed, as President of this sage and martial assembly.

At the opposite end, under a small gallery, his natural curiosities were arranged in a most romantic and amusing manner. There was a mound of earth, considerably raised and covered with green turf, from which a number of trees ascended and branched out in different directions. On the declivity of this mound was a small thicket, and just below it an artificial pond; on the other side a number of large and small rocks of different kinds, collected from different parts of the world, and appearing in the rude state in which they were found. At the foot of the mound were holes dug and the earth thrown up, to show the different kinds of clay, ochre, coal, marl, etc., which he had collected from different parts, also, various ores and minerals. Around the pond was a beach, on which was exhibited an assortment of shells of different kinds, turtles, frogs, toads, lizards, water-snakes, etc. In the pond was a collection of fish with their skins stuffed, water fowls, such as the different species of geese, ducks, cranes, herons, etc., all having the appearance of life, for their skins were admirably preserved. On the mound were those birds which commonly walk on the ground, as the partridge, quail, heath-hen, etc.; also, different kinds of wild animals—bear, deer, leopard, tiger, wild-cat, fox, raccoon, rabbit, squirrel, etc. In the thickets and among the rocks, land-snakes, rattlesnakes of an enormous size, black, glass, striped, and a number of other snakes. The boughs of the trees were loaded with birds, some of almost every species in America, and many exotics.

In short, it is not in my power to give any particular account of the numerous species of fossils and animals, but only their general arrangement. What heightened the view of this singular collection was that they were all real, either their substance or their skins finely preserved. . . . Mr. Peale's animals reminded me of *Noah's Ark*, into which was received every kind of beast and creeping thing in which there was life. But I can hardly conceive that even Noah could have boasted of a better collection.

Mr. Peale was very complaisant, and gave us every information we desired. He requested me to favor him with any of the animals and fossils from this part of America, not already in his museum, which it might be in my power to collect.

—*from Life, Journals and Correspondence
of Rev. Manasseh Cutler*

The Reverend Manasseh Cutler

CHURCHES BEFORE
THE REVOLUTION

EDITOR'S NOTE: *The religion of the American colonists played an important part in their daily lives and influenced the spirit that made them independent. The following article is adapted from one written by historian Edward Eggleston for the "Century Magazine" about the churches of the 1700s.*

The earliest houses of worship in America belonged to the makeshift order of architecture—four walls of logs, or a rude framework of wood, clay-plastered outside and in, or of rived clapboards with earth filled in-between the rough siding without and the rough ceiling within. The roof was sometimes of thatch, and there was usually a floor. Very few communities built substantial churches at the outset, but as soon as the pioneer struggle was over, better places for worship were provided. In New England the first meeting-houses, after the log and thatched ones, were generally framed buildings, nearly square, with what was familiarly called a "tunnel roof"—that is, a roof sloping on all four sides to a point in the middle—with a belfry perched on the apex from which the bell-rope dangled to the floor in the very center of the assembly. Nothing could have less of aesthetic sentiment in it; nothing could have been more baldly utilitarian and more entirely Puritan than this foursquare inclosure.

These buildings were appropriately called "meeting-houses;" they were mere places for assemblage and nothing more—the work of a people who at first repelled with earnestness the notion of any special sacredness in consecrated places. In this same building assembled the town meeting with its contentious wrangles; here the magistrates decided the disputes of a litigious people; and here the court sentenced petty criminals and immoral people to the stocks or the whipping-post, which stood conveniently in front of the door. Architecture of this kind was not quite confined to New England. This almost square house with pyramidal roof was found sometimes among the New York Dutch. The Dutch church at New Utrecht, on Long Island, had a steep funnel roof and the building was six-sided. The first Quaker meeting-house in Burlington, New Jersey, was also hexagonal with a steep roof.

The New Englanders refused to apply the name of church to a building, and when the primitive meeting-house fell into disuse they gave it to the minister to shelter his hay, his horses, and his cows in, or they applied it to some other ignoble use. One Long Island Puritan meetinghouse when discarded served the town for a jail. This very secularization of the old building was a solemn protest against what they deemed a papistical or idolatrous notion that holiness could inhere in wood or stone. The Virginians built their first churches with equal rudeness, but when the primitive building of mud-daubed logs and sedge-thatched roof fell into disuse, they surrounded it with a ditch to protect the ruins from profanation by the beasts of the field. This was an act of pure sentiment, for no colonial building ever received consecration from the hands of a bishop.

The greater part of what we may call the secondary churches in the Southern colonies were, even down to the Revolution, "composed of wood, without spires or towers or steeples or bells, and placed like those of our remotest ancestors in Great Britain in retired and solitary spots, and contiguous to springs or wells," says Jonathan Boucher, the well-known colonial clergyman. Ladles were secured by chains at the springs; there were horse-blocks in front of the church, and in some places sundials. But all the buildings were not so simple. The Anglican body in America had its roots in England, and wherever there was wealth enough, efforts were made to follow the prevailing fashion in English ecclesiastical architecture.

Some of the early churches, such as Christ Church in Philadelphia and St. Michael's in Charleston, succeeded in attaining considerable beauty of an imitative sort. There have come down in the mid-1800s a few ancient country churches in the Southern colonies that show the ambition of their builders for decoration—as a Virginia church with Corinthian pillars the capitals of which are elaborately carved and painted white. But the parish church was rarely more than four wooden walls with a commonplace roof; sometimes the latter was relieved

Interior of St. John's Church in Richmond, Virginia, where Patrick Henry declared on March 23, 1775, "We must fight; an appeal to arms and to the God of hosts in all that is left to us."

The Augustus Trappe Lutheran Church in Trappe, Pennsylvania, dating back to 1743, the oldest Lutheran Church still standing and in use.
—From a wash sketch by Kay Smith

by a curious dip over the front gables. Within, the churches of the Establishment often had upon the walls tablets containing the Creed, the Lord's Prayer, and the Commandments, usually in gilt letters on a sky-blue ground. There was also erected, according to law, a table of marriages to keep the parishioners in continual memory that a man might not marry his grandmother or any other of a long list of relatives within the prescribed limit, including the sister of a deceased wife. Stone baptismal fonts were erected in some of the Virginia parish churches before 1692.

The ecclesiastical architecure of New England, which had never been quite uniform, underwent considerable modification when Puritanism itself molted. After the 1600s there came a new era: the most austere form of Puritanism disappeared; the crusade against long hair, wigs, and witchcraft had spent itself; the increase of luxury softened manners; a slight tendency toward regular ceremonials appeared; by degrees the Bible came to be read in church without exposition, and the psalms to be sung by note and without dictation; prayers were presently offered at funerals; and the prevailing squarish meeting-houses with pyramidal roofs began to give way to buildings with some ambition for architectural effect. Even where traces of the old form of meeting-house showed themselves in buildings erected after 1700, the house was in most cases distinctly longer than broad, and the belfry instead of capping a tunnel roof was made to mark the middle of a roof-ridge hipped at both ends. In one case "pinnacles or other ornaments" were to be set upon each end of a house apparently with a plain ridge roof. But in the later buildings the belfry often gave place to a tower standing at one of the rear angles of the building and surmounted by a spire. The church porch, which had been present in some of the early meeting-houses, always, perhaps, on one of the longer sides of the building, was sometimes in the later structures at the end, and this, no doubt, marked a change in the internal arrangement of the house, for the pulpit was usually on the side or end opposite the porch. The putting of the pulpit on one of the longer sides in the first meeting-houses may have been a protest against the location of altars or chancels in one end of a church.

The Lutheran Church on Fourth Street in Philadelphia as it appeared in 1799 —From an engraving by Wm. Birch & Son

FROM A WATERCOLOR PAINTING BY KAY SMITH

*The Carlyle House in Alexandria dates back to 1752, when it was constructed by John Carlyle
of Dunfries, Scotland, one of the incorporators of Alexandria in 1748. It is alleged that it was built
over the foundation of an old stone fort that protected the area from the Indians. It was occupied
for a time by British General Braddock in 1755 before he met his death in the battle of Fort Duquesne.
The following inscription appears on the wall of this house, which is being restored for 1976:*

> This house is said to be the place where the revolution was born, for within its walls, ten years
> before the Stamp Act, first came the demand from the officials of the British Government
> for taxation of the colonies by Act of Parliament, which, when finally carried out, resulted in
> its resistance, the independence of the colonies, and the formation of the United States.

*A replica of George Washington's surveying office in Alexandria, Virginia,
which he used in the period between his service in the French and Indian War
and the beginning of the American Revolution.*

FROM A WATERCOLOR SKETCH BY KAY SMITH

Open cooking in iron pots and kettles was a common practice in other than the winter months because of the heat generated in the cramped quarters of most colonial homes.

FROM A WATERCOLOR PAINTING BY KAY SMITH

Gunston Hall, dating back to 1758, was the residence of George Mason, author of the Virginia Bill of Rights, the first Constitution of Virginia, and the Fairfax County Resolves, one of the first and most important protests by the colonists. The architect was James Buckland of Oxfordshire, England, who was brought to America as an indentured craftsman by George Mason's brother Thomson, who found him to be so skilled and talented that he recommended him to his brother and all his friends. This well preserved mansion is near Alexandria.

FROM A WATERCOLOR PAINTING BY KAY SMITH

Gadsby's Tavern, built in 1752 in Alexandria, Virginia, and known then as City Tavern, is one of the most historic buildings in the country. On at least three occasions Washington used it as his headquarters and in 1775 he presided at a public meeting in this building which resulted in the adoption of the Fairfax County Resolves—resolutions drawn up by George Mason which served as a model for other protests of a similar nature. In 1788 the celebration here of the adoption of the Federal Constitution was attended by Washington and other dignitaries, and on February 22, 1799, General and Mrs. Washington celebrated Washington's last lifetime birthday in this venerable building. The smaller building on the left was the original City Tavern, and in 1793 it was joined by the larger building on the right by John Gadsby to become Gadsby's Tavern.

*Christ Church in Alexandria,
Virginia, was completed in
1773 and through the years
has been the place of worship
for many of the nation's leaders,
including George Washington,
who was a vestryman and remained
a member until his death, and
Robert E. Lee, who attended
services here during his boyhood
and again later in life.*

FROM A WATERCOLOR PAINTING BY KAY SMITH

FROM A WATERCOLOR PAINTING BY KAY SMITH

This courtyard of Gadsby's Tavern was regularly used by couriers and stage coaches from all the principal colonial towns and cities, as it was on the King's Highway that extended from Savannah and Charleston through Williamsburg all the way to Boston. Here during the Revolution John Paul Jones met Lafayette and the Baron de Kalb, and again, in 1824, when Lafayette was the nation's guest, he was entertained at Gadsby's Tavern by the Alexandria Masonic Lodge and the citizens of Alexandria. The restoration of the two buildings has been participated in by a number of organizations, including Daughters of the American Revolution, the Colonial Dames of America, the Women's Auxiliary of the American Legion, the Garden Club of Alexandria, and the Alexandria Association.

St. Mary's Church and burial ground on Fourth Street, one of the first Roman Catholic churches in Philadelphia, along with St. Joseph's, St. Augustine's and Holy Trinity.

Called to church by beaten drum

In the years following the first planting of the colonies, church bells were few and the custom in vogue at Jamestown, of calling the congregation to service by beat of drum, prevailed very generally where the people lived within hearing distance. We should, perhaps, mistake if we supposed this to be merely the adaptation of a military usage; the village drummer was only a variety of the town-crier or bell-man. In the absence of newspapers and handbills, he beat his drum in the most public places whenever anything of importance was to be cried, and time-pieces being wanting, he was in some towns engaged to announce the hour for beginning daily labor and the arrival of bedtime. Nothing was more natural than that he should also rattle his drum in the streets on Sunday morning to bring the clockless people to meeting in time. In primitive New Haven the Sunday morning drum was beaten by the drummer standing on top of the meeting-house, that those who lived afar might hear. The old New England meeting-house was often perched on the top of a high hill, and a flag was sometimes raised as a signal to worshipers living too remote to hear a drum. It was a more common plan to blow a conch-shell dinner-horn in the streets. An old verse with a good anti-climax preserves the memory of this custom:

New England's Sabbath-day
Is heaven-like still and pure;
Then Israel walks the way
Up to the temple's door;
The time we tell
When there to come
By beat of drum
Or sounding shell.

The Sunday morning drum-beat, the conch-shell blown in the streets, and the signal flag flying from the top of the meeting-house, lingered in some places until well on toward the close of the colonial period.

A time for meeting neighbors

In the Middle and Southern colonies where dwelling-houses were widely scattered on large private plantations and where boats, small piraguas, and canoes were favorite vehicles for travel, some of the earliest churches stood conveniently by the waterside, and meetings held in private houses were located with reference to the prevailing modes of getting about. Nothing could be more animated than the scene upon the water at such gatherings. The concourse of boats in which the Maryland settlers had come to one of George Fox's meetings made the stream in front of the house "look like the Thames." An Italian traveler at a later period gives us a lively picture of a similar scene in the Maine woods, where the people, after listening to a sermon preached in a barn and then dining together at a neighboring house off a large boiled cod, embarked in a fleet of canoes, discussing the doctrine of the preacher as they paddled homeward.

Eating together after the service was a very common practice in thinly settled regions, and it afforded a good opportunity for the gratification of the social instinct. To Sheldon Church, in South Carolina, there came seldom less than sixty or seventy carriages, but a neighboring planter was accustomed to entertain the whole assembly; those of higher social position he invited to his own table, while common-folk were provided for by his overseer at the planter's expense. At great Quaker meetings a similar unstinted hospitality was dispensed by the wealthier Friends. In New England care was taken at first that every family should live so near to the meeting-house that people could attend church without straining the fiber of the fourth commandment. But when the common lands came to be more and more divided, and farms and out-hamlets were settled, people had to travel farther. In the wintertime the people from a distance spent the time between the two services by the fireside in the kitchen of the parsonage-house, or in that of some other neighbor who heaped up wood against the great back-log to cheer the worshipers when they came chilled to the marrow from the frosty air of the meeting-house.

Unheated meeting-houses

The custom of building churches without appliances for warming them was very general, especially in the colonies north of Pennsylvania, and was no doubt brought from Europe; one may yet sit through service in fireless churches in Holland, Switzerland, and elsewhere on the continent. In a climate so severe as that of New England, it must have added much to the grizzly rigor of the religious observances. Judge

Walloon Church
New Paltz, N.Y.

Kay Smith

The Walloon Dutch Church and cemetery on Huguenot Street in New Paltz, New York, dating back to the early eighteenth century—now authentically restored.
—From a wash sketch by Kay Smith

Friends Meeting House near Cornwall, New York, dating back to 1792.

Sewall records in his diary, on a certain Sunday in January, 1686, when Boston harbor was covered with ice: "This day so cold that the Sacramental Bread is frozen pretty hard and rattles sadly as broken into the plates." Though in most places no one ever dreamed of warming the building, yet measures were sometimes taken to mitigate the cold; the first church in Lynn, for example, was made to descend to low eaves on the side exposed to the northwest wind, and the floor was sunk below the ground. In New York, in 1714, servants are described as carrying foot-stoves to church for the use of their masters and mistresses, and foot-stoves were likewise used in New England in the 1700s.

In one Quaker meeting in Pennsylvania it was provided, in 1699, that a fire should be kept in an upper room, "for such as are weak through sickness, or age, or otherwise, to warm at, and come down again modestly." But at a later period we find some of the Friends' meeting-houses warmed with German stoves. The Southern parish churches were probably not generally warmed, but it was provided in a colonial parish, as far south as North Carolina, that the clerk and lay-reader should also build fires whenever they were needed. There were even some exceptional towns in New England that had iron stoves in their meeting-houses as early as 1730, though most of them resisted the improvement until after the beginning of the 1800s.

The custom of sabbath-day houses

In Connecticut, perhaps more than anywhere else, Sunday was a sort of popular idol, nor did the rigor of its observance abate perceptibly until long after the Revolution. This extreme scrupulosity about Sabbath-keeping was doubtless the moving cause of the building of the "Sabbath-day houses." These were little shanties standing on the meeting-house green, each intended to accommodate a family during the interval between the two services. Some Sabbath-day houses were built with a stall at one end to shelter the horse, while the family took refuge in the other, where there was a chimney and meager furniture of rude seats and a table. Here, on arrival, before the first service the owners lighted a fire and deposited their luncheon, and to this camp-like place they came back to eat their doughnuts and thaw themselves out after their first long sitting in the arctic climate of the meeting-house.

Sometimes two families had a Sabbath-day house together; sometimes there were two rooms in a Sabbath-day house that the sexes might sit apart—for nothing so agreeable as social converse between boys and girls was permitted during the consecrated time. But some parishes in Massachusetts, and perhaps elsewhere, had a common "noon-house" for all comers to rest in. Fireside assemblages on Sunday, whether in the parsonage or the noon-house, were in danger of proving delightful to those who were prone to enjoy the society of other human beings, and hence the pastors "were put upon their best contrivances" to have most of the interval between the services filled up with the reading aloud of edifying books and other exercises calculated to keep the mind in a becomingly irksome frame.

Week-day lectures

The New England reverence for the Sabbath tended to repress social enjoyment in the accidental encounters of Sunday, but the week-day lecture suffered from no such restriction, and was for a long time much more in favor than even the Sunday service. From all the country round, in spite of the poverty and difficult conditions of pioneer life, people flocked to these week-day assemblages. Cotton's lecture in Boston was so attractive that it was found convenient to establish a

Christ Church, the Old North Church in Boston designed after the manner of Sir Christopher Wren—famous in United States history for the signal lanterns of Paul Revere.

69

A view of Second Street north from Market Street in Philadelphia showing the court house, which was the seat of legislature before the State House was built, and Christ Church, in continuous use since 1727, where many colonial leaders worshiped. —Drawn and engraved by W. Birch & Son, 1799

market on the same day; punishments in the stocks, in the pillory, at the whipping post, or on the gallows, were generally set down for a lecture-time, perhaps in order that as large a number of people as possible might be edified by the sight of a sinner brought to a just retribution. Nor did these exhibitions of flogging, of cutting off ears, and of men sitting in the stocks, or dangling from a gallows, tend to diminish the attendance. At one period during Philip's war, scarcely a Boston lecture-day passed for a number of weeks without the congregation being regaled with the sight of the execution of one or more Indians.

When heretical or seditious books were condemned, it was decreed that they should be solemnly burned "just after lecture." Elections were appointed for the same time at first, and the early popularity of the Thursday lectures in Boston and Ipswich fixed the annual Thanksgiving festival on that day of the week.

The largeness of the assemblies at lecture-time gave some uneasiness to the magistrates in the first years of the colony;

they were concerned to see people who could ill spare the time going to three or four lectures in different places during the same week. They saw that young people made attendance on lectures a pretext for enjoying themselves, and they had a reasonable fear that the hospitality exercised on such occasions might become burdensome. As early as 1633 the magistrates interfered to fix the hour of the lecture at one o'clock or later, that the people might take their midday meal at home. The next year they persuaded the ministers about Boston to arrange their lectures in alternate weeks so that four contiguous towns might have two lectures a week.

In 1639 the rulers again sought to regulate the hour of lecture, but this brought the clergy on their backs, and the next year all restrictions were repealed, and the week-day lecture long remained a time of common assemblage, of business convenience, of hospitality, and of great social enjoyment.

Social standing dictated seating arrangements

In the churches of the English Establishment in the colonies, the people of consequence sat in family seats or pews, which were in some places accounted private property and descended from father to son. At Williamsburg, in Virginia, the pew seems to have been an appurtenance of the residence, and to have been sold with it. In many churches the gallery was the place of dignity, a conventional idea that is yet retained in parts of Britain. In the old Virginia church at Grub Hill the leading families were so jealous of their rights of property in the very uncomfortable pews under the roof that they refused to suffer the gallery to be taken down after its decay rendered it necessary to support it by props.

The church at Annapolis is a good example of the spirit of the time. Here, in the new building of 1774, pews were set apart for the governor, the speaker, the members of the Upper and those of the Lower House, and the judges. Even jurymen had a reserved seat, and everybody was, by act of the legislature, assigned to his proper position in the church according to his official dignity or the amount of money he had given to the building; only the gallery was reserved for those who had no pews. In the older Annapolis church the same system seems to have prevailed, for in 1745, after Whitefield had preached a fifth of November sermon to a great congregation, the iron ornament used to designate and decorate the pew of the speaker fell and hurt seriously two of the members of the Assembly in the next pew to that of their presiding officer. It was thus that a provincial government made the worship of God a public act, performed by all its functionaries in their due order and array, and with all proper fuss and parade.

Indeed, among all sorts of religious people at that time the house of worship was believed to be the proper place to air one's superiority. In the primitive New England meeting-house it was not accounted safe to permit the two sexes to

St. Michael's Church, Charleston, South Carolina, the beacon of which guided the mariners into the harbor.

71

occupy the same seats or even to sit upon the same side of the house, but the heads of families on each side were sedulously pigeon-holed according to what was deemed their relative rank, and sometimes even the young people in the galleries were thus classified. There was no trace of democratic sentiment in the earlier days, and respect for social rank was a very important department of religion.

Seated according to taxes paid

In some places the seating was adjusted mathematically by the tax-book, according to the amount of estate set down to each householder; in others, as in Brookhaven, on Long Island, and elsewhere, it was shrewdly fixed by the relative liberality of contributors to the church treasury, but in most New England towns an anxious committee undertook the dreadful task of weighing all those considerations, palpable and impalpable, of property, family, professional dignity, official position, age, and what not besides, that go to make up social standing. Preliminary to this, another committee was appointed to "dignify the meeting-house"—that is, to fix a relative rank to the several seats. Such was the ambition for the higher seats in the synagogue that the villagers sometimes refused to accept the places assigned them, and shameful disorders were the result of a contest for place, so that some towns found it needful to impose a sharp fine on aspiring people who endeavored "to advance themselves in the meeting-house."

The matter of ecclesiastical rank was more definite and more easily settled. The New England hierarchy was carefully ranged in the light of the apostle Paul's epistles. The "teaching elders," or ministers, of whom most churches in the first years of the colonies had two, occupied the highest seat behind the pulpit, or, as Cotton took pains to call it, "the scaffold." When the minister and his family entered the door, the congregation rose and remained reverently standing until he had mounted to his place. The ruling elders' seat was a high bench in front of the pulpit and facing the people, and the deacons sat in a seat yet one degree lower down. In the like spirit we find the Goose Creek parish church in South Carolina setting apart in perpetuity the front pews of the middle row for the church-wardens and vestrymen and their successors forever, while some churches built pews specially for the church-wardens. And notwithstanding the protest of Friends against man-worship, the Quaker meeting-houses had "galleries" or raised seats, in order to give this sort of precedence to leading members and ministers; though when it came to preaching, the Public Friend had no pulpit, but mounted upon a preaching-stool.

The problem of keeping the congregation awake

The seating of church officers in conspicuous places had a certain justification in the practical necessity that there was in

During the earlier years of his married life Washington attended Pohick Church, seven miles from Mount Vernon, more frequently than any other. This present Pohick Church was completed in 1773, the general plan of the building having been worked out by George Washington.

—From a wash sketch by Kay Smith

*The old ship
meeting house at Hingham,
Massachusetts, 1681.*
—Sketch by Kay Smith

that ruder time for awing into decent behavior inconsiderate and disorderly youths. In New England meeting-houses, a tithing-man or some equivalent official was put in charge of the boys, whose meditations were rendered appropriately solemn by a rod held in plain sight and sometimes rapped against the wall in an admonitory way. In Lynn, and perhaps elsewhere, the tithing-man went about the meeting-house with a long wand having a ball on one end with which to tap any man who should be overcome by sleep; from the other end of his wand there dangled a fox's tail; with this he politely brushed the faces of the women when he caught them dozing. One frequent sleeper incontinently struck the tithing-man for disturbing his repose; he was thereupon sent to the whipping post for "common sleeping at the public exercises."

The tithing-man had an arduous time of it, between waking up the sleepers, keeping the disorderly quiet, and driving away the rabble of dogs which were bred in that day as a defense against wolves, and which appear to have given almost as much trouble in meeting-time as the boys.

The pestiferous boys were relegated to the galleries; and in one church two men were specially appointed to watch them "that they might be contained in order." On report of the tithing-man, a lad was liable to be "called forth" and reproved by the minister, and if this were not sufficient he could be made to answer to the justice, and one boy was sent to the whipping post for fighting in meeting.

In New London the sexton was charged with digging graves, sweeping the meeting-house, "ordering the youth in meeting-time, and beating out the dogs;" but the Andover people hit upon a plan of settling the dog question by levying sixpence on the owner of every dog that should intrude into the service.

With the increase of luxury and refinement and the relaxation of religious rigor, the narrow slips with their hinged seats, which were raised when the people stood up and let down again with a great clatter, gradually gave way to square pews topped with turned balusters, in which the families sat together to the increase of decorum in the congregation. The tithing-man and his stick went out of existence, but even in the pews the irrepressible youngsters found chances to beguile the tedious Sunday hours by whispering between the balusters to their friends in the adjoining compartments.

*An old lamp from
St. Joseph's Church, Philadelphia*

MEETINGS OF
THE CONTINENTAL CONGRESS

The first Continental Congress met in Carpenters' Hall in Philadelphia, beginning on September 5, 1774. Eleven colonies were represented by forty-four delegates at the first meeting. Three delegates from a twelfth colony, North Carolina, arrived on September 14, and other delegates coming late eventually swelled the total to fifty-four colonial leaders. Because each colony could appoint as many delegates as it wished, the Congress decided that each colony should have just one vote. Peyton Randolph of Virginia was elected as the first president of the first Continental Congress.

Patrick Henry of Virginia made the keynote speech in which he said: " . . . British oppression has effaced the boundaries of the several colonies; the distinction between Virginians, Pennsylvanians, and New Englanders is no more. *I am not a Virginian, but an American.*" This sentiment was echoed in other speeches by other delegates.

Radicals and conservatives

Some delegates were radical, such as Sam Adams of Massachusetts. Some were conservative, such as John Dickinson of Pennsylvania. Many were timid and sought to compromise the issues. But the first important resolution, adopted on October 8, stated:

"That this Congress approve the opposition of the inhabitants of Massachusetts Bay to the execution of the late acts of Parliament; and if the same shall be attempted to be carried into execution by force, in such case all Americans ought to support them in their opposition."

The Congress adopted the *American Association,* on October 20, calling on the colonies to cease importing and exporting goods with Britain until the British acts punishing the people of Boston had been repealed. After sending appeals and addresses to the people of Britain, to the king, and to the people of Canada, the Congress adjourned on October 26, 1774, after having agreed to meet again in May 1775.

Short-tempered John Adams, who had hoped for more radical action from the Congress, wrote in his diary on October 24, 1774: "There is no greater mortification than to sit with half a dozen wits, deliberating upon a petition, address or memorial. These great wits, these subtle critics, these refined geniuses, these learned lawyers, these wise statesmen, are so

Chandeliers of this style were a luxury because of the many candles used but they were used in large entrance halls, parlors, dining rooms and meeting halls.

fond of showing their parts and powers as to make their consultations very tedious."

The second Continental Congress began meeting in Philadelphia on May 10, 1775. Peyton Randolph again was elected president, but later was replaced by John Hancock when Randolph was called to Virginia to a session of legislature, of which he was speaker. The two Adamses and Hancock were the focus of attention by the delegates as they told of their dramatic escape from Lexington, Massachusetts, just ahead of the British redcoats and of having heard the first shots of the battle fired before they galloped off to Philadelphia. Georgia was represented in this Congress for the first time by Lyman Hall, who arrived on May 25. Because he had been sent as a special delegate by the parish of St. Johns, rather than by the colony as a whole, he was admitted to a seat, but was not given a vote.

Where the first Continental Congress had been considered a committee of conference among the colonies, the second Congress clearly was regarded as a provisional government uniting all powers of executive, legislative, and judicial functions.

The Congress solemnly resolved on May 26 that war had been begun by Britain. But the delegates were not yet ready to end their allegiance to the king. New petitions and addresses were adopted and sent to the king, to Canada, and to other British colonies stating the case of the American colonies and expressing the desire for peace.

Washington named commander-in-chief

On June 15, 1775, Congress appointed George Washington as commander-in-chief of the new Continental Army, absorbing the militia troops currently assembled at Cambridge, Massachusetts, outside Boston. Four major generals and eight brigadier generals also were appointed. So strong were the ties with Britian that it was more than a year later before Thomas Jefferson's *Declaration of Independence* was adopted, and even then many conservative members of Congress, such as John Dickinson, refused to vote for it or sign it.

In December 1776 when Washington's army retreated to New Jersey from New York and the British were feared to be en route to capture Philadelphia, Congress fled to Baltimore, where it continued meeting until March 1777. By then Washington had won victories at Trenton and Princeton, so Congress returned to conduct its business in Philadelphia.

After the failure of the Continental Army to stop the British advance on Philadelphia at the battle of Brandywine on September 11, 1777, Congress again had to flee from the city, this time to York, Pennsylvania, west of the Susquehanna River, pausing on the way for a one-day session in Lancaster. After the British army decided to evacuate Philadelphia in June 1778 and marched back to New York City, Congress returned to the capital and continued sessions there until 1783. Begin-

A street lamp powered by candles in a four-sided globe suggested by Benjamin Franklin to give more draft and prevent smoking.
—Sketch by Kay Smith

ning in 1781, after the Articles of Confederation had been ratified, Congress began meeting regularly on November 1 each year. Congress again left Philadelphia in 1783. After holding sessions in Princeton, New Jersey; Annapolis, Maryland; and Trenton, New Jersey, Congress settled on New York City as the capital.

Long before the Revolutionary War was over the quality of the Congress had begun to decay. Less qualified delegates were sent from the states because many of the best leaders either were fighting in the war or were needed at home because of the monumental problems that had to be solved at the state level. After the new United States Constitution was drafted in 1787, rigor mortis began to set in. From November 3, 1788, to January 1, 1789, only six delegates showed up.

The first United States Congress under the new United States Constitution was appointed to meet for the first time on March 4, 1789. The City Hall in New York City, renovated and refurbished as Federal Hall under the direction of architect Pierre L'Enfant, was designated as the place of meeting. Most of the members were late arriving, and it was not until March 30 that thirty members of the House of Representatives had assembled to make up the necessary quorum to begin business. Frederick A. Mühlenberg of Pennsylvania was elected as the first Speaker of the House. A week later, on April 6, the U.S. Senate was able to begin business, electing John Langdon of New Hampshire as President of the Senate, and then counting the votes of the Electoral College that showed George Washington had been unanimously chosen as President of the United States and that John Adams had been elected by a majority to be Vice President.

*A portable desk
and writing utensils
of the colonial period*
—From a wash sketch by Kay Smith

★ ★ ★ ★ ★ ★ ★ ★ ★ ★ ★ ★ ★

Meeting dates of the Continental Congress

1774 (Sept. 5 to Oct. 26) . . . . Philadelphia
1775–1776 (May 10, 1775 to Dec. 12, 1776) . Philadelphia
1776–1777 (Dec. 20, 1776 to March 4, 1777) . Baltimore, Md.
1777 (March 5, 1777 to Sept. 18, 1777) . . . Philadelphia
1777–1778 (Sept. 30, 1777 to June 27, 1778) . York, Pa.
1778–1783 (July 2, 1778 to June 21, 1783) . Philadelphia
1783 (June 30 to Nov. 4) . . . . Princeton, N.J.
1783–1784 (Nov. 26, 1783 to June 3, 1784) . Annapolis, Md.
1784 (Nov. 1 to Dec. 24) . . . . Trenton, N.J.
1785 (Jan. 11 to Nov. 4) . . . . New York City
1785–1786 (Nov. 7, 1785 to Nov. 3, 1786) . . New York City
1786–1787 (Nov. 6, 1786 to Oct. 30, 1787) . New York City
1787–1788 (Nov. 5, 1787 to Oct. 21, 1788) . New York City
1788–1789 (Nov. 3, 1788 to March 2, 1789) . New York City

★ ★ ★ ★ ★ ★ ★ ★ ★ ★ ★ ★ ★

PRESIDENTS OF THE CONGRESS

PEYTON RANDOLPH,[1] of Virginia . . . . Elected September 5, 1774
HENRY MIDDLETON, of South Carolina . . . . . . Elected October 22, 1774
PEYTON RANDOLPH,[2] of Virginia . . . . Elected May 10, 1775
JOHN HANCOCK, of Massachusetts . . . . Elected May 24, 1775
HENRY LAURENS, of South Carolina . . . . Elected November 1, 1777
JOHN JAY, of New York . . . . Elected December 10, 1778
SAMUEL HUNTINGTON, of Connecticut . . . . . Elected September 28, 1779
THOMAS McKEAN, of Delaware . . . . Elected July 10, 1781
JOHN HANSON, of Maryland . . . . Elected November 5, 1781
ELIAS BOUDINOT, of New Jersey . . . . Elected November 4, 1782
THOMAS MIFFLIN, of Pennsylvania . . . . Elected November 3, 1783
RICHARD HENRY LEE, of Virginia . . . . Elected November 30, 1784
JOHN HANCOCK,[3] of Massachusetts . . . . Elected November 23, 1785
NATHANIEL GORHAM, of Massachusetts . . . . . Elected June 6, 1786
ARTHUR ST. CLAIR, of Pennsylvania . . . . Elected February 2, 1787
CYRUS GRIFFIN, of Virginia . . . . Elected January 22, 1788

★ ★ ★ ★ ★

SECRETARY OF THE CONGRESS

CHARLES THOMSON, of Pennsylvania . . . . Elected September 5, 1774

★ ★ ★ ★ ★

DELEGATES IN THE CONGRESS

CONNECTICUT[4]

Andrew Adams	1777–1780	Stephen M. Mitchell	1781–1784
Andrew Adams	1781–1782	Stephen M. Mitchell	1785–1786
Joseph P. Cook	1784–1788	Stephen M. Mitchell	1787–1788
Silas Deane	1774–1776	Jesse Root	1778–1783
Eliphalet Dyer	1774–1779	Roger Sherman	1774–1784
Eliphalet Dyer	1780–1783	Joseph Spencer	1778–1779
Pierrepont Edwards	1787–1788	Jedediah Strong	1782–1784
Oliver Ellsworth	1777–1784	Jonathan Sturges	1774–1787
William Hillhouse	1783–1786	John Treadwell	1785–1786
Titus Hosmer	1775–1776	Joseph Trumbull	1774–1775
Titus Hosmer	1777–1779	James Wadsworth	1783–1784
Benjamin Huntington	1780–1784	James Wadsworth	1785–1786
Benjamin Huntington	1787–1788	Jeremiah Wadsworth	1787–1788
Samuel Huntington	1776–1784	William Williams	1776–1778
William S. Johnson	1784–1787	William Williams	1783–1784
Richard Law	1778	Oliver Wolcott	1775–1778
Richard Law	1783–1784	Oliver Wolcott	1780–1784

[1] *Resigned October 22, 1774*
[2] *Died October 22, 1775*
[3] *Resigned May 29, 1786, not having served, owing to continued illness.*
[4] *No Delegates attended from Connecticut, Delaware, and Georgia in 1788–1789, and no credentials from these States for those years are in the Papers of the Continental Congress.*

DELAWARE[1]

Gunning Bedford[2]	1786–1787	William Peery	1785–1786
Gunning Bedford, Jr.	1783–1785	George Read	1774–1777
John Dickinson[3]	1776–1777	Caesar Rodney	1774–1776
John Dickinson	1779–1780	Caesar Rodney	1777–1778
Philemon Dickinson	1782–1783	Caesar Rodney	1782–1784
John Evans[3]	1776–1777	Thomas Rodney	1781–1783
Dyre Kearney[4]	1787–1788	Thomas Rodney	1785–1787
Eleazer McComb	1782–1784	James Sykes[5]	1777–1778
Thomas McKean	1774–1776	James Tilton	1783–1785
Thomas McKean	1778–1783	Nicholas Van Dyke[5]	1777–1782
Nathaniel Mitchell	1786–1788	John Vining	1784–1786
John Patten	1785–1786	Samuel Wharton	1782–1783

GEORGIA[1]

Benjamin Andrew[6]	1780	Richard Howley	1780–1781
Abraham Baldwin	1785	Noble Wimberly Jones	1775
Abraham Baldwin	1787–1789	Noble Wimberly Jones	1781–1782
Nathan Brownson	1777	Lachlan McIntosh[6]	1784
Nathan Brownson	1783	Edward Langworthy	1777–1779
Archibald Bulloch	1775–1776	William O'Bryen[6]	1789
Joseph Clay[6]	1778	Henry Osborne[6]	1786
Joseph Clay	1783	Nathaniel Pendleton[6]	1789
Samuel Elbert[7]	1784	William Pierce	1787
William Few	1780–1788	Samuel Stirk[6]	1781
William Gibbons	1784–1785	Edward Telfair	1778–1782
James Gunn[6]	1788–1789	Edward Telfair	1784–1785
Button Gwinnett	1776–1777	Edward Telfair	1788–1789
John Habersham	1785	John Walton	1778
Joseph Habersham	1783–1784	George Walton	1776–1778
Lyman Hall	1775–1778	George Walton	1780–1781
Lyman Hall	1780	George Walton	1787–1788
John Houstoun	1775–1777	Joseph Wood	1777–1778
John Houstoun	1779	John Zubly[8]	1775
William Houstoun	1783–1786		

MARYLAND

Robert Alexander	1775–1777	Charles Carroll ("Barrister")	1776–1777
William Carmichael	1778–1780		

---

1 *No Delegates attended from Connecticut, Delaware, and Georgia in 1788–1789 and no credentials from these States for those years are in the Papers of the Continental Congress.*
2 *Resigned January 15, 1787.*
3 *Resigned April 4, 1777.*
4 *Elected to fill vacancy caused by resignation of Gunning Bedford.*
5 *Elected to fill vacancies caused by resignations of John Dickinson and John Evans.*
6 *Did not attend.*
7 *Declined January 21, 1784.*
8 *Resigned in November 1775.*

Charles Carroll of Carrollton	1776–1777		Thomas Sim Lee	1783–1784
Daniel Carroll	1780–1784		Edward Lloyd	1783–1784
Jeremiah T. Chase	1783–1784		James McHenry	1783–1786
Samuel Chase	1774–1778		Luther Martin	1784–1785
Samuel Chase	1784–1785		William Paca	1774–1779
Benjamin Contee	1787–1788		George Plater	1778–1781
James Forbes[1]	1778–1780		Richard Potts	1781–1782
Uriah Forrest	1786–1787		Nathaniel Ramsay	1785–1787
Robert Goldsborough	1774–1775		Richard Ridgely	1785–1786
John Hall	1775		John Rogers	1775–1776
John Hall	1783–1784		David Ross	1786–1787
John Hanson	1780–1783		Benjamin Rumsey	1776–1778
William Harrison	1785–1787		Gustavus Scott	1784–1785
William Hemsley	1782–1784		Joshua Seney	1787–1788
John Henry	1784–1787		William Smith	1777–1778
William Hindman	1784–1787		Thomas Stone	1775–1779
John E. Howard	1787–1788		Thomas Stone	1784–1785
Daniel Jenifer of St. Thomas	1778–1782		Matthew Tilghman	1774–1777
Thomas Johnson	1774–1777		Turbutt Wright	1781–1783

MASSACHUSETTS

John Adams	1774–1778		Samuel Holten	1784–1785
Samuel Adams	1774–1782		Samuel Holten	1786–1787
Thomas Cushing	1774–1776		Jonathan Jackson	1782
Francis Dana	1776–1778		Rufus King	1784–1787
Francis Dana	1784		James Lovell	1776–1782
Nathan Dane	1785–1788		John Lowell	1782–1783
Elbridge Gerry	1776–1781		Samuel Osgood	1780–1784
Elbridge Gerry	1782–1785		Samuel A. Otis	1787–1788
Nathaniel Gorham	1782–1783		Robert Treat Paine	1774–1778
Nathaniel Gorham	1785–1787		George Partridge	1779–1782
John Hancock	1775–1780		George Partridge	1783–1785
John Hancock	1785–1786		Theodore Sedgwick	1785–1788
Stephen Higginson	1782–1783		James Sullivan	1782
Samuel Holten	1778–1780		George Thacher	1787
Samuel Holten	1782–1783		Artemas Ward	1780–1781

NEW HAMPSHIRE

Josiah Bartlett	1775–1778		Abiel Foster	1783–1785
Jonathan Blanchard	1783–1784		George Frost	1777–1779
Jonathan Blanchard	1787		John Taylor Gilman	1782–1783
Nathaniel Folsom	1774–1775		Nicholas Gilman	1786–1789
Nathaniel Folsom	1777–1778		John Langdon	1775–1777
Nathaniel Folsom	1779–1780		John Langdon	1786–1787

[1] *Died March 25, 1780.*

Woodbury Langdon	1779–1780	John Sullivan	1780–1781
Samuel Livermore	1780–1783	Matthew Thornton	1776–1778
Samuel Livermore	1785–1786	John Wentworth Jr	1778–1779
Pierce Long	1784–1786	William Whipple	1776–1779
Nathaniel Peabody	1779–1780	Phillips White	1782–1783
John Sullivan	1774–1775	Paine Wingate	1787–1788

NEW JERSEY

John Beatty	1783–1785	Frederick Frelinghuysen	1782–1783
Elias Boudinot	1777–1778	John Hart[10]	1776
Elias Boudinot[1]	1781–1783	Francis Hopkinson	1776
William Burnet[2]	1780–1781	Josiah Hornblower	1785–1786
Lambert Cadwalader	1784–1787	William C. Houston	1779–1782
Abraham Clark	1776–1778	William C. Houston	1784–1785
Abraham Clark[3]	1779–1783	James Kinsey	1774–1775
Abraham Clark	1786–1789	William Livingston	1774–1776
Silas Condict	1781–1784	James Schureman	1786–1787
John Cooper	1776	Nathaniel Scudder	1777–1779
Stephen Crane	1774–1776	Jonathan D. Sergeant[12]	1776
Jonathan Dayton[4]	1787–1788	Jonathan D. Sergeant[13]	1776–1777
John De Hart[6]	1774–1775	Richard Smith[14]	1774–1776
John De Hart[6]	1776	John Stevens	1783–1784
Samuel Dick	1783–1785	Charles Stewart	1784–1785
Jonathan Elmer[7]	1776–1778	Richard Stockton	1776
Jonathan Elmer[8]	1781–1784	John C. Symmes	1785–1786
Jonathan Elmer	1787–1788	John Witherspoon	1776–1779
John Fell	1778–1780	John Witherspoon	1780–1781
Frederick Frelinghuysen[9]	1778–1779	John Witherspoon[15]	1782

NEW YORK

John Alsop	1774–1776	Egbert Benson	1786–1788
Egbert Benson	1784–1785	Simon Boerum[16]	1775

---

1 *Elected to fill vacancy caused by declination of William Paterson.*
2 *Resigned April 1, 1781.*
3 *Elected to fill vacancy caused by declination of Thomas Henderson.*
4 *Elected to fill vacancy caused by declination of William Paterson.*
5 *Resigned November 22, 1775.*
6 *Resigned June 13, 1776.*
7 *Resigned October 2, 1778.*
8 *Elected to fill vacancy caused by resignation of William Burnet.*
9 *Resigned May 25, 1779.*
10 *Seat vacated August 30, 1776, by his election as Speaker of House of Assembly.*
11 *Resigned November 22, 1775.*
12 *Resigned June 22, 1776.*
13 *Resigned September 6, 1777.*
14 *Resigned June 12, 1776.*
15 *Elected to fill vacancy caused by declination of William C. Houston.*
16 *Died July 11, 1775.*

George Clinton	1775–1777	Philip Livingston[1]	1774–1778
Charles DeWitt	1783–1785	Robert R. Livingston	1775–1777
James Duane	1774–1784	Robert R. Livingston	1779–1781
William Duer	1777–1778	Walter Livingston	1784–1785
William Floyd	1774–1777	Isaac Low	1774–1775
William Floyd	1778–1783	Gouverneur Morris	1777–1780
Leonard Gansevoort	1787–1788	Lewis Morris	1775–1777
David Ghelston	1788–1789	Alexander McDougall	1781–1782
Alexander Hamilton	1782–1783	Alexander McDougall	1784–1785
Alexander Hamilton	1787–1788	Ephraim Paine	1784–1785
John Haring	1774–1775	Philip Pell	1788–1789
John Haring	1785–1788	Zephaniah Platt	1784–1786
John Jay	1774–1777	Philip Schuyler	1775–1777
John Jay	1778–1779	Philip Schuyler	1778–1781
John Lansing, Jr	1784–1788	John Morin Scott	1780–1783
John Laurance	1785–1786	Melancthon Smith	1785–1788
Francis Lewis	1774–1779	Henry Wisner	1774–1776
Ezra L'Hommedieu	1779–1783	Abraham Yates	1787–1788
Ezra L'Hommedieu	1787–1788	Peter W. Yates	1785–1787

NORTH CAROLINA

John B. Ashe[2]	1787	Samuel Johnston	1780–1782
Timothy Bloodworth	1786–1787	Allen Jones	1779–1780
William Blount	1782–1783	Willie Jones	1780–1781
William Blount	1786–1787	Abner Nash	1782–1784
Thomas Burke	1777–1781	Abner Nash[4]	1785–1786
Robert Burton	1787–1788	John Penn	1775–1776
Richard Caswell	1774–1776	John Penn	1777–1780
William Cumming	1784	William Sharpe	1779–1782
Cornelius Harnett	1777–1780	John Sitgreaves	1784–1785
Benjamin Hawkins	1781–1784	Richard D. Spaight	1783–1785
Benjamin Hawkins	1786–1787	John Swan[5]	1787–1788
Joseph Hewes	1774–1777	James White	1786–1788
Joseph Hewes[3]	1779	John Williams	1778–1779
Whitmil Hill	1778–1781	Hugh Williamson	1782–1785
William Hooper	1774–1777	Hugh Williamson	1787–1788

PENNSYLVANIA

Andrew Allen	1775–1776	Samuel J. Atlee	1778–1782
John Armstrong	1778–1780	John B. Bayard	1785–1787
John Armstrong	1787–1788	Edward Biddle	1774–1776

---

[1] *Died June 12, 1778*
[2] *Resigned November 1, 1787.*
[3] *Died November 10, 1779.*
[4] *Died December 2, 1786.*
[5] *Elected to fill vacancy caused by resignation of John B. Ashe.*

Edward Biddle	1778–1779	Cadwalader Morris	1783–1784
William Bingham	1787–1788	Robert Morris	1776–1778
Matthew Clarkson	1785–1786	John Morton	1774–1777
William Clingan	1777–1779	Frederick A.C. Muhlenberg	1778–1780
George Clymer	1776–1778	Richard Peters, Jr	1782–1783
George Clymer	1780–1783	Charles Pettit	1785–1787
Tench Coxe	1787–1788	Joseph Reed	1777–1778
John Dickinson	1774–1776	James R. Reid	1787–1789
Thomas Fitzsimons	1782–1783	Samuel Rhoads	1774–1775
Benjamin Franklin	1775–1776	Daniel Roberdeau	1777–1779
Joseph Galloway	1774–1775	George Ross	1774–1777
Joseph Gardner	1784–1785	Benjamin Rush	1776–1777
Edward Hand	1784–1785	Arthur St. Clair	1785–1787
William Henry	1784–1786	James Searle	1778–1780
Charles Humphreys	1774–1776	William Shippen	1778–1780
Jared Ingersoll	1780–1781	James Smith	1776–1778
William Irvine	1786–1788	Jonathan B. Smith	1777–1778
David Jackson	1785–1786	Thomas Smith	1780–1782
James McClene	1779–1780	George Taylor	1776–1777
Timothy Matlack	1780–1781	Thomas Willing	1775–1776
Samuel Meredith	1787–1788	James Wilson	1775–1776
Thomas Mifflin	1774–1776	James Wilson	1782–1783
Thomas Mifflin	1782–1784	James Wilson	1785–1787
Joseph Montgomery	1783–1784	Henry Wynkoop	1779–1783

RHODE ISLAND

Jonathan Arnold	1782–1784	David Howell	1782–1785
Peleg Arnold	1787–1789	James Manning	1785–1786
John Collins	1778–1783	Henry Marchant	1777–1780
Ezekiel Cornell	1780–1783	Henry Marchant	1783–1784
William Ellergy[1]	1776–1781	Nathan Miller	1785–1786
William Ellery	1783–1785	Daniel Mowry, Jr	1780–1782
John Gardiner	1789	James M. Varnum	1780–1782
Sylvester Gardiner[2]	1788–1789	James M. Varnum	1786–1787
Jonathan J. Hazard	1787–1789	Samuel Ward	1774–1776
Stephen Hopkins	1774–1780		

SOUTH CAROLINA

Robert Barnwell	1788–1789	William H. Drayton[3]	1778–1779
Thomas Bee	1780–1782	Nicholas Eveleigh	1781–1782
Richard Beresford	1783–1785	Christopher Gadsden	1774–1776
John Bull	1784–1787	John L. Gervais	1782–1783
Pierce Butler	1787–1788	Thomas Heyward, Jr.	1776–1778

---

1 *Elected to fill vacancy caused by death of Samuel Ward.*
2 *Did not take his seat.*
3 *Died September 3, 1779.*

Daniel Huger	1786–1788	Isaac Motte	1780–1782
Richard Hutson	1778–1779	John Parker	1786–1788
Ralph Izard	1782–1783	Charles Pinckney	1777–1778
John Kean	1785–1787	Charles Pinckney	1784–1787
Francis Kinloch	1780–1781	David Ramsay	1782–1784
Henry Laurens	1777–1780	David Ramsay	1785–1786
Thomas Lynch, Sr	1774–1776	Jacob Read	1783–1785
Thomas Lynch, Jr	1776–1777	Edward Rutledge	1774–1777
John Mathews	1778–1782	John Rutledge	1774–1777
Arthur Middleton	1776–1778	John Rutledge	1782–1783
Arthur Middleton	1781–1783	Paul Trapier	1777–1778
Henry Middleton	1774–1776	Thomas T. Tucker	1787–1788

VIRGINIA

Thomas Adams	1778–1780	Joseph Jones	1780–1783
John Banister	1778–1779	Arthur Lee	1781–1784
Richard Bland	1774–1775	Francis Lightfoot Lee	1775–1780
Theodorick Bland	1780–1783	Henry Lee	1785–1788
Carter Braxton[1]	1775–1776	Richard Henry Lee	1774–1780
John Brown	1787–1788	Richard Henry Lee	1784–1787
Edward Carrington	1785–1786	James Madison	1780–1783
John Dawson	1788–1789	James Madison	1786–1788
William Fitzhugh	1779–1780	James Mercer	1779–1780
William Fleming	1779–1781	John F. Mercer	1782–1785
William Grayson	1784–1787	James Monroe	1783–1786
Cyrus Griffin	1778–1781	Thomas Nelson, Jr.	1775–1777
Cyrus Griffin	1787–1788	Thomas Nelson, Jr.	1779–1780
Samuel Hardy[2]	1783–1785	Mann Page	1777
Benjamin Harrison	1774–1778	Edmund Pendleton	1774–1775
John Harvie	1777–1779	Edmund J. Randolph	1779–1782
James Henry	1780–1781	Peyton Randolph[3]	1774–1775
Patrick Henry	1774–1776	Meriwether Smith	1778–1782
Thomas Jefferson	1775–1776	George Washington	1774–1775
Thomas Jefferson	1783–1785	George Wythe	1775–1777
Joseph Jones	1777–1778		

---

1   *Elected to fill vacancy caused by death of Peyton Randolph.*
2   *Died October 17, 1785.*
3   *Died October 22, 1775.*

FIRST CONGRESS

MARCH 4, 1789, TO MARCH 3, 1791

FIRST SESSION — March 4, 1789,[1] to September 29, 1789
SECOND SESSION — January 4, 1790, to August 12, 1790
THIRD SESSION — December 6, 1790, to March 3, 1791

❖   ❖   ❖

VICE PRESIDENT OF THE UNITED STATES
John Adams, of Massachusetts

PRESIDENT PRO TEMPORE OF THE SENATE
John Langdon,[2] of New Hampshire

SECRETARY OF THE SENATE
Samuel A. Otis,[3] of Massachusetts

DOORKEEPER OF THE SENATE
James Mathers,[4] of New York

❖   ❖   ❖

SPEAKER OF THE HOUSE OF REPRESENTATIVES
Frederick A.C. Muhlenberg,[5] of Pennsylvania

CLERK OF THE HOUSE
John Beckley,[6] of Virginia

SERGEANT AT ARMS OF THE HOUSE
Joseph Wheaton,[7] of Rhode Island

DOORKEEPER OF THE HOUSE
Gifford Dalley

---

[1] *Neither a quorum of the Senate nor of the House of Representatives appeared in their respective chambers
on Wednesday, March 4, 1789. But eight Senators appeared and the minority adjourned from day to day
until Monday, April 6, when a quorum of the Senate was first present. Thirteen Members of the House
of Representatives appeared on March 4 and a quorum was not present until April 1, when the body
proceeded to the transaction of business. When both Houses were organized, on April 6, they met in joint
convention, in the hall of the Senate, and proceeded to open and count the electoral vote for
President and Vice President. John Adams, the Vice President elect, appeared in the Senate Chamber
and assumed the duties of the chair on Tuesday, April 21, 1789. On May 15, 1789, the Senate
determined by lot the classes into which the membership should be divided agreeably to paragraph 2,
section 3, of Article I of the Constitution, as follows:*
   Class 1, term expires March 3, 1791-Messres. Carroll, Dalton, Ellsworth, Elmer, Maclay, Read,
   and Grayson.
   Class 2, term expires March 3, 1793 — Messrs. Bassett, Butler, Few, Lee, Strong, Paterson, and Wingate.
   Class 3, term expires March 3, 1795 — Messrs. Gunn, Henry, Johnson, Izard, Langdon, and Morris.
[2] *Elected April 6, 1789.*
[3] *Elected April 8, 1789.*
[4] *Elected April 7, 1789.*
[5] *Elected April 1, 1789.*
[6] *Elected April 1, 1789.*
[7] *Elected May 12, 1789.*

CONNECTICUT
SENATORS
  Oliver Ellsworth
  William S. Johnson
REPRESENTATIVES
  Benjamin Huntington
  Roger Sherman
  Jonathan Sturges
  Jonathan Trumbull
  Jeremiah Wadsworth

DELAWARE
SENATORS
  Richard Bassett
  George Read
REPRESENTATIVE
  John Vining

GEORGIA
SENATORS
  William Few
  James Gunn
REPRESENTATIVES
  Abraham Baldwin
  James Jackson
  George Matthews

MARYLAND
SENATORS
  John Henry
  Charles Carroll, of
    Carrollton

MARYLAND (*continued*)
REPRESENTATIVES
  Daniel Carroll
  Benjamin Contee
  George Gale
  Joshua Seney
  William Smith
  Micheal Jenifer Stone

MASSACHUSETTS
SENATORS
  Tristram Dalton
  Caleb Strong
REPRESENTATIVES
  Fisher Ames
  Elbridge Gerry
  Benjamin Goodhue
  Jonathan Grout
  George Leonard
  George Partridge[1]
  Theodore Sedgwick
  George Thacher

NEW HAMPSHIRE
SENATORS
  John Langdon
  Paine Wingate
REPRESENTATIVES
  Abiel Foster
  Nicholas Gilman
  Samuel Livermore

NEW JERSEY
SENATORS
  Jonathan Elmer
  William Paterson[2]
  Philemon Dickinson[3]
REPRESENTATIVES[4]
  Elias Boudinot
  Lambert Cadwalader
  Thomas Sinnickson
  James Schureman

NEW YORK
SENATORS
  Rufus King[5]
  Philip John Schuyler[6]
REPRESENTATIVES
  Egbert Benson
  William Floyd
  John Hathorn[7]
  John Laurance
  Peter Silvester[8]
  Jeremiah Van Rensselaer[9]

NORTH CAROLINA
SENATORS
  Benjamin Hawkins[10]
  Samuel Johnston[11]
REPRESENTATIVES
  John Baptista Ashe[12]
  Timothy Bloodworth[13]
  John Sevier[14]
  John Steele[15]
  Hugh Williamson[16]

1 *Resigned August 14, 1790*
2 *Resigned November 13, 1790, having been elected governor.*
3 *Elected to fill vacancy caused by resignation of William Paterson, and took his seat December 6, 1790*
4 *The election of all four Representatives was contested, but owing to the burning of the papers and documents from the First to the Sixth Congress, by the British in 1814, it is not possible to ascertain the grounds upon which the contest was based. It is known that it related to questions of regularity and procedure, and that the decision was favorable to the sitting Members.*
5 *Took his seat July 25, 1789; term to expire, as determined by lot, March 3, 1795.*
6 *Took his seat July 27, 1789; term to expire, as determined by lot, March 3, 1791*
7 *Took his seat April 23, 1789.*
8 *Took his seat April 22, 1789.*
9 *Took his seat May 9, 1789*
10 *Took his seat January 13, 1790; term to expire, as determined by lot, March 3, 1795.*
11 *Took his seat January 29, 1790; term to expire, as determined by lot, March 3, 1793,*
12 *Took his seat March 24, 1790.*
13 *Took his seat April 6, 1790.*
14 *Took his seat June 16, 1790.*
15 *Took his seat April 19, 1790.*
16 *Took his seat March 19, 1790.*

Benjamin Franklin's visit to the House of Commons in 1766. —From a painting by C.E. Mills

PENNSYLVANIA

SENATORS
  William Maclay
  Robert Morris

REPRESENTATIVES
  George Clymer
  Thomas Fitzsimons
  Thomas Hartley
  Daniel Hiester
  Frederick A.C. Muhlenberg
  John Peter G. Muhlenberg
  Thomas Scott
  Henry Wynkoop

RHODE ISLAND

SENATORS
  Theodore Foster[1]
  Joseph Stanton, Jr.[2]

REPRESENTATIVE
  Benjamin Bourn[3]

SOUTH CAROLINA

SENATORS
  Pierce Butler
  Ralph Izard

REPRESENTATIVES
  Aedanus Burke
  Daniel Huger
  William L. Smith[4]
  Thomas Sumter
  Thomas Tudor Tucker

VIRGINIA

SENATORS
  William Grayson[5]
  John Walker[6]
  James Monroe[7]
  Richard Henry Lee

REPRESENTATIVES
  Theodoric Bland[8]
  William B. Giles[9]
  John Brown
  Isaac Coles
  Richard Bland Lee
  James Madison
  Andrew Moore
  John Page
  Josiah Parker
  Alexander White
  Samuel Griffin

---

[1] *Took his seat June 25, 1790; term to expire, as determined by lot, March 3, 1791.*

[2] *Took his seat June 25, 1790; term to expire, as determined by lot, March 3, 1793.*

[3] *Took his seat December 17, 1790.*

[4] *Took his seat April 13, 1789; on April 15, 1789, David Ramsay presented a petition claiming that Smith was ineligible because at the time of his election he had not been a citizen of the United States the term of years required by the Constitution, which was referred to the Committee on Elections; the committee reported on April 18, 1789, and on May 22, 1789, the House adopted a resolution that Mr. Smith was eligible at the time he was elected.*

[5] *Died March 12, 1790*

[6] *Appointed to fill vacancy caused by death of William Grayson, and took his seat April 26, 1790.*

[7] *Elected to fill vacancy caused by death of William Grayson, and took his seat December 6, 1790*

[8] *Died June 1, 1790*

[9] *Elected to fill vacancy caused by death of Theodoric Bland, and took his seat December 7, 1790.*

Ethan Allen, the redoubtable leader of the Green Mountain Boys, who was declared an outlaw for enforcing a form of pioneer justice and later became a hero of the Revolutionary War for capturing Fort Ticonderoga.

MEN AND WOMEN
OF THE REVOLUTION

In the five hundred biographies that follow an attempt has been made to highlight the known facts about a cross-section of the Americans who gave their time, money, effort, and often their lives to help achieve and secure independence for the United States. All the Founding Fathers who signed the Declaration of Independence and the United States Constitution are included. All the delegates who sat in the Continental Congresses and the first United States Congress have biographies. Military figures include most of the generals of the Continental Army. The section also encompasses biographies of other officers, soldiers, politicians, writers, artists, poets, and housewives.

Few, if any, generalizations can be drawn about these Americans, other than that each was an individual and proud of it. No two people wore exactly the same kind of clothes, lived in exactly the same kind of houses, or believed in exactly the same ideas. Mass production and mass media had not yet been invented. And many of the patriots or their parents had come to America primarily to be free of the conformity demanded by kings and religious leaders.

Individuality was respected to such a great extent that even during the heat of the Revolutionary War those Americans who preferred to remain loyal to the British crown were allowed to live in their own houses, remain at their same jobs, and carry on a normal life—so long as they did not spy for the British or actively try to restore British rule.

What a person could do counted for much more than what a person was or had been. Age didn't matter: at nineteen the Marquis de Lafayette was commissioned a major general in the Continental Army, and at seventy Seth Pomeroy died while leading his troops in the field in the middle of winter. Social position counted for little: a general might be a farmer (George Washington), a tavern-keeper (Israel Putnam), a bookseller (Henry Knox), or a physician (Joseph Warren). And you didn't have to have been born in America to die in battle for independence: Richard Montgomery (Ireland); Hugh Mercer (Scotland); Casimir Pulaski (Poland); and Baron de Kalb (Bavaria). Many had graduated from Harvard, Princeton, Yale, and other American colleges. Others had spent many years at English and European schools. But there were others who had taught themselves to read and write.

A comb-back chair
—Sketch by Kay Smith

89

Historians of the Revolutionary War period recorded little biographical information about women, largely because women were not allowed to participate openly in politics or war. Those women who did take an active role had to act with circumspection (such as Mercy Otis Warren, who planted her ideas in the minds of men and let them take the credit), or act surreptitiously (such as Deborah Sampson, who disguised herself as a man in order to fight the British). Most of the women of the times are more typically identifiable with Abigail Adams, who kept the home fires burning and reared children while her husband was away winning the war; with Mary Draper, who sent her cherished pewter off to be made into bullets; or even with Nancy Hart, who secretly buried the enemies she killed.

★ ★ ★ ★ ★

A plate warmer

• ABIGAIL (SMITH) ADAMS   1744–1818

The only woman to be the wife of one President and the mother of another, Abigail Smith was the second of three daughters of a clergyman. She was born in Weymouth, Massachusetts, November 23, 1744. She, like most other girls of the time, did not attend school, but became well educated by reading the books in her father's library. At the age of nineteen she married John Adams on August 25, 1764. At the time he was a rising young lawyer, who was ten years older than she. They had five children, the eldest being John Quincy Adams, who became the sixth President of the United States.

Abigail Adams' contribution to American history came in the patriotism she inspired in her husband and in her children. Following is an extract from one of her letters written during the Revolutionary War:

"Heaven is our witness that we do not rejoice in the effusion of blood or the carnage of the human species—but, having been forced to draw the sword, we are determined never to sheathe it—*slaves to Britain.* Our cause, Sir, I trust, is the cause of truth and justice and will finally prevail, though the combined force of earth and hell should rise against it."

While Adams served as a diplomat in Europe during the Revolutionary War he took John Quincy Adams with him, while Mrs. Adams cared for the other children at home. But, after the war, when he was appointed as the first American ambassador to Britain, she joined him in London. That she received her share of slights is apparent from this comment she wrote in a letter home: "Whoever in Europe is known to have adopted republican principles must expect to have all the engines of every court and courtier in the world displayed against him."

Shortly before returning from Europe she wrote to one of her sisters: "When I reflect on the advantages which the people of America possess over the most polished of other na-

Abigail Adams, the only woman to be the wife of one President and the mother of another, John Quincy Adams, oldest of her five children.
—From a wash sketch by Kay Smith

tions—the ease with which property is obtained, the plenty which is so equally distributed, their personal liberty and security of life and property—I feel grateful to Heaven who marked out my lot in that happy land; at the same time I deprecate that restless spirit, and that baneful ambition and thirst for power, which will finally make us as wretched as our neighbors.''

When Adams became Vice-President and then President, Abigail, or Abby as her husband called her, served as a charming and graceful hostess. After Adams' retirement, she kept up a constant flow of letters to friends and relatives discussing the happenings of the times. She died in Quincy, Massachusetts, on October 28, 1818.

• ANDREW ADAMS 1736–1797

A delegate to the Continental Congress from Connecticut, Andrew Adams was born in Stratford, Connecticut, January 7, 1736. He was graduated from Yale College in 1760, studied law, and then was admitted to the Fairfield County bar. In 1772 he became prosecuting attorney of Litchfield County. He was a member of the Connecticut council of safety for two years, and then served in the Revolutionary War with the rank of colonel. A member of the Connecticut house of representatives from 1776 to 1781, he served as speaker in 1779–80. As a delegate to the Continental Congress from 1777–82, he signed the Articles of Confederation. Appointed chief justice of the Connecticut supreme court in 1793, he continued in that office until his death in Litchfield on November 26, 1797.

• JOHN ADAMS 1735–1826

One of the most important of the Founding Fathers of the United States, John Adams helped bring about the American Revolution, helped win it, and then helped establish the new nation as the first Vice President and second President.

Born in Braintree (now Quincy), Massachusetts, on October 30, 1735, Adams was graduated from Harvard College at the age of twenty. After teaching school and studying law, he was admitted to the bar and began practicing law in Braintree in 1758. When the British parliament passed the Stamp Act, Adams wrote essays in the *Boston Gazette*, appealing for popular opposition. The next year he moved to Boston, where he began to take a more active role in colonial politics. After the Boston Massacre of March 5, 1770, Adams and his friend Josiah Quincy acted as defense lawyers for the British soldiers who were accused of murder. Adams defended them on the grounds that the real culprits were the members of the British government in London who had sent them there, obtaining acquittal for all but two who were convicted on lesser charges of manslaughter and released with only a reprimand.

During the next several years Adams served in the colonial legislature, and then was elected as one of the Massachusetts delegates to the first Continental Congress in 1774. There he met George Washington, Patrick Henry, and patriots from other colonies, but he was disappointed in the mildness of the actions of the Congress.

Attending the second session of the Continental Congress in 1775, shortly after fighting had begun at Lexington and Concord, Adams nominated George Washington as commander in chief of the Continental Army that was to be formed. During the next several months he was active on many committees of the Congress, helping gather together men and supplies for the fight against the British.

A member of the committee to draft the Declaration of In-

John Adams, one of the most influential leaders of the colonial period, the second President of the United States.

dependence, he deferred the task of writing it to Thomas Jefferson, and then enthusiastically helped win its approval by the Congress.

After continuing to serve in the Continental Congress through 1777, Adams was sent to France in 1778 to help Benjamin Franklin negotiate for aid from France. He returned to Massachusetts in 1779, where he was elected to the state constitutional convention and did much of the work in writing the first Massachusetts constitution.

In 1780 Adams returned to France, appointed by Congress as minister plenipotentiary to negotiate a peace treaty with

Samuel Adams, older cousin of John Adams, one of the real firebrands of revolutionary fervor who firmly believed in the rights to life, liberty, and property, and the right to defend all.

Britain and a treaty of trade and friendship with the Netherlands. He successfully concluded the treaty with the Netherlands in October 1782, and then joined Franklin and other American peace commissioners in negotiating the peace treaty with Britain that finally was concluded on September 3, 1783. He remained in Europe for five years, first negotiating trade treaties with various countries, and then serving as the first American ambassador to Britain.

Adams returned to the United States in 1788, just as the new United States Constitution was made effective by ratification by nine states. In February 1789 he was elected as the nation's first Vice-President to serve under George Washington, the first President. As political parties formed out of the rivalry between Thomas Jefferson and Alexander Hamilton, Adams received the support of Hamilton's Federalists in winning a second term as Vice-President in 1793.

After Washington announced he would not run for a third term in 1796, the Federalists supported Adams as their candidate for President against Jefferson. When the electoral votes were counted, Adams received 71 and Jefferson 68, so Adams became the nation's second President with Jefferson as his Vice-President.

During Adams' administration, the United States was drawn into an undeclared naval war with France. Adams lost popularity, especially because of the Alien and Sedition Acts passed by Congress under which newspapermen were jailed for printing criticisms of him and the government. Adams lost the election of 1800 to Jefferson and retired to Quincy, Massachusetts, at the end of his term in 1801.

In the last twenty-five years of his life Adams devoted much of his time to writing of the events that led up to the Revolutionary War. He died on July 4, 1826, on the same day that Thomas Jefferson died—the 50th anniversary of the adoption of the Declaration of Independence, to which they had both devoted their lives.

• SAMUEL ADAMS   1722–1803

More than any other man, Samuel Adams fanned the sparks of patriotism until they burst into the flames of the American Revolution. Thirteen years older than his cousin John Adams, he was born in Boston, Massachusetts, on September 27, 1722. At the age of seventeen he was graduated from Harvard College, and then continued his studies there, receiving a master's degree in 1743, after taking as his thesis the proposition: "Whether it be lawful to resist the supreme magistrate if the commonwealth cannot otherwise be preserved."

The son of a brewer, he inherited his father's business, but soon lost it because he was more interested in politics than making money. He became a member of the Caucus Club, the behind-the-scenes political organization of the city, and in

An earthenware teapot

1756 was elected to his first public office as tax collector.

When the British parliament passed the Stamp Act, Adams organized the secret patriotic society, the Sons of Liberty, to oppose it, and inspired the mobs who sacked the homes and offices of British officials to show their displeasure. Elected to the Massachusetts legislature in 1765, he became clerk of that body, and in effect became the "political boss" of the colony.

His agitation against the quartering of British troops in Boston led to the Boston Massacre in 1770, and two years later he organized the first committees of correspondence that became the underground communications network for patriots in various towns of Massachusetts and eventually among the colonies. He expressed his views simply and forthrightly, as in this report he wrote in 1772: "Among the natural rights of the colonists are these: First, a right to life. Second, to liberty. Thirdly, to property; together with the right to support and defend them in the best manner they can. These are evident branches of, rather than deductions from, the duty of self-preservation, commonly called the first law of nature."

Boston Tea Party

Adams' Sons of Liberty, dressed as Indians, carried out the Boston Tea Party in 1773, bringing about the British reprisals against Boston that shocked all of the colonies into action. As a delegate from Massachusetts, he attended and helped organize the first Continental Congress in Philadelphia in 1774.

Along with John Hancock, Samuel Adams was regarded by the British military governor of Boston, Lt. Gen. Thomas Gage, as a prime traitor against the crown. When Hancock and Adams were preparing to leave for the second Continental Congress in 1775, Gage sent out troops from Boston to arrest them for treason, and it was this force that was stopped by minutemen at Lexington and Concord. Adams was said to have seen the first shots fired at Lexington on April 19, 1775, declaring, "This is a glorious day for America."

Adams continued to serve in the Continental Congress until 1782, signing the Declaration of Independence in 1776 and grumbling that it "should have been made immediately after the 19th of April, 1775." In 1779 he and John Adams did most of the work in drawing up Massachusetts' first constitution, and he was a member of the state convention that ratified the United States Constitution in 1788 after he had obtained promises that it would be amended to include a bill of rights.

Defeated in his efforts to be elected to the first U.S. Congress because of his anti-Federalist views, he was elected lieutenant governor of Massachusetts from 1789 to 1793, serving under his old friend John Hancock, who was governor. Upon Hancock's death in 1793, he became acting governor, and then was elected governor each year from 1794 through 1797. At the age of seventy-six he retired from public life, and died five years later in Boston on October 2, 1803.

*Faneuil Hall, Boston meeting and market place dating back to colonial times,
where many of the grievances were publicly asserted by such rebels as James Otis,
Samuel Adams, John Hancock, and others.*

The Concord North Bridge just 21 miles from Boston, where the first major confrontation of the colonial and British forces, on April 19, 1775, ignited a war that lasted six years and ended in American freedom from England.

FROM A WATERCOLOR PAINTING
BY KAY SMITH

The Wayside Inn, near Lexington and Concord, where many of the colonial leaders, including George Washington, dined during the late eighteenth century — immortalized through Tales of a Wayside Inn *by Henry Wadsworth Longfellow.*

Raising the Liberty Pole in 1776 —Engraved by J.C. McRae after F.A. Chapman

• THOMAS ADAMS   1730−1788

A delegate to the Continental Congress from Virginia, Thomas Adams was born in New Kent County, Virginia, in 1730. He attended common schools and then became clerk of Henrico County. In 1762 he went to England to represent various business interests, remaining there until 1774. Returning to Virginia shortly before the Revolutionary War, he was elected to the Virginia house of burgesses and signed the Articles of Association on May 27, 1774. He served as chairman of the New Kent County committee of safety in 1774. A member of Virginia's delegation to the Continental Congress from 1778 to 1780, he signed the Articles of Confederation. Adams died on his estate, "Cowpasture," in Augusta County, Virginia, in August 1788.

• ROBERT ALEXANDER[1]

One of the handful of members of the Continental Congress to turn traitor, Robert Alexander was born on his family's estate in Cecil County, Maryland, which is now part of the city of Elkton. After studying law and being admitted to the bar, he was elected to the provincial convention of Maryland in 1774–1776, became secretary of the Baltimore committee of observation and member of the council of safety in 1775, and was commissioned a first lieutenant in the Baltimore militia on June 6, 1776. Alexander became a member of the Maryland delegation to the Continental Congress on December 9, 1775, and was re-elected July 4, 1776. Opposing the adoption of the Declaration of Independence, he soon after fled from Maryland to seek protection from the British and joined the Associated Loyalists of America. In 1780 he was adjudged guilty of high treason and his property was confiscated. When it became clear that the British had lost the war, Alexander sailed to London in 1782, where he later died.

• WILLIAM ALEXANDER (LORD STIRLING)   1726–1783

One of George Washington's most faithful generals, William Alexander was born in New York City in 1726, the son of a prominent lawyer, James Alexander, who was secretary and then attorney general of New York. He came naturally by his love of liberty, learning of the importance of freedom from his father, who was disbarred for a year in 1735 because of his defense of John Peter Zenger in his battle for freedom of the press.

In the French and Indian War he served as aide-de-camp to Gen. William Shirley, commander of British forces in America and governor of Massachusetts. In 1756 he accompanied Shirley to England to help defend him against charges of mismanagement of the war. While in England he unsuccessfully claimed the estates and title of the earldom of Shirley, and thereafter when he returned to America was known as Lord Stirling.

Married to a sister of William Livingston, who later became the first governor of the state of New Jersey, the wealthy Alexander settled in an elegant home in Basking Ridge, New Jersey. An astronomer and mathematician, he was appointed surveyor-general of New Jersey, a post that his father also at one time had held.

Upon the outbreak of the Revolutionary War, Alexander was appointed as a colonel of the 1st New Jersey regiment. The first action in which he distinguished himself was when he and Elias Dayton led four boats in the capture of a British supply ship, the *Blue Mountain Valley*, on January 22–23, 1776, off the coast of Sandy Hook, New Jersey. In March he was promoted to brigadier general and given command of pre-

[1]*Exact dates of birth and death unknown.*

Lord Stirling at the Battle of Long Island —After a painting by Chappel

*General William Alexander, Lord Stirling,
one of Washington's favorite generals*
—From a drawing by Chappel

paring the defenses of New York City. At the Battle of Long Island on August 27, 1776, he commanded battalions from Maryland and Delaware with about 1,600 men who bravely beat back a force of 7,000 British troops for several hours until surrounded and forced to surrender.

Alexander was released after about a month in a prisoner exchange for the governor of the Bahamas and rejoined Washington's troops. He took part in the Battle of Trenton on Christmas night 1776, and two months later was promoted to major general. He fought at the battles of Brandywine and Germantown in 1777 and commanded the artillery on the left wing of the Battle of Monmouth in 1778. Washington appointed him president of the court-martial that found Gen. Charles Lee guilty of disobedience in the Monmouth battle. In January 1780 he led an unsuccessful raid against British troops on Staten Island, and later that year sat on the board of inquiry that sentenced John André to be hanged as a spy for his part in Gen. Benedict Arnold's treason. In October 1781 he was placed in command of the Northern Department of the Continental Army with orders to prepare for an expected British attack from Canada. A hard drinker, he died of gout in Albany, New York, on January 15, 1783, at the age of fifty-six.

• ANDREW ALLEN   1740−1825

One of the most distinguished members of the Continental Congress to turn against his countrymen and join the British, Andrew Allen was born in Philadelphia, Pennsylvania, in June 1740. After graduation from the University of Pennsylvania in 1759, he completed law studies at the Temple in London. Returning to Philadelphia, he was admitted to the bar in 1765, and was appointed as the colony's attorney general the next year. From 1765 to 1775 he was elected to the Pennsylvania assembly and served as a member of the committee of safety in 1775−76. He was elected as a member of Pennsylvania's delegation to the Continental Congress in 1775 and 1776, but disapproved of the growing movement for independence and withdrew in June 1776. After the British army entered New York, he crossed over the British lines, took an oath of allegiance to the King, and renounced the oaths he had taken as a member of the Continental Congress. After the patriots confiscated his estates for his treason, the British government compensated him with an annual pension of 400 pounds. He died in London on March 7, 1825.

• ETHAN ALLEN   1737−1789

Commander of the rough-and-ready Green Mountain Boys of Vermont, Ethan Allen was born on January 10, 1737, in Litchfield, Connecticut. He apparently had little or no schooling, but by the age of twenty-five was co-owner of an ironworks in Salisbury, Connecticut. Four years later, in 1776, he decided to seek his fortune in the wilderness region that later became Vermont. This region was claimed both by New Hampshire and New York. To resist New York claims, Allen organized his band of Green Mountain Boys who beat up New York officials, burned the homes of New York settlers, and enforced their own frontier justice. In turn, the government of New York declared Allen an outlaw and offered a reward for his capture. After learning of the outbreak of the Revolutionary War at Lexington and Concord, Allen devised a plan to capture the British Fort Ticonderoga on Lake Champlain. Before setting off at the head of about 200 to 300 men, Allen was joined by Benedict Arnold, who had been commissioned a colonel by Massachusetts. About dawn on May 10, 1775, Allen and his men burst into the fort while the commander was still in bed. Allen said later that he demanded the surrender of the fort "in the name of the Great Jehovah and the Continental Congress." He captured 50 prisoners and a large amount of guns and military supplies in this first American victory of the war.

Allen led his Green Mountain Boys on two expeditions into Canada later in 1775 to try to persuade the settlers there to join the American cause against the British. He decided to try

The Continental soldier equipped for battle —From an engraving by J.C. McRae after Chappel

to capture Montreal largely with Canadian volunteers he had recruited while another few hundred men under Col. John Brown of Massachusetts attacked the city from the other side. On the night of September 24–25, 1775, Allen ferried his men across the St. Lawrence River in canoes and was ready to attack before dawn, when he learned that Brown had been unable to get his men into position to help. Sighted by the British, Allen and about 40 of his men were captured after a brief fight. When the British commander, Col. Richard Prescott, learned of Allen's identity as the captor of Fort Ticonderoga, he bound him hand and foot in shackles and threw him in the hold of a ship bound for England.

Allen gained his freedom in 1778 in a prisoner exchange, and upon reporting to George Washington at Valley Forge was given a commission of colonel in the Continental Army "in reward of his fortitude, firmness and zeal in the cause of his country, manifested during his long and cruel captivity, as well as on former occasions."

Returning to Vermont, Allen was appointed major general of the militia. He also was sent to the Continental Congress in an unsuccessful effort to get that body to recognize Vermont's independence from New Hampshire and New York. During the latter part of the Revolutionary War the British negotiated with Allen in an effort to get Vermont to unite with Canada. He died in Burlington, Vermont, February 13, 1789, two years before Vermont gave up its independence and joined the United States.

• JOHN ALSOP   1724–1794

A member of the Continental Congress from New York, John Alsop was born in New Windsor, Orange County, New York, in 1724. After completing his education, he moved to New York City where he built up an importing business. Alsop represented New York City in the colonial legislature, and was one of the incorporators of New York Hospital, serving as its governor from 1770 to 1784. Elected a member of the New York delegation to the Continental Congress, he served from September 14 to October 26, 1774, and from May 10, 1775 to 1776. The citizens of New York City chose him in 1775 as a member of the committee of one hundred who ran the government until a convention could be assembled. He later served as the eighth president of the New York Chamber of Commerce in 1784–85. Alsop died in Newtown, Long Island, New York, on November 22, 1794. His body was buried in Trinity Church cemetery in New York City.

John Alsop

• FISHER AMES   1758–1808

A member of the First U.S. Congress from Massachusetts, Fisher Ames was born in Dedham, Massachusetts, April 9,

Fisher Ames

1758. After attending the town school in Dedham and receiving private tutoring, he attended Harvard College, graduating in 1774. During the next seven years he taught school and studied law. After being admitted to the bar, he began law practice in Dedham in 1781. He served in the state house of representatives in 1788, and that same year was a member of the Massachusetts convention that ratified the new United States Constitutuion. Ames was elected as a Federalist to the first four Congresses, from 1789 to 1797. In Congress he distinguished himself with his powers of oratory. His speech in favor of the adoption of Jay's Treaty with Britain in 1796 was so powerful that opponents asked postponement of a vote on the measure, fearing the emotions he had aroused would sway too many in favor of the treaty. Ames did not seek re-election in 1796, returning to the practice of law in Dedham. He was a member of the Massachusetts governor's council in 1799 and 1800. Chosen president of Harvard University in 1804, he declined to accept because of failing health. He died in Dedham at the age of fifty, on July 4, 1808.

• BENJAMIN ANDREW 1730—1799

A Georgia delegate to the Continental Congress, Benjamin Andrew was born in Dorchester, South Carolina, in 1730. He moved to Georgia in 1754 where he farmed in St. John's Parish. Andrew became president of the state executive council in 1777 and was elected a delegate to the Continental Congress in 1780. He died in Liberty County, Georgia, about 1799.

• JOHN ARCHER 1741—1810

The first person graduated with a medical degree in America and a Revolutionary War hero, John Archer was born near Churchville, Maryland, May 5, 1741. He was graduated from Princeton College in 1760, and then studied medicine at the College of Philadelphia, graduating in 1768 with the first medical diploma issued by a school in the American colonies. While practicing medicine in Maryland, he became active in pre-Revolutionary patriotic committees. He raised a military company and served as aide-de-camp to Gen. Anthony Wayne, rising to the rank of major. After the battle of Stony Point, New York, in 1779, he carried news of Wayne's victory to Washington's headquarters. Also active in politics during the war, Archer was a member of Maryland's first constitutional convention in 1776 and was a member of the state legislature from 1777 to 1779. A supporter of Thomas Jefferson, he was elected to three terms in Congress, serving from 1801 to 1809. He died at his country home, "Medical Hall," near Churchville, Maryland, on September 28, 1810.

• JOHN ARMSTRONG 1717—1795

A general in the Revolutionary War and a member of the Continental Congress, John Armstrong was born in Brookbor, County Fermanagh, Ireland, October 13, 1717. He became a

View of Pittsburgh in the eighteenth century

civil engineer and then moved to Pennsylvania. In the French and Indian War he led Pennsylvania militia in destroying the Indian villages at Kittanning and became a friend of George Washington during the expedition against Fort Duquesne in 1758. At the age of fifty-eight he was commissioned a brigadier general in the Continental Army in 1776. He helped defend Charleston, South Carolina, from British attack later that year, but, feeling his services were not appreciated, he resigned in 1777. Appointed as a major general in the Pennsylvania militia, he served in that capacity throughout the rest of the Revolution, taking part in the battles of Brandywine and Germantown. He was elected as a delegate to the Continental Congress in 1778–80 and 1787–88. His two sons John, Jr., and James both served in the Revolution and later in the U.S. Congress. At the age of seventy-seven, General Armstrong died in Carlisle, Pennsylvania, on March 9, 1795.

• JOHN ARMSTRONG, JR.   1755–1843

A son of General John Armstrong, John Armstrong, Jr., was born in Carlisle, Pennsylvania, on November 25, 1755. A seventeen-year-old student at Princeton College when the Revolutionary War began, Armstrong left college to become aide-de-camp to Brig. Gen. Hugh Mercer. When Mercer was fatally wounded during the Battle of Princeton in 1777, Armstrong carried the dying general off the battlefield. He then became aide-de-camp to Maj. Gen. Horatio Gates, serving with him at the battle of Saratoga and throughout the rest of the war.

In 1783, while the Continental Army was encamped at Newburg, New York, awaiting the end of peace negotiations, great discontent arose among the officers and men because Congress was so slow in sending them their back pay. Because Major Armstrong was noted for his ability as a writer, he was chosen to write the grievances of the officers, which were circulated anonymously as the "Newburg Addresses." This document called on the army to take matters into their own hands and threaten to take over the government, if necessary, if their back pay demands were not met. At a meeting of the disgruntled officers on March 15, 1783, General Washington calmed their fears, assuring them they would be justly treated, and ended the plot to revolt.

After the war, Armstrong successively became secretary of state and adjutant-general of the state of Pennsylvania. In 1789, he married a sister of Chancellor Robert Livingston of New York and moved to that state. He served as U.S. Senator from New York from 1800 to 1804 and as minister to France in 1804–10. During the War of 1812 he was appointed Secretary of War in 1813, but resigned a year later when he was blamed for the loss of the nation's capital. He died in Red Hook, New York, on April 1, 1843.

The most notorious traitor of the Revolutionary War, Benedict Arnold was born in Norwich, Connecticut, on January 14, 1741, the great-grandson of a governor of Rhode Island who had the same name. Apprenticed to a druggist at the age of fourteen, he ran away, joined the army, and then deserted. He enlisted again at the age of nineteen, and again deserted after brief service in upstate New York. Returning to Connecticut, he completed his apprenticeship as a pharmacist, and then opened a store of his own in New Haven, Connecticut. Successful as a businessman, he financed voyages of a merchant ship and accompanied it on voyages to the West Indies and to Canada.

Elected a captain of militia in New Haven in 1774, Arnold saw the coming conflict with Britain as an opportunity to win fame and glory. As soon as he heard of the outbreak of fighting at Lexington and Concord, he marched his men to Massachusetts to volunteer his services. He talked the authorities there into commissioning him as a colonel with permission to raise men to capture Fort Ticonderoga. Learning of Ethan Allen's plans to capture the fort, he hurried the Vermont, taking with him only a servant, and demanded that Allen turn over command of the operation to him. Allen refused, but let Arnold accompany him. A few days after Allen's men had captured Ticonderoga, Arnold led a detachment that captured the British garrison at St. Johns, Canada, on May 17, 1775.

In September 1775, Arnold was placed in command of a thousand troops with the assignment to capture Quebec. He led his men on a long march through the wilderness of Maine, reaching the Canadian city two months later, on November 9, after having lost about a fourth of his men to cold and sickness. He was joined by Gen. Richard Montgomery and troops from New York, and they laid siege to Quebec until the end of December. Finally, on New Year's eve they began an unsuccessful attack that ended with Montgomery being killed and Arnold badly wounded. Arnold was promoted to brigadier general and remained with his troops outside of Quebec until relieved of his command in April 1776. In the summer and fall of 1776, Arnold commanded a fleet of boats on Lake Champlain, where he battled the British gunboats with skill and bravery.

After British troops destroyed an important Continental Army depot at Danbury, Connecticut, Arnold distinguished himself by leading militia attacks on the British as they retreated to their ships. As a result, he was appointed major general on May 2, 1777, but Arnold was angered because five other generals had been promoted ahead of him and he felt he should not be their junior.

Although Gen. Horatio Gates, who was in overall command of American forces, received most of the credit for the

Benedict Arnold —From an engraving by H.B. Hall

defeat of British Gen. John Burgoyne at the Battles of Saratoga in September and October 1777, Burgoyne himself and most historians believe Arnold was responsible for the victory. As a reward for his actions, Congress asked Washington to give Arnold a new commission as major general, dating it to give him seniority over the other five generals he believed should be his junior. Washington complied. Arnold had been badly wounded at Saratoga and it took him many months to recover.

After the British evacuated Philadelphia in June 1778, Arnold was placed in command of that city. There he married the daughter of a prominent Tory and lived extravagantly, falling deeply into debt. Accused of using his position to fatten his purse, Arnold was court-martialed and found guilty on two counts in January 1780, but was sentenced merely to receive a reprimand.

Long before the court-martial, Arnold had been in touch with the British, plotting and negotiating to get the best deal

The Hudson River from Fort Putnam at West Point, New York

for turning traitor. Finally, the British agreed to pay 20,000 pounds if he could surrender West Point, New York, to them. After much maneuvering, Arnold managed to get command of West Point in August 1780. Then, on September 23, the plot began to unravel when three militiamen captured British Maj. John André, who was acting as a go-between with Arnold. On September 25, Arnold learned of André's capture and fled to seek protection from the British. After a court-martial, André was hanged as a spy. But Arnold escaped without penalty.

The British gave Arnold a commission as a brigadier general, and for the rest of the war he led a series of raids against his countrymen in Connecticut and in Virginia. After the war he lived for a few years in Canada, and then moved to England in 1791. He died in London ten years later on June 14, 1801.

• **JONATHAN ARNOLD   1741–1793**

A delegate to the Continental Congress from Rhode Island, Jonathan Arnold was born in Providence, Rhode Island, December 3, 1741. After studying medicine, he began practice in Providence. During the Revolutionary War he served as director of the army hospital in Providence. He was elected a member of Rhode Island's delegation to the Continental Congress in 1782–84. Arnold moved to St. Johnsbury, Vermont, in 1787. There he was appointed a member of the governor's council and as a judge. He died in St. Johnsbury on February 1, 1793.

• **PELEG ARNOLD   1751–1820**

A tavern-keeper, delegate to the Continental Congress, and chief justice of Rhode Island, Peleg Arnold was born in Smithfield, Rhode Island, on June 10, 1751. After attending Brown University, Arnold studied law, and began practice in Smithfield, where he also was keeper of the "Peleg Arnold Tavern." He served in the general assembly of Rhode Island 1777–78 and 1782–83, and was chosen as a delegate to the Continental Congress 1787–89. In 1790 he was incorporator of the Providence Society for Abolition of Slavery. Arnold was appointed chief justice of the supreme court of Rhode Island 1795–1809 and 1810–12. He completed his years of public service by serving again in the state legislature 1817–19. Arnold died in Smithfield on February 13, 1820.

• **JOHN ASHE   1720–1781**

A militia general during the Revolutionary War, John Ashe was born in Grovely, North Carolina, in 1720. As speaker of the North Carolina assembly from 1762 to 1765, he led the colony's opposition to the Stamp Act. As an officer in the colony's militia, he and his men tried to capture the colony's royal governor, Josiah Martin, at the outbreak of the Revolution. He and his men captured Fort Johnston at the mouth of the Cape Fear River, but the governor escaped to a British ship.

   Appointed a brigadier general of North Carolina's militia, Ashe suffered a military disaster at Briar Creek on March 3, 1779. While leading a force of 1,600 militia toward Savannah, Georgia, Ashe paused at Briar Creek to rebuild a bridge the British had destroyed. British Lt.Col. Marc Prevost launched a surprise attack, trapping Ashe and his men between the creek and a swamp. After holding their ground briefly, the militia panicked. Some leaped into the water. Some headed for the swamp. About 200 Americans were killed and about 170 captured. Only five British soldiers were killed. Ashe asked for and received a court-martial, which found that he should have been better prepared for the attack.

In 1781, the British captured Ashe and threw him in prison where he contracted smallpox. Paroled because of his illness, he died shortly after, on October 24, 1781, in Sampson County, North Carolina.

• JOHN BAPTISTA ASHE   1748−1802

A soldier and a politician, John Baptista Ashe was born in 1748 in Rocky Point, North Carolina. He served with North Carolina troops throughout the Revolutionary War, advancing to the rank of colonel. Elected to the state legislature in 1784, he became speaker of the house in 1786, and the next year was elected as a delegate to the Continental Congress. He was a member of the state convention that ratified the United States Constitution, and then was elected to the First and Second U.S. Congresses. In 1802 he was elected governor of North Carolina, but died on November 27, 1802, in Halifax, North Carolina, before being inaugurated.

• SAMUEL JOHN ATLEE   1739−1786

A soldier and a politician, Samuel John Atlee was born in Trenton, New Jersey, in 1739. He grew up in Lancaster, Pennsylvania, and at the age of sixteen volunteered for service in the French and Indian War. He fought in the battle of Fort Duquesne in 1758 as a lieutenant, and the next year was promoted to captain. At the beginning of the Revolutionary War, he was appointed as colonel in command of the Pennsylvania musketry battalion. He and his men fought bravely at the battle of Long Island, but were surrounded and captured on August 27, 1776. Atlee was held prisoner for more than two years before being exchanged. Upon his return home in 1778, he immediately was elected as a delegate to the Continental Congress from 1778 to 1782. After the war he was elected to the Pennsylvania legislature, dying while serving in that body in Philadelphia on November 25, 1786.

• CRISPUS ATTUCKS   c.1723−1770

Crispus Attucks, according to legend and some records, was over six feet in stature, mulatto, and at the time of the Boston Massacre about fifty years old. He was born in Framingham, Massachusetts, about 1723, and had gone to the Bahamas to work. He had returned to Boston with the intention of going to work there or seeking employment elsewhere.

John Adams, who represented the British soldiers accused of murder in the massacre, described Attucks as the leader of the "rowdy mob" fired at by the British. Adams said:

"This Attucks . . . appears to have undertaken to be the hero of the night, and to lead this army with banners, to form them in the first place in Dock square and march them up to

A broadside reminding the citizens of Boston
of the massacre of five young men

Crispus Attucks

King Street with their clubs . . . this man with his party cried
do not be afraid of them . . ."

Several years later Adams used Attucks' deed to help stir
patriotic enthusiasm. In a letter to the press which he signed
with Attucks' name he said the British were "chargeable before
God and Man with our Blood."

Cornwallis cannon in Savannah, Georgia —Sketch by Kay Smith

• ABRAHAM BALDWIN   1754–1807

A signer of the United States Constitution, Abraham Baldwin was born in North Guilford, Connecticut, on November 22, 1754. Entering Yale College at the age of thirteen, he was graduated in 1772, and then stayed on studying law and tutoring other students. From 1777 until 1783 he served as a chaplain for Connecticut troops in the Revolutionary War. After the war, he went to Savannah, Georgia, where he was admitted to the bar in 1784. Three months later he was elected to the state legislature, where he drew up the charter for the University of Georgia, the first university chartered by a state. In 1785 he was elected as a member of Georgia's delegation to the Continental Congress, and in 1786 attended the Annapolis Convention that called for the convening of a national constitutional convention.

Baldwin represented Georgia at the Constitutional Convention in 1787, helping draft and then signing the United States Constitution. Elected to the first U.S. Congress in 1788, he served with James Madison on the committee that drafted the Bill of Rights amendments. He was reelected every two years to the U.S. House of Representatives until 1798 when he was elected to the U.S. Senate. He served as a senator until his death in Washington, D.C., on March 4, 1807.

• JOHN BANISTER   1734—1788

A signer of the Articles of Confederation, John Banister was born on his family's estate near Petersburg, Virginia, on December 26, 1734. He attended private school in England and was graduated in law from the Temple in London. After returning to Virginia, he practiced law in Petersburg. He was a member of Virginia's legislature for most of the period 1765–83. Banister served as an officer of Virginia militia during the Revolutionary War, and in 1778 was elected as a member of the state's delegation to the Continental Congress where he helped write and signed the Articles of Confederation. He died on his estate, "Hatcher's Run," near Petersburg on September 30, 1788.

• JOSHUA BARNEY   1759—1818

A naval hero of both the Revolutionary War and the War of 1812, Joshua Barney was born July 6, 1759, in Baltimore, Maryland. At the age of twelve, he made his first voyage across the Atlantic as an apprentice seaman. By the time he was fifteen, he became captain of the *Sidney*, when the captain of that vessel died at sea on a voyage to France. Barney sailed the ship on to France, discharged its cargo, and then sailed it back to America. He first learned of the outbreak of the Revolutionary War when British officers boarded his vessel when he entered Chesapeake Bay in October 1775. He joined the Continental Navy, which was just then being formed in Philadelphia, and was appointed mate of the 10-gun sloop *Hornet*, aboard which he took part in the successful raid on the Bahama Islands in March 1776. In ensuing actions he often was placed in command of captured ships, and himself was captured and exchanged three times. In 1781 he again was captured and sent to prison in England, but escaped and made his way back to the United States by way of the Netherlands. In 1782 he was given command of the 16-gun *Hyder Ali* and in April captured the larger 20-gun British brig *General Monk* in a battle off Cape May, New Jersey. Later that year he was placed in command of the *General Monk*, in which he sailed to France and back with dispatches to and from Benjamin Franklin. In the War of 1812 he served in the U.S. Navy, serving first as a captain and later as a commodore. While leading 500 marines in the Battle of Bladensburg in defense of Washington, D.C., in 1814, he was wounded and taken prisoner. He died in Pittsburgh, Pennsylvania, on December 1, 1818, while preparing to take his family to land he had bought in Kentucky.

Joshua Barney

• ROBERT BARNWELL   1761—1806

A soldier and politician, Robert Barnwell was born in Beaufort, South Carolina, on December 21, 1761. At sixteen, he joined the army to fight in the Revolutionary War. While serving as a lieutenant at the siege of Charleston in 1780, he was captured by the British and sent aboard the prison ship *Pack Horse*. After his release in a general exchange of prisoners in June 1781, Barnwell rejoined his company and was wounded seventeen times in a battle at Johns Island, South Carolina. At the age of twenty-seven, he was elected to the Continental Congress in 1788 and to the South Carolina convention that ratified the United States Constitution. As a Federalist, Barnwell won election to the Second U.S. Congress 1791–93. After declining renomination to Congress, he was elected to the state house of representatives 1795–97 and to the state senate 1805–06. He died in Beaufort, South Carolina, on October 24, 1814.

• JOHN BARRY   1745–1803

One of the outstanding captains of the Continental Navy, John Barry was born in Tacumshane, Ireland, in 1745. He went to sea when he was a boy and quickly rose to command. He settled in Philadelphia at age fifteen and in the 1760s became a well-to-do shipmaster and shipowner. When the Continental Navy was formed, he was given command of the 14-gun brig *Lexington*, and on April 17, 1776, captured the British tender *Edward*, the first prize taken in combat by the new American navy. In command of the 32-gun *Effingham* in Delaware Bay when the British took Philadelphia in 1777, Barry burned the ship rather than surrender it, rejecting a bribe offered by the British to turn the ship over to them. While commanding the 32-gun *Raleigh* in 1778, he was forced to run the ship aground in Penobscot Bay to avoid being captured by British cruisers. While in command of the 32-gun *Alliance* in 1781 and 1782, he captured many prizes, including the British ships *Atlanta* and *Trespass*, which he defeated in a long battle. Barry fought the last naval engagement of the Revolutionary War in January 1783, when his *Alliance* fought off the larger British warship *Sybille* in a battle that lasted about an hour. When the United States Navy was created in 1794, Barry was commissioned as the senior officer. He supervised the building of the 44-gun frigate *United States*, but never saw action again. He died in Philadelphia on September 13, 1803.

Captain John Barry

• JOSIAH BARTLETT   1729–1795

The first member of the Continental Congress to vote for adoption of the Declaration of Independence, Josiah Bartlett was born in Amesbury, Massachusetts, on November 21, 1729. He received his early education from tutors, mastering Greek and Latin by the age of sixteen. He then turned to the study of medicine and began practicing medicine at the age of twenty-one in Kingston, New Hampshire. A member of the

Josiah Bartlett

colonial legislature from 1765 to 1775, he became an increasingly vocal opponent of the royal governor. Elected to the first Continental Congress in 1744, he was unable to serve because loyalists burned down his home. He represented New Hampshire in the Continental Congress in 1775 and 1776, and had the honor of having his name called first in the roll of states to vote on adoption of the Declaration of Independence, answering with a loud "Yea and Amen." As a lieutenant colonel of the state militia, he fought in the Battle of Bennington in 1777. He again served in the Continental Congress in 1778, where on July 9 he was the first delegate to sign the Articles of Con-

The Battle of Bennington —From an engraving by St. Memin

federation. He served as chief justice of the New Hampshire court of common pleas from 1779 to 1782, associate justice of the state's supreme court from 1782 to 1788, and chief justice of the state supreme court from 1788 to 1790. After ratification of the United States Constitution, the state legislature elected Bartlett as one of its first U.S. Senators, but he declined the office. He was elected as the president of New Hampshire from 1790 to 1793, and when a new constitution went into effect he was elected as the state's first governor from 1793 to 1794. After retiring from public life because of failing health, he died on May 19, 1795, in Kingston, New Hampshire.

• WILLIAM BARTON   1748–1831

A heroic officer in the Revolutionary War, William Barton was born on May 26, 1748, in Warren, Rhode Island. While serving as a major in the Rhode Island militia in 1777, Barton with a small party of men crossed Narragansett Bay in boats on the night of July 10, captured the British General Richard Prescott, and brought him back to the American lines. Prescott was especially hated because of the harshness of his treatment of Ethan Allen when that hero was captured at Montreal. The Continental Congress voted Barton a sword and a commission as a colonel in appreciation of his service. Wounded at Bristol Ferry in August, 1778, Barton ended his military service. Many years later, when Barton was in his seventies, the Marquis de Lafayette learned that the old soldier was being held in jail in Vermont because he could not pay a judgment levied on land he owned in that state. Lafayette paid the claim and obtained Barton's release. Barton died in Providence, Rhode Island, at the age of eighty-three on October 22, 1831.

Colonel William Barton

Richard Bassett

• RICHARD BASSETT   1745–1815

A signer of the United States Constitution, Richard Bassett was born April 2, 1745, in Cecil County, Maryland. The son of a tavern-keeper, he was adopted by a wealthy lawyer who educated him in the law and left him a large estate. During the Revolutionary War, Bassett was captain of a troop of Delaware light-horse militia, and from 1776 to 1786 he served in

the Delaware legislature. In 1786 Bassett represented Delaware at the Annapolis Convention and the next year was a
member of the state's delegation to the Constitutional Convention, where he helped write and signed the United States
Constitution. From 1789 to 1793 he served in the U.S. Senate. For six years, from 1793 to 1799, he was chief justice of
Delaware's court of common pleas, and then was elected as
governor of the state for the term of 1799 to 1801. At the end
of his term as governor, he was appointed as a federal circuit
judge by President John Adams. Bassett died at his estate,
"Bohemia Manor," in Cecil County, Maryland, on September
15, 1815.

- **JOHN BUBENHEIM BAYARD   1738–1807**

A soldier and politician, John Bubenheim Bayard was born in
Cecil County, Maryland, on August 11, 1738. In 1756 he
moved to Philadelphia, where he became one of the city's
leading merchants during the next twenty years. A militia
colonel during the Revolutionary War, he served in the battles
of Princeton, Brandywine, and Germantown. He was a member of Philadelphia's council of safety in 1776–77 and was
elected to the Pennsylvania general assembly 1776–79 and in
1784. From 1785 to 1787 he was elected a member of Pennsylvania's delegation to the Continental Congress. Bayard
moved to New Brunswick, New Jersey, in 1788, where he
became mayor in 1790 and later a judge of the court of common pleas. He died in New Brunswick on January 7, 1807.

- **JOHN BEATTY   1749–1826**

A physician, soldier, and politician, John Beatty was born in
Neshaminy, Pennsylvania, on December 10, 1749. A graduate
of the College of New Jersey in 1769, he studied medicine in
Philadelphia and then became a physician in Bucks County,
Pennsylvania. Joining the Continental Army in 1775, Beatty
was a major when he was captured by the British at the surrender of Fort Washington, New York, November 16, 1776.
After his exchange, Beatty was appointed commissary general
of prisoners with the rank of colonel in 1778. He resigned
from the army in 1780 and returned to the practice of medicine, settling in Princeton, New Jersey. In 1784–85 he served
in the Continental Congress, where he was a member of a
special committee that thanked Marquis de Lafayette for his
services in the American cause before his departure for
France. Beatty later served as a member of the state general
assembly 1789–90, in the Third U.S. Congress 1793–95, and
as secretary of state of New Jersey 1795–1805. He became
president of the Trenton (N.J.) Banking Company in 1815,
remaining in that position until his death in Trenton on May
30, 1826.

GUNNING BEDFORD 1742–1797

A Delaware soldier and politician, Gunning Bedford was born in Philadelphia on April 7, 1742, five years older than his cousin Gunning Bedford, Jr. As a lieutenant colonel in the crack Delaware Continentals Regiment, Bedford was wounded in the battle of White Plains on October 28, 1776. Subsequently he was appointed Muster Master General for the period 1776–77. Leaving the army, he was admitted to the bar in Delaware in 1779. Bedford won election to the Delaware general assembly 1784–86, and was elected a member of the Continental Congress for the term 1786–87. He was a delegate to the Delaware convention in 1787 that ratified the United States Constitution, and was a presidential elector in 1788. Elected governor of Delaware in 1796, he served in that office until his death in New Castle, Delaware, September 30, 1797.

GUNNING BEDFORD, JR. 1747–1812

A signer of the United States Constitution, Gunning Bedford, Jr., was born in Philadelphia in 1747. He was graduated from the College of New Jersey (now Princeton University) in

Gunning Bedford, Jr.

The waterfront on the Delaware River in Philadelphia about 1800 —From an engraving by W. Birch & Son

119

1771, where James Madison was one of his classmates. He studied law in Philadelphia, and during the Revolutionary War served for a time as an aide to George Washington. In 1779 he was admitted to the bar in Dover, Delaware, and began practicing law there. From 1783 to 1785 he was a member of Delaware's delegation to the Continental Congress, in 1786 was a delegate to the Annapolis Convention, and in 1787 was a delegate to the Constitutional Convention. His arguments in the interests of small states were a major factor in the decision to give each state two senators in the new United States government. After signing the United States Constitution, Bedford helped win its ratification by Delaware, the first state to do so. In 1789 George Washington appointed Bedford as the first U.S. district judge for Delaware, a position he held until his death on March 30, 1812, in Wilmington, Delaware.

- ## THOMAS BEE   1725–1812

A delegate to the Continental Congress from South Carolina, Thomas Bee was born in Charleston, South Carolina, in 1725. After graduation from Oxford University in England, he studied law and was admitted to the bar in Charleston in 1761. He was regularly elected to the colonial legislature from 1762 to 1776, and took an active part in the pre-Revolutionary movement as a member of the council of safety 1775–76. Bee then won election to the new state house of representatives 1776–79 and in 1782, serving as speaker of the house 1777–79. He was South Carolina's lieutenant governor in 1779–80, and then was elected to the Continental Congress for the period 1780–82. President George Washington appointed him as a federal district judge in 1790. Bee died in Pendleton, South Carolina, February 18, 1812.

- ## CORNELIA (VAN CORTLANDT) BEEKMAN   1752–1847

A patriot whose judgment of the honesty of men contributed to the exposure of Benedict Arnold's treason, Cornelia Van Cortlandt was born in 1752 at Van Cortlandt Manor in Croton-on-Hudson, New York, which is still preserved as a historic residence. Her father later was lieutenant governor of New York from 1777 to 1795, and her older brother Philip was promoted to brigadier general for his bravery in the Battle of Yorktown. At the age of seventeen, Cornelia married Gerard G. Beekman, a wealthy businessman. Throughout the Revolutionary War, she and her husband lived in a large brick manor house her husband had built north of Peekskill, New York. Here she had many encounters with foraging British soldiers, when they were in the vicinity, and entertained George Washington and his officers when they passed through. Her most notable contribution to history came about because Lt. John Webb, an aide to General Washington, had left in her care

A chest on a chest

*Margaret Beekman, daughter of Henry Beekman
and wife of Robert R. Livingston* —Courtesy of Beekman Arms Inn

a valise containing a new uniform and some gold. In September 1780 an acquaintance, Joshua Smith, whose brother had been royal chief justice of New York, called at the house and asked for the valise, saying: "You know me very well, Mrs. Beekman; and when I assure you that Lieutenant Jack sent me for the valise, you will not refuse to deliver it to me, as he is greatly in want of his uniform." She answered: "I do know you very well—*too well* to give you the valise without a written order from the owner." Smith appealed to her husband, who urged her to give up the valise, but she was adamant, so the angered Smith rode off. Later, it was learned that Smith had overheard Webb mention that he had left the uniform with Mrs. Beekman, and that he had been trying to obtain it so that it could be worn by the British spy Maj. John André in trying to escape through American lines after his last meeting with Benedict Arnold. Had not Mrs. Beekman stood firm in her suspicions of Smith, André might have escaped, and Benedict Arnold's treason would not have been exposed. Having lived to the age of ninety-five, Mrs. Beekman died on March 14, 1847, in her birthplace, Van Cortlandt Manor.

• EGBERT BENSON   1746–1833

A delegate to the Continental Congress from New York, Egbert Benson was born in New York City on June 21, 1746.

Coat of Arms,
King's College, New York

After graduation from King's (now Columbia) College in 1765, he studied law and was admitted to the bar. In 1777 he was appointed as the first attorney general of the state of New York, serving until 1789. He also was a member of the state assembly 1777–81 and again in 1788. Benson was appointed as one of three commissioners in 1783 who directed the deportation of Tory loyalists to Canada and other British colonies. From 1784 to 1788 Benson was a delegate to the Continental Congress, and then was elected to the First and Second U.S. Congresses 1789–93. He was an associate judge of the New York supreme court from 1784 to 1801, when he then was appointed by President John Adams as a federal circuit judge. In 1812 he was elected to the Thirteenth U.S. Congress, but resigned in 1813 after serving only five months. Benson died in Jamaica, New York, on August 24, 1833.

• **RICHARD BERESFORD**   **1755–1803**

A soldier and politician, Richard Beresford was born in Berkeley County, South Carolina, in 1755. After studying law at the Middle Temple in London, England, he was admitted to the bar in 1773 in Charleston, South Carolina. A member of the state militia, Beresford served under Gen. Isaac Huger in the Georgia campaign in 1778. At the fall of Charleston in 1780 he was captured by the British and imprisoned at St. Augustine, Florida, until 1781 when he was exchanged. Upon his return home the twenty-six-year-old Beresford immediately was elected to the state house of representatives, and the next year was appointed to the privy council. He was elected lieutenant governor in 1783, but resigned shortly afterward, having been elected to the Continental Congress for the period of 1783–84. He retired from politics at the age of twenty-nine and devoted the rest of his life to managing his extensive plantations and to writing. He died in Charleston, South Carolina, at the age of forty-eight, on February 6, 1803.

• **EDWARD BIDDLE**   **1738–1779**

A delegate to the Continental Congress who opposed the Declaration of Independence, Edward Biddle was born in Philadelphia in 1738. Joining the army in 1754 at the age of sixteen, he served throughout the French and Indian War, advancing to the rank of captain. After resigning from the army in 1763, he studied law and began practice in Reading, Pennsylvania. Biddle was elected to the Pennsylvania assembly from 1767 to 1775, serving as speaker in 1774. Elected as a delegate to the First and Second Continental Congresses in 1774 to 1776, he opposed the Declaration of Independence and did not sign it. He again was elected to the Continental Congress for the period 1778–79. At the age of forty-one, he died at Chatsworth, Maryland, on September 5, 1779.

Nicholas Biddle —From a painting by C.W. Peale

- **NICHOLAS BIDDLE   1750–1778**

A heroic American naval captain who went down with his ship, Nicholas Biddle was born in Philadelphia on September 10, 1750. He shipped out to sea at the age of thirteen, making his first voyage to Quebec. Two years later, he and two shipmates were castaway on an uninhabited island in the West Indies for two months before being rescued. In 1770 he joined the royal navy as a midshipman. But, seeking further adventure, he deserted in 1773 in order to sign on as a seaman on the polar exploration ship *Carcass*. On this voyage he was a shipmate of fifteen-year-old Horatio Nelson, who served as coxswain. Returning to Philadelphia in 1775, the city's committee of safety engaged him to take a ship to Cuba to bring back gunpowder. After this successful mission, Benjamin Franklin commissioned him as a captain in the newly formed Pennsylvania Navy, giving him command of the galley *Franklin*, which was just being built. When the Continental Congress

William and Mary College is the second oldest advanced institution of learning in the United States, having been founded in 1693 by the Reverend James Blair, its first president and rector of the Church at Jamestown and of Bruton Church in Williamsburg. Sir Christopher Wren, the noted English architect who introduced pure Renaissance style in designing St. Paul's Cathedral in London, drew the plans for William and Mary College, with some modifications to adapt to the needs of the colonies. The college was named for the reigning sovereigns and the college colors are orange and white, like the House of Orange. A president and six professors composed the original faculty. The college was burned three times—in 1705, 1859, and 1863—each time being restored within the same brick walls. The list of the many distinguished Americans who attended William and Mary College includes George Wythe, distinguished lawyer and professor, Thomas Jefferson, John Marshall, Edmund Randolph, Peyton Randolph, James Monroe, John Tyler, General Winfield Scott, and many others.

—From a wash sketch by Kay Smith

created the Continental Navy, he was one of the first four captains commissioned in December 1775. Given command of the 14-gun brig *Andrea Doria*, he took part in the successful raid on the Bahamas in March 1776. Later in 1776 he captured two British transports carrying 400 Highland troops bound for Boston. In 1777 in command of the new 32-gun frigate *Randolph* he sailed to the West Indies where he captured the 20-gun British *True Briton* and three merchantmen, all of which he sailed into Charleston, South Carolina. The people of Charleston fitted out four small warships and placed them under Biddle's command. After slipping out of the British blockade of the port, Biddle's *Randolph* was overtaken on March 7, 1778, by the 64-gun British *Yarmouth*. Biddle was seriously wounded early in the engagement, and then a broadside from the larger warship blew up *Randolph*. Biddle and all but four of his 315-man crew were lost.

• **WILLIAM BINGHAM**   1752–1804

A member of the Continental Congress from Pennsylvania, William Bingham was born in Philadelphia on March 8, 1752. At the age of sixteen he was graduated from Philadelphia College in 1768. During the Revolutionary War, he was an agent from 1777 to 1780 for the Continental Congress in the West Indies at Martinique and St. Pierre. He was elected to the Continental Congress for the period 1787–88, and then became a member of the Pennsylvania house of representatives in 1790–91, serving as speaker in 1791. He became president of the state senate in 1794, and next served one term in the U.S. Senate from 1795 to 1801. Bingham then withdrew from public life, moving to Bath, England, where he lived with his daughter until his death there on February 7, 1804.

• **JOHN BLAIR**   1732–1800

A signer of the United States Constitution, John Blair was born in 1732 in Williamsburg, Virginia. After graduation from William and Mary College about 1752, he went to London where he studied law in the Middle Temple. He was regularly elected to the Virginia house of burgesses from 1765 to 1775. In 1776 he helped draw up Virginia's declaration of rights and its first state constitution, and then served on Governor Patrick Henry's executive council. In 1787 he was a member of the Virginia delegation to the Constitutional Convention, where he signed the United States Constitution despite some objections to centering all executive power in one man. In 1789 George Washington appointed him as one of the first associate justices of the United States Supreme Court, a position he held until illness forced him to resign in 1796. He died in Williamsburg on August 31, 1800.

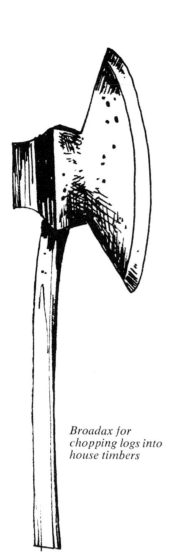

Broadax for chopping logs into house timbers

• **JONATHAN BLANCHARD** 1738–1788

A delegate to the Continental Congress from New Hampshire, Jonathan Blanchard was born in Dunstable, New Hampshire on September 18, 1738. Active in the patriotic movement, he was chosen a member of the colony's council of twelve in 1775 and served in the state's first legislature in 1776. The next year he was appointed as attorney general of the state. Blanchard represented New Hampshire in the Continental Congress in 1783–84 and in 1787. He became the first judge of probate under the state constitution in 1784. Blanchard died in Dunstable on July 16, 1788.

• **RICHARD BLAND** 1710–1776

A Virginia statesman, Richard Bland was born in Orange County, Virginia, on May 6, 1710. He graduated from William and Mary College and then studied law at the University of Edinburgh. First elected to the Virginia house of burgesses in 1745, he served thirty-one years in that body, becoming its most senior member, and was given the nickname "The Virginia Antiquary." A leader in the patriotic movement, he published "Inquiry into the Rights of the British Colonies," during the Stamp Act controversy of 1765, and was one of the first men chosen to serve on Virginia's committee of correspondence in 1773. Along with Patrick Henry, George Washington, and other distinquished Virginians, he was a delegate to the First Continental Congress in 1774. Although elected again in 1775, he declined to serve, regarding his presence at the Virginia Revolutionary convention of 1776 as more critical to the patriotic cause. But before he could play a larger part in the Revolutionary War, Bland died in Williamsburg, Virginia, on October 26, 1776.

• **THEODORICK BLAND** 1742–1790

A cavalry commander and delegate to the Continental Congress, Theodorick Bland was born near Petersburg, Virginia, on March 21, 1742, a descendant of the Indian princess Pocahontas and a nephew of Richard Bland (see above). After being educated in England, he studied medicine at the University of Edinburgh. Returning to Virginia in 1759 at the age of seventeen, he developed an extensive medical practice. One of the patriots who captured the arms from the governor's residence in Williamsburg, Virginia, in 1775, he joined the Continental Army the next year as captain of the 1st Troop of Virginia Cavalry. Subsequently he advanced to become colonel of the 1st Continental Dragoons and commanded General Washington's cavalry at the battle of the Brandywine. In 1778 he was given the job of escorting the 5,000 British troops that had surrendered at the battle of Saratoga on their long march from Connecticut to Virginia, and after he got them there he was made commander of their prison camp, where he earned the nickname of "Alexander the Great."

Resigning from the army in 1779, Bland was elected as one of Virginia's delegates to the Continental Congress from 1780 to 1783. A follower of Patrick Henry, he opposed ratification of the United States Constitution at the Virginia convention in 1788. Elected to the First U.S. Congress, he was a member of the Congressional committee that escorted General Washington from New Jersey to New York City for his inauguration as President in 1789. While still serving in Congress, Bland died in New York City on June 1, 1790.

• TIMOTHY BLOODWORTH   1736—1814

A gunsmith for the Continental Army and a politician, Timothy Bloodworth was born in New Hanover County, North

The team of oxen was a familiar sight in the colonial period. —Sketch by Kay Smith

Carolina, in 1736. Self-educated, he became a master of many trades. At the outbreak of the Revolutionary War he made muskets and bayonets for the Continental Army. Entering politics in 1778, he was elected in turn to the state legislature 1778–79, the Continental Congress 1786–87, the First U.S. Congress 1790–91, again to the state legislature 1793–94, and finally to the U.S. Senate 1795–1801. After leaving the Senate, he became collector of customs at Wilmington, North Carolina, where he died on August 24, 1814.

• WILLIAM BLOUNT   1749–1800

A signer of the United States Constitution and the first man ever impeached by the U.S. House of Representatives, William Blount was born March 26, 1749, in Bertie County, North Carolina, the son of a wealthy plantation owner. During the Revolutionary War he served for a time as paymaster of the 3rd North Carolina Battalion of the Continental Army. When Gen. Horatio Gates became commander of the southern American armies in 1780, Blount won appointment as chief commissary agent. In 1781 he was elected to the North Carolina legislature and the next year became a member of the state's delegation to the Continental Congress. He continued to be elected to both bodies for the next several years, while at the same time carrying on large land speculations in the western lands that later became Tennessee. He was a member of the Constitutional Convention in 1787, but explained in signing the United States Constitution that he did not mean to show he endorsed it but merely wanted to show that he was present. In 1790 Blount received appointment from George Washington as governor of the newly formed Territory of the United States South of the Ohio River, a post that he held for the next six years. In 1796 he presided over the territory's convention at which a constitution was drawn up for the new state of Tennessee, and then was elected as one of the new state's first U.S. Senators. Because of his interest in buying and selling western land, Blount entered into a conspiracy to help the British stir up an Indian war against the Spanish to prevent the Louisiana territory that they then held from falling into the hands of the French. The plan called for casting blame for the ensuing trouble on George Washington. When documents incriminating Blount fell into the hands of the government, the House of Representatives voted to impeach him on July 7, 1797, and the next day the U.S. Senate voted to expel him. Andrew Jackson was elected Senator to fill Blount's unexpired term. Blount did not attend his impeachment trial by the U.S. Senate which ended in 1799 with a 14–11 vote to dismiss the impeachment on the basis that Senators are not impeachable civil officers. The next year the fifty-year-old Blount died at his home in Knoxville, Tennessee, on March 21, 1800.

William Blount

FROM A WATERCOLOR PAINTING BY KAY SMITH

*The Rising Sun Tavern in Fredericksburg, Virginia, was built about 1760 by Charles Washington,
the youngest brother of George, and was then known as Washington Tavern and later as Eagle Tavern,
or the Golden Eagle. Many of the patriots of the colonial period gathered in this friendly atmosphere
to discuss the problems of the day. Such leaders as George Washington, Thomas Jefferson, Patrick Henry,
George Mason, Hugh Mercer, John Marshall, the Lees, and many others stopped here for rest, food,
beverages, and talk. It was a social center, the post office, and the stagecoach stop. Extensive restoration
of the building and the refurnishing of the interior with authentic period pieces make it possible
to visualize the life of those days of the birth of the American republic.*

Mount Vernon is one of America's most revered shrines. A majestic structure with all the complementary adjoining buildings necessary to a large plantation, it occupies a commanding view of the Potomac River nine miles from Alexandria, Virginia. Built by George Washington's half brother, Lawrence, it was inherited from him upon his death in 1752 by the future great leader of the American Revolution and the first American President. George Washington took his farming seriously and was known as a very progressive agronomist, being one of the first proponents of crop rotation. Though he dearly loved his beautiful plantation estate, he was absent for many years, including all the years of the American Revolution and the eight years that he served as President. He passed away here on December 14, 1799.

FROM A WATERCOLOR PAINTING BY KAY SMITH

FROM A WATERCOLOR SKETCH BY KAY SMITH

The Mary Washington House in Fredericksburg, Virginia, which George Washington bought for his mother in 1772. He came here to visit his ailing mother before leaving for his inauguration in New York. She died here in 1789 without seeing her son again.

• SIMON BOERUM   1724—1775

A member of the Continental Congress, Simon Boerum was born in New Lots (now Brooklyn), New York, on February 29, 1724. After graduation from the Dutch school in Flatbush, New York, he became a farmer and miller. Appointed in 1750 by Governor Clinton as clerk of Kings County and as clerk of the county board of supervisors, he held both positions for the next twenty-five years until his death. He also was elected to the colonial assembly from 1761 to 1775, and to the Continental Congress in 1775. His role in the Revolutionary War was cut short by his death in Brooklyn on July 11, 1775.

• DANIEL BOONE   1734—1820

The pioneer woodsman who led the first settlers west to Kentucky, Daniel Boone was born November 2, 1734, on a farm in Berks County, Pennsylvania. His schooling was limited to learning how to read, write, and do a little arithmetic. When Daniel was about sixteen, his family moved to the wilderness area along the Yadkin River in North Carolina. The boy's skill at hunting kept the Boone family supplied with game. During the French and Indian War, the twenty-year-old Boone was one of the wagon drivers during Gen. Edward Braddock's unsuccessful attempt to capture the French Fort Duquesne (now Pittsburgh). Upon his return home from this expedition, Boone married seventeen-year-old Rebecca Bryan and settled down to become a farmer. But he had been made restless by tales he had heard of the good hunting in the lands west of the Appalachians. In 1767 he made his first journey to Kentucky and back with a few woodsman friends. He set out again in 1769 with a larger group of hunters, and this time found an Indian trail that led through the Cumberland Gap to Kentucky. Several members of the party were killed by Indians, and Boone was captured by them but escaped. Joined by his younger brother, Squire Boone, who had followed his trail, Boone stayed in Kentucky two years hunting and exploring.

After selling his farm on the Yadkin River, Boone set out with his family and a party of settlers in 1773, determined to establish a settlement in Kentucky. But before reaching the Cumberland Gap the party was attacked by Indians and Boone's seventeen-year-old son James was killed along with five other young men. Disheartened and distressed by the calamity, the settlers turned back and settled down for the winter on the Clinch River in southwestern Virginia. In June 1774 a message arrived from Governor Dunmore of Virginia asking Boone to travel into Kentucky and guide out a party of surveyors that the governor feared were in danger. Boone effected the rescue, traveling on foot eight hundred miles in sixty-two days.

The Shawnee Indian chief Cornstalk led an uprising against

settlers in western Virginia in 1774, and Boone was commissioned as a captain in the militia to help fight them. Boone took part in the great battle at Point Pleasant, Virginia, in October 1774 in which Cornstalk was defeated.

In 1775 a group of colonists who had purchased land in Kentucky from the Cherokee Indians employed Boone to build a road through the Cumberland Gap and erect a fort at their settlement. Thus, Boone laid out what became known as the Wilderness Road and built the fort, which he called Boonesborough, completing it by the middle of June 1775. Boone then brought his wife and family from Virginia, later describing this journey in these words: "We arrived safe, without any other difficulty than such as are common to this passage, my wife and daughter being the first white women that ever stood on the banks of the Kentucky River."

More settlers followed in 1776 and 1777 despite Indian raids that came with increasing frequency as the British instigated them to kill the American settlers. In February 1778 Boone and ten other settlers were captured by the Indians and taken to Detroit where the British commander offered to pay ransom for their release but which the Indians refused. The Indians then took Boone to their village of Chillicothe, where the Shawnee chief Blackfish adopted him as his son. In June, when he learned the Indians were planning an attack on Boonesborough, he escaped, traveling the 160 miles home in five days. He found that his wife, believing he had been killed or taken to Canada by the British, had returned to North Carolina with his younger children. In September Boone led the defense of Boonesborough against an attacking force of 144 Indians and 12 Canadians. Although Boone had less than half as many men under his command as did the enemy, he successfully resisted. The Canadian-Indian force gave up the attack and departed after three weeks, carrying with them the bodies of at least 37 of their comrades who had been killed.

In the fall of 1778 Boone headed back to Virginia taking with him $20,000 of his own and of his neighbors to pay for land grants from the Virginia government. On the way he was robbed of all the money. Thus, he and many of his neighbors lost the opportunity to hold the land they had been struggling for. Nevertheless, Boone brought his family back to Kentucky once more in 1780.

On August 19, 1782, Boone, now a lieutenant colonel in the militia, took part in the battle of Blue Licks in which the Kentucky settlers, pursuing a band of about 250 maurauding Indians and Tories, suffered a costly defeat. One of Boone's sons was killed in the fight along with 76 others, almost half of the entire militia.

Having lost title to his land in Kentucky, Boone moved his family to Point Pleasant, in what is now West Virginia, in 1788. But soon he heard tales that there were better unsettled lands farther west. So about 1795 the sixty-one-year-old Boone

Daniel Boone, great wilderness scout

again headed west with his wife and some of his children, and settled about forty-five miles west of St. Louis, Missouri, in territory that was then under control of Spain. In 1800 the Spanish government appointed him commandant of the Femme Osage district where he had settled, and he was given about 8,500 acres of land in payment for his services. But when the United States purchased the Louisiana Territory, Boone again lost title to most of his land because of legal technicalities. In 1814 the U.S. Congress passed special legislation returning 850 acres to Boone as a reward for his efforts in opening the way west. Boone died at the age of eighty-five in Charette, Missouri, on September 26, 1820.

Elias Boudinot

• ELIAS BOUDINOT 1740–1821

The tenth President of the Continental Congress, Elias Boudinot was born in Philadelphia on May 2, 1740. After receiving a classical education, he studied law under Richard Stockton, who would become one of the signers of the Declaration of Independence, and married Stockton's sister, Hannah. At the age of twenty, Boudinot was admitted to the bar in 1760, and commenced practice in Elizabethtown, New Jersey. An early advocate of liberty from England, he became a member of the New Jersey committee of correspondence in 1774 and a member of the committee of safety in 1775. He was appointed in 1776 as commissary general of prisoners for the Continental Army, serving in that capacity until 1779. Elected to the Continental Congress for the periods 1777–78 and 1781–1783, he was chosen President in 1782 and 1783. As President, Boudinot signed the treaty of peace with England ending the Revolutionary War in 1783. He was elected to the First U.S. Congress, and continued to serve as a representative for New Jersey for the period 1789–95. President Washington appointed Boudinot as Director of the Mint in 1795, a position he held for the next ten years. As a wealthy philanthropist. Boudinot gave time and money to many projects. For forty-nine years, from 1772 to his death he was a trustee of Princeton College, and in 1816 he was elected as the first president of the American Bible Society. Boudinot also wrote several books and journals. At the age of eighty-one, he died in Burlington, New Jersey, on October 24, 1821.

• CARTER BRAXTON 1736–1797

A signer of the Declaration of Independence, Carter Braxton was born September 10, 1736, at "Newington," on the Mattaponi River in Virginia, the son of a wealthy tobacco planter. After graduating at nineteen from William and Mary College, he spent three years in England attending the University of Cambridge. Upon his return, Braxton began managing the extensive estates he had inherited. He was elected to the Vir-

Residence of Carter Braxton, Newington, Virginia

Carter Braxton

ginia house of burgesses from 1761 to 1771 and in 1775. He also served as sheriff of King William County from 1772 to 1773. After the royal governor dissolved the house of burgesses, Braxton was elected a delegate to the patriotic convention that determined Virginia's support of the Revolution. Elected a member of Virginia's delegation to the Continental Congress to fill the vacancy caused by the death of Peyton Randolph, Braxton signed the Declaration of Independence in 1776. He served in the state legislature most of the remaining twenty-one years of his life, and was a member of the governor's executive council most of the period 1793–97. Having lost much of his fortune during the Revolutionary War, Braxton died in reduced circumstances in Richmond, Virginia, on October 10, 1797.

• **DAVID BREARLEY   1745–1790**

An officer in the Continental Army and a signer of the United States Constitution, David Brearley was born June 11, 1745, in Spring Grove, New Jersey. After studying law and being admitted to the bar, he began practicing law in 1767 in Allentown, New Jersey. At the beginning of the Revolutionary War he was a captain in the state militia, but in 1776 was appointed as a lieutenant colonel in the Continental Army. While leading his troops to fight the Indians in the Wyoming Valley of Pennsylvania in 1779, he received word that the state legislature had elected him chief justice of New Jersey. Resigning his commission, he served as chief justice for the next ten years, establishing the precedent that his court had the power to decide whether a law was constitutional. In 1787 he attended the Constitutional Convention as one of New Jersey's delegates, where he spoke out strongly for the rights of the smaller states, helping achieve the compromises that enabled him to sign the United States Constitution. George Washington appointed him in 1789 as U.S. district judge for New Jersey, but he died less than a year later on August 16, 1790, in Trenton, New Jersey.

Ann Broom,
oldest daughter of Jacob Broom,
from a painting by James Peale
—Courtesy of National Archives

• **JACOB BROOM**　1752—1810

The only Delaware-born delegate to sign the United States Constitution, Jacob Broom was born in 1752 in Wilmington, Delaware. A surveyor and businessman, Broom served on the town council of Wilmington from 1776 to 1785 and as a member of the Delaware legislature from 1784 to 1786. As a delegate to the Constitutional Convention in 1787, Broom played an important role in helping prevent the convention from breaking up in July over the issue of representation between large and small states. After signing the United States Constitution, Broom devoted the rest of his life to private business, opening the first cotton mill in Wilmington in 1795. He died in Philadelphia on April 25, 1810.

• **JOHN BROWN**　1736—1803

Organizer of the patriots who burned the British tax vessel *Gaspee*, John Brown was born in Providence, Rhode Island, on January 27, 1736. Angered by the British tax policies, he gathered the party of patriots who burned the British revenue cutter *Gaspee* in Narragansett Bay on June 17, 1772, one of the major pre-Revolutionary incidents that aroused patriotic fervor. Sent in irons to Boston for trial, Brown eventually was released because the British could not gather any witnesses to testify against him. Brown laid the cornerstone for the first building of the College of Rhode Island (now Brown University) in 1770, and served as a trustee of the school for the rest of his life. He was a member of the Rhode Island legislature in 1782–84, and was elected a delegate to the Continental Congress in 1784 but did not serve. As a Federalist he was elected to the Sixth U.S. Congress 1799–1801. He died in Providence on September 20, 1803.

• **JOHN BROWN**　1744—1780

A Massachusetts patriot who gave his life during the Revolutionary War, John Brown was born in Sandisfield, Massachusetts, on October 19, 1744. After graduation from Yale College at the age of sixteen in 1761, he became a lawyer. In 1774–75 he went to Canada as a spy for the Boston committee of correspondence to set up a chain of informers about British troop movements. In 1775 he helped Ethan Allen capture Fort Ticonderoga. Commissioned a major, Brown operated as a spy behind British lines during General Montgomery's invasion of Canada in September 1775. During the Canadian operations he became an opponent of Benedict Arnold, and filed court-martial charges against the future traitor, accusing him of misappropriating funds to his own use. When the army failed to act on the charges, Brown published handbills about Arnold in the spring of 1776 that prophetically said of Arnold:

"Money is this man's god, and to get enough of it he would sacrifice his country." After the British recaptured Ticonderoga in July 1777, Brown, who had been promoted to lieutenant colonel, led a raid on the fort in September, freeing 100 American prisoners and capturing about 300 British regulars. Angered because the army did not act on his charges against Benedict Arnold, Brown resumed his law practice and was elected to the Massachusetts legislature in 1778. In 1780 when the British and Iroquois Indians began to ravage the Mohawk Valley of New York, Colonel Brown led a company of militia to protect the settlers. He and his 130 men attacked a force of British and Indians nearly ten times larger, and, because expected reinforcements did not arrive, Brown and about 40 of his men were killed near Fort Keyser, New York, on October 19, 1780.

• **JOHN BROWN**   1757–1837

The last member of the Continental Congress to die, John Brown was born in Staunton, Virginia, on September 12, 1757. After attending Washington College (now Washington and Lee University), Brown was furthering his studies at Princeton College when the Revolutionary War began. Leaving school, he enlisted in the army and served for several years. He then completed his studies at William and Mary

The death warrant of Major André

College and taught school for several years while studying law. Admitted to the bar in 1782, he began practice in Frankfort, in the Kentucky district of Virginia. He was elected as a member of the Virginia senate 1784–88, and was chosen as a delegate to the Continental Congress 1787–88. After ratification of the United States Constitution, Brown was elected from Virginia to the First and Second U.S. Congresses 1789–92. When Kentucky became a separate state, he was elected and re-elected as a U.S. Senator from 1792 to 1805, serving as president pro tempore of the Senate from 1803 to 1805. Brown had become the last surviving member of the Continental Congress by the time he died in Frankfort, Kentucky, on August 29, 1837, at the age of eighty.

- **NATHAN BROWNSON   1742–1796**

A delegate from Georgia to the Continental Congress, Nathan Brownson was born in Woodbury, Connecticut, on May 14, 1742. After graduation from Yale College in 1761, he studied medicine and began medical practice in Woodbury. About 1764 he moved to Liberty County, Georgia. At the outbreak of the Revolutionary War in 1775, he was chosen as a member of Georgia's assembly, and then volunteered as a surgeon in the army. He was elected as a representative of Georgia to the Continental Congress in 1777 and 1783. Brownson served as speaker of the Georgia house of representatives in 1781 and 1788, and was chosen governor of Georgia in 1782. From 1789 to 1791 he was president of the state senate. Brownson died at his plantation near Riceboro, Georgia, on November 6, 1796.

A pewter baby bottle

- **JOHN BULL   1740–1802**

A delegate to the Continental Congress from South Carolina, John Bull was born in Prince William's Parish, South Carolina, about 1740. A member of South Carolina's legislature throughout most of the period 1772 to 1784, he was chosen as a member of the state's delegation to the Continental Congress 1784–87. Bull died in Prince William's Parish, South Carolina, in 1802.

- **ARCHIBALD BULLOCH   1730–1777**

The head of Georgia's government in the early years of the Revolutionary War and the great-great-grandfather of President Theodore Roosevelt, Archibald Bulloch was born in Charleston, South Carolina, about 1730. A lawyer, Bulloch moved to Savannah, Georgia, about 1762, where he soon became a leading figure in the pre-Revolutionary patriotic movement. He was appointed a member of the committee to correspond with Benjamin Franklin for redress of grievances in

1768 and of the committee to sympathize with the citizens of Boston in 1774. He was elected speaker of the Georgia royal assembly in 1772 and for the rest of his life was the acknowledged leader of Georgia's people. Upon the outbreak of the Revolutionary War he was elected president of the Georgia provincial congress and commander in chief of Georgia's military forces. Although elected a member of the state's delegation to the Continental Congress in 1775–76, his duties in Georgia prevented his being present in Philadelphia at the adoption of the Declaration of Independence. However, he became the first person in the state to receive a copy of it and read it aloud. His death on February 22, 1777, in Savannah left Georgia leaderless until his position was filled by Button Gwinnett.

• **AEDANUS BURKE   1743–1802**

A soldier, politician, and judge, Aedanus Burke was born in Galway, Ireland, June 16, 1743. He was educated at the theological college at St. Omer, France. After immigrating to South Carolina, he began practicing law in Charleston, South Carolina. Throughout the Revolutionary War he served in the state's militia. In 1778 he was appointed judge of the state circuit court, and from 1779 to 1782 was a member of South Carolina's house of representatives. He opposed the state's ratification of the United States Constitution in 1788, but was elected to the First U.S. Congress 1789–91. He declined reelection in 1790 because the legislature had passed a law prohibiting a state judge from leaving the state. Burke was elected chancellor of the courts of equity in 1799, holding this office until his death in Charleston on March 30, 1802.

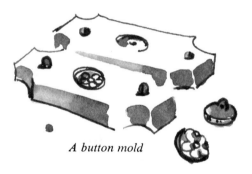

A button mold

• **THOMAS BURKE   1747–1783**

A delegate to the Continental Congress and governor of North Carolina, Thomas Burke was born in Galway, Ireland, about 1747. After studying medicine, he immigrated to America at seventeen in 1764, settling in Accomac County, Virginia, where he practiced medicine. He then began to study law, was admitted to the bar, and became a lawyer in Norfolk, Virginia. In 1771 Burke moved to Hillsboro, North Carolina. He was elected as a delegate to the state patriotic conventions in 1775 and 1776. From 1776 to 1781 he represented North Carolina in the Continental Congress, where he became a leading advocate of states' rights and of civilian authority over the military. Burke was elected as the third governor of North Carolina in June 1781 at a time when British troops were overrunning the South. Tories kidnaped Burke and his council on September 13, 1781, and held them prisoner on James Island near Charleston, South Carolina. In January 1782 Burke escaped and resumed his duties as governor for three months until retiring

to his estate, "Tyaquin," near Hillsboro, where he died on
December 2, 1783.

• WILLIAM BURNET   1730–1791

Military surgeon general and a delegate from New Jersey to
the Continental Congress, William Burnet was born in Newark, New Jersey, on December 2, 1730. After graduation at
eighteen from Princeton College in 1749, Burnet studied medicine in New York and then commenced practice in Newark.
Throughout the Revolutionary War, he served the Continental
Army as surgeon general of the eastern district of the United
States, and also represented New Jersey for a few months in
the Continental Congress 1780–81. As well as medicine,
Burnet pursued a judicial career, having been appointed in
1776 as presiding judge of the court of the New Jersey court
of common pleas and in 1781 as the first judge of Essex County. He died in Newark on October 7, 1791.

• AARON BURR   1756–1836

Revolutionary War soldier and politician, Aaron Burr was
born in Newark, New Jersey, on February 6, 1756, the son of
the second president of the College of New Jersey (now
Princeton University). After graduation from the College of
New Jersey at the age of sixteen in 1772, he studied theology
until 1774, and then abandoned it to take up law. At nineteen
he enlisted in the Continental Army as a private and marched
with Benedict Arnold to Quebec in 1775. In Canada he became aide-de-camp to General Montgomery with the rank of
captain. He narrowly escaped death when Montgomery was
killed at Quebec, and carried the body of the dead general
from the battlefield. In May 1776 he joined General George
Washington as his aide-de-camp with the rank of major, but
wishing to be closer to the battles he left after a few weeks to
become aide to General Putnam. He served bravely in the battle of Long Island in 1776, and the next year was given
command of a regiment with the rank of lieutenant colonel. At
the battle of Monmouth in 1778 he commanded a brigade. He
and his regiment were stationed in Westchester County, New
York, in the winter of 1778–79 and for a short time he was in
command of the fort at West Point. Ill health caused him to
resign from the army in 1779.

Burr resumed the study of law, was admitted to the bar in
1782, and after practicing law briefly in Albany, New York,
moved to New York City in 1783. He rose swiftly in politics
as a member of the Democratic-Republican Party, winning
election to the state legislature in 1784, appointment as attorney general of New York in 1789, and election as a U.S. Senator in 1790. As Thomas Jefferson's vice-presidential running-
mate in 1800, Burr received an equal number of electoral votes

Aaron Burr

to Jefferson, and took the opportunity of a flaw in the Constitution to try to obtain the Presidency for himself. Burr failed in his attempt, and became the third Vice President of the United States under President Jefferson. In July 1804, while still Vice President, he killed Alexander Hamilton in a duel. Having ruined himself in politics, Burr headed West with a scheme to take Mexico and the Mississippi Valley and make himself king. Burr was arrested and tried for treason in August 1807, but was acquitted. After spending several years abroad, Burr resumed the practice of law in New York City in 1812. He died on Staten Island, New York, on September 14, 1836.

• **ROBERT BURTON   1747–1825**

A delegate to the Continental Congress, Robert Burton was born near Chase City, Virginia, on October 20, 1747. He moved in 1775 to Granville County, North Carolina, where he owned a plantation. During the Revolutionary War he served the Continental Army as a quartermaster general, attaining the rank of colonel. Burton became a member of the North Carolina governor's council in 1783–84, and then was elected a member of the state's delegation to the Continental Congress 1787–88. Burton died in Granville (now Vance) County, North Carolina, on May 31, 1825.

• PIERCE BUTLER   1744–1822

A former British army officer and signer of the United States Constitution, Pierce Butler was born July 11, 1744, in County Carlow, Ireland, the son of an Irish baron. Joining the British army at the age of seventeen, he had risen to the rank of major when sent with other troops to Boston before the Revolutionary War. In 1771 he married the daughter of a wealthy South Carolina planter and two years later resigned his British commission to live in South Carolina and support the cause of the American patriots. He was elected to the state legislature in 1778 and served in that body for the next ten years. In 1787 he was chosen as a member of South Carolina's delegation to the Continental Congress and also to the Constitutional Convention. He spoke up often in the convention on any point in which he thought the Northern States were trying to take away rights from the Southern States, and succeeded in having the Constitution include a clause to protect the rights of slave owners in having escaped slaves returned from other states. In 1789 he was elected to the First U.S. Congress as one of South Carolina's first U.S. Senators. Butler resigned from the Senate in 1796 to attend to personal affairs, was reelected in 1802, but resigned again two years later. In his later years he lived in Philadelphia, where he died on February 15, 1822.

• JOHN CADWALADER   1742–1786

A militia general in the Revolutionary War, John Cadwalader was born in Philadelphia on January 10, 1742, a cousin of John Dickinson, the "Penman of the Revolution." At the beginning of the Revolutionary War, Cadwalader was a member of the Philadelphia committee of safety and captain of a company of militia. In 1776 he was made commander of a Pennsylvania militia regiment with the rank of colonel, and cooperated with General Washington in the battles of Trenton and Princeton. He was appointed a brigadier general of Pennsylvania militia in 1777 and turned down repeated offers of a brigadier general's commission in the Continental Army, preferring to stay with his own troops. Cadwalader took part in the battles of Brandywine and Germantown in 1777, and in the battle of Monmouth in 1778. On July 4, 1778, Cadwalader fought a duel with Gen. Thomas Conway because of disparag-

General John Cadwalader

ing remarks Conway had made about General Washington. In the duel Conway was badly wounded in the mouth. After the war Cadwalader lived in Maryland for a while, serving in that state's legislature. He died in Shrewsbury, Pennsylvania, on February 11, 1786.

• LAMBERT CADWALADER   1742–1823

A soldier and a Congressman, Lambert Cadwalader was born near Trenton, New Jersey, in 1742. After attending the College of Philadelphia, he became a member of the common council of Philadelphia. At the beginning of the Revolution he was elected a delegate to the provincial convention in Pennsylvania in 1775 and to the state constitutional convention in 1776. Joining the Continental Army as a lieutenant colonel, he was in command of Pennsylvania troops at the battle for Fort Washington on New York's Manhattan Island on November 16, 1776. Although he and his troops fought bravely against overwhelming odds, he was captured when the fort surrendered. After being released by the British, Cadwalader resigned from the army. He was elected a member of New Jersey's delegation to the Continental Congress 1784–87 and to the First U.S. Congress 1789–91. He retired from politics after again serving in Congress 1793–95. Cadwalader died on his estate, "Greenwood," near Trenton, New Jersey, on September 13, 1823.

• WILLIAM CAMPBELL   1745–1781

A frontiersman and militia officer during the Revolutionary War, William Campbell was born in Augusta County, Virginia, in 1745. At twenty-nine, as a captain of militia, he fought the Shawnee Indians at the battle of Point Pleasant in Lord Dunmore's War in 1774. The next year he served as a captain in Patrick Henry's 1st Virginia Regiment, which drove Lord Dunmore, the royal governor, out of the colony. Having been promoted to colonel in the militia, Campbell marched his company of Virginia riflemen 200 miles in September 1780 to take part in the battle of King's Mountain, South Carolina, where British Maj. Patrick Ferguson had assembled an army of several thousand American Loyalists and was threatening to hang any rebels that fell into his hands. Other militia units arrived from North Carolina, South Carolina, and from "over the mountains," that later was to be Tennessee. On September 29 over 1,500 frontiersmen and militia had assembled. Because the giant-sized Campbell was the biggest officer among the assembled militia colonels, he was elected to lead the operation. On the afternoon of October 7, 1780, Campbell surrounded Ferguson's army, which had taken up positions on the 60-foot-high ridge of King's Mountain. Having slipped up like Indians, Campbell called for the attack, yelling: "Shout

The Battle of King's Mountain —After an engraving by Chappel

like hell and fight like devils." Ferguson tried to charge the rebels, but was shot dead with seven bullets from the frontier marksmen in his body. The British Loyalist troops then threw down their arms and surrendered. Over 300 of the Loyalists were killed or fatally wounded and about 700 captured. The next day a trial was held in which 30 of the prisoners were convicted of atrocities against the patriots, and nine were hanged. Campbell's victory became the high-water mark for American militia operations in the South and rallied new volunteers to the cause.

Campbell later fought in the battle of Guilford, North Carolina, in March 1781, and was promoted to brigadier general. He then helped Lafayette in battling Cornwallis in Virginia, commanding the light infantry and riflemen. But he became ill and died on August 22, 1781, at Rocky Mills, Virginia, a few weeks before Cornwallis' surrender at Yorktown.

• WILLIAM CARMICHAEL ?–1795

A Congressman and diplomat, William Carmichael was born at "Round Top," near Chestertown, Maryland. He studied law and began practice in Centerville, Maryland. At the beginning of the Revolution he was assistant to Silas Deane, secret agent of Congress in Paris. In 1776 he went to Berlin, Prussia, seeking help for the United States. He was named secretary to the American commissioners in France in 1777, but did not serve. Returning to the United States in May 1778, Carmichael was elected a member of Maryland's delegation to the Continental Congress 1778–80. Congress sent him to Spain in 1779, where he served first as secretary of the legation 1779–82, and then as chargé d'affaires 1782–94. He died in Madrid, Spain, on February 9, 1795.

The Old Treasury Building, Annapolis, Maryland, built in 1737, where paper money was printed during the colonial period—still preserved on the grounds of the State House.
　　　　　　　　　　　　　　　　　　　　　　—Sketch by Kay Smith

143

• EDWARD CARRINGTON   1748–1810

A soldier and delegate to the Continental Congress, Edward Carrington was born in Goochland County, Virginia, on February 11, 1748. He served throughout the Revolutionary War as a lieutenant colonel of artillery, taking part in the battles of Monmouth, New Jersey, in 1778, of Hobkirk's Hill, South Carolina, in 1781, and at Yorktown, Virginia, in 1781. Of even more importance, though less glamorous, was his service during 1780–81 as quartermaster general for Gen. Nathanael Greene's army, keeping the Continental soldiers supplied with food and clothing during their successful campaign in the South. After the war Carrington was elected as a member of Virginia's delegation to the Continental Congress in 1785–86. President Washington appointed Carrington as federal marshal of Virginia in 1789. His only other notable contribution to history was as foreman of the jury during the trial of Aaron Burr for treason in 1807. Carrington died in Richmond, Virginia, on October 28, 1810.

• CHARLES CARROLL   1723–1783

A cousin of Charles Carroll of Carrollton and Daniel Carroll, Charles "Barrister" Carroll was born in Annapolis, Maryland, on March 22, 1723. Sent to England for his education, he was graduated from the University of Cambridge, and studied law in the Middle Temple. At the age of twenty-three he returned to Annapolis, Maryland, in 1746 and commenced the practice of law. He was elected to the Maryland lower house of assembly in 1755 to fill the vacancy caused by the death of his father, Dr. Charles Carroll. He framed many important state documents and public papers, among them the "Declaration of Rights" adopted by the convention of Maryland on November 3, 1776. He was elected a delegate to the Continental Congress on November 10, 1776, to succeed his cousin, Charles Carroll of Carrollton. In 1777 he was elected to the first state senate. Carroll died at his residence, Mount Clare, near Baltimore, Maryland, on March 23, 1783.

• CHARLES CARROLL   1737–1832

The last surviving signer of the Declaration of Independence, Charles Carroll of Carrollton was born in Annapolis, Maryland, on September 19, 1737. Educated in Europe, Carroll attended the College of St. Omer in France, and then studied civil law at the College of Louis le Grand in Rheims and common law in London. Returned to Annapolis in 1765, he became active in the pre-Revolutionary movement, being barred by law from holding public office in Maryland because he was a Roman Catholic. One of the wealthiest landowners in Maryland, he was elected as a delegate to the Continental

Charles Carroll of Carrollton

Congress on July 4, 1776, where he signed the Declaration of Independence and was a member of the Board of War 1776–77. After resigning from the Continental Congress in 1778, he was regularly elected to the state senate throughout the period 1777 to 1800. In 1789 he was elected as one of Maryland's U.S. Senators to the First United States Congress, where he served until November 30, 1792, when, preferring to remain a state senator, he resigned because of a law passed by the Maryland legislature disqualifying members of the state senate from holding seats in Congress. He retired to private life in 1801. His last public act was setting the stone marking the beginning of the Baltimore & Ohio Railroad on July 4, 1828. At the age of ninety-five he was the last signer of the Declaration of Independence to die, on November 14, 1832, in Baltimore.

• **DANIEL CARROLL**   **1730–1796**

A cousin of the two Charles Carrolls, Daniel Carroll was born in Prince Georges County, Maryland, on July 22, 1730. Educated abroad at St. Omer's College, France, he returned to Maryland in 1748, and proceeded to build a fortune as a slave

Daniel Carroll

owner and merchant. Like his cousins, he was barred from holding public office until the Revolution because of his Roman Catholic religion. Elected as a delegate to the Continental Congress 1780–84, Carroll signed the Articles of Confederation as the representative of the thirteenth state to ratify the Articles, bringing them into effect on March 1, 1781. In 1787 he was one of Maryland's delegates to the convention that framed the United States Constitution. A strong believer in democracy, he tried to convince the convention that the President should be elected directly by the people, but, when he failed to win his argument, he signed the Constitution anyhow. Elected to the first state senate of Maryland, Carroll served in that body or in the state's executive council the rest of his life. He was elected as a Federalist to the First U.S. Congress 1789–91, where he was appointed by President Washington as one of the commissioners to locate the District of Columbia. He received much criticism when the commission selected Carroll's own farm as part of the area for the new capital city. Carroll died at his home near the present site of the capitol on May 7, 1796.

• RICHARD CASWELL   1729–1789

A militia general, governor, and delegate to the Continental Congress, Richard Caswell was born in what is now Baltimore County, Maryland, on August 3, 1729. At seventeen he moved to North Carolina, where he was appointed deputy surveyor of the colony in 1750. After studying law as clerk of the court of Orange County 1752–54 he was admitted to the bar and commenced practice in Hillsboro, North Carolina. From 1754 he was elected regularly as a member of North Carolina's house of delegates, serving as speaker in 1770–71. Caswell commanded the right wing of Governor William Tryon's army at the Battle of Almance against the Regulators in 1771. He was a member of North Carolina's delegation to the Continental Congress 1774–76. As a militia colonel, he commanded 800 patriots at the Battle of Moores Creek Bridge, North Carolina, in February 1776, helping capture an army of Scot Loyalists. After presiding over the state constitutional convention in 1776, Caswell was elected as the state's first governor 1776–80. As a major general of militia he commanded North Carolina troops at the Battle of Camden, South Carolina, in August 1780, in which the Continental Army under Gen. Horatio Gates was disastrously defeated by the British general Lord Cornwallis. After serving as speaker of the state senate 1782–84, Caswell again was elected governor 1784–87. Although appointed as a delegate from North Carolina to the convention that framed the United States Constitution in 1787, Caswell did not attend. He was serving as speaker of the state assembly at his death in Fayetteville, North Carolina, on Novmeber 10, 1789.

• JOHN CHAMPE   1752–c.1798

A Revolutionary War soldier who went on a dangerous spy mission at the request of General Washington, John Champe was born in Loudon County, Virginia, in 1752. In October 1780, after Benedict Arnold had turned traitor, Washington received a rumor that a second American general was soon to desert to the British (possibly Horatio Gates or Robert Howe). Champe, a sergeant-major in Henry Lee's cavalry, volunteered for the assignment, and was instructed to discover the second traitor and find out whether it was possible to capture Arnold. Champe left the American camp at Tappan, New York, at night, pursued as a deserter, and reached Paulus Hook where British warships were anchored. After being examined, he was sent to Arnold, who was recruiting a regiment. Arnold appointed Champe as a sergeant-major in his command. Champe found evidence to prove that the suspected second American general was not a traitor, and sent his information to Washington. Champe also devised a plan to kidnap Arnold, who regularly took an evening walk in his garden.

Washington's telescope

147

But on the night set for the kidnap attempt, Arnold moved to different quarters. Before new plans could be made, Arnold and his forces, including Champe, were loaded aboard ship and sailed for operations in the South. Champe later escaped, and rejoined the American army in North Carolina. He died in Kentucky about 1798.

• **JEREMIAH CHASE   1748−1828**

A Maryland delegate to the Continental Congress, Jeremiah Townley Chase was born in Baltimore, Maryland, on May 23, 1748. He took part in pre-Revolutionary activities as a member of the committees of observation and correspondence in 1774. Chase was a delegate to the Maryland constitutional convention of 1776, and a member of the governor's council 1780–84 and 1786–88. He became mayor of Annapolis in 1783, and then became a member of the Continental Congress in 1783–84. Chase was appointed judge of the general court in 1789, and then served as chief justice of the court of appeals until his resignation in 1824. He died in Annapolis on May 11, 1828.

• **SAMUEL CHASE   1741−1811**

A signer of the Declaration of Independence and an associate justice of the Supreme Court, Samuel Chase was born in Somerset County, Maryland, on April 17, 1741. After studying law, he was admitted to the bar at the age of twenty and commenced practice in Annapolis, Maryland. First elected to the general assembly of Maryland in 1764, he served in the legislature for the next twenty years. From the time of the Stamp Act in 1765, he was the acknowledged leader of patriots in Maryland, inciting mobs against the British officials. As a delegate to the Continental Congress 1774–78, he served on a commission to try to induce Canada to join the Revolution and then helped persuade Maryland to join the other colonies in letting him and other Maryland delegates sign the Declaration of Independence. After the war, Chase went to England in 1783 as agent for the state of Maryland to recover stock in the Bank of England that had been purchased when the state was a colony. He again served as a member of Congress in 1784–85. Chase was appointed judge of the Baltimore criminal court in 1788, and judge of the general court of Maryland in 1791. President Washington appointed Chase an associate justice of the U.S. Supreme Court in 1796. Articles of impeachment were filed against Chase in 1804 on charges of malfeasance in his conduct of sedition trials five years earlier and for a speech he made to a Maryland grand jury denouncing efforts to extend voting privileges to persons not owning property. Tried by the U.S. Senate, he was acquit-

Samuel Chase

ted of all charges on March 5, 1805. Chase then resumed his seat on the bench, and retained it until his death in Washington, D.C., on June 19, 1811.

• ABRAHAM CLARK   1726−1794

A signer of the Declaration of Independence, Abraham Clark was born on a farm near present-day Elizabeth, New Jersey, on February 15, 1726. Although he studied law, Clark never practiced other than to give advice to friends and neighbors. His popularity with his fellow-farmers won him election as sheriff of Essex County. At the outbreak of the Revolutionary War, he was elected to the New Jersey provincial congress in 1775. The next year he was elected to the Continental Congress, where he signed the Declaration of Independence. He remained in Congress throughout the Revolutionary War to 1783, a cautious conservative who acted as a watchdog against excessive spending. He was particularly critical of George Washington for granting amnesty to loyalists who would swear allegiance to the United States. After serving as a member of the State legislature 1783–85, he again was sent to the Continental Congress 1787–89. Because he opposed ratification of the new U.S. Constitution, he was defeated for election to the First U.S. Congress in 1789. But he won election to the Second and Third Congresses, serving from 1791 until his death in Rahway, New Jersey, on September 15, 1794.

Abraham Clark

George Rogers Clark
—Sketch by Kay Smith

• GEORGE ROGERS CLARK   1752–1818

A fearless frontiersman who won the Northwest Territory from the British and Indians with only a handful of men, George Rogers Clark was born near Charlottesville, Virginia, on November 19, 1752. As he grew up, he developed a father-son friendship with a neighbor, the Virginia statesman George Mason, who helped Clark become widely read. Like George Washington, Clark has little formal schooling, but learned to become a surveyor while in his teens. And, like Washington, he enjoyed most going on long journeys of exploration on Virginia's frontier, where he became an excellent woodsman and frontiersman. At the age of twenty-one, he served as a militia captain in Lord Dunmore's War against the Shawnee Indians on the Ohio River. The next year he was appointed deputy surveyor of Kentucky.

Upon the outbreak of the Revolutionary War, Clark went to the Virginia legislature and got an agreement for Kentucky to be organized as one of the state's counties. Gov. Patrick Henry commissioned Clark a major and put him in charge of the defense of Kentucky, giving him 500 pounds of gunpowder.

In 1777 it became clear that the British were inciting the Indians to attack the American frontier settlements. The lieutenant governor of Canada, Henry Hamilton, who was stationed at Detroit, had become known as the "Hair Buyer" because of the British practice of paying the Indians for white scalps that they brought in. Clark devised an audacious plan to capture all the British forts west of the Alleghenies.

In January 1778 Governor Henry approved Clark's plan and promoted the twenty-five-year-old frontiersman to lieutenant colonel. Clark enlisted 200 men for a three-month expedition, and set out down the Ohio River from Pittsburgh. In June he reached the Falls of the Ohio and established a base on an island opposite the present site of Louisville, Kentucky. Taking 175 men with him, he made a six-day march to the French settlement of Kaskaskia (now in Illinois), reaching it on July 4, 1778, and taking the fort by surprise under cover of darkness. When Clark explained to the French settlers that France was in alliance with the United States against the British, they readily swore allegiance to the new government. Clark sent some of his troops back to Louisville to build Fort Nelson, and decided to remain in Kaskaskia for the winter.

A Revolutionary War cannon
—Sketch by Kay Smith

Detroit, Michigan, July 25, 1796

News from a Spanish trader came to Clark late in January 1779 that Lieutenant Governor Hamilton was at Vincennes (now in Indiana), planning a spring offensive against the American settlements. Clark, now promoted to colonel, set off with 130 men, many of whom were French volunteers, for an 18-day march across prairies flooded with icy water to reach the vicinity of Vincennes on February 23. Clark later wrote in his memoirs:

"Our situation was now truly critical—no possibility of retreating in case of defeat, and in full view of a town that had, at this time, upward of 600 men in it—troops, inhabitants, and Indians . . . . We were now in the position that I had labored to get ourselves in. The idea of being made prisoner was foreign to almost every man, as they expected nothing but torture from the savages, if they fell into their hands. Our fate was now to be determined, probably in a few hours. We knew that nothing but the most daring conduct would insure success."

What to do? Clark sat down and wrote the following message to be sent into the fort by a messenger:

"TO THE INHABITANTS OF POST VINCENNES:

Gentlemen—Being now within two miles of your village with my army, determined to take your fort this night, and not being willing to surprise you, I take this method to request such of you as are true citizens and willing to enjoy the liberty I bring you to remain still in your houses; and those, if any

151

there be, that are friends to the King will instantly repair to the fort, and join the hair-buyer general, and fight like men. And if any such as do not go to the fort shall be discovered afterwards, they may depend on severe punishment. On the contrary, those who are true friends to liberty may depend on being well treated; and I once more request them to keep out of the streets. For every one I find in arms on my arrival I shall treat him as an enemy.

(Signed) G.R. Clark"

Receiving no response, Clark attacked at sunset. Surrounding the fort, his men fired at the fort all night. Meanwhile, inhabitants of the town opened their doors to Clark, and brought out food and ammunition to help in the attack. About nine o'clock in the morning, Clark sent a note to Hamilton demanding unconditional surrender. There followed a parley. On the afternoon of February 24 Hamilton and his men surrendered, and the next day marched out of the fort. Clark sent Hamilton to Williamsburg, Virginia, under guard.

Clark wanted to push on to Detroit, the British headquarters in the West, but he was unable to get reinforcements or supplies from Virginia, which was then being ravaged by the British. In 1780 he beat off a British—Indian attack at Cahokia, on the east side of the Mississippi River from St. Louis. That same year, at the age of twenty-seven, he was promoted to brigadier general. Clark's final major action of the Revolutionary War came in November 1782 when he attacked and destroyed the capital of the Shawnee tribe, Chillicothe (now in Ohio). This expedition was so successful that the Indians never again attacked the settlers in Kentucky. The British willingly gave up claims to the region in the peace treaty ending the Revolutionary War because Clark had wrested it from them.

After the war Clark led an unsuccessful expediton in 1786 against the Indians on the Wabash River. Clark was relieved of his command and replaced by James Wilkinson, who was discovered many years later to have been a spy in the pay of Spain and had plotted to have Clark removed so that Spain would win the West.

Having paid the expenses of many of his expeditions out of his own pocket, Clark was left a poor man when Virginia refused to repay him. He lived on in relative obscurity until his death near Louisville, Kentucky, at the age of sixty-five on February 18, 1818.

His younger brother, William Clark (1770–1838), was co-leader with Meriwether Lewis of the famous expedition of 1804–06 that explored the vast Louisianan Territory.

• **JOSEPH CLAY** 1741–1804

A soldier, politician, and judge, Joseph Clay was born in Beverly, England, October 16, 1741. At eighteen he immigrated to America, settling in Savannah, Georgia, where he engaged in the general commission business. Clay was elected a member of the Georgia council of safety and as a delegate to the Georgia provisional congress in 1775. He was commissioned a major in the Georgia Line of the Continental Army at the beginning of the Revolutionary War, and then was advanced to colonel when he was appointed deputy paymaster general in Georgia in 1777. He was elected a member of the state's delegation to the Continental Congress in 1778 and 1783. After the ratification of the U.S. Constitution, Clay became a judge of the U.S. district court of Georgia. He died in Savannah on November 15, 1804.

• **WILLIAM CLINGAN**   **?–1790**

A delegate to the Continental Congress, William Clingan was born near Wagontown, Pennsylvania. Elected as one of Pennsylvania's delegation to the Continental Congress 1777–79, Clingan was one of the first signers of the Articles of Confederation in 1778. He served twenty-nine years as a justice of the peace in Chester County 1757–86, and as president of the county courts 1780–86. He died on May 9, 1790, in Chester County, Pennsylvania.

• **GEORGE CLINTON**   **1739–1812**

A Revolutionary War general and fourth Vice President of the United States, George Clinton was born in Little Britain, New York, on July 26, 1739. During the French and Indian War, he served as an eighteen-year-old lieutenant of rangers in the expedition against Fort Frontenac. After studying law, he was admitted to the bar and commenced practice in Little Britain, where he was appointed district attorney in 1765. He was elected to the colonial assembly in 1768, and became a member of the New York committeee of correspondence in 1774. As a delegate to the Continental Congress from 1775 to 1776, he voted for the Declaration of Independence but did not have an opportunity to sign it because he was called to duty as a brigadier general of militia on July 8, 1776, to defend the Hudson River highlands. In 1777 Congress appointed Clinton as brigadier general of the Continental Army, but he had little opportunity to serve because a month later he was elected as the first governor of the state of New York. Clinton remained as governor eighteen years, being elected to six successive terms from 1777 to 1795. He did not run for a seventh successive term, but returned to become governor again in 1801–04. Clinton, an anti-Federalist, unsuccessfully ran for Vice President against John Adams in 1792. In 1804 he again ran for Vice President on the ticket headed by Thomas Jefferson and won. He was re-elected Vice President in 1808, serving under President James Madison. While still Vice President, he died in Washington, D.C., on April 20, 1812.

General George Clinton

George Clymer —From a painting by Charles Willson Peale

• GEORGE CLYMER   1739–1813

One of the few men to sign both the Declaration of Independence and the United States Constitution, George Clymer was born in Philadelphia on March 16, 1739. Orphaned while a small boy, he was reared by an uncle who was a well-to-do merchant. After attending the College of Philadelphia, he soon became a successful merchant and financier in his own right. Before the outbreak of the Revolutionary War, Clymer became a member of the committee of safety and a captain of a company of volunteers. Although Clymer was elected a member of the Continental Congress on July 20, 1776, after the Declaration of Independence already had been approved, he expressed such a strong desire to sign it that he was allowed to do so. Both the national government and the Pennsylvania government made extensive use of his financial abilities during his service in the Continental Congress 1776–78 and 1780–83 and in the state legislature 1785–88. During this time he helped charter the first national bank, the Bank of North America, in 1781. In 1787 he helped write and signed the United States Constitution. After being elected as a Representative from Pennsylvania to the 1st U.S. Congress 1789–91, Clymer was appointed in 1791 by President Washington as federal collector of the whisky tax in Pennsylvania. After one of Clymer's sons was killed in the ensuing Whisky Insurrection, Clymer resigned the post. In 1795 he went to Georgia at President Washington's request where he negotiated a treaty with the Cherokees and the Creeks on June 29, 1796. During the last years of his life he devoted himself to his business and to civic duties in Philadelphia. He died in Morrisville, Pennsylvania, on January 23, 1813.

• **ISAAC COLES   1747–1813**

A soldier and Congressman, Isaac Coles was born in Richmond, Virginia, on March 2, 1747. He was educated at William and Mary College, and served as a colonel of militia during the Revolutionary War. From 1783 to 1787 he was elected to the Virginia legislature. An anti-Federalist, Coles opposed ratification of the United States Constitution, and then was elected to the U.S. Congress, serving in 1789–91 and 1793–97. At the age of fifty he retired to his plantation, "Coles Hill," near Chatham, Virginia, where he died sixteen years later on June 3, 1813.

• **JOHN COLLINS   1717–1795**

A delegate to the Continental Congress and governor of Rhode Island, John Collins was born in Newport, Rhode Island, on June 8, 1717. He was a member of the committee sent by the Rhode Island general assembly in September 1776 to inform General Washington of the condition of the colony and to obtain his views on the best method to adopt for its defense. Collins was a member of Rhode Island's delegation to the Continental Congress 1778–83, and then was elected governor of Rhode Island 1786–90. Although elected to the First U.S. Congress in 1789, he did not take his seat. Collins died in Newport on March 4, 1795.

• **SILAS CONDICT   1738–1801**

A large landowner and New Jersey legislator, Silas Condict was born in Morristown, New Jersey, March 7, 1738. He was a member of the New Jersey committee of safety and of the State council from its organization in 1776 until 1780. After serving as a member of the Continental Congress 1781–84 he was elected to the state general assembly 1791–94, 1796–98, and in 1800, serving as speaker 1792–94 and again in 1797. Condict died in Morristown on September 6, 1801.

• **BENJAMIN CONTEE   1755–1815**

A soldier, Congressman, and minister, Benjamin Contee was born at "Brookefield," near Nottingham, Maryland, in 1755. After military service in the Revolutionary War as lieutenant and captain in the 3rd Maryland Battalion, Contee was elected to the Maryland house of delegates 1785–87. He served in the Continental Congress in 1787–88, and was elected to the First U.S. Congress 1789–91. Refusing to be a candidate for renomination in 1790, Contee traveled to Europe, where he studied theology. Upon his return to the United States, Contee completed his studies and then was ordained a minister of the Episcopal Church in 1803. He became pastor of the Episcopal

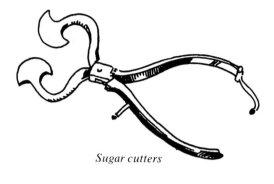

Sugar cutters

Church at Port Tobacco, Maryland. Later he became presiding judge of the county orphans' court, a position he held at the time of his death in Charles County on November 30, 1815.

• **THOMAS CONWAY   1733–c.1800**

A general in the Continental Army, best known for taking part in a conspiracy called the Conway Cabal to replace General Washington as commander-in-chief, Thomas Conway was born in Ireland on February 27, 1733. He grew up in France, and served more than twenty-five years in the French army, advancing to the rank of colonel before coming to America in 1777 to join the Continental Army. Commissioned a brigadier general by Congress, Conway fought with distinction in the battles of Brandywine and Germantown. In November 1777 General Alexander wrote to Washington to tell of a letter he had been shown that Conway had written to General Gates containing disparaging remarks about the commander-in-chief. When confronted by Washington, Conway admitted writing the letter, but denied that he meant to undercut Washington. He offered to resign, and sent his resignation to Congress. In that body several members, including Thomas Mifflin and Benjamin Rush, disliked Washington and wanted him replaced by General Gates. So instead of accepting Conway's resignation, Congress promoted him in December 1777 to major general and inspector general of the army. When Conway visited Washington at his Valley Forge winter headquarters, the commander-in-chief gave Conway a cool reception. The impetuous Irish-Frenchman then wrote Washington a letter complaining of his treatment and invidiously comparing Washington to Frederick the Great of Prussia. Washington forwarded the letter to Congress, describing Conway as his "enemy." At the same time nine brigadier generals petitioned Congress complaining about Conway having been promoted over their heads. When Conway then protested to Congress in March that he had not been given a separate command, the Congressmen decided to wash their hands of the affair and accepted his previous resignation. On July 4, 1778, Gen. John Cadwalader fought a duel with Conway over remarks that Conway had made about Washington, wounding Conway severely in the mouth. After recovering, Conway returned to France and rejoined the French army, where he continued to advance, being made commanding general of French forces in India in 1787. During the French Revolution, he went into exile with other royalists, and is believed to have died about 1800.

• **JOSEPH PLATT COOK   1730–1816**

A soldier, Congressman, and judge, Joseph Platt Cook was born in Stratford (now Bridgeport), Connecticut, on January 4, 1730. At twenty he was graduated from Yale College, in 1750.

For twenty years he represented his town in the Connecticut general assembly 1763–83. As colonel of the 16th Regiment of Connecticut militia, Cook accompanied General Wolcott's forces to New York in 1776. Cook was in command of militia when the British burned Danbury, Connecticut, on April 26–27, 1777. Resigning his colonelcy in 1778, Cook became a member of the state council of safety in 1778, and was elected to the Continental Congress 1784–88. For thirty-seven years he served as judge of the probate court for Danbury district 1776–1813. Cook died in Danbury on February 3, 1816.

The Battle of Germantown, showing the Chew residence under siege. —After an engraving by Chappel

• JOHN COOPER 1729–1785

A New Jersey legislator and judge, John Cooper was born near Woodbury, New Jersey, on February 5, 1729. He was elected to the New Jersey provincial congress in 1775–76 and served on the committee that drafted the first state constitution. He represented Gloucester County on the state legislative council in 1776–80 and 1784. Cooper served as a delegate to the Continental Congress from February 14 to June 22, 1776. Elected judge of Gloucester County in 1779, Cooper served in that position until his death in Woodbury on April 1, 1785.

The commemorative plaque marking the grave of Margaret Corbin at West Point

• MARGARET COCHRAN CORBIN 1751–1800

A Revolutionary War heroine who manned her husband's cannon after he was killed in battle, Margaret Cochran was born in Franklin County, Pennsylvania, on November 12, 1751. When she was about four or five years old, Indians killed her father and carried off her mother. She grew up in the home of an uncle, and when she was twenty married John Corbin in 1772. Her husband enlisted in the 1st Company of Pennsylvania Artillery at the beginning of the Revolutionary War, and Margaret went with him when his company was called up for duty in New York. During the battle of Fort Washington, New York, on November 16, 1776, John Corbin was killed during a Hessian attack. Having seen her husband die, Margaret Corbin took his place as an assistant gunner, keeping the gun firing until she too was severely wounded. After the fort surrendered, she was taken to Philadelphia with the other wounded. Nearly three years later, in July 1779, Congress voted her a pension for life at the half-pay of a soldier, and in addition paid for "one suit of cloaths." After the war, she lived in Westchester County, New York, dying in poverty at the age of forty-eight on January 16, 1800. On the 150th anniversary of her heroism, her body was moved from an obscure grave to a place of honor in the military cemetery at West Point, New York.

• EZEKIEL CORNELL 1732–1800

A militia general and Congressman, Ezekiel Cornell was born in Scituate, Rhode Island, in 1732. Employed as a mechanic, he had risen to lieutenant colonel in Hitchcock's Rhode Island Regiment by the outbreak of the Revolutionary War. He served with the militia at the siege of Boston in 1775–76. Cornell was appointed brigadier general of state troops in 1776 and served until March 16, 1780, when he resigned to become a member of the Continental Congress 1780–83. After the war Cornell retired to his farm at Scituate. He died in Milford, Massachusetts, on April 25, 1800.

• TENCH COXE   1755—1824

A turncoat soldier, Congressman, public official, and economist, Tench Coxe was born in Philadelphia on May 22, 1755. At the beginning of the Revolutionary War he resigned from the Pennsylvania militia in 1776, turned Loyalist, and joined the British Army under Howe. He was arrested, paroled, and then rejoined the patriot cause. After the war he was appointed as one of Pennsylvania's delegates to the Convention at Annapolis in 1786 and then became a member of the Continental Congress in 1787–88. President Washington appointed him assistant secretary of the treasury 1789–92. He next was revenue commissioner 1792–96, and purveyor of public supplies under Presidents Jefferson and Madison from 1803 to 1812. A prolific writer on political and economic subjects, he was called the father of the cotton industry in America because of books and articles he wrote on the subject. Coxe died in Philadelphia on July 17, 1824.

• STEPHEN CRANE   1709—1780

A New Jersey delegate to the Continental Congress, Stephen Crane was born in Elizabethtown (now Elizabeth), New Jersey, in July 1709. Prominent in colonial affairs, he was sheriff of Essex County and was chosen by the Elizabethtown Associates to go to England and lay a petition before the king in 1743. He was elected to the New Jersey general assembly 1766–73 and served as speaker in 1771. Crane was mayor of Elizabethtown 1772–74, and then sent to the Continental Congress 1774–76. After formation of the new state government, Crane served as a member of the state council in 1776–77 and in 1779. He died in Elizabeth on July 1, 1780.

• WILLIAM CRAWFORD   1732—1782

A frontiersman and Revolutionary War colonel who was tortured to death by Indians, William Crawford was born in Berkeley County, Virginia, in 1732. He became a friend of George Washington when both were seventeen-year-old surveyors on the Virginia frontier, and later served with Washington in the French and Indian War. In the years before the Revolutionary War Crawford established himself as an Indian trader in the wilderness near Pittsburgh. In Lord Dunmore's War in 1774 he was commissioned a major in the militia and led a band of about 500 frontiersmen against the Indians. In 1776 Crawford was commissioned colonel in command of the 7th Virginia Regiment of militia, and with his men took part in the battles of Long Island, Trenton, and Princeton. He led scouting parties in the battles of Brandywine and Germantown in 1777, and then was sent back to the frontier to command a newly recruited militia regiment in protecting settlers from

Sewing table clamp
—Sketch by Kay Smith

British-inspired Indian attacks. In 1782 Washington prevailed on his fifty-year-old friend to lead a major expedition against the Indians in the region of Sandusky in what is now northern Ohio. In May 1782 Crawford and about 500 frontiersmen made their way for about 150 miles through the forests, reaching the Sandusky area at the beginning of June. News of the approaching American expedition already had reached the British, and they were prepared. On June 4-5 an army of British Loyalists and Indians equipped with artillery attacked the Americans. As in many another battle the militiamen panicked and ran. On June 7, while rounding up stragglers, Crawford and ten others were taken prisoner by a large band of Delaware Indians. On June 11 the Indians killed and scalped nine of the prisoners and tortured Crawford to death while British Loyalists looked on and laughed. The official British report of Crawford's death by the officer in charge said: "Crawford died like a hero; never changed his countenance, tho' they scalped him alive, and then laid hot ashes on his head; after which they roasted him by a slow fire." The remaining prisoner, Dr. John Knight, the expedition's surgeon, escaped and brought news of Crawford's death to Fort Pitt on July 4, 1782.

Interior of an old prison ship in the Revolutionary War —From a wood engraving

FROM A WATERCOLOR PAINTING BY KAY SMITH

When Washington decided to spend the winter of 1779–80 in Morristown, New Jersey, because of its strategic location and relatively safe defensive position, he is quoted as having said, "I understand my quarters are to be at Mrs. Ford's." Jacob Ford built this impressive mansion upon 200 acres of land in the years 1772–74. A barn, a well, ice and carriage houses served the family needs. Ford passed away early in the war and Mrs. Ford stayed on in the mansion with her four children. She generously shared the mansion with Washington and his aides, moving into a single bedroom along with her four children for that bitter winter. When Washington arrived and observed the crowded quarters, he ordered construction of a kitchen building and a stable. Washington conferred here with Lafayette, Ambassador Luzerne Don Juan De Miralles representing the Spanish government, and key members of the Continental Congress.

Kay Smith
Nassau Hall - Princeton

Nassau Hall, Princeton, New Jersey,
erected in 1756 by the College of
New Jersey and named Nassau Hall
in honor of King William III, was
seized by the British forces for
military purposes in 1776 and retaken
by the American army January 3, 1777.
From June 30, 1783, until
November 4, 1783, the Continental
Congress met in this building, when
it served as the Capitol of the United
States, and on August 26 during
that session they received and honored
General George Washington
for his services in establishing
the freedom and independence of
the United States of America.

FROM A WATERCOLOR PAINTING BY KAY SMITH

FROM A WATERCOLOR PAINTING BY KAY SMITH

Two settlers from England acquired a section of land in New Jersey located about forty miles west of New York City where they set up a blast furnace, refinery, and forge which attracted workers who established the village of Andover Forge, later renamed Waterloo. This stone house was built between 1762 and 1764 as a duplex having three stories to house two families of mill workers. The iron produced here was the finest quality, and during the Revolutionary War orders were issued specifying that cannon balls for the colonial army be procured from Andover Forge. The English owners were loyal to the King, so the plant was confiscated and run by the Continental government until the end of the war. Wounded Revolutionary soldiers were housed in the village and this house was used as a hospital. When the Morris Canal was built between 1824 and 1830, it went through Waterloo just in front of this house, which then housed canal workers, and thus it became known as the Canal House.

• THOMAS CUSHING 1725–1788

A close associate of Samuel Adams in the pre-Revolutionary activities in Massachusetts, Thomas Cushing was born in Boston on March 24, 1725. At nineteen he was graduated from Harvard College where he had become a friend of Samuel Adams, and his father, a prominent merchant, gave Adams his first job. Cushing became a lawyer and was first elected to the Massachusetts legislature in 1761. Two years later he became speaker of the legislature, a post he held until the outbreak of the Revolution, working closely with Adams who was clerk of the legislature. He served with both John and Samuel Adams in the Continental Congress 1774–76, helping fan the fires of patriotism in wavering delegates from other colonies. Elected as lieutenant governor of Massachusetts in 1779, he was repeatedly re-elected to that office until his death in Boston on February 28, 1788.

Thomas Cushing

• TRISTRAM DALTON 1738–1817

One of the first U.S. Senators from Massachusetts, Tristram Dalton was born in Newbury, Massachusetts, on May 28, 1738. After being graduated from Harvard College at the age of seventeen, he studied law and was admitted to the bar. He was elected to the Massachusetts house of representatives 1782–88, serving as speaker in 1784–85. Elected as a U.S. Senator to the First U.S. Congress, he served in 1789–91, but was an unsuccessful candidate for re-election. He was surveyor of the port of Boston from 1814 until his death in Boston on May 30, 1817.

• FRANCIS DANA 1743–1811

A diplomat, statesman, and jurist, Francis Dana was born in Charlestown, Massachusetts, on June 13, 1743, the son of Richard Dana, a prominent member of the Sons of Liberty in the pre-Revolutionary period. Francis Dana was graduated from Harvard College in 1762, studied law, was admitted to the bar, and commenced practice in Boston in 1767. He carried confidential correspondence to Benjamin Franklin in England in 1774 as conditions worsened between the crown and the American colonies. Returning to America, he was elected a member of the Massachusetts delegation to the Continental Congress 1776–78, where he was a member of the board of war and signed the Articles of Confederation on July 9, 1778. Congress appointed Dana in 1779 to accompany John Adams to Europe as secretary on the mission to negotiate a treaty of peace with Great Britain and a treaty of commerce with Holland. In 1780 Congress appointed Dana as minister to Russia. He traveled to St. Petersburg with fourteen-year-old John Quincy Adams as his secretary, but, despite two years of

161

trying, was unable to gain official recognition from the Russian court. Having returned to the United States, he again was elected to the Continental Congress in 1784. The next year Dana was appointed to the supreme court of Massachusetts, and six years later was made chief justice, a position he held for the next fifteen years. Dana also served as a presidential elector in 1788, 1792, 1800, and 1808. He died in Cambridge, Massachusetts, on April 25, 1811. He was the grandfather of Richard Henry Dana, Jr., author of *Two Years Before the Mast*.

• NATHAN DANE   1752–1835

A delegate to the Continental Congress from Massachusetts, Nathan Dane was born in Ipswich, Massachusetts, on December 29, 1752. After graduation from Harvard College at the age of sixteen, he taught school, studied law, was admitted to the bar, and commenced practice in Beverly, Massachusetts, in 1782. He was elected to the state house of representatives 1782–85, and then to the Continental Congress 1785–88. Dane next served in the state senate in 1790–91 and 1794–97. He became judge of the court of common pleas for Essex County in 1794. He was appointed commissioner to codify the laws of Massachusetts in 1795 and in 1812. He died in Beverly on February 15, 1835.

• WILLIAM LEE DAVIDSON   1746–1781

A militia general who died fighting during the Revolutionary War, William Lee Davidson was born in Lancaster County, Pennsylvania, in 1746. While he was a child his family moved to what is now Iredell County, North Carolina. Active in the pre-Revolutionary movement, Davidson was a member of the local committee of safety in 1775. He was commissioned a major in the 4th North Carolina Regiment in 1776, and marched north with his men to join Washington's army. After taking part in the battles of Brandywine and Germantown in 1777, he was promoted to lieutenant colonel. He fought at the battle of Monmouth in 1778. Then in 1779 the remnants of the North Carolina troops were sent to the South, and Davidson left the Continental Army to join the North Carolina militia. In 1780 Davidson commanded a force of 300 militia in the American victory over British Loyalists at Ramseur's Mill in North Carolina. Later that year he was severely wounded in a battle with Loyalists at Calson's Mill. He then received a promotion to brigadier general of militia. Two weeks after the major American victory at Cowpens, South Carolina Cornwallis and his troops were pursuing the American army of Gen. Nathanael Greene to seek revenge. Davidson and 800 militia he had recruited were stationed along the flooded Catawba River to prevent Cornwallis from crossing. When Corn-

A town meeting —From a painting by John Trumbull

wallis and his crack British Guards plunged across the river at Cowan's Ford on the morning of February 1, 1781, the militia fell back and Davidson was killed while trying to prevent their retreat.

- ## JOHN DAWSON   1762–1814

A Congressman from Virginia, John Dawson was born in Virginia in 1762. After graduation from Harvard in 1782, he studied law and was admitted to the bar. At twenty-four he was elected to the Virginia house of delegates 1786–89, and at twenty-six became a member of the Continental Congress 1788–89. Beginning in 1796, he was elected as a U.S. Representative of Virginia to nine succeeding U.S. Congresses, serving there until his death in Washington, D.C., on March 31, 1814.

- ## ELIAS DAYTON   1737–1807

A Revolutionary War officer who believed fighting was more important than holding political office, Elias Dayton was born in Elizabethtown (now Elizabeth), New Jersey, on May 1, 1737. After completing an apprenticeship as a mechanic, Dayton fought in the French and Indian War as a lieutenant of the "Jersey Blues" militia under Gen. James Wolfe at Quebec in 1759. As a captain, he led his militia company to Detroit in 1763 to fight the Indians in Pontiac's War. In the dozen years before the Revolutionary War, Dayton became proprietor of a

Fort William and Mary on the Piscataqua River in New Hampshire

Elias Dayton —From a painting by James Sharples

general store at Elizabethtown, an alderman of the town, and in 1774 a member of the committee of safety to enforce measures recommended by Continental Congress. In 1775, Dayton was one of Essex County's four muster-masters to enlist troops for the Continental Army. He was commissioned a colonel of the 3rd Regiment of the New Jersey Line on January 10, 1776. Twelve days later, he and Gen. William Alexander led seventy-seven volunteers in three shallops who captured the British supply ship *Blue Mountain Valley* which was anchored off Sandy Hook. Dayton marched his regiment to New York's Mohawk Valley in May 1776, where he rebuilt Fort Stanwix and built Fort Dayton at Herkimer, New York, to ward off Indian raids. Rejoining Washington's main army at Morristown, New Jersey, in March 1777, he fought in skirmishes at Bound Brook, New Jersey, and at Staten Island. After taking part in the battles of Brandywine and Germantown, Dayton spent the winter of 1777–1778 at Valley Forge with Washington's army. In 1778 he and his regiment fought in the battle of Monmouth, New Jersey. Dayton was elected to the Continental Congress in December 1778, but declined to serve, saying his place was with his men. In 1779 Dayton and his regiment joined Gen. John Sullivan's expedition in western New York that attacked and destroyed the towns of the Iroquois Indians. In June 1780 Dayton fought off a large British force at Springfield, New Jersey. In 1781 Dayton led the New Jersey brigade at the siege of Yorktown, Virginia. Dayton was promoted to brigadier general in January 1783. After the war Dayton returned to Elizabethtown and operated his general store, becoming a major general of militia. He was elected a member of the New Jersey general assembly 1791–92 and 1794–96, and was mayor of Elizabethtown 1796–1805. He died in Elizabethtown on October 22, 1807. He was the father of Jonathan Dayton.

• JONATHAN DAYTON   1760–1824

A Revolutionary War soldier and the youngest man to sign the United States Constitution, Jonathan Dayton was born in Elizabethtown (now Elizabeth), New Jersey, on October 16, 1760, the son of Elias Dayton. At sixteen he was graduated from Princeton College, and joined the Continental Army as ensign in his father's 3rd New Jersey Regiment on February 7, 1776. He fought at his father's side throughout most of the war. During the expedition against the Iroquois Indians in 1779, he served as aide-de-camp to Maj. Gen. John Sullivan, and then rejoined his father's regiment as a captain. He was taken prisoner at Elizabethtown on October 5, 1780, and later exchanged, rejoining the army in January 1781. The twenty-one-year-old Dayton distinguished himself by bravely storming a redoubt at the battle of Yorktown in 1781. After the war he studied law and began practice in Elizabethtown. He was elected to the state legislature in 1786. The next year he was sent as a New Jersey delegate to the federal Constitutional Convention. At twenty-six he became the youngest delegate to sign the new United States Constitution. He was elected to the Continental Congress 1787–88, became speaker of the house of the New Jersey legislature in 1790, and then won election to the U.S. Congress, serving in 1791–99. During his last four years as a Congressman he was Speaker of the House. In 1798 Dayton won election to the U.S. Senate, where he served one term 1799–1805. Dayton became a close friend of Aaron Burr and invested in western land in Ohio, where the city of Dayton was named in his honor. He

A Revolutionary War shelter house as reconstructed at the New Windsor Cantonment near Newburgh, New York. —Sketch by Kay Smith

was arrested in 1807 on a charge of conspiring with Burr in treasonable projects. He gave bail and was subsequently released, having never been brought to trial. He died in Elizabethtown on October 9, 1824.

• **SILAS DEANE** **1737—1789**

A secret agent for the Continental Congress, Silas Deane was born in Groton, Connecticut, on December 24, 1737. After graduation from Yale College in 1758, he studied law and commenced practice in Wethersfield, Connecticut, in 1761. He was elected to the Connecticut general assembly 1768–75, and as a member of the Continental Congress 1774–76.

Silas Deane

The Secret Committee of Congress sent him to France in March 1776 as a secret political and financial agent to purchase supplies for the Continental Army and recruit for engineers. Unfortunately his mission was not secret from the British because Deane became a close friend of Edward Bancroft, an American double agent, who, although Deane did not realize it, reported all of Deane's transactions to the British government. Deane was successful in obtaining supplies, but also arranged to profit on the transactions himself. His liberality in promising commissions to French adventurers plagued Congress with many incompetent foreign officers, but also resulted in the recruitment of such outstanding officers as the Marquis de Lafayette. In September 1776 Deane was commissioned by Congress as an ambassador with Benjamin Franklin and Arthur Lee to negotiate a treaty between France and the United States. Lee and others believed Deane was engaged in dishonest deals, so Congress recalled him in 1777 for investigation. Unable to prove to Congress that his large claims for expenses were valid, Deane returned to France to procure transcripts of his transactions. He wrote letters saying that he had lost confidence in the American cause and believed arrangements should be made with Britain. Bancroft secretly gave these letters to the British government, which had them published. Charges of treason by Deane were now added to the previous charges of dishonesty. After living in poverty for several years, Deane decided to return to the United States, but died aboard ship on September 23, 1789. Over fifty years later, Congress voted $37,000 in 1842 to pay Deane's heirs for his expenses.

• **HENRY DEARBORN   1751−1829**

A young officer in the Revolutionary War and later the senior American general in the War of 1812, Henry Dearborn was born in North Hampton, New Hampshire, on February 23, 1751. After studying medicine, he commenced practice in Nottingham Square at the age of twenty-one in 1772. On the outbreak of the Revolutionary War in 1775, he led a company of New Hampshire militia to Boston where he fought in the Battle of Bunker Hill under command of Col. John Stark. Dearborn commanded a company of musketmen during Arnold's expedition to Canada in 1775 and was taken prisoner during the storming of Quebec. Released on parole in May 1776, Dearborn fought in the battles of Stillwater, Saratoga, Monmouth, and Newton. He joined Washington's staff in 1781 as deputy quartermaster general with rank of colonel and served at the siege of Yorktown. After the war, Dearborn moved to Monmouth, Massachusetts (now Maine), where he became major general of militia and was appointed U.S. marshal for the district of Maine in 1789. He was elected as a

Henry Dearborn

Democrat from a Maine district to the Third and Fourth U.S. Congresses 1793–97. President Jefferson appointed Dearborn as Secretary of War, an office he held throughout Jefferson's administration from 1801 to 1809. After holding the office of collector of the port of Boston for three years, he was appointed by President Madison as the senior major general in the U.S. Army on January 27, 1812. During the War of 1812, he was in command of the frontier with Canada and was blamed for American defeats in that area. Recalled from the frontier in July 1813, he was placed in command of the city of New York. In 1815 President Madison nominated Dearborn as Secretary of War, but the Senate refused to confirm the appointment. His last public service was as minister to Portugal during President Monroe's administration from 1822 to 1824. He returned to Roxbury, Massachusetts, where he died on June 6, 1829.

• **JOHN DE HART   1728–1795**

A New Jersey delegate to the Continental Congress, John De Hart was born in Elizabethtown (now Elizabeth), New Jersey, in 1728. After studying law, he became a successful lawyer in Elizabethtown. In 1774 he was chosen as one of New Jersey's delegates to the Continental Congress, where he was one of the signers of the Articles of Association, as the nonimportation agreement was called. He resigned from Congress on November 22, 1775, was again elected on February 14, 1776, and again resigned on June 13, 1776. He was a member of the committee that drafted the New Jersey state constitution in June 1776. De Hart was elected chief justice of the state supreme court in September 1776, but declined to serve. He became mayor of Elizabethtown in 1789 and was repeatedly re-elected until his death there on June 1, 1795.

• JOHN PHILIP DE HAAS   1735–1786

A colonel in the Continental Army who resigned rather than be a brigadier general, John Philip De Haas was born in the Netherlands in 1735 and was brought to America by his parents, while he was still a baby. They settled in Lancaster, Pennsylvania. When De Haas was twenty-two, he was commissioned an ensign in the Pennsylvania militia, and fought in the French and Indian War and Pontiac's War. After leaving the army in 1763, he became an iron-maker at Lancaster. When the Revolutionary War began, De Haas was colonel of the 1st Pennsylvania Regiment. In 1776 he led his regiment to Canada, bringing needed support at a time when Benedict Arnold's forces were in danger of being captured. He then marched his regiment from Lake Champlain to New York City, taking part in the battle of Long Island. In October 1776 his regiment was absorbed into the 2nd Pennsylvania Continental Regiment, and De Haas was commissioned a colonel in the Continental Army. Four months later, in February 1777, Congress named him as one of ten new brigadier generals. De Haas did not respond to the new appointment, so General Washington wrote him four months later to inquire why he was so slow in answering. Apparently feeling that he deserved a higher rank or else just not wishing to serve in the army on a permanent basis, De Haas replied by resigning his commission. He died in Philadelphia on June 3, 1786.

• CHARLES DE WITT   1727–1787

An editor and politician, Charles De Witt was born in Kingston, New York, in 1727. An editor of the *Ulster Sentinel* for many years, he was a member of the colonial assembly 1768–76, and of the New York provisional congress that approved the Declaration of Independence 1775–77. De Witt was a delegate to the Continental Congress in 1784, and a representative in the state assembly in 1781 and 1785–86. He died in Kingston on August 27, 1787.

• SAMUEL DICK   1740—1812

A military surgeon and Congressman, Samuel Dick was born in Nottingham, Maryland, on November 14, 1740. After studying medicine in Scotland, he commenced practice in Salem, New Jersey, in 1770. At the beginning of the Revolutionary War he was a member of the New Jersey provincial congress and colonel of the 1st Battalion Salem County militia. He served as an assistant surgeon in the Continental Army in the Canadiam campaign 1775–76. He was appointed collector of customs for the western district of New Jersey in 1778 and then was elected to the Continental Congress in 1783–84. Dick was surrogate of Salem County 1785–1804. He died in Salem on November 16, 1812.

The struggle at Concord Bridge —From a sketch by Chappel

A sketch of John Dickinson showing his versatility as a student of the law and a man of letters.

• JOHN DICKINSON   1732–1808

Called the "Penman of the Revolution" because of the many important documents he wrote during the birth of the United States, John Dickinson was born on November 8, 1732, on his father's estate "Crosiadore," near Trappe, Maryland. When he was about eight, he moved with his parents to an estate near Dover, Delaware, where he grew up as a devout Quaker. After studying law at the Middle Temple in London, England, he began practice in Philadelphia in 1757.

He began a career of public service that was to go on for more than thirty years when he was elected in 1760 at the age of twenty-four to a term in the colonial assembly of Delaware. Two years later he was elected to the Pennsylvania general assembly, beginning one of the most unusual aspects of his career, in that he regularly switched his public duties back and forth between Delaware and Pennsylvania because he had residences and owned property in each.

At the age of twenty-nine he won prominence throughout the colonies as a delegate from Pennsylvania to the 1765 Stamp Act Congress in New York. There he wrote one of the most important documents adopted by the Congress, the "Declaration of Rights and Grievances of the Colonists of America" in which he said in part:

". . . it is inseparably essential to the freedom of a people, and the undoubted rights of Englishmen, that no taxes be imposed on them but with their own common consent, given personally or by their representatives."

Two years later he wrote a series of twelve newspaper articles called "Letters from a Farmer in Pennsylvania to the Inhabitants of the British Colonies." In these articles he explained in terms understandable by laymen the points at issue between the colonies and the English government, but warned the colonists not to be swayed by agitators to take rash acts in the name of patriotism.

Continuing to serve in the Pennsylvania general assembly during the pre-war years of the 1770s, he wrote articles inveighing against the British-imposed tax on tea in 1773, warning that the measure threatened to "sacrifice the lives of thousands."

At the first Continental Congress in 1774 the delegates adopted Dickinson's "Petition to the King" and "Address to the Inhabitants of Quebec" because they were more conservative and conciliatory in nature than those suggested by the more hot-headed delegates from New England and Virginia.

When the Continental Congress met again in 1775, after fighting already had begun at Lexington and Concord, the delegates adopted Dickinson's "Declaration on the Causes and Necessity of Taking Up Arms," which declared that the colonists were determined "to die freemen rather than like slaves" but at the same time cautioned that "we mean not to dissolve that union" between the colonies and England. In the months that followed Dickinson stood firmly against any proposal that the colonies should separate from the mother country, and he opposed and refused to sign the "Declaration of Independence." At the same time, however, he recognized that the colonies must have a more solidly based government than the loose collection of rules adopted by the Continental Congress, so he devoted his time to writing the Articles of Confederation, which he presented to Congress on July 12, 1776. He left Congress a few days later, having failed to be re-elected as a delegate by the Pennsylvania legislature because of his opposition to the Declaration of Independence.

To demonstrate his continued patriotism, Dickinson joined the militia as a private, and in January 1777 helped capture Elizabethtown, New Jersey, from the British. Later in 1777 he fought at Brandywine in trying to prevent the British capture of Philadelphia. Then in October 1777 he accepted a commission as a brigadier general of Pennsylvania militia.

Dickinson returned to the Continental Congress in 1779–80 as a delegate from Delaware, and had the pleasure of signing the Articles of Confederation to indicate their ratification by Delaware.

During the next five years, Dickinson was elected in turn president of Delaware 1781–82 and president of Pennsylva-

A flail used for the separation of the grain from the chaff

173

nia 1782–85. Also during this period he donated land to and helped found Dickinson College at Carlisle, Pennsylvania.

Urging the necessity of a stronger government for the United States, Dickinson presided at the Annapolis Convention in 1786 that initiated the calling of a federal Constitutional Convention. He attended the Constitutional Convention in Philadelphia the next year as a delegate from Delaware, and acted as a spokesmen for the smaller states. Unable to be present at the final signing ceremony, he authorized a fellow-delegate to sign his name by proxy to the new United States Constitution. In 1788 he wrote a series of articles over the name "Fabius" advocating ratification of the Constitution, helping win its early approval by Delaware and Pennsylvania.

Dickinson accepted his last elective office at the age of sixty, when he served as a delegate to the Delaware state constitutional convention in 1792, where he helped write a new constitution establishing the office of governor. After retiring from public office, Dickinson continued to write and express his views on current issues, until his death at the age of seventy-five on February 14, 1808, in Wilmington, Delaware.

• PHILEMON DICKINSON   1739–1809

Commanding general of the New Jersey militia during the Revolutionary War, a delegate to the Continental Congress, and a U.S. Senator, Philemon Dickinson was born at "Crosiadore," near Trappe, Maryland, on April 5, 1739, a younger brother of John Dickinson. After graduation in the first class from the College of Philadelphia in 1757, he studied law, but never practiced. In 1767 he moved to an estate, "The Hermitage," near Trenton, New Jersey. At the beginning of the Revolutionary War in 1775 he was commissioned as colonel of the Hunterdon County militia, and in October was promoted to brigadier general of militia. In 1776 he was elected as a delegate to New Jersey's Revolutionary provincial congress. In January 1777 Dickinson led 400 of his militia in a raid on a British foraging party near Somerset Court House, New Jersey, capturing about forty wagons of supplies and several prisoners. In June 1777 he was appointed major general in command of all New Jersey militia, a post he held throughout the rest of the war. Dickinson's militia took part in the battle of Monmouth in 1778, helping obstruct the retreat of the British to New York. When his cousin John Cadwalader dueled Gen. Thomas Conway on July 4, 1778, Dickinson was Cadwalader's second. Dickinson represented New Jersey in the Continental Congress in 1782–83, and the following year served on a commission to choose the site for a national capital. He was elected by the New Jersey legislature as a U.S. Senator in 1790–93, and after that retired to his estate, "The Hermitage," where he died on February 4, 1809.

A view of Boston in the eighteenth century

• MARY DRAPER

EDITOR'S NOTE: *The following account is from "Women of the American Revolution" by Elizabeth F. Ellet, a collection of anecdotes about women of the period collected in the early 1800s. The author says of this sketch: "The facts were communicated by a lady who was well acquainted with Mrs. Draper, and has often heard her relate particulars of the war."*

Mary Draper was the wife of Captain Draper of Dedham, Massachusetts, and lived on a farm. When the first call to arms sounded throughout the land, she exhorted her husband to lose no time in hastening to the scene of action; and with her own hands bound knapsack and blanket on the shoulders of her only son, a stripling of sixteen, bidding him depart and do his duty. To the entreaties of her daughter that her young brother might remain at home to be their protector, she answered that every arm able to aid the cause belonged to the country. "He is wanted and must go. You and I, Kate, have also service to do. Food must be prepared for the hungry; for before tomorrow night, hundreds, I hope thousands, will be on their way to join the continental forces. Some who have traveled far will need refreshment, and you and I, with Molly, must feed as many as we can."

Captain Draper was a thriving farmer; his granaries were well filled, and his wife's dairy was her special care and pride. All the resources at her command were in requisition to contribute to her benevolent purpose. Assisted by her daughter and the domestic, she spent the whole day and night, and the succeeding day, in baking brown bread. The ovens of that day were not the small ones now in use, but were suited for such

A bonnet called a calash

175

an occasion, each holding bread sufficient to supply a neighborhood. By good fortune two of these monster ovens appertained to the establishment, as is frequently the case in New England. These were soon in full blast, and the kneading trough was plied by hands that shrank not from the task.

At that time of hurry and confusion, none could stop long enough to dine. The people were under such haste to join the army, that they stayed only to relieve the cravings of hunger, though from want of food, and fatigue, many were almost exhausted.

With the help of a disabled veteran of the French war, who had for years resided in her family, Mrs. Draper had soon her stores in readiness. A long form was erected by the roadside; large pans of bread and cheese were placed upon it, and replenished as often as was necessary; while old John brought cider in pails from the cellar, which, poured into tubs, was served out by two lads who volunteered their services. Thus were the weary patriots refreshed on their way.

Mrs. Draper presided, and when her own stock of provisions began to fail, applied to her neighbors for aid. By their contributions her hospitable board was supplied, till in a few days the necessity for extraordinary exertion had in a measure passed, and order and discipline took the place of popular tumult. When each soldier carried his rations, the calls on private benevolence were less frequent and imperative.

But ere long came the startling intelligence, after the battle of Bunker Hill, that a scarcity of ammunition had been experienced. General Washington called upon the inhabitants to send to headquarters every ounce of lead or pewter at their disposal, saying that any quantity, however small, would be gratefully received.

This appeal could not be disregarded. It is difficult at this day to estimate the value of pewter as an ornamental as well as indispensable convenience. The more precious metals had not then found their way to the tables of New Englanders; and throughout the country, services of pewter, scoured to the brightness of silver, covered the board, even in the mansions of the wealthy. Few withheld their portion in that hour of the country's need; and noble were the sacrifices made in presenting their willing offerings.

Mrs. Draper was rich in a large stock of pewter, which she valued as the ornament of her house. Much of it was precious to her as the gift of a departed mother. But the call reached her heart, and she delayed not obedience, thankful that she was able to contribute so largely to the requirements of her suffering country. Her husband before joining the army had purchased a mould for casting bullets, to supply himself and son with this article of warfare. Mrs. Draper was not satisfied with merely giving the material required, when she could possibly do more; and her platters, pans, and dishes were soon in process of transformation into balls.

—Sketch by Kay Smith

William Henry Drayton

• WILLIAM HENRY DRAYTON   1742–1779

A major spokesman for civil liberties at the beginning of the American Revolution, William Henry Drayton was born at "Drayton Hall" on the Ashley River in South Carolina in September 1742. He received a classical education at Westminster School and Balliol College, Oxford, in England. After returning to South Carolina in 1764, he studied law and was admitted to the bar. He again visited England in 1770 and was appointed royal privy councilor and assistant judge for South Carolina. In 1774 he wrote an address to the Continental Congress specifying the grievances of the American people and spelling out a bill of rights. That same year he addressed a grand jury in Camden, South Carolina, on the subject of civil liberties. His remarks were published and widely distributed, contributing to the rising sentiment for independence. He said in part: "I know no master but the law. I am a servant, not to the king, but to the constitution; and, in my estimation, I shall best discharge my duty . . . when I boldly declare the laws to the people and instruct them in their civil rights." When Drayton became president of the South Carolina council of safety in 1775, the royal government fired him from both his government positions. He was made chief justice of the state in 1776, and was elected president of South Carolina the following year. Chosen a member of the state's delegation to the Continental Congress in 1778 he served until his death in Philadelphia on September 3, 1779.

• JAMES DUANE   1733–1797

A New York delegate to the Continental Congress throughout the Revolutionary War, James Duane was born in New York

City on February 6, 1733. After studying law, he was admitted to the bar in 1754, became clerk of the chancery court in 1762, and attorney general of the colony of New York in 1767. Although he had served as an officer of the crown, his patriotic views were well known, and he was chosen as a member of New York's Revolutionary committee of one hundred in 1775. He served eleven years as a member of New York's delegation to the Continental Congress 1774–84. In 1775 he angered John Adams and the other Massachusetts delegates by introducing resolutions that delayed the Declaration of Independence, which Duane believed was unnecessary and refused to sign. After New York City was recovered from the British at the end of the war, Duane was elected as its first mayor, serving 1784–89. For the next five years he was U.S. district judge for New York 1789–94. Duane died in Duanesburg, New York, February 1, 1797.

• WILLIAM DUER   1747–1799

A businessman and delegate to the Continental Congress who died in debtor's prison, William Duer was born in Devonshire, England, on March 18, 1747. After attending Eton College in England, at seventeen he became aide-de-camp to Lord Clive, Governor General in India. Duer immigrated to America in 1768 and settled in Fort Miller, New York. At twenty-six he was appointed the first royal judge of Charlotte (now Washington) County. He built the first saw and grist mills at Fort Miller, and later erected a snuff mill and a powder mill. Taking an active part in the pre-Revolutionary movement, he became a member of the New York provincial congress in 1776–77, served in the state senate in 1777, and was chosen a delegate to the Continental Congress in 1777–78. Duer also was appointed judge of the court of common pleas in 1777–78. He built the first cotton mills in Paterson, New Jersey, and Westchester County, New York. Duer became prominent in New York society after marrying Lady Kitty Alexander, the daughter of wealthy Gen. William (Lord Stirling) Alexander, in a marriage in 1779 in which Gen. George Washington gave the bride away. He became secretary of the Treasury Board of the Continental Congress and then assisted Alexander Hamilton in organizing the U.S. Treasury Department in 1789–90. Duer's arrest for debt in 1792 brought on a financial panic in New York. He spent most of the rest of his life in prison, dying there in New York City on May 7, 1799.

• ELIPHALET DYER   1721–1807

A judge and member of the Continental Congress throughout most of the Revolutionary War, Eliphalet Dyer was born in Windham, Connecticut, on September 14, 1721. After graduation from Yale College at nineteen, he studied law and com-

Lieutenant Moody, a British officer who was rescued from an American prison. —From an English engraving of 1783

menced practice in Windham. A founding member of the Susquehanna Company in 1753, he served as a member of the
committee to purchase the Indian title to lands selected for
colonization at Wyoming, Pennsylvania, then believed to be
within the charter limits of Connecticut. During the French
and Indian War, Dyer was colonel of a militia regiment sent
against Canada in 1758. For more than thirty years he was a
member of Connecticut's general assembly, both before and
after the Revolutionary War. He was sent as a delegate to the
Stamp Act Congress in 1765 and to the Continental Congress
1774–79 and 1780–83. A justice of the peace since 1746,
Dyer was appointed a member of Connecticut's superior court
in 1766, and held the position of chief justice from 1789 until
he retired in 1793. He died in Windham on May 13, 1807.

179

The Battle of Eutaw Springs —After a painting by Chappel

• **PIERREPONT EDWARDS**   1750–1826

A Connecticut delegate to the Continental Congress, Pierrepont Edwards was born in Northampton, Massachusetts, on April 8, 1750. He was the youngest son of Jonathan Edwards, the Puritan minister whose sermons at revival meetings had brought about the religious movement called "The Great Awakening" in the 1730s to 1740s. After graduation from Princeton College at eighteen, Edwards studied law and began practice in New Haven, Connecticut, in 1771. After Benedict Arnold was found guilty of treason, Edwards was made administrator of his estate. He was a member of the Continental Congress in 1787–88. Elected to the Connecticut house of representatives in 1789, he served as speaker in 1790. Edwards was appointed district judge for Connecticut in 1806. He died in Bridgeport, Connecticut, on April 5, 1826.

JOSEPH EGGLESTON   1754–1811

A daring cavalry officer during the Revolutionary War and later a Virginia Congressman, Joseph Eggleston was born in Middlesex County, Virginia, on November 24, 1754. After graduation from William and Mary College in 1776, he joined the Continental Army. He was captured by the British at Elizabethtown, New Jersey, in January 1780. After being exchanged, he joined Henry Lee's Lighthorse Cavalry with the commission of captain. He won special distinction for his rear guard cavalry actions in the battle of Guilford Courthouse, North Carolina, on March 15, 1781, and was promoted to major. He further distinguished himself for his bold command of the cavalry during 1781 at the battle of Fort Galphin, South Carolina, the capture of Augusta, Georgia, and the battle of Eutaw Springs, South Carolina. Eggleston was elected to the Virginia house of delegates 1785–88 and 1791–99 and then to the U.S. Congress 1798–1801. After retiring from Congress he served as justice of the peace from 1801 until his death on his estate in Amelia County, Virginia, on February 13, 1811.

SAMUEL ELBERT   1743–1788

A Revolutionary War infantry commander and later governor of Georgia, Samuel Elbert was born in Prince William Parish, South Carolina, in 1743. In his twenties he became a merchant in Savannah, Georgia. A member of the Sons of Liberty and a militia captain, he became a member of the Savannah council of safety in 1775. In 1776 he was commissioned a colonel in command of the 2nd Georgia Continental Regiment. He led his regiment into East Florida the next year, but was forced to return to Georgia because of lack of supplies. Although Elbert and the 100 Continentals under his command fought bravely at the battle of Briar Creek, South Carolina, in 1779, he was wounded and captured. After being exchanged two years later in June 1781, he commanded a brigade at the battle of Yorktown. Before being discharged from the army at the end of the war in 1783, he was advanced to the rank of brigadier general. In 1784 he was elected as a delegate to the Continental Congress, and the next year was elected governor of Georgia. Elbert died in Savannah on November 2, 1788.

WILLIAM ELLERY   1727–1820

A signer of the Declaration of Independence, William Ellery was born in Newport, Rhode Island, on December 22, 1727. After graduation from Harvard College at twenty, Ellery became a successful businessman and lawyer. After Rhode Island declared its independence from Britain in May 1776, Ellery was sent as a delegate to urge the Continental Congress

William Ellery

to follow suit. His pleasure in participating in the signing of the Declaration of Independence several months later was described in these words he wrote: "I was determined to see how they all looked, as they signed what might be their death warrant. I placed myself beside the secretary, Charles Thomson, and eyed each closely as he affixed his name to the document. Undaunted resolution was displayed in every countenance." When the British occupied Newport, they took revenge on Ellery by burning his house and destroying his property. Ellery served over seven years in the Continental Congress 1776–81 and 1783–85. As a member of the Congress' committee on naval affairs, he was credited with planning and executing the use of fire ships against the British fleet. Ellery was appointed chief justice of Rhode Island in 1785. President Washington named him collector of the port of Newport in 1790, a post he held until his death in Newport on February 15, 1820.

• OLIVER ELLSWORTH   1745–1807

One of Connecticut's first U.S. Senators and later Chief Justice of the United States, Oliver Ellsworth was born in Windsor, Connecticut, on April 29, 1745. He attended Yale College and then was graduated from Princeton College in 1766. After studying law, he began practice in Windsor. He was elected a representative in the Connecticut general assembly in 1775–76, was appointed state attorney in 1777, and was chosen as a member of the state's delegation to the Continental Congress 1777–84. He was a member of the governor's council 1780–85 and judge of the Connecticut superior court 1785–89. Chosen as a Connecticut delegate to the federal Constitutional Convention of 1787, Ellsworth played an important part in helping write the United States Constitution,

A view of New York Harbor in the eighteenth century

Oliver Ellsworth, Chief Justice —From a painting by W. R. Wheeler

but was forced to leave the convention because of illness, and therefore was not present when it finally was signed. He was elected as one of Connecticut's Senators to the First U.S. Congress in 1789, serving until 1796, when he resigned to accept appointment as Chief Justice of the United States. He retired from the bench in 1800 after President John Adams appointed him as an envoy to negotiate an end to the country's undeclared war with France. After successfully concluding the treaty, Ellsworth returned to the United States in 1801 and again became a member of the governor's council, serving in that body until his death in Windsor on November 26, 1807.

- ● JONATHAN ELMER   1745–1817

A physician and one of New Jersey's first U.S. Senators, Jonathan Elmer was born in Cedarville, New Jersey, on November 29, 1745. At the age of twenty-three he was graduated from the first medical class of the College of Philadelphia and began practice in Bridgeton, New Jersey. Elmer was elected high sheriff of Cumberland County in 1772, and was chosen captain of a light infantry company in 1775. He then served nine years as a member of the Continental Congress 1776–78, 1781–84, and 1787–88. He was elected as one of New Jersey's Senators to the First U.S. Congress 1789–91. Elmer then served as presiding judge of the county court of common pleas in 1802–04 and 1813–14. He died in Bridgeton on September 3, 1817. His younger brother, Ebenezer Elmer, was also a physician and represented New Jersey in the U.S. Congress 1801–07.

- ### NICHOLAS EVELEIGH   c. 1748–1791

A Revolutionary War officer and delegate from South Carolina to the Continental Congress, Nicholas Eveleigh was born in Charleston, South Carolina, about 1748. After being educated in England, he returned to Charleston in 1774. Appointed captain in the 2nd South Carolina Continental Regiment, he fought in the battle with the British fleet and forces at Fort Moultrie, South Carolina, on June 28, 1776. Eveleigh was promoted to colonel and appointed deputy adjutant general for South Carolina and Georgia on April 3, 1778. After the British conquered Georgia in 1778–79, Eveleigh resigned from the army. In 1781–82 he represented South Carolina in the Continental Congress. After formation of the new United States government in 1789, he was appointed Comptroller of the U.S. Treasury, a position he held until his death in Philadelphia on April 16, 1791.

- ### JOHN FELL   1721–1798

A New Jersey delegate to the Continental Congress, John Fell was born in New York City on February 5, 1721. A farmer and businessman, he moved to New Jersey where he became judge of the court of common pleas 1766–74. A zealous patriot, he helped overthrow the royalist government of New Jersey, and was chairman of the committee of safety of Bergen County. Captured by the British, he was held as a political prisoner from 1777 to 1778. After his release he was elected a member of the Continental Congress 1778–80. He died at the home of his son in Coldenham, New York, on May 15, 1798.

- ### WILLIAM FEW   1748–1828

A signer of the United State Constitution and one of Georgia's first U.S. Senators, William Few was born near Baltimore, Maryland, June 8, 1748. He moved with his parents to Orange County, North Carolina, in 1758, where he educated himself by reading books. At the age of twenty-eight he was admitted to the bar and commenced practice in Augusta, Georgia. At the outbreak of the Revolutionary War he joined the state militia, later describing his feelings in these words: "Although at that time I knew but little of politics, nor had I much studied the principles of free governments, I felt the spirit of an American, and without much investigation of the justice of her cause, I resolved to defend it." He was promoted to lieutenant colonel in the militia, taking part in the

William Few
—From a painting by James Sharples

One of the most charming colonial homes in Charleston, South Carolina, dates back to an original land grant of 1692 and has been preserved through nearly three centuries, including the Revolutionary and Civil Wars, countless hurricanes, an earthquake, and various owners. The original builder, George Eveleigh, was a merchant from Augusta, Georgia.

—Sketch by Kay Smith

185

guerrilla fighting after the British conquered Georgia in 1778–79. For eight years he represented Georgia in the Continental Congress 1780–88. He also represented Georgia at the federal Constitutional Convention in 1787, where he signed the United State Constitution. He then was elected as one of Georgia's U.S. Senators to the First U.S. Congress, serving from 1789 to 1793. He sat as judge of the circuit court of Georgia 1794–97. Few moved to New York City in 1799, and three years later was elected to the New York assembly 1802–05. He became director of the Manhattan Bank 1804–14, and its president in 1814–16, during which time he also served as a New York City alderman in 1813–14. Few died at the home of his son-in-law in Fishkill, New York, on July 16, 1828.

• **WILLIAM FITZHUGH**   **1741–1809**

A plantation owner and delegate to the Continental Congress from Virginia, William Fitzhugh was born in Eagles Nest, Virginia, on August 24, 1741. One of the small handful of close friends of George Washington, Fitzhugh first began to take an interest in politics at the outbreak of the Revolutionary War. He was elected to the state constitutional convention in 1776, and as a member of the state house of delegates in 1776–77. He was one of Virginia's delegates to the Continental Congress in 1779–80. Fitzhugh again was a member of the Virginia house of delegates in 1780–81 and 1787–88. He also served in the state senate 1781–85. Fitzhugh died at his estate "Ravensworth" in Fairfax County, Virginia, on June 6, 1809.

• **THOMAS FITZSIMONS**   **1741–1811**

A signer of the United States Constitution and the first Roman Catholic elected to office in Pennsylvania, Thomas Fitz-Simons was born in County Tubber, Wicklow, Ireland, in 1741. He immigrated to America and served an apprenticeship as a clerk in a counting-house in Philadelphia. Active in the pre-Revolutionary patriotic movement, he was a member of Philadelphia's committee of correspondence and was elected to Pennsylvania's first provincial congress in 1774. Upon the outbreak of war he raised a company of militia and served as their captain in fighting in New Jersey in 1776–77. With Robert Morris and others he helped found the Bank of North America in 1781 and then served as one of its directors for the next twenty-two years. FitzSimons was elected as one of Pennsylvania's delegates to the Continental Congress 1782–83 and to the state legislature in 1786–87. He was one of the state's delegates to the federal Constitutional Convention in 1787 and signed the new United States Constitution. Fitz-Simons was elected as one of Pennsylvania's representatives to the First U.S. Congress in 1789 where he continued to serve until 1795, having been defeated for re-election. Fitz-Simons lost a sizeable fortune in a financial panic in the early 1800s and died in obscurity in Philadelphia, on August 26, 1811.

• WILLIAM FLEMING   1736–1824

A judge and legislator, William Fleming was born in Cumberland County, Virginia, on July 6, 1736. After graduation from William and Mary College in 1763, he became a lawyer. Fleming was elected to the Virginia house of burgesses 1772–75, to the Virginia Revolutionary conventions 1775–76, and to the state house of delegates 1776–78. He served as a member of the Continental Congress 1779–81. For the last thirty-five years of his life, Fleming sat as a judge of the state's supreme court of appeals, and was president of the court from 1809 to his death at his country home "Summerville" in Chesterfield County, Virginia, on February 15, 1824.

The Bank of the United States on Third Street in Philadelphia in 1799 —From an engraving by W. Birch & Son

187

William Floyd

• **WILLIAM FLOYD**   **1734−1821**

A signer of the Declaration of Independence, William Floyd was born at the family estate "Brookhaven" on Long Island, New York, on December 17, 1734. By the time of the Revolutionary War, Floyd was commander of the Suffolk County militia. When the British were reported to be preparing to land troops on Long Island in the winter of 1774−75, Floyd assembled the militia to stave off the invasion. But the report proved false and no action ensued. Floyd served as a member of New York's delegation to the Continental Congress throughout the Revolutionary War. Although he did not vote for the Declaration of Independence because he had not been authorized to do so by the New York assembly, he signed the document after it was adopted by the Continental Congress. After the British took New York in 1776, they seized his estate, leaving him and his family without a home or income until after 1783. Floyd also served in the state senate in 1777−78 and 1784−88. He was elected to the First U.S. Congress 1789−91, but was defeated for re-election. To rebuild his fortune he moved in 1794 to Westernville in Oneida County, New York, to develop a large tract of land. He served as a presidential elector in 1792, 1800, 1804, and 1820. Floyd died in Westernville at the age of eighty-six on August 4, 1821.

• NATHANIEL FOLSOM   1726–1790

A major general of militia and a delegate to the Continental Congress, Nathaniel Folsom was born in Exeter, New Hampshire, on September 18, 1726. He served in the French and Indian War, rising to colonel of the 4th Regiment of New Hampshire militia. Although he was major general of the New Hampshire militia at the beginning of the Revolutionary War, he largely was involved in logistics rather than field command. He was elected a member of New Hampshire's delegation to the Continental Congress in 1774–75 and 1777–80. He was president of the state constitutional convention of 1783, and then served as chief justice of the court of common pleas. He died in Exeter on May 26, 1790.

• JAMES FORBES   c. 1731–1780

A delegate to the Continental Congress, James Forbes was born near Benedict, Maryland, about 1731. A justice of the peace and tax commissioner of Charles County, Maryland, he was elected a member of the state general assembly in 1777 and a representative member to the Continental Congress 1778–80. He died in Philadelphia on March 25, 1780, while serving in Congress.

• URIAH FORREST   1756–1805

An officer in the Revolutionary War and a delegate to the Continental Congress, Uriah Forrest was born near Leonardtown, Maryland, in 1756. Forrest was nineteen at the beginning of the Revolutionary War when he joined the Maryland militia as a lieutenant. He rose rapidly to major. Forrest was wounded at the Battle of Germantown and lost a leg at the Battle of Brandywine. He was elected a member of Maryland's delegation to the Continental Congress 1786–87, and as a Representative to the Third U.S. Congress 1793–94. He was commissioned major general of Maryland Militia in 1795. Forrest served as clerk of the circuit court of the District of Columbia from 1800 to his death at his home, "Rosedale," near Georgetown in Washington, D.C., on July 6, 1805.

• ABIEL FOSTER   1735–1806

A minister, judge, and Congressman, Abiel Foster was born in Andover, Massachusetts, August 8, 1735. After graduation from Harvard College in 1756, he studied theology and became a pastor in Canterbury, New Hampshire, from 1761 to 1779. Elected a member of the Continental Congress 1783–85, he then became judge of the court of common pleas of Rockingham County 1784–88. Foster was elected to the First U.S. Congress, serving 1789–91 and again in 1795–1803. He died in Canterbury, New Hampshire, February 6, 1806.

An interview aboard ship between Lord Howe and a committee of Congress —From a painting by Chappel

• BENJAMIN FRANKLIN   1706–1790

Recognized at home and abroad as America's leading statesman of the Revolutionary period, Benjamin Franklin was born in Boston on January 17, 1706, the youngest son in a family of seventeen children of a poor candle-maker. When he was ten, young Ben was taken out of school and put to work making candles. At twelve he was apprenticed to his brother James Franklin to learn the trade of printing. During the next five years, while becoming an expert printer, he also educated himself by reading every book he could borrow. At seventeen he decided he had had enough of his brother's bad temper, and he ran away to find a job on his own, going first to New York City, and finally settling in Philadelphia in 1723.

The royal governor of Pennsylvania, Sir William Keith, became interested in the boy, suggested that he should set up his own printing shop, and offered to give Franklin letters of credit in England so that he could buy a press and type. But when Franklin got to England in 1725, he discovered there were no letters of credit, and he was unable to interest anyone in loaning him the money to become a printer. After spending eighteen months leading a carefree life in London, Franklin returned to Philadelphia in 1726.

At twenty-three Franklin began publishing a newspaper, *The Pennsylvania Gazette*, in partnership with another printer. In 1731 he founded the first subscription library, the Library Company of Philadelphia.

When Franklin was twenty-seven, in 1733, he began his most successful publishing enterprise, *Poor Richard's Almanac*. This book became a best-seller for its time, with about 10,000 customers a year buying the *Almanac* to read Franklin's latest proverbs and witticisms.

Franklin began his career of public service that was to last for more than fifty years, when at thirty he became clerk of the Pennsylvania general assembly, serving 1736–51. The next year he became deputy postmaster of Philadelphia, a position he held sixteen years, 1737–53, until he was appointed deputy postmaster for all the American colonies, an office he filled for twenty-one more years, 1753–74. After that he was appointed postmaster of the United States by the Continental Congress in 1775. When Franklin was thirty-eight, he won his first election as a representative to the Pennsylvania general assembly, where he served for the next eleven years, 1744–54.

Though busy enough as a newspaper and book editor and holder of three public offices, Franklin turned his genius to science. He invented the Franklin stove in 1740 to conserve fuel and improve home heating. He discovered in 1747 that there were two kinds of electricity, positive and negative, in 1749 invented the lightning rod, and three years later, in 1752, used a kite to prove that lightning is electricity. He continued to invent and make scientific discoveries for the rest of his life.

A pottery jug dating back to 1667, with the words: If God be for us, who can be against us?

In 1754 Franklin made his first contacts with the leaders of other colonies when he went as a delegate to a Congress called in Albany, New York, by the seven northern colonies to determine how they could best defend themselves in the French and Indian War. Franklin wrote and presented a Plan of Union that the Congress adopted, but which the English government later rejected. Franklin's plan called for a grand council to be chosen from the several colonies and a president-general appointed by the crown.

When Franklin was fifty-one, he began a new career as a foreign diplomat. He was sent to London to represent the Pennsylvania legislature. He remained in London for the next eighteen years, 1757–75, except for a tour of the colonies he made in 1763 in his capacity as deputy postmaster general. As time went on, Franklin gained a greater and greater influence with the leaders of the English government, and other colonies asked him to be their representative. In addition to Pennsylvania, he represented Massachusetts, New Jersey, and Georgia. But, despite Franklin's best efforts he was unable to sway the English government from its determination to make an issue over the "Boston Tea Party." Realizing that war was likely to begin at any time, Franklin sailed for America, arriving in Philadelphia in May 1775 to learn that the battles of Lexington and Concord had been fought while he was crossing the Atlantic.

Immediately Franklin was chosen as a delegate from Pennsylvania to the second Continental Congress that was about to meet, was made a member of the Pennsylvania council of safety, and in 1776 presided at the Pennsylvania constitutional convention that drew up a plan for the state government. At seventy Franklin was the oldest delegate to the Continental Congress of 1775–76. Speaking out strongly for independence, he served with Thomas Jefferson and John Adams on the committee assigned to write the Declaration of Independence, and then voted for and signed the document.

In September the Continental Congress voted to send Franklin to France as one of three commissioners to obtain help for Washington's army. Franklin immediately packed his bags, but before boarding ship turned over his entire personal fortune to the Congress to use in fighting the war. He reached Paris in December, where he was to remain for the next nine years. After months of negotiation, he signed a treaty of alliance with France in February 1778, and soon help in the form of money, supplies, troops, and warships was sent to aid the American cause, culminating in the British defeat at Yorktown in 1781. Franklin then turned his attention to negotiating a peace treaty with the British that finally was concluded and signed in September 1783. Franklin stayed on in Paris for two more years until Thomas Jefferson arrived to take up the duties of American minister to France.

On his way home, Franklin stopped briefly in England, and

*The interior of Carpenters' Hall, Philadelphia, where
the First Continental Congress met in September 1774.*

*John Hanson (1715-1783), born in Charles County, Maryland, and three times elected
to the Continental Congress, was president of the Continental Congress in 1781-1783.
so that in a sense he was the first President of the United States of America.*

*(At right) The Old Swedes Church, founded in Philadelphia in 1677
by Swedish settlers who first worshiped in a cabin on the same site
as this church, which was constructed between 1698 and 1703.*

*The Brandywine headquarters of Marquis de Lafayette, who
at the age of nineteen volunteered to fight for American liberty.*

Benjamin Franklin —From a painting by Charles Willson Peale

then arrived back in Philadelphia in September 1785 to be greeted by a celebration of bells, bonfires, and artillery salutes. The seventy-nine-year-old Franklin almost immediately was elected by the general assembly as president of Pennsylvania, an office he held for the next three years 1785-88. In 1787 Franklin was one of the state's delegates to the Federal Con-

Arch Street and the waterfront in Philadelphia in 1799—From an engraving by W. Birch & Son

stitutional Convention, where on the last day of the convention, September 17, he made an impassioned speech asking all the delegates to support the new United States Constitution, which at eighty-one he then signed as the oldest delegate. Franklin lived to see George Washington become the first President of the new United States government, and then died at the age of eighty-four in his home in Philadelphia on April 17, 1790.

His natural son, William Franklin (1731–1813), was the last royal governor of New Jersey in 1763–76. After being removed as governor by the patriots, he was imprisoned until 1778, when he was turned over to the British in a prisoner exchange. Benjamin Franklin said of his son in his will: "The part he acted against me in the late war, which is of public notoriety, will account for my leaving him no more of an estate he endeavored to deprive me of."

• FREDERICK FRELINGHUYSEN   1753–1804

An officer in the Revolutionary War and a delegate to the Continental Congress, Frederick Frelinghuysen was born near Somerville, New Jersey, on April 13, 1753. After graduation from Princeton College at seventeen, he studied law and commenced practice in 1774 in Somerset County, New Jersey. He was elected a member of the provincial congress of New Jersey in 1775–76. Then he served in the Revolutionary War as a captain of artillery with the New Jersey militia, as colonel of the 1st Battalion of Somerset County militia, and as aide-de-camp to Brig. Gen. Philemon Dickinson. He was chosen as a member of New Jersey's delegation to the Continental Congress in 1778–79 and 1782–83. President Washington appointed him as a brigadier general in 1790 in a campaign against the western Indians, and he served as a major general during the Whiskey Rebellion in 1794. He was elected as a Federalist to the U.S. Senate 1793–96. He died in Millstone, New Jersey, April 13, 1804. His son Theodore and grandson Frederick both served as U.S. Senators, the latter also becoming Secretary of State under President Arthur.

• PHILIP FRENEAU   1752–1832

Called the "Poet of the Revolution," Philip Freneau was born in New York City on January 2, 1752. At fifteen he entered the College of New Jersey, where one of his classmates was James Madison, the future President. While still in college, at seventeen, he wrote the poem, "History of the Prophet Jonah." With the collaboration of a classmate, H.H. Brackenridge, he wrote the patriotic poem, "Rising Glory of America." After graduation from college in 1771, Freneau taught school, and then went to the West Indies, where he earned his living as secretary to a planter in Santa Cruz, while writing poetry about the islands. During the Revolutionary War, he sailed as a privateer in command of the ship *Aurora*. After several successful cruises, he was captured by a British warship in May 1780. After his release the following year, he wrote several poems about his treatment aboard British prison ships. He settled in Philadelphia and for the rest of the war wrote and published many patriotic poems. In the late 1780s he went to sea again, and wrote poems of his experiences with storms and the ocean. Beginning in 1789 he worked for several years as a newspaper editor, first in New York and then in Philadelphia. As a newspaper editor he was partisanly Democratic-Republican and Anti-Federalist. After his newspaper the *National Gazette* went bankrupt in 1793, Freneau worked for newspapers in New Jersey and New York for several years. At the age of eighty he died while struggling through a snowstorm near his home in Freehold, New Jersey, on December 18, 1832.

• GEORGE FROST 1720–1796

A sea captain, judge, and delegate to the Continental Congress, George Frost was born in Newcastle, New Hampshire, on April 26, 1720. After following the sea for many years as a merchant ship captain, he retired to Durham, New Hampshire, in 1770, where he became judge of the court of common pleas of Strafford County 1773–91. He was chosen as a member of New Hampshire's delegation to the Continental Congress 1777–79. He died in Durham on June 21, 1796.

• CHRISTOPHER GADSDEN 1723–1805

A Revolutionary War general and the first patriot in South Carolina to call for independence, Christopher Gadsden was born in Charleston, South Carolina, on February 16, 1723. After being educated in England, he worked in a counting house in Philadelphia 1742–45 before returning to South Carolina. During the protests over the Stamp Act in 1765, he helped organize the Sons of Liberty in South Carolina and constructed the first Liberty Tree in the colony. He was chosen to represent the colony in the Stamp Act Congress that met in New York. He was chosen as a member of South Carolina's delegation to the Continental Congress 1774–76, but left that body in January 1776 to assume command of the Continental Army troops in defense of Charleston. The next month he shocked conservatives in South Carolina by calling on the provincial congress to vote for independence from England. After Maj. Gen. Robert Howe was placed in command of troops in South Carolina, the fiery Gadsden challenged Howe to a duel in August 1778, which resulted only in Gadsden receiving a minor wound on his ear. He was elected lieutenant governor 1778–80. General Gadsden was captured by the British at the surrender of Charleston in May 1780. He was temporarily paroled and then dragged back to prison with a threat by the British to hang him in reprisal for the execution of Maj. John André, to which Gadsden replied: "I am always ready to die for my country." After being imprisoned in St. Augustine, Florida, for ten months, he was released in 1781 and was elected governor of South Carolina, but declined to serve because of illness. He died in Charleston on September 15, 1805. Interment in St. Philip's Churchyard. His grandson, James Gadsden, negotiated the acquisition of land in the Southwest in 1853 that became known as the Gadsden Purchase.

• GEORGE GALE 1756–1815

One of Maryland's first U.S. Congressmen, George Gale was born in Somerset County, Maryland, on June 3, 1756. In his twenties he served with Maryland troops during the Revolu-

The Castillo de San Marcos of St. Augustine, Florida—the oldest masonry fort in the United States. —Sketch by Kay Smith

tionary War. He was a member of the Maryland convention that ratified the U.S. Constitution in 1788, and then was elected to the First U.S. Congress 1789–91. Gale was appointed by President Washington on March 4, 1791, as supervisor of distilled liquors for the district of Maryland. He died at his estate "Brookland" in Cecil County, Maryland, on January 2, 1815.

• JOSEPH GALLOWAY   c.1729–1803

A member of the Continental Congress who opposed independence and then joined the British as a Loyalist, Joseph Galloway was born in Anne Arundel County, Maryland, about 1729. He became a lawyer in Philadelphia where he rose to

197

prominence as the colonial political leader of Pennsylvania. He was a close friend of Benjamin Franklin. Galloway was elected to the colony's house of representatives 1757–75, serving as speaker 1766–74. As a member of the Continental Congress in 1774–75, he signed the nonimportation agreement, but was opposed to independence of the colonies. He presented a plan of union in which a president-general would be the chief executive officer, responsible directly to the king. This plan was at first accepted by the Continental Congress in 1774, and then rejected. In December 1776 he joined the British Army of General Howe in New York and was placed in charge of the civil government during the British occupation of Philadelphia 1777–78. When the British evacuated Philadelphia in 1778, Galloway fled to England. The same year the general assembly of Pennsylvania convicted Galloway of high treason and confiscated his estates. He petitioned to be allowed to return to the United States in 1793, but was denied permission. He died in Watford, England, on August 29, 1803.

• LEONARD GANSEVOORT   1751–1810

A delegate to the Continental Congress and judge, Leonard Gansevoort was born in Albany, New York, on July 14, 1751, a younger brother of Gen. Peter Gansevoort. At the age of twenty he was admitted to the bar and commenced practice in Albany. Although commissioned a colonel of light cavalry in the Revolutionary War, he devoted his attention to politics. He was a member of New York's provincial congress in 1775–76, and a member of the state assembly in 1778–79 and 1788. He was chosen as a member of New York's delegation to the Continental Congress in 1787–88. After serving in the state senate 1791–93, he was appointed judge of Albany County 1794–97, and then judge of the probate court in 1799. He held the latter post until his death in Albany on August 26, 1810.

• PETER GANSEVOORT   1749–1812

An officer whose heroic defense of Fort Stanwix in the Mohawk Valley prevented an army of Indians and Canadians from reinforcing Burgoyne at Saratoga, Peter Gansevoort was born in Albany on July 17, 1749. In 1775 he was commissioned a major in the 2nd New York Regiment, and marched with the regiment to Canada under General Montgomery. In 1776 he commanded Fort George, New York, and was promoted to colonel of the 3rd New York Regiment. In 1777 he was made commander of Fort Stanwix (now at Rome, New York), which was the main defense post to prevent an invasion from Canada down the Mohawk Valley. In the summer of 1777 an army of about 2,000 Indians, Loyalists, and British regulars under British Lt. Col. Barry St. Leger entered the

This residence in Kinderhook, New York, was frequently visited by the leaders of the colonial period.

Mohawk Valley from Canada with the intention of joining up with British General Burgoyne, who was leading a larger army down the Hudson Valley. On August 2 St. Leger's army reached Fort Stanwix, where Gansevoort had a garrison of about 750 soldiers. St. Leger put the fort under siege, and on August 6 at the battle of Oriskany successfully turned back an American army of 800 militiamen marching to the relief of Fort Stanwix. Meanwhile, the same day Gansevoort had sent a column out of the fort, which destroyed the camps of the Indians and Loyalists. Despite constant attacks and threats of massacre, Gansevoort held the fort until a relief column led by Bendict Arnold raised the siege on August 23, forcing St. Leger's retreat and preventing the reinforcements from reaching Burgoyne. Gansevoort received the thanks of Congress for his defense of the fort. He continued to serve in upstate New York during the rest of the war, and in 1781 was promoted to brigadier general of militia. After the war he was a commissioner of Indian affairs, and in 1793 was promoted to major general of militia. He died in Albany on July 2, 1812.

Peter Gansevoort

199

• JOHN GARDINER   1747–1808

A farmer who served briefly in the Continental Congress, John Gardiner was born in South Kingstown, Rhode Island, in 1747. He served in the Revolutionary War as captain of the "Kingstown Reds" in 1775–76. After the war he was elected as a representative to the Rhode Island general assembly by the Paper Money Party in 1786–87. He served briefly as a member of Rhode Island's delegation to the last session of the Continental Congress in 1789. He died in South Kingstown on October 18, 1808.

• JOSEPH GARDNER   1752–1794

A physician and legislator, Joseph Gardner was born in Chester County, Pennsylvania, in 1752. After studying medicine, he began practice in Chester County in his early twenties. He raised a company of volunteers in 1776 and commanded the 4th Battalion of militia from Chester County in the Revolutionary War. He was a member of the local committee of safety in 1776–77 and of the Pennsylvania assembly 1776–78. Gardner was chosen as a delegate to the Continental Congress in 1784–85. He practiced medicine in Philadelphia 1785–92, and then moved to Elkton, Maryland, where he died in 1794.

• HORATIO GATES   1728–1806

An American hero for his defeat of British Gen. John Burgoyne at the battles of Saratoga, Horatio Gates was born at Maldon, England, in 1728, where his mother was a servant to the Duke of Leeds. He joined the British army as a boy. He had risen to the rank of major by the age of twenty-seven, when he came to America in 1755 with General Braddock's army during the French and Indian War. He took part in Braddock's disastrous expedition against Fort Duquesne (Pittsburgh) in July 1755, and during this time became a friend of George Washington, who also was in the action. Gates continued to serve in the British army until 1765, when he retired to live in England. At Washington's invitation, Gates returned to America in 1772, settling in Virginia as a neighbor of Washington's brother Samuel.

When the Continental Army was being formed by Washington in June 1775, Gates was appointed adjutant general with the rank of brigadier general, and in 1776 was promoted to major general. When Burgoyne invaded the United States from Canada in 1777 with an army of about 7,000, easily capturing Fort Ticonderoga on July 5, Congress' board of war ordered Gates to take command of the Northern Department and repel the invasion. Gates relieved Gen. Philip Schuyler

General Horatio Gates —From a mezzotint by John Morris

just three days after Col. John Stark of New Hampshire had defeated a column of Burgoyne's army at the battle of Bennington, killing 200 and capturing 700.

Burgoyne's weakened army, almost out of supplies, crossed the Hudson River early in September, and on September 19 about 4,000 American troops under Gen. Benedict Arnold fought Burgoyne to a standstill at Freeman's Farm, near Saratoga. Although his army was now reduced to about 6,000, Burgoyne advanced on the main American position at Bemis Heights, where Gates had stationed about 11,000 troops, and attacked on October 7. Although Gates later was to receive most of the credit for Burgoyne's defeat, the battle was largely won by an attack led by General Arnold. About 600 British troops were killed or severely wounded, while American losses were about 150. Ten days later Burgoyne surrendered to Gates, who counted 2,139 British prisoners, 2,022 Germans, and 830 Canadians.

The American victory, the biggest of the war until Yorktown four years later, buoyed American hopes and convinced the French that it was worthwhile to aid the American cause. It also caused intrigue in Congress to replace Washington with Gates as commander-in-chief. Congress appointed Gates as president of the board of war, but upon the exposure of some of the intriguing against Washington, talk of making him commander-in-chief ceased.

When the British moved their main action to the Southern States in 1780, Congress appointed Gates as commander of the Southern Department. There he launched a campaign against General Cornwallis that ended in the worst American defeat of the war at the battle of Camden, South Carolina, August 16, 1780, in which Gates' army of 4,000 was annihilated. Gates brought further disgrace on himself by fleeing by fast horse from the scene and reaching Charlotte, sixty miles away, before the day was over.

Gates retired from active duty after the battle, living on his Virginia plantation for the next two years while Congress debated whether or not to hold an investigation of the debacle. In 1782 Gates was restored to active duty, joining Washington at his headquarters in Newburgh, New York. After the war Gates lived in Virginia until 1790, when he moved to New York. He died in New York City on April 10, 1806.

• DAVID GELSTON   1744–1828

A delegate to the last Continental Congress, David Gelston was born in Bridgehampton, Long Island, New York, on July 4, 1744. From the beginning of the Revolutionary War he was elected for eleven years to New York's provincial congress and state assembly 1775–85, serving as speaker in 1784–85. He was chosen as one of New York's delegates to the last session of the Continental Congress in 1789. He was a member of the state senate 1791–94, 1798, and 1802; and then served as collector of the port of New York 1801–20. He died in New York City on August 21, 1828.

Elbridge Gerry

• ELBRIDGE GERRY   1744–1814

A signer of the Declaration of Independence and the fifth Vice President of the United States, Elbridge Gerry was born in Marblehead, Massachusetts, on July 17, 1744. After graduation from Harvard College at eighteen, he helped his father sell codfish in Marblehead. Active in the pre-Revolutionary patriotic movement, he was elected to the Massachusetts colonial assembly 1772–75. Throughout the Revolutionary War he served almost continuously as a delegate to the Continental Congress 1776–85, where he signed both the Declaration of Independence and the Articles of Confederation. Gerry was a delegate to the federal Constitutional Convention in Philadelphia in 1787, where he refused to sign the new United States Constitution, because he believed the new government would be too democratic. He was elected as an Anti-Federalist to the First and Second U.S. Congresses 1789–93. President John Adams sent Gerry to France in 1797 as a diplomatic envoy to try to settle the undeclared war between the two nations, but the mission was unsuccessful. Gerry was elected governor of Massachusetts in 1810–12, and then was elected Vice President in 1812 on the ticket headed by James Madison. While serving as Vice President he died in Washington, D.C., on November 23, 1814.

• JOHN LEWIS GERVAIS   ?–1798

A delegate to the Continental Congress, John Lewis Gervais was believed to have been born in France of Huguenot parents who were forced to flee to Germany. After being educated in Hanover, Germany, Gervais immigrated to Charleston, South Carolina, in 1764. There he became a merchant, planter, and landowner. He was chosen as a delegate to the provincial conventions and was a member of the council of safety in 1775–76. During the Revolutionary War he helped in the defense of Charleston in 1780, and was a member of the state senate in 1781–82, serving as president. He was a delegate to the Continental Congress in 1782–83. Gervais died in Charleston on August 18, 1798.

• WILLIAM GIBBONS   1726–1800

A legislator and judge, William Gibbons was born at Bear Bluff, South Carolina, on April 8, 1726. After studying law, he began practice in Savannah, Georgia. A member of the Sons of Liberty, he was one of the party that broke open the royal magazine in Savannah on May 11, 1775, and removed 600 pounds of the king's powder. Gibbons was a delegate to the Georgia provincial congress and a member of the committee of safety in 1775. He served on the state's executive council 1777–81, and was chosen as a delegate to the Continental Congress in 1784–85. Gibbons was elected to the Georgia house of representatives in 1783, 1785–89, and 1791–93, serving as speaker in 1783 and 1786–87. He was president of the state constitutional convention in 1789. His last public service was as justice of the inferior court of Chatham County 1790–92. He died in Savannah on September 27, 1800.

• JOHN TAYLOR GILMAN   1753–1828

A delegate to the Continental Congress and governor of New Hampshire, John Taylor Gilman was born in Exeter, New Hampshire, December 19, 1753, an older brother of Nicholas Gilman. A farmer and shipbuilder, he was one of the Minutemen of 1775. He was chosen as a delegate to the Continental Congress in 1782–83. He served as governor of New Hampshire 1794–1805 and 1813–16. He died in Exeter on September 1, 1828.

• NICHOLAS GILMAN   1755–1814

A Continental Army officer throughout the Revolutionary War and a signer of the United States Constitution, Nicholas Gilman was born in Exeter, New Hampshire, on August 3, 1755, a younger brother of John Taylor Gilman. Joining Col. Alexander Scammell's New Hampshire regiment at the begin-

Building a frigate in 1799 in Philadelphia, with the Swedish Church in the background
(*See the inside color insert opposite page 193.*)   —From an engraving by W. Birch & Son

ning of the Revolutionary War, he rose from lieutenant to captain. At the battle of Yorktown he acted as General Washington's deputy adjutant general to take an accounting of the number of prisoners surrendered by Lord Cornwallis. After the war he was chosen as a delegate to the Continental Congress 1786–88, and then to the federal Constitutional Convention in 1787, where he signed the new United States Constitution. He won election to the First to Fourth U.S. Congresses 1789–97, and then served as a U.S. Senator from 1805 until his death in Philadelphia, on May 2, 1814.

Mordecai Gist

• MORDECAI GIST   1743–1792

A Continental Army general during the Revolutionary War, Mordecai Gist was born in Baltimore on February 22, 1742, a nephew of the frontiersman Christopher Gist who was a companion of George Washington in exploring the frontier. Before the Revolutionary War, Gist was a merchant in Baltimore. In 1776 he was commissioned a major in the 1st Maryland Regiment. He and his men fought bravely in the battles of Long Island and White Plains, and he was promoted to colonel in December 1776. He commanded the 3rd Maryland Regiment in the battle of Germantown in 1777. In 1779 he was promoted to brigadier general. In 1780 at the disastrous battle of

The death of DeKalb in the Battle of Camden —From a painting by Chappel

Camden, South Carolina, he and his Maryland brigade carried the brunt of the fighting, while most of the rest of the army panicked. He was credited with saving the remnants of the army after General Gates fled from the battlefield. At the battle of Combahee Ferry, South Carolina, on August 27, 1782, Gist took part in one of the last skirmishes of the war, attacking a large foraging party of British and Loyalist troops, and driving them off. After the war he settled on a plantation near Charleston, South Carolina, where he died on August 2, 1792. In an unusual exhibition of patriotism, Gist named one of his sons Independence and another States Rights. The latter was killed during the Civil War as a Confederate brigade commander.

• JOHN GLOVER   1732–1797

A Continental Army general during the Revolutionary War, John Glover was born in Salem, Massachusetts, on November 5, 1732. He grew up in Marblehead, Massachusetts, where he became a successful fisherman and shipowner. As soon as he heard of the outbreak of fighting at Lexington and Concord, Glover raised a regiment of 1,000 Marblehead fishermen and marched them to Boston as their colonel. His regiment became known as the "Amphibious Regiment," because he and his men manned the boats that enabled Washington's army to escape to Manhattan Island after the battle of Long Island in August 1776. Later that year Glover and his fishermen operated the boats in which Washington crossed the icy Delaware River to make his surprise attack at Trenton, New Jersey. Promoted to brigadier general in 1777, Glover fought at the battles of Saratoga, and was in charge of leading Burgoyne's captured army to Cambridge, Massachusetts. He took part in the attempt to recapture Rhode Island in 1778, and served actively in Rhode Island and New York until 1782 when illness forced him to retire from the army. He was brevetted a major general in 1783. Glover was a delegate to the Massachusetts convention in 1788 that ratified the United States Constitution, and he was elected to the Massachusetts legislature 1788–89. He died in Marblehead on January 30, 1797.

General John Glover

• ROBERT GOLDSBOROUGH   1733–1788

A Maryland delegate to the Continental Congress, Robert Goldsborough was born at "Horns Point" in Dorchester County, Maryland, on December 3, 1733. After studying law at the Inner Temple in London, England, he was admitted to the bar at the age of twenty-one and practiced in London until 1759. After returning to America, he was graduated from Philadelphia College (now the University of Pennsylvania) in 1760, and began a law practice in Cambridge, Maryland. He was elected high sheriff of Dorchester County 1761–65, burgess to the Maryland assembly in 1765, and attorney general of Maryland in 1766. Goldsborough was chosen as a delegate to the Continental Congress in 1774–75, and to the Maryland constitutional convention in 1776. After serving in the state senate in 1777, he retired from public life to his estate "Horns Point," near Cambridge, where he died on December 22, 1788.

• BENJAMIN GOODHUE   1748–1814

A Congressman and U.S. Senator, Benjamin Goodhue was born in Salem, Massachusetts, on September 20, 1748. He was graduated from Harvard College in 1766. He was elected to the Massachusetts house of representatives 1780–82 and to the state senate 1786–88. Goodhue won election to the first and three succeeding U.S. Congresses 1789–96, and then served as one of Massachusetts' U.S. Senators 1796–1800. He died in Salem on July 28, 1814.

• NATHANIEL GORHAM   1738–1796

The fourteenth President of the Continental Congress, Nathaniel Gorham was born in Charlestown, Massachusetts, on May 27, 1738. He became a well-to-do merchant in Charlestown and was elected to the Massachusetts provincial legislature 1771–75, and to the state legislature 1779–89, serving as speaker of the house in 1781–82 and 1785. He was chosen as a delegate to the Continental Congress in 1782–83 and 1785–87, and was elected its President from June 6, 1786, to February 2, 1787. A delegate to the federal Constitutional Convention at Philadelphia in 1787, he signed the new United State Constitution. When he ran for election as a representative to the First U.S. Congress, Gorham was defeated by Elbridge Gerry, who had refused to sign the Constitution. He and a partner purchased for $1 million a huge tract of land that had been ceded to Massachusetts by New York. They sold more than a million acres of the land to Pennsylvania financier Robert Morris—a speculation that ultimately ended with Morris being sent to debtor's prison. Gorham served as judge of the court of common pleas 1785–96, resigning from the bench less than two weeks before his death in Charlestown, on June 11, 1796.

• WILLIAM GRAYSON   1740–1790

An aide to George Washington in the Revolutionary War and one of Virginia's first U.S. Senators, William Grayson was born in Prince William County, Virgina, in 1740. He attended the University of Pennsylvania, was graduated from the University of Oxford, in England, and then studied law at the Temple in London. After returning to Virginia, he practiced law in Dumfries, Virginia. During the early years of the Revolutionary War, Grayson served as aide-de-camp to General Washington. He then was commissioned colonel of a Virginia Continental Army regiment on January 1, 1777, which he commanded at the Battle of Monmouth, New Jersey, in 1778. Colonel Grayson was appointed as a member of the board of war in 1780–81. After the war he was chosen as a delegate to the Continental Congress 1784–87. Although he was a friend of Washington, he sided with Patrick Henry in opposing ratification of the new United States Constitution at the Virginia convention of 1788. With Henry's support, Grayson was elected to the U.S. Senate in 1789, serving in that capacity until his death in Dumfries on March 12, 1790.

The Battle of Princeton—After John Trumbull

General Nathanael Greene —After a painting by Chappel

• NATHANAEL GREENE   1742—1786

George Washington's most trusted general during the Revolutionary War and the liberator of the Southern States from British occupation, Nathanael Greene was born in Warwick, Rhode Island, on May 27, 1742, and reared as a member of the Quaker faith. He worked as a blacksmith and iron-maker before the Revolutionary War. Elected to the Rhode Island legislature in 1770, he was re-elected each year for the next ten years. In 1773 he was excommunicated from the Friends church because he attended a military parade. The next year he helped recruit a militia company in which he served as a private. In May 1775 the Rhode Island legislature named Greene to command the Rhode Island militia being sent to the aid of Boston, and the next month he was commissioned a brigadier general in the Continental Army at the age of thirty-three. His organizational talents were quickly recognized by Washington, and he was given command of Boston after British forces evacuated in March 1776.

Greene led his troops to the defense of New York in April 1776, and was placed in command of the defense of the city. In August he was promoted to major general, the youngest in the army at age thirty-four. Unfortunately, illness caused him to be relieved of his command just a week before the battle of Long Island, and he took no part in that action. He commanded the left wing of Washington's army in the victory at Trenton later in the year. In 1777 Greene led his division in a rapid march at the battle of Brandywine that saved the American army from encirclement, and he later fought at Germantown.

In 1778, while the army was suffering in the winter headquarters at Valley Forge, Greene was appointed quartermaster general, replacing Thomas Mifflin. Greene took on the job only on the condition that he also would continue as a field commander. While straightening out the army's supply problems, he also led the army's right in the battle of Monmouth in 1778, and later that year took part in the battle of Rhode Island.

After General Gates' disaster at the battle of Camden, South Carolina, in 1780, General Washington sent Greene to command the Southern army. After taking command from Gates on December 3, he reorganized the army and sent Daniel Morgan to harass Cornwallis while he assembled a large enough army to try to defeat the British. The tide in the South began to turn when Morgan and his men defeated the hated British Lt. Col. Banastre Tarleton at the battle of Cowpens, South Carolina, on January 17, 1781. Greene led his army north across the Carolinas to Virginia, thwarting British efforts to trap him, and crossing the flooded Dan River into Virginia with his army intact on February 14. During the next five months in a series of battles and minor engagements Greene reconquered the South, leaving the British only with

A fire bucket

A provision train of General Washington —From a painting by Chappel

Savannah, Georgia, and Charleston, South Carolina. But, even after Cornwallis' surrender at Yorktown, Virginia, to General Washington, the war continued in the South because of the large number of British Loyalist partisans. The British gave up Savannah in July 1782 and left Charleston in December.

During the war Greene had pledged most of his own fortune to obtain supplies for the army, including his home in Rhode Island. In appreciation for his services, the state of Georgia gave him a plantation near Savannah that formerly had belonged to the royalist lieutenant governor of the colony, and Greene settled there in the fall of 1785. Less than a year later he died there on June 19, 1786, at the age of forty-four.

• RICHARD GRIDLEY   1711–1796

Chief engineer and commander of artillery for the Continental Army in the early months of the Revolutionary War, Richard Gridley was born in Boston on January 3, 1711. A surveyor and civil engineer, he was commissioned a lieutenant colonel in 1745 and commanded the bombardment of Louisbourg at the mouth of the St. Lawrence River during King George's War. During the French and Indian War he also served as chief engineer of the British army with the rank of colonel, designing and building many of the frontier forts. At the beginning of the Revolutionary War, the Massachusetts legislature commissioned Gridley as a major general and chief engineer of the militia. He supervised the construction of fortifications at Bunker Hill and was wounded in the subsequent action June 1775. In September 1775 the Continental Congress commissioned him colonel in the Continental Army and made him chief of the army's artillery, but he was replaced in that post two months later by Henry Knox. Although Gridley retained his commission as a colonel, he performed little in the way of active military duty during the rest of the war. But he made a major contribution by manufacturing artillery pieces at an iron foundry he owned at Sharon, Massachusetts. He died in Stoughton, Massachusetts, on June 20, 1796.

• **CYRUS GRIFFIN   1748–1810**

The sixteenth and last President of the Continental Congress, Cyrus Griffin was born in Farnham, Virginia, on July 16, 1748. After studying law at the University of Edinburgh and at the Temple in London, he returned to Virginia and began a law practice in 1774. He was elected to the Virginia house of burgesses in 1777–78 and then was sent as a delegate to the Continental Congress 1778–81. After serving from 1780–87 as president of the supreme court of admiralty, he again was chosen as a delegate to the Continental Congress. Griffin was elected by its members as President on January 22, 1788, presiding over its final sessions until it dissolved on March 2, 1789. For the last twenty-one years of his life he was U.S. district judge for Virginia 1789–1810. Griffin died in Yorktown, Virginia, on December 14, 1810.

• **SAMUEL GRIFFIN   ?–1810**

A Revolutionary War officer and one of Virginia's first U.S. Representatives, Samuel Griffin was born in Richmond County, Virginia. He studied law and began practice in Richmond County. Commissioned a colonel in the Revolutionary War, he was wounded in the battle of Harlem Heights, New York, in September 1776. After the war he was elected a member of Virginia's house of delegates 1786–88, and then won election to the First, Second, and Third U.S. Congresses in 1789–95. Griffin died on November 3, 1810.

• **JONATHAN GROUT   1737–1807**

One of Massachusetts' first Representatives in the U.S. Congress, Jonathan Grout was born in Lunenburg, Massachusetts (now Vermont), on July 23, 1737. During the French and Indian War, he served in the expedition that conquered Canada 1758–1760. After studying law, he commenced practice in

Petersham, Massachusetts. Grout served in the Revolutionary War, and then won election to the Massachusetts legislature in 1781, 1784, 1787, and 1788. He was elected as an Anti-Federalist to the First U.S. Congress 1789–91. He died in Dover, New Hampshire, on September 8, 1807.

• **JAMES GUNN**   **1753–1801**

A Revolutionary War officer and one of Georgia's first U.S. Senators, James Gunn was born in Virginia, on March 13, 1753. After studying law, he commenced practice in Savannah, Georgia. During the Revolutionary War, as a captain of dragoons he took part in the relief of Savannah in 1782, and subsequently was promoted to brigadier general of Georgia militia. He was elected to the Continental Congress in 1788–89 but did not serve. Elected as a U.S. Senator from Georgia to the First U.S. Congress in 1789, he served until 1801. Gunn died in Louisville, Georgia, on July 30, 1801.

Button Gwinnett

• **BUTTON GWINNETT**   **c. 1735–1777**

A signer of the Declaration of Independence, Button Gwinnett was born in Down Hatherly, Gloucestershire, England, about 1735. He came to America and settled in Charleston, South Carolina, about 1763. Two years later he moved to Georgia, where he established a plantation on St. Catherines

Island, Georgia. He was chosen as one of Georgia's delegates to the Continental Congress in 1776–77, where he was the first delegate to sign the Declaration of Independence, after the President, John Hancock. At the Georgia constitutional convention in February 1777, he was the main architect of the first state constitution. When Archibald Bullock, Georgia's president (governor) died at the end of the convention, a group of patriotic leaders named Gwinnett as acting president and commander in chief of the state militia. In May 1777 he was defeated in a bid to be elected to a full term as governor. He blamed his defeat on Gen. Lachlan McIntosh, who had been assigned by the Continental Congress to raise a brigade in Georgia for the Continental Army. When McIntosh called Gwinnett a "lying scoundrel," Gwinnett challenged him to a duel. Both men were wounded in the pistol duel, and Gwinnett died eleven days later on May 27, 1777, in Savannah.

A bed wrench used for tightening rope springs

• JOHN HABERSHAM   1754–1799

A Revolutionary War officer and delegate to the Continental Congress, John Habersham was born at "Beverly," near Savannah, Georgia, December 23, 1754, a younger brother of Joseph Habersham. After attending Princeton College, he was sent to England for experience in business. Returning to Georgia at the beginning of the Revolutionary War, he joined the Continental Army as a first lieutenant, but soon was advanced to major. He was captured in the battle of Savannah in December 1778. Upon being exchanged he rejoined the army and was captured again at the battle of Briar Creek in March 1779. Exchanged again, he continued to serve with the army to the war's end. After the war he was selected as a delegate to the Continental Congress in 1785. He was appointed an Indian agent by President Washington, and then became collector of customs at Savannah from 1789 until his death there on December 17, 1799.

• JOSEPH HABERSHAM   1751–1815

Leader of the patriots who overthrew the royal governor of Georgia, Joseph Habersham was born in Savannah, Georgia, on July 28, 1751. His father, James, who was considered the wealthiest man in the colony, was a close friend of the British governor, Sir James Wright, and had been acting governor during Wright's absence in England 1769–72. Joseph attended Princeton College and then was sent to England for three years for business experience. Upon his return to Georgia in 1771, he soon became active in the pre-Revolutionary patriotic movement. When news of the fighting at Lexington and Concord reached Georgia, he and a group of Sons of Liberty seized a quarter of a ton of gunpowder from the royal arsenal on May 11, 1775. Two months later he helped capture a

Joseph Habersham

215

British supply ship carrying 15,000 pounds of gunpowder. As head of the Georgia committee of safety, Habersham led a group which captured the royal governor in January 1776, and held him prisoner until his escape to a British warship a month later. As a colonel in the Continental Army he took part in the siege of Savannah in 1779. After the war Habersham was chosen as a delegate to the Continental Congress in 1783–84, and was elected mayor of Savannah in 1792. President Washington appointed him Postmaster General of the United States in 1795, an office he held until 1801. He then became president of the branch Bank of the United States at Savannah from 1802 until his death on November 17, 1815.

• NATHAN HALE   1755–1776

An American patriot whose dying statement, "I only regret that I have but one life to lose for my country!" gave him immortality as a hero, Nathan Hale was born in Coventry, Connecticut, on June 6, 1755. After graduation from Yale College at eighteen in 1773, he taught school for several months in East Haddam, Connecticut, and then became master of the New London, Connecticut, grammar school. He was commissioned a lieutenant in the Connecticut militia in July 1775, and after marching his men to the siege of Boston in September he was promoted to captain. In April 1776 Hale and the rest of his rangers were transferred to New York to prepare for the impending British invasion there. Shortly after their arrival, Hale and his men distinguished themselves by capturing a British supply sloop. When General Washington in September asked for a volunteer to go behind British lines and

(At left) Nathan Hale. (Below) The birthplace of Nathan Hale in Connecticut

gather information, Hale volunteered. On about September 12, disguised as a school teacher, Hale left the army's camp on Harlem Heights and made his way to Long Island. After spending more than a week taking notes on the size and location of various British units, Hale was captured on September 21, apparently betrayed by a cousin, Samuel Hale, who was a Loyalist and was a deputy commissioner of prisoners for the British army. He was immediately taken before the British commander, Gen. Sir William Howe, who is said to have offered Hale a British commission if he would change allegiance. When Hale refused, Howe ordered him executed the next morning without a trial. Hale's executioner, William Cunningham, the British provost marshal, is said to have refused Hale the services of a clergyman or Bible and to have torn up letters that Hale wrote to his mother and sisters. Just before he was hanged, Hale made a speech containing the famous sentence quoted above.

• JOHN HALL   1729−1797

A delegate to the Continental Congress, John Hall was born near Annapolis, Maryland, on November 27, 1729. After studying law, he practiced in Annapolis. At the beginning of the Revolutionary War, he became a member of the local council of safety and delegate to the Maryland convention in 1775. He was chosen as a Maryland delegate to the Continental Congress in 1775, 1777, 1780, and 1783–84. He continued the practice of law until his death on his plantation, "The Vineyard," near Annapolis on March 8, 1797.

• LYMAN HALL   1724−1790

A signer of the Declaration of Independence and governor of Georgia, Lyman Hall was born in Wallingford, Connecticut, on April 12, 1724. After graduating from Yale College in 1747, he studied theology and in 1749 began preaching at Fairfield, Connecticut. He was dismissed from the church on charges of immorality, in 1751, but continued to preach as a visiting minister for two years. He then took up the study of medicine, and moved to Georgia, where he became a physician in Sunbury, St. John's Parish. Hall had a strong influence in inciting revolutionary sentiments in Georgia. He was elected a delegate to the Continental Congress in 1775–78 and 1780, where he helped promote and signed the Declaration of Independence. Upon the fall of Savannah and the capture of Sunbury in 1778, his property was destroyed, so he took his family north to live. After returning to Savannah in 1782, Hall was elected governor of Georgia for a one-year term in 1783. Hall then retired to a plantation in Burke County, where he died on October 19, 1790. His body is buried beneath a monument in front of the courthouse in Augusta, Georgia.

Lyman Hall

• ALEXANDER HAMILTON   1757–1804

An aide to General Washington in the Revolutionary War, a signer of the United States Constitution, and the first United States Secretary of the Treasury, Alexander Hamilton was born in Charlestown on the island of Nevis in the West Indies on January 11, 1755 or 1757. He was the natural son of a Scottish trader who deserted Hamilton's mother. When the boy's mother died in 1769, young Alexander was apprenticed to a storekeeper on St. Croix island. Befriended by a Presbyterian minister who helped him borrow money for his passage, Hamilton came to America in 1772, bringing with him a letter of introduction to William Livingston, a prominent Presbyterian layman who many years later would also sign the Constitution. He entered King's College in New York City in 1773, but when the Revolutionary War began, he left school, joining the Continental Army as a captain of artillery in March 1776. His company fought in the rear guard in the retreat from Long Island. He then fought in the battles of White Plains, Trenton, and Princeton. In March 1777 he was appointed as an aide to General Washington with the rank of lieutenant colonel. After three years helping Washington, Hamilton asked for an opportunity to show his ability as a military leader. He was given command of a New York infantry battalion and distinguished himself at the battle of Yorktown in 1781 by leading an attack on fortifications.

The birthplace of Alexander Hamilton

Alexander Hamilton

Leaving the army immediately after Cornwallis' surrender, Hamilton studied law, and was chosen by the New York legislature as a representative in the Continental Congress 1782–83 and 1787–89. In 1786 Hamilton was one of New York's delegates to the Annapolis Convention that called for the preparation of a new federal constitution. And in 1787 he became a delegate to the federal Constitutional Convention. He spoke strongly for establishing an elective monarchy, but when his proposal was discarded he signed the completed United States Constitution after remarking that the only alternative was anarchy. During the next year he joined with John Jay and James Madison in writing a series of articles called

Washington's reception for Alexander Hamilton after his marriage to the daughter of General Schuyler

Mrs. Alexander Hamilton

The Federalist that explained the need for the new government. In 1788 he was elected to New York's convention in which he helped win the state's ratification of the Constitution.

President Washington appointed Hamilton in September 1789 as his first Secretary of the Treasury. During the next four years Hamilton worked hard establishing the new government on a sound financial basis. At the same time his conflicts with Secretary of State Thomas Jefferson led to the creation of the American two-party political system as Hamilton became the spokesman for the Federalists and Jefferson became the spokesman for the anti-Federalists or Democratic-Republicans. After leaving the Cabinet in 1795, Hamilton resumed his law practice, but also continued to lead the Federalist party.

When the United States and France became involved in an undeclared war with each other in the 1790s, President John Adams appointed Hamilton in 1798 as a major general, second in command after General Washington, in a newly formed United States Army.

When Hamilton made disparaging remarks about Vice President Aaron Burr in a political campaign in 1804, Burr challenged him to a duel. The duel was fought on the west bank of the Hudson River, near Weehawken, New Jersey, and Hamilton was fatally wounded, dying the next day in New York on July 12, 1804.

John Hancock
—Sketch by Kay Smith

- **JOHN HANCOCK**   **1737−1793**

The fourth and thirteenth President of the Continental Congress and first signer of the Declaration of Independence, John Hancock was born in Braintree (now Quincy), Massachusetts, on January 12, 1737. After graduation from Harvard College at the age of seventeen, he worked in the family shipping business that he inherited ten years later, becoming one of the wealthiest men of Boston. As a member of the Massachusetts legislature 1766−72 and as president of the provincial congress in 1774, he became a leader of the pre-Revolutionary movement. He and Samuel Adams were denounced as the two leading rebels and were exempted from pardon in a proclamation by Governor Gage in 1775. He was a delegate to the Continental Congress 1775−80 and 1785−86, serving as the fourth President of the Congress from May 24, 1775, to November 1, 1777. As President he was the first signer of the Declaration of Independence. Disappointed at not being chosen to lead the Continental Army, he served as senior major general of Massachusetts militia during the Revolutionary War and led 6,000 troops in an unsuccessful effort to free Rhode

The John Hancock house in Boston

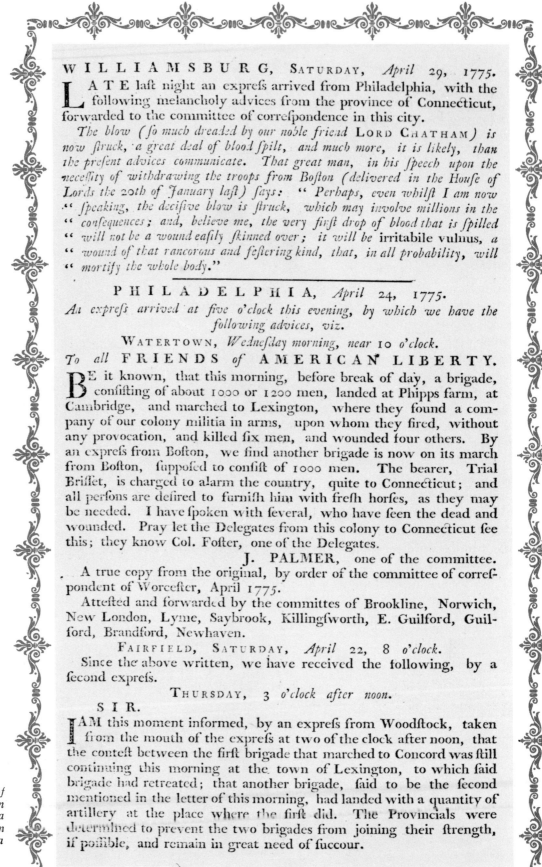

WILLIAMSBURG, SATURDAY, *April* 29, 1775.

LATE laſt night an expreſs arrived from Philadelphia, with the following melancholy advices from the province of Connecticut, forwarded to the committee of correſpondence in this city.

The blow (ſo much dreaded by our noble friend LORD CHATHAM*) is now ſtruck, a great deal of blood ſpilt, and much more, it is likely, than the preſent advices communicate. That great man, in his ſpeech upon the neceſſity of withdrawing the troops from Boſton (delivered in the Houſe of Lords the 20th of January laſt) ſays:* " *Perhaps, even whilſt I am now* " *ſpeaking, the deciſive blow is ſtruck, which may involve millions in the* " *conſequences; and, believe me, the very firſt drop of blood that is ſpilled* " *will not be a wound eaſily ſkinned over; it will be* irritabile vulnus, *a* " *wound of that rancorous and feſtering kind, that, in all probability, will* " *mortify the whole body.*"

PHILADELPHIA, *April* 24, 1775.

An expreſs arrived at five o'clock this evening, by which we have the following advices, viz.

WATERTOWN, *Wedneſday morning, near* 10 *o'clock.*

To all FRIENDS of AMERICAN LIBERTY.

BE it known, that this morning, before break of day, a brigade, conſiſting of about 1000 or 1200 men, landed at Phipps farm, at Cambridge, and marched to Lexington, where they found a company of our colony militia in arms, upon whom they fired, without any provocation, and killed ſix men, and wounded four others. By an expreſs from Boſton, we find another brigade is now on its march from Boſton, ſuppoſed to conſiſt of 1000 men. The bearer, Trial Biſſet, is charged to alarm the country, quite to Connecticut; and all perſons are deſired to furniſh him with freſh horſes, as they may be needed. I have ſpoken with ſeveral, who have ſeen the dead and wounded. Pray let the Delegates from this colony to Connecticut ſee this; they know Col. Foſter, one of the Delegates.

J. PALMER, one of the committee.

A true copy from the original, by order of the committee of correſpondent of Worceſter, April 1775.

Atteſted and forwarded by the committes of Brookline, Norwich, New London, Lyme, Saybrook, Killingſworth, E. Guilford, Guilford, Brandford, Newhaven.

FAIRFIELD, SATURDAY, *April* 22, 8 *o'clock.*

Since the above written, we have received the following, by a ſecond expreſs.

THURSDAY, 3 *o'clock after noon.*

SIR.

IAM this moment informed, by an expreſs from Woodſtock, taken from the mouth of the expreſs at two of the clock after noon, that the conteſt between the firſt brigade that marched to Concord was ſtill continuing this morning at the town of Lexington, to which ſaid brigade had retreated; that another brigade, ſaid to be the ſecond mentioned in the letter of this morning, had landed with a quantity of artillery at the place where the firſt did. The Provincials were determined to prevent the two brigades from joining their ſtrength, if poſſible, and remain in great need of ſuccour.

The first report of the battles at Lexington and Concord in a broadside printed in Williamsburg, Virginia

Island from British occupation. He was elected as the first state governor of Massachusetts 1780–85. He again was elected thirteenth President of the Continental Congress on November 23, 1785, but resigned May 29, 1786, not having served on account of illness. He again was elected governor of Massachusetts from 1787 until his death in Quincy, Massachusetts, October 8, 1793.

• EDWARD HAND   1744–1802

A Revolutionary War general and a delegate to the Continental Congress, Edward Hand was born in Clyduff, County Kings, Ireland, December 31, 1744. He came to Pennsylvania in 1767 as surgeon's mate of the 18th Royal Irish Regiment. He resigned from the British army in 1774 and settled in Pennsylvania to practice medicine. At the beginning of the Revolution he helped organize and train a regiment of Pennsylvania riflemen whom he commanded as colonel during the battles of Long Island, White Plains, and Princeton in 1776–77. He was promoted to brigadier general April 1, 1777. He succeeded Gen. John Stark in command at Albany, New York, in 1778 and served in the expedition against the Iroquois Indians. He took command of a brigade of light infantry in August 1780. General Washington appointed him adjutant general of the Continental Army in January 1781 and he served in that capacity to the end of the war, being brevetted major general in 1783. After the war he was elected a member of Pennsylvania's delegation to the Continental Congress 1784–85. He was appointed major general in the U.S. Army in 1798 when an invasion by France was feared. He died in Rockford, Pennsylvania, on September 3, 1802.

• JOHN HANSON   1715–1783

The ninth President of the Continental Congress, John Hanson was born at Mulberry Grove, Maryland, on April 3, 1715. A planter, he regularly was elected to the Maryland senate 1757–73. He was active in the pre-Revolutionary patriotic movement, and was chosen as one of Maryland's delegates to the Continental Congress 1780–83, where he worked for ratification of the Articles of Confederation, signing them himself in 1781. He then was elected President of the Continental Congress on November 5, 1781. He served one year as President, until November 4, 1782, and in that capacity tendered General Washington the thanks of Congress for the victory at Yorktown. Retiring from public life, he died at the home of his nephew at Oxon Hill, Prince Georges County, Maryland, on November 15, 1783. His grandson, Alexander Contee Hanson (1786–1819), became a prominent Federalist newspaper editor in Baltimore, and later was a Congressman and U.S. Senator.

John Hanson, first President of the Confederation of the United States

223

• SAMUEL HARDY   c.1758–1785

A Virginia delegate to the Continental Congress, Samuel Hardy was born in Isle of Wight County, Virginia, about 1758. After graduation from William and Mary College, he studied law and commenced a law practice. He was first elected to the Virginia legislature at the age of twenty, and at the age of twenty-five was elected lieutenant governor. The next year, 1783, he was elected as a delegate to the Continental Congress 1783–85. But his promising career was cut short when he died at the age of twenty-eight while attending Congress in Philadelphia on October 17, 1785.

• JOHN HARING   1739–1809

A New York delegate to the Continental Congress, John Haring was born in Tappan, New York, on September 28, 1739. After studying law, he began a law practice in New York City and Rockland County. He was elected a member of the four New York Provincial Revolutionary congresses 1775–77, serving as president pro tempore 1776–77; and was chosen as a member of New York's delegation to the Continental Congress 1774–75 and 1785–88. He opposed adoption of the United States Constitution at the state convention in 1788, and after its ratification had little part in public affairs except for election as a member of the state assembly for one year in 1806. He died in Blauveltville, New York, on April 1, 1809.

• CORNELIUS HARNETT   1723–1781

Head of the North Carolina Revolutionary government at the beginning of the American Revolution, Cornelius Harnett was born near Edenton, North Carolina, April 20, 1723. After completing his education, he became a wealthy merchant in Wilmington, North Carolina. For more than twenty years he was regularly elected to the colonial assembly 1754–75. He led the colony's resistance to the Stamp Act in 1765 as chairman of the Sons of Liberty of North Carolina. As the Revolution approached he was a member of the committee of correspondence 1773–74 and chairman of the Wilmington committee of safety 1774–75. As president of the provincial council 1775–76, he was chief executive of the Revolutionary government. As such, he was excepted by Sir Henry Clinton from his proclamation offering general amnesty in 1776. He served as one of North Carolina's delegates to the Continental Congress 1777–80. Harnett was captured by the British when they occupied Wilmington in January 1781, and he died three months later as a prisoner in Wilmington on April 20, 1781.

FROM A WATERCOLOR PAINTING BY KAY SMITH

*The Amstel House in New Castle, Delaware, was built about 1730 for Dr. John Finney.
For a time it was occupied by Nicholas Van Dyke, an early Delaware governor. In 1784
George Washington attended the wedding here of Anne Van Dyke to Kensey Johns.*

FROM A WATERCOLOR PAINTING BY KAY SMITH

This State House in New Castle, Delaware, was a colonial meeting place for forty-three years before the Revolution. It was the first capitol of Delaware before the seat of government was transferred to Dover. In this handsome Georgian-style building the Declaration of Independence was approved by the Delaware delegation and the first Delaware constitution was approved in 1777. The central part was built in 1732, the year of George Washington's birth. Two small wings were added in 1765 and the roof and cupola were modified toward the end of the eighteenth century.

FROM A WATERCOLOR SKETCH BY KAY SMITH

The Old Dutch House in New Castle, Delaware, dates back to the seventeenth century and has been restored to its original condition with authentic furnishings.

Benjamin Harrison

- **BENJAMIN HARRISON**   1726–1791

A signer of the Declaration of Independence, Benjamin Harrison was born on the family plantation "Berkeley" in Charles City County, Virginia, on April 5, 1726. He attended William and Mary College, but had to leave school to manage the family estate upon the death of his father. From the time he was twenty-three he served almost continuously for more than forty years in the Virginia legislature. In 1773 he was one of the original eleven-man pre-Revolutionary Virginia committee of correspondence. As a delegate from Virginia to the Continental Congress 1774–78, he was chairman of the committee of the whole and head of the board of war. He presided over the debates that led to the adoption of the Declaration of Independence, and then signed it after joking that his weight of more than 200 pounds insured him a quick death if the British hanged him. During the Revolutionary War, the British destroyed most of his property and reduced him to near-poverty. At the end of the war he was elected governor of Virginia 1782–84. He served as speaker of the Virginia house of delegates from 1785 to his death at "Berkeley" on April 24, 1791. He was the father of President William Henry Harrison and the great-grandfather of President Benjamin Harrison.

John Hart

- **JOHN HART**   c.1711–1779

A signer of the Declaration of Independence, John Hart was born in Stonington, Connecticut, about 1711. He became a farmer in Hunterdon County, New Jersey, and was elected to the New Jersey colonial assembly 1761–72. Hart was active in the pre-Revolutionary movement, serving as a member of New Jersey's committee of safety 1775–78 and as a member of the New Jersey provincial congress 1775–76. As a delegate to the Continental Congress in 1776, he signed the Declaration of Independence. He served as speaker of the first state general assembly under the state constitution in 1776–78. When British troops invaded New Jersey in 1776 his home was devastated, and he and his family were forced to flee to the forests, his wife dying of the hardship. Hart died at his home near Hopewell, New Jersey, on May 11, 1779.

Nancy Hart, heroine of the revolution

• NANCY HART   c. 1765—1840

EDITOR'S NOTE: *The following account is adapted from Eliza-beth F. Ellet's "Women of the American Revolution." The story was verified many years later when a railroad excavation through the site of Nancy Hart's cabin uncovered six skeletons.*

Nancy Hart was a woman entirely uneducated and ignorant of all the conventional civilities of life, but a zealous lover of liberty and of the "liberty boys," as she called the American patriots. She had a husband whom she denominated a "poor stick," because he did not take a decided and active part with the defenders of his country. This vulgar and illiterate, but hospitable and valorous female patriot could boast no share of beauty—a fact she would herself have readily acknowledged, had she ever enjoyed an opportunity of looking in a mirror. She was cross-eyed, with a broad, angular mouth—ungainly in figure, rude in speech, and awkward in manners—but having a woman's heart for her friends, though that of a tigress for the enemies of her country. She was well known to the Loyalists, who stood somewhat in fear of her vengeance for any grievance or aggressive act; though they let pass no opportunity of teasing and annoying her, when they could with impunity.

On the occasion of an excursion from the British camp at Augusta, a party of Loyalists penetrated into the interior; and having savagely massacred Colonel Dooly in bed in his own house, proceeded up the country with the design of perpetrating further atrocities. On their way, a detachment of five from the party diverged to the east, and crossed Broad River to examine the neighborhood and pay a visit to their old acquaintance Nancy Hart.

When they arrived at her cabin, they unceremoniously entered it, although receiving from her no welcome but a scowl, and informed her they had come to learn the truth of a story in circulation, that she had secreted a noted rebel from a company of "King's men" who were pursuing him, and who, but for her interference, would have caught and hung him. Nancy undauntedly admitted her help in the fugitive's escape. She had, she said, at first heard the tramp of a horse, and then saw a man on horseback approaching her cabin at his utmost speed. As soon as she recognized him to be a patriot fleeing from pursuit, she let down the bars in front of her cabin, and motioned him to pass through both doors, front and rear, of her single-roomed house—to take to the swamp, and secure himself as well as he could. This he did without loss of time; and she then put up the bars, entered the cabin, closed the doors, and went about her usual work. Presently, some Loyalists rode up to the bars, calling vociferously for her. She muffled up her head and face, and opening the door, inquired why they disturbed a sick, lone woman. They said they had traced a man they wanted to catch near to her house, and asked if anyone on horseback had passed that way. She answered, no—but she saw someone on a sorrel horse turn out of the path into the woods, some two or three hundred yards back. "That must be the fellow!" said the Loyalists; and asking her direction as to the way he took, they turned about and went off, "*well fooled*," concluded Nancy, "in an opposite course to that of my patriot boy; when, if they had not been so lofty minded—but had looked on the ground inside the bars, they would have seen his horse's tracks up to that door, as plain as you can see the tracks on this here floor, and out of t'other door down the path to the swamp."

The bold story did not much please the Loyalist party but they would not wreak their revenge upon the woman who so unscrupulously avowed the cheat she had put upon the pursuers of a rebel. They contented themselves with ordering her to prepare them something to eat.

She replied that she never fed traitors and King's men if she could help it—the villains having put it out of her power to feed even her own family and friends, by stealing and killing all her poultry and pigs, "except that one old gobbler you see in the yard."

"Well, and *that* you shall cook for us," said one who appeared to be a leader of the party; and raising his musket he shot down the turkey, which another of them brought into the house and handed to Mrs. Hart to be cleaned and cooked without delay. She stormed and swore awhile—for Nancy occasionally swore—but seeming at last disposed to make a merit of necessity, began with alacrity the arrangements for cooking, assisted by her daughter, a little girl ten or twelve years old, and sometimes by one of the party, with whom she seemed in a tolerably good humor—now and then exchanging rude jests with him. The Loyalists, pleased with her freedom, invited her to drink some of the liquor they had brought with them—an invitation that was accepted with jocose thanks.

The spring—of which every settlement had one nearby—was just at the edge of the swamp; and a short distance within the swamp was hid among the trees a high snag-topped stump, on which was placed a conch-shell. This rude trumpet was used by the family to convey information, by variations in its notes, to Mr. Hart or his neighbors, who might be at work in a field, or clearing, just beyond the swamp—to let them know that the "Britishers" or Loyalists were about—that the master was wanted at the cabin—or that he was to keep close, or make tracks for another swamp. Pending the operation of cooking the turkey, Nancy had sent her daughter Sukey to the spring for water, with directions to blow the conch for her father in such a way as should inform him there were Loyalists in the cabin, and that he was to "keep close" with his three neighbors who were with him, until he should again hear the conch.

The party had become merry over their jug, and sat down to feast upon the slaughtered gobbler. They had cautiously stacked their arms where they were in view and within reach; and Mrs. Hart, assiduous in her attentions upon the table and to her guests, occasionally passed between the men and their muskets. Water was called for; and our heroine having contrived that there should be none in the cabin, Sukey was a second time despatched to the spring, with instruction to blow such a signal on the conch as should call up Mr. Hart and his neighbors immediately.

Meanwhile, Nancy had managed, by slipping out one of the pieces of pine which forms a "chinking" between the logs of a cabin, to open a space through which she was able to pass to the outside two of the five guns. She was detected in the act of putting out the third. The whole party sprang to their feet; when quick as thought Nancy brought the piece she held to

A ladder-back chair
—Sketch by Kay Smith

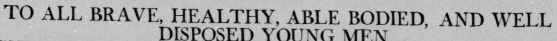

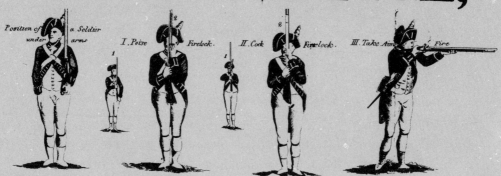

A Revolutionary War recruiting poster

her shoulder, declaring she would kill the first man who approached her. All were terror-struck; for Nancy's crossed eyes caused each to imagine himself her destined victim.

At length one of them made a movement to advance upon her; and true to her threat, she fired and shot him dead! Seizing another musket, she leveled it instantly, keeping the others at bay. By this time Sukey had returned from the spring; and taking up the remaining gun, she carried it out of the house, saying to her mother—"Daddy and them will soon be here." This information much increased the alarm of the Loyalists, who perceived the importance of recovering their arms immediately; but each one hesitated, in the confident belief that Mrs. Hart had one eye at least on him for a mark.

They started a general rush. No time was to be lost by the bold woman—she fired again, and brought down another of the enemy. Sukey had another musket in readiness, which her mother took, and posting herself in the doorway, called upon the party to surrender "their damned Loyalist carcasses to a patriot woman."

They agreed to surrender, and proposed to "shake hands upon the strength of it." But the victor, unwilling to trust their word, kept them in their places for a few minutes, till her husband and his neighbors came up to the door.

They were about to shoot down the Loyalists, but Mrs. Hart stopped them, saying they had surrendered to *her;* and her spirit being up to boiling heat, she swore that "shooting was too good for them."

This hint was enough. The dead man was dragged out and the others were bound, taken out beyond the bars and hung!

The tree upon which they were suspended was shown in 1828 by one who lived in those bloody times, and who also pointed out the spot once occupied by Mrs. Hart's cabin; accompanying the mention of her name with the emphatic remark: "Poor Nancy! She was a honey of a patriot—but the devil of a wife!"

• THOMAS HARTLEY   1748–1800

A colonel during the Revolutionary War and one of Pennsylvania's first Representatives in the U.S. Congress, Thomas Hartley was born in Reading, Pennsylvania, on September 7, 1748. After studying law, he commenced practice in Yorktown (now York), Pa. He was elected a member of the provincial Revolutionary convention at Philadelphia in 1775. During the Revolutionary War, he was appointed colonel of the 6th Pennsylvania Regiment, and helped defend upstate New York from invasion from Canada in 1776. He commanded an expedition against the Indians in 1778, and later that year was elected to the Pennsylvania legislature. Elected to the First U.S. Congress in 1789, he was regularly re-elected until his death in Yorktown on December 21, 1800.

Delaware troops under General Haslet leaving Dover, Delaware, in July 1776. —From a painting by Stanley M. Arthurs

• JOHN HARVIE 1742–1807

A signer of the Articles of Confederation, John Harvie was born in Albemarle County, Virginia, in 1742. After studying law, he began practice in Albemarle County. He was appointed commissioner to treat with the western Indians in 1774. Harvie was a member of the Virginia Revolutionary conventions of 1775–76, and was chosen as a delegate to the Continental Congress 1777–79. In Congress he was one of the signers of the Articles of Confederation and was a member of the committee appointed to explore reorganization of the Continental Army in 1777. Harvie died as the result of a construction accident in Richmond, Virginia, on February 6, 1807.

• JOHN HATHORN 1749–1825

A militia officer and U.S. Congressman, John Hathorn was born in Wilmington, Delaware, on January 9, 1749. A surveyor and school teacher, Hathorn served in the Revolutionary War as colonel of the 4th Regiment Orange County (N.Y.) militia, and was one of the few survivors in a battle with Indians and Tories in July 1779 near the present site of Port Jervis, New York. First elected to the New York state assembly in 1778, Hathorn served as speaker in 1783–84. He was elected as a Federalist to the First U.S. Congress 1789–91. He was defeated for re-election in 1790 and 1792, but again won a seat in the Fourth U.S. Congress 1795–97. After defeat for re-election in 1796, he retired to private business. Hathorn died in Warwick, New York, on February 19, 1825.

*A spice chest
dating back to 1679*

• BENJAMIN HAWKINS   1754—1816

One of North Carolina's first U.S. Senators, Benjamin Hawkins was born in Granville (now Warren) County, North Carolina, on August 15, 1754. A senior at Princeton College when the Revolutionary War began, he was appointed on the staff of George Washington to act as interpreter because of his fluency in French. First elected to the North Carolina legislature at the age of twenty-three in 1778, Hawkins was chosen by the legislature in 1780 to procure arms and munitions to defend the State. Chosen as a member of North Carolina's delegation to the Continental Congress 1781–84, and 1786–87, he was appointed by Congress to negotiate treaties with the Creek and Cherokee Indians in 1785. Hawkins was elected as a Federalist as one of North Carolina's U.S. Senators in 1789–95. Appointed by President Washington in 1796 as Indian agent for all tribes south of the Ohio River, he held the office until his death in Crawford County, Georgia, June 6, 1816.

• ISAAC HAYNE   1745—1781

A South Carolina militia colonel hanged without a trial by the British, Isaac Hayne was born at "Hayne Hall" near Jacksonboro, South Carolina, on September 23, 1745. A wealthy planter and iron-maker, Hayne served in the militia both as a captain and a private in the early years of the war. He was captured by the British at the fall of Charleston, South Carolina, on May 12, 1780, and was paroled to his home. Early in 1781 the British ordered him to join the British army as a British subject or be imprisoned in Charleston. Because his wife and children were ill with smallpox, he went to Charleston to plead that he be left to care for them. The authorities told him that if he would sign a declaration of allegiance to the British crown he would not be required to bear arms against his countrymen, so he signed the oath, and returned home. Later, he was summoned to join the British army. Hayne felt that this broke all his obligations, and relieved him of observing his parole as a prisoner of war. He joined the American forces and was commissioned a colonel. In July Hayne led a band of guerrillas in capturing the turncoat militia Gen. Andrew Williamson. In turn, a British force rescued Williamson and captured Hayne. The British commander of Charleston, Lt. Col. Nisbet Balfour, declared that Hayne had led an insurrection and that Hayne should be hanged as "an example." Lt. Col. Lord Rawdon-Hastings, leader of the British army in South Carolina, concurred. So on August 4, 1781, Hayne was hanged without a trial. The "example" backfired, because Hayne's death caused an outpouring of anger in the South that brought militiamen flocking to join General Greene's army and helped ensure the defeat of the British forces in the South. Over thirty years later Lord Rawdon-Hastings still was writing letters trying to explain that the action was justified.

• JONATHAN J. HAZARD   1744–c.1824

A Rhode Island delegate to the Continental Congress, Jonathan J. Hazard was born in Newport, Rhode Island, in 1744. He became paymaster in the Continental Army battalion from Rhode Island in 1777, and later that year joined General Washington's troops in New Jersey. In 1778 he was elected to the Rhode Island house of representatives and was a member of the state's council of war. Hazard was chosen as one of Rhode Island's delegates to the Continental Congress 1787–89. After that he served fifteen years in the state legislature 1790–1805. He moved to a Quaker settlement at Verona, New York, in 1805, where he died about 1824.

• WILLIAM HEMSLEY   1737–1812

A Maryland delegate to the Continental Congress, William Hemsley was born at "Clover Fields Farm," near Queenstown, Maryland, in 1737. A planter and surveyor, he became colonel of the 20th Battalion of the Queen Anne's County militia in 1777. He was elected to the state senate 1779–81, and was selected as a delegate to the Continental Congress 1782–84. After serving several more years in the state senate, he retired to "Clover Fields Farm," where he died on June 5, 1812.

• JAMES HENRY   1731–1804

A judge and a delegate to the Continental Congress, James Henry was born in Accomac County, Virginia, in 1731. After studying law at the University of Edinburgh, he returned to Virginia to begin his practice. He was elected to the Virginia house of burgesses 1772–74, and to the state house of delegates in 1776–77 and 1779. He was chosen as a Virginia delegate to the Continental Congress in 1780–81. He served as judge of the state court of admiralty 1782–88, and judge of the general court 1788–1800. He died at his home, "Fleet Bay," in Northumberland County, Virginia, December 9, 1804.

• JOHN HENRY   1750–1798

One of Maryland's first U.S. Senators, John Henry was born at "Weston," Maryland, in November 1750. After graduation from Princeton College at eighteen, he studied law in the Temple in London. Returning to Maryland in 1775, he began a law practice in Dorchester County. He was sent as a Maryland delegate to the Continental Congress 1778–81 and 1784–87, where he was a member of the committee that prepared the Northwest Ordinance of 1787. He was elected as one of Maryland's first U.S. Senators, serving from 1789 until he resigned in 1797 to accept election as governor of Maryland. While serving as governor he died at his country estate "Weston" on December 16, 1798.

Patrick Henry

• PATRICK HENRY   1736—1799

Virginia's "Firebrand of the Revolution," Patrick Henry was
born at "Studley" in Hanover County, Virginia, on May 29,
1736. He had little or no formal education, and worked as a
storekeeper and farmer from the age of fifteen. Then at the age
of twenty-four he decided to become a lawyer, so he studied
intensively for six weeks, passed his bar examination, and
began to practice law in Hanover, Virginia. In 1763 he won a
state-wide reputation for his eloquence when he won a case
called the "Parsons' Cause" by arguing that the British crown
had no right to invalidate a law passed by the Virginia house
of burgesses. Two years later in 1765 at the age of twenty-
eight Henry was elected to the house of burgesses for a career
that would make him a power in Virginia politics for the rest
of his life. Nine days after taking his seat in the legislature, the
brash young frontier lawyer presented a series of resolutions
condemning the British Stamp Act. In a speech supporting the
resolutions, Henry declared: "Tarquin and Caesar each had
his Brutus, Charles the First his Cromwell, and George the
Third may profit by their example!" As his speech was interrupted by cries of "Treason!" from conservative members of
the legislature, Henry added: "If this be treason make the
most of it!" His resolutions against the Stamp Act were approved by a narrow margin, but after Henry went home the
leaders by a parliamentary maneuver killed the most controversial of his resolutions.

Henry was elected and re-elected to the legislature in succeeding years, becoming the leader of the most active patriots, and was chosen as one of Virginia's delegates to the Continental Congress of 1774–76. At the first Continental Congress in 1774 he was disappointed when the delegates rejected a fiery petition to the King that he had written, and adopted instead a milder one prepared by John Dickinson. In March 1775 Henry electrified Virginia and other colonies, when in a speech before Virginia's second Revolutionary convention, he called for the colony to arm itself for defense, and ended with the declaration: "I know not what course others may take; but as for me, give me liberty, or give me death!" Less than a month later, the royal governor of Virginia, Lord Dunmore, ordered British marines to seize the colony's supply of gunpowder and put it aboard British warships. Henry called out the Hanover County militia, and started marching at their head on the Virginia capital at Williamsburg. The frightened governor got Henry to turn back by sending him a bill of exchange for the value of the gunpowder. Virginia's Revolutionary convention appointed Henry commander of the colony's militia in July 1775, and a year later elected him as the state's first governor 1776–79. Because he was so busy in Virginia, Henry missed the debates on the Declaration of Independence in the Continental Congress, and therefore did not sign the Declaration.

Michie Tavern near Monticello—a place for food, lodging, recreation, and revelry dating back to the colonial period. —Sketch by Kay Smith

After turning the governorship over to Thomas Jefferson in 1780, Henry was again elected as a member of the legislature 1780–84. After the war he again was elected governor 1784–86, and then resumed his seat in the legislature 1786–90. He led the opposition in the state to the ratification of the United States Constitution, and when it was approved over his objections he angrily prevented James Madison, the "Father of the Constitution," from being chosen by the legislature as one of the state's first U.S. Senators.

Henry retired from the legislature in 1791, and accepted no more public offices, even though President Washington offered him several Cabinet positions and the office of Chief Justice of the United States. When the Virginia legislature elected Henry as governor again in 1796, he also declined that position. However, at Washington's urging he did come out of public retirement to accept election to the Virginia legislature in 1799 to fight Virginia's nullification of the Alien and Sedition Acts. But before he could take his seat in the legislature, Henry died at the age of sixty-three at his home "Red Hill" in Charlotte County, Virginia, on June 6, 1799.

- **WILLIAM HENRY   1729–1786**

A Pennsylvania delegate to the Continental Congress, William Henry was born near Downington, Pennsylvania, on May 19, 1729. Throughout the Revolutionary War he was assistant commissary general with the rank of colonel for the district of Lancaster, Pennsylvania. He was chosen as a member of Pennsylvania's delegation to the Continental Congress 1784–86. Known for his ingenuity, Henry is credited with inventing the screw auger and being an early advocate of the use of steam as a motive power. He died in Lancaster on December 15, 1786.

- **JOSEPH HEWES   1730–1779**

A signer of the Declaration of Independence, Joseph Hewes was born a Quaker in Kingston, New Jersey, on January 23, 1730. After serving an apprenticeship with a merchant in Philadelphia, Hewes became a well-to-do shipowner in Edenton, North Carolina. He was elected to the North Carolina house of commons 1766–75, and was one of the first members of the committee of correspondence in 1773. He also was one of the first three delegates chosen to represent North Carolina in the Continental Congress 1774–77. During this period of service he signed the Declaration of Independence and headed the naval committee of Congress, being in effect the first Secretary of the Navy. He again served in the North Carolina legislature in 1778–79. He was returned as a delegate to Congress in 1779, but became ill and died in Philadelphia on November 10, 1779.

Joseph Hewes

Thomas Heyward, Jr.

• **THOMAS HEYWARD, Jr. 1746–1809**

A signer of the Declaration of Independence and of the Articles of Confederation, Thomas Heyward, Jr., was born on his father's plantation "Old House" in what is now St. Luke's Parish, South Carolina, on July 28, 1746. After studying law in the Middle Temple in London, he returned to South Carolina in 1771 and established himself in the practice of law. He was a delegate to the provincial Revolutionary convention in 1774, and a member of the council of safety in 1775–76. While serving in the South Carolina legislature 1776–84, he was chosen as a delegate to the Continental Congress 1776–78, where he signed both the Declaration of Independence and the Articles of Confederation. As a captain of a militia artillery battalion he was wounded at the battle of Port Royal Island, South Carolina, in February 1779, and was captured

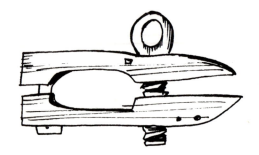

by the British in the fall of Charleston, South Carolina, on May 12, 1780. He was held prisoner at St. Augustine, Florida, for over a year, during which time the British plundered his plantation and his wife died. After his return he served as judge of the circuit court until 1789. His last major public service was as a member of the State constitutional convention in 1790. He died on his plantation, "White Hall," in St. Luke's Parish on March 6, 1809.

• DANIEL HIESTER   1747—1804

One of the first U.S. Representatives from Pennsylvania, Daniel Hiester was born in Berks County, Pennsylvania, on June 25, 1747. He served as a brigadier general of militia in the Revolutionary War. He then was a member of the supreme executive council of Pennsylvania 1784–86. He was elected from Pennsylvania to the U.S. Congress from 1789 to 1796, when he resigned and moved to Hagerstown, Maryland. He then won election to Congress from Maryland from 1801 until his death in Washington, D.C., March 7, 1804. His brother, Joseph Hiester (1752–1832), served as a colonel in the Revolutionary War, as a Congressman from Pennsylvania 1797–1805, 1815–20, and as governor of Pennsylvania 1820–24.

• STEPHEN HIGGINSON   1743—1828

A Massachusetts delegate to the Continental Congress, Stephen Higginson was born in Salem, Massachusetts, November 28, 1743. In the years before the Revolutionary War he became a successful shipmaster. He was selected as a member of the Massachusetts delegation to the Continental Congress in 1782–83. He served as naval officer at the port of Boston 1797–1808. Higginson died in Boston on November 22, 1828.

• WHITMEL HILL   1743—1797

A North Carolina delegate to the Continental Congress, Whitmel Hill was born in Bertie County, North Carolina, on February 12, 1743. After graduation from the College of Philadelphia in 1760, he took a prominent part in the early Revolutionary movements. In the Revolutionary War he attained the rank of colonel in the militia. He was a delegate to the assembly of freemen at Hillsboro in 1775, to the North Carolina revolutionary congress at Halifax in 1776, and to the State constitutional convention in 1776. A member of the state legislature 1777–80 and 1784–85, he was a delegate to the Continental Congress 1778–81. He died on his plantation "Hills Ferry" near Hamilton, North Carolina, on September 26, 1797.

• WILLIAM HILLHOUSE   1728–1816

A delegate to the Continental Congress and a judge, William Hillhouse was born in Montville, Connecticut, on August 25, 1728. After studying law, he began practice in Montville. He served over fifty years in the Connecticut legislature, as a representative and then as a senator 1756–60 and 1763–1808. He was a major in the 2nd Regiment of the Connecticut cavalry in the Revolutionary War. Hillhouse was a delegate to the Continental Congress 1783–86. He served as judge of the court of common pleas 1784–1806, and as judge of probate for the New London district 1786–1807. He died in Montville on January 12, 1816. His son, James Hillhouse (1754–1832), was a captain in the Revolutionary War, a U.S. Representative from Connecticut (1791–96), and a U.S. Senator (1796–1810).

• WILLIAM HINDMAN   1743–1822

A Maryland delegate to the Continental Congress, William Hindman was born in Dorchester County, Maryland, on April 1, 1743. After graduation from the College of Philadelphia at eighteen, he studied law at the Inns of Court in London. Returning to Maryland in 1765, he began a law practice in Talbot County. He was active in the pre-Revolutionary movement and was elected to the state senate 1777–84. He was sent as a delegate to the Continental Congress 1784–88. He then became a member of the state executive council 1789–92. He was elected as a U.S. Representative to Congress 1793–99 and as a U.S. Senator 1800–01. He died in Baltimore, Maryland, on January 19, 1822.

• SAMUEL HOLTEN   1738–1816

A Massachusetts delegate to the Continental Congress, Samuel Holten was born in Danvers, Massachusetts, on June 9, 1738. After studying medicine, he became a physician in Danvers. Holton was elected to the provincial Revolutionary congress 1774–75, and was a member of the committee of safety in 1775. He became a delegate to the Continental Congress 1778–80 and 1782–87, where he was one of the signers of the Articles of Confederation. From 1780 to 1792 he served regularly in the state senate and on the governor's council. He was elected to the Third U.S. Congress 1793–95, and then was appointed judge of the probate court for Essex County, serving 1796–1815. He died in Danvers on January 2, 1816.

William Hooper

• WILLIAM HOOPER   1742–1790

A signer of the Declaration of Independence, William Hooper was born in Boston on June 17, 1742. After graduation from

Harvard College at the age of eighteen, he studied law under the leading patriot, James Otis, and then moved to Wilmington, North Carolina, where he began practice in 1767. Shortly before the Revolutionary War he published a series of articles against the crown which aroused the people to the issues involved, and as a result the royal government disbarred him for one year. He was chosen as one of North Carolina's delegates to the Continental Congress 1774–1777, where he signed the Declaration of Independence. He was elected a member of the North Carolina legislature 1773–78. He died in Hillsboro, North Carolina, on October 14, 1790. His body is buried in Guilford Courthouse National Military Park.

• **ESEK HOPKINS   1718–1802**

The first commander in chief of the Continental Navy, Esek Hopkins was born in Scituate, Rhode Island, on April 26, 1718, the younger brother of Stephen Hopkins. At the age of twenty he went to sea and became a ship captain. During the French and Indian War he served as a privateer. At the outbreak of the Revolutionary War, Hopkins was appointed a brigadier general of Rhode Island militia. In December 1775, when Congress appointed the officers of the new Continental Navy, Hopkins was commissioned commander in chief, largely through the influence of his brother who was then serving on the naval committee of the Congress. He put to sea with the first squadron in February 1776, consisting of four ships and three sloops under instructions to sail along the southern coast of the colonies and harass British shipping. Disregarding his instructions, Hopkins sailed for the Bahamas, where on March 3–4 he put ashore a contingent of marines who captured the British fort at Nassau, taking 100 cannons and other supplies. On his return voyage Hopkins captured two British vessels, but a British frigate, the *Glasgow*, shot up his ships in a night action on Long Island sound before he got into port at New London, Connecticut, in April. Hopkins then was called before a hearing of the naval committee of Congress, which voted to censure him for disobeying orders, even though he was defended by John Adams. In the following months Hopkins was unable to instill sufficient discipline in the crews of his fleet to get them to put to sea again. Congress finally suspended him from his command in March 1777, and the following year he was dismissed from the service. Hopkins remained active in Rhode Island politics until his death in North Providence, Rhode Island, on February 26, 1802.

Esek Hopkins
—Sketch by Kay Smith

• **STEPHEN HOPKINS   1707–1785**

The only former colonial governor and chief justice to sign the Declaration of Independence, Stephen Hopkins was born in Providence, Rhode Island, March 7, 1707. He married and

An early view of Providence, Rhode Island

began farming his own land when he was nineteen. He was first elected to the Rhode Island legislature when he was twenty-five and remained a member most of the rest of his life except when he held higher public offices. He became chief justice of the court of common pleas in 1739 and chief justice of the superior court 1751–1754. He was a delegate to the colonial congress which met in Albany in 1754, where he became a good friend of Benjamin Franklin. He was elected and re-elected the governor of Rhode Island for all but four years of the period 1755–68. He was again appointed chief justice of the superior court in 1773. He became an abolitionist in 1773, freed his own slaves, and wrote legislation forbidding further importation of slaves into Rhode Island, which he persuaded the legislature to adopt in 1774. He was a delegate to the Continental Congress 1774–1780, where he signed the Declaration of Independence and helped write the Articles of Confederation. He died in Providence on July 13, 1785.

Stephen Hopkins

241

Francis Hopkinson

- **FRANCIS HOPKINSON**   **1737—1791**

A signer of the Declaration of Independence, a political satirist, and a judge, Francis Hopkinson was born in Philadelphia on October 2, 1737. He was the first graduate of the College of Philadelphia (now the University of Pennsylvania) in 1757. After studying law, he commenced practice in Philadelphia in 1761. Having married a wealthy heiress, Ann Borden, he moved to her estate in Bordentown, New Jersey, in 1774. That year he began publishing patriotic satires about the king and was elected to the Revolutionary provincial council of New Jersey 1774—76. He was selected as a delegate to the Continental Congress in 1776, where he signed the Declaration of Independence. The following year he is said to have designed the American flag of thirteen stars and thirteen stripes. He was appointed judge of the admiralty court of Pennsylvania in 1779—89, and then as U.S. district court judge for eastern Pennsylvania 1789—91. He died in Philadelphia on May 9, 1791. His son, Joseph Hopkinson (1770—1842), also was a lawyer and judge and wrote the patriotic song "Hail, Columbia."

- **JOSIAH HORNBLOWER**   **1729—1809**

A New Jersey delegate to the Continental Congress, Josiah Hornblower was born in Staffordshire, England, on February 23, 1729. A civil engineer, he came to America and settled in Belleville, New Jersey, in 1753. During the French and Indian War he was captain of New Jersey militia. Elected to the state general assembly in 1779—80, he served as speaker in the latter year. He was chosen as a member of New Jersey's delegation to the Continental Congress in 1785—86. He was appointed judge of the Essex County court in 1798, a position he held at his death on January 21, 1809.

- **TITUS HOSMER**   **1736—1780**

A Connecticut delegate to the Continental Congress, Titus Hosmer was born in what is now West Hartford, Connecticut, in 1736. After graduation from Yale College in 1757, he studied law and commenced practice in Middletown, Connecticut, in 1760. He was elected to the Connecticut legislature 1773—80, serving as speaker of the house in 1776 and 1778. Hosmer was a member of the council of safety 1776—77, and was a delegate to the Continental Congress 1775—79. He died in Middletown on August 4, 1780.

- **WILLIAM CHURCHILL HOUSTON**   **c. 1745—1788**

A college professor and New Jersey delegate to the Continental Congress, William Churchill Houston was born in Cabarrus County, North Carolina, about 1745. Graduated from Princeton College in 1768, he remained on at Princeton as a professor 1769–83. During the Revolutionary War he was a captain in the 2nd Regiment, Somerset militia. He was appointed deputy secretary of the Continental Congress in 1775–76. Houston was elected to the New Jersey Revolutionary provincial congress in 1776, and to the New Jersey assembly 1777–79. He was named a delegate to the Continental Congress 1779–81 and 1784–85. Appointed clerk of the supreme court of New Jersey 1781–88, he took up the study of law and was admitted to the bar in 1783. He was a delegate to the Annapolis Convention in 1786, and to the federal Constitutional Convention in 1787, but was forced to leave the meeting by illness before the new U.S. Constitution was completed. He died the next year in Frankfort, Pennsylvania, on August 12, 1788.

- **JOHN HOUSTOUN   1744–1796**

A delegate to the Continental Congress and governor of Georgia, John Houstoun was born in Waynesboro, Georgia, on August 31, 1744. After studying law, he began practice in Savannah, Georgia. Prominent in the early Revolutionary movement, he was one of the four original Georgia members of the Sons of Liberty. A delegate to the Continental Congress 1775–77 and 1779, he was absent in Georgia when the Declaration of Independence was signed. He was elected governor of Georgia in 1778 and 1784, and was appointed chief justice of Georgia in 1786. Defeated for election as governor in 1787, he won election as mayor of Savannah in 1789–90. He was appointed judge of the state superior court in 1792. Houstoun died at his estate "White Bluff" near Savannah on July 20, 1796.

- **WILLIAM HOUSTOUN   1755–1813**

A Georgia delegate to the Continental Convention, William Houstoun was born in Savannah, Georgia, in 1755. After studying law in the Inner Temple in London, he returned to Savannah to practice in 1776. He was a delegate to the Continental Congress 1783–86, and to the federal Constitutional Convention in 1787, but left the meeting before the new U.S. Constitution was completed. He died in Savannah on March 17, 1813.

- **JOHN EAGER HOWARD   1752–1827**

A heroic Revolutionary War officer who received one of only eight medals awarded by Congress during the war, John Eager Howard was born near Baltimore, Maryland, June 4, 1752. Born to wealth, he owned much of the land of the city of Balti-

Lieutenant Colonel
John Eager Howard,
holder of the Medal of Honor

243

The Battle of Cowpens, the conflict between Colonel Washington and the British General Tarleton

more. During the Revolutionary War he advanced from captain to lieutenant colonel of infantry, fighting in the battles of White Plains (N.Y.), Germantown (Pa.), Monmouth (N.J.), Camden (S.C.), Cowpens (S.C.), Guilford Courthouse (N.C.), Hobkirk Hill (S.C.), and Eutaw Springs (S.C.). The Congressional medal was awarded for his action at the battle of Cowpens in January 1781, when he commanded the main battle line that gave the British their worst defeat since the battle of Saratoga. After the war Howard became a delegate to the Continental Congress 1784–88, was elected governor of Maryland 1789–91, declined President Washington's appointment as Secretary of War in 1795, and won election as a U.S. Senator 1796–1803. He was an unsuccessful candidate for Vice President on the Federalist ticket in 1816. Howard died at his estate "Belvedere" near Baltimore on October 12, 1827. He was the father of Benjamin Chew Howard (1791–1872) who was a Maryland Congressman (1829–33 and 1835–39).

• ROBERT HOWE   1732–1786

A general in the Continental Army, Robert Howe was born in Brunswick County, North Carolina, in 1732, the son of a wealthy planter. After receiving a formal education in England, he returned to North Carolina where he became a successful rice planter. He was elected to the North Carolina legislature in 1772, becoming an active and vocal member of the patriotic movement. Howe and a fellow assemblyman, Cornelius Harnett, busied themselves raising and training militia for what they were sure was an inevitable struggle with the British. They were honored for their efforts by being the only North Carolina rebels not offered amnesty in a proclamation by British general Sir Henry Clinton in 1776. In September 1775 Howe was commissioned colonel in command of the 2nd North Carolina regiment. Howe marched with his troops to Virginia in December, where he took command of forces that drove the British governor out of Virginia. Hailed as a hero, Howe was appointed a brigadier general of the Continental Army in March 1776.

British spite against Howe was exhibited on May 12, 1776, when Sir Henry Clinton ordered Lord Cornwallis and his men to ravish Howe's plantation at Old Brunswick, North Carolina. Howe was promoted to major general and placed in command of all forces in the South in October 1777. He soon set out for Florida with 2,000 militia from South Carolina and Georgia. They proceeded south with little opposition until reaching the British base at St. Augustine, Florida. There the

West Point in 1780

troops were struck down by fever, causing about 500 to die. Howe was forced to retreat with the remainder of his men. When criticized for his failure by South Carolina Gen. Christopher Gadsden, Howe fought a duel with Gadsden, wounding him in the ear. When the British captured Savannah, Georgia, in December 1778, Howe was court-martialed, but was acquitted with honor.

Howe was commander of West Point in 1780, where he was succeeded by Benedict Arnold. Later that year he was a member of the military court that sentenced Maj. John André to death for his part in Arnold's treason. In 1781 Howe helped put down the mutiny by New Jersey troops, and in 1783 restored order in Philadelphia after rioting mobs forced Congress to flee from the city. He died at his home in Brunswick County on December 14, 1786.

The mansion of the governor general
in St. Augustine, Florida, as it appeared in 1764.
—Sketch by Kay Smith

• DAVID HOWELL   1747–1824

A college professor, judge, and delegate to the Continental Congress, David Howell was born in Morristown, New Jersey, on January 1, 1747. After graduation from Princeton College at nineteen, he studied law and began practice in Providence, Rhode Island, in 1768. Earlier, he had become a tutor at Brown University in Providence 1766–69, and was promoted to professor of natural philosophy 1769–79. He was appointed justice of the peace in 1779, and justice of the court of common pleas in 1780. He was chosen as a delegate from Rhode Island to the Continental Congress 1782–85. He next became justice of the state supreme court 1786–87, and then attorney general of the state in 1789. He was appointed by Brown University as professor of law 1790–1824, and was acting president of the university in 1791–92. He finally served as U.S. district judge for Rhode Island from 1812 until his death in Providence, on July 21, 1824.

• RICHARD HOWLEY   1740–1784

A governor of Georgia and delegate to the Continental Congress, Richard Howley was born in Liberty County, Georgia, in 1740. After studying law, he commenced practice in St. John's Parish. He was elected to the state house of representatives 1779–83, and as governor of Georgia in 1780. He was selected as a delegate to the Continental Congress in 1780–81. His final public office was as chief justice of Georgia 1782–83. He died in Savannah, Georgia, in December 1784.

• DANIEL HUGER   1742–1799

The eldest of five patriotic brothers who served their country in the formative years of the United States, Daniel Huger was born on "Limerick" plantation in St. John's Parish, South Carolina, on February 20, 1742. He was prominent in pre-Revolutionary activities, and was elected a member of the state house of representatives in 1778–79. As a member of the governor's council in 1780, he was present in Charleston, South Carolina, during the siege, but left the town with Governor Rutledge to continue the defense of the state. He later was captured by the British, but was paroled. He served as a delegate to the Continental Congress 1786–88, and then was elected to the new U.S. Congress 1789–93. His remaining years were spent in managing his extensive estates. He died in Charleston on July 6, 1799. His brothers were: *Isaac* (1743–1797), a brigadier general of the Continental Army, who especially distinguished himself at the battles of Guilford Courthouse (N.C.) and Hobkirk's Hill (S.C.). *John* (1744–1804), the first Secretary of State of South Carolina. *Benjamin* (1746–1779), a major in the Continental Army who was killed at Charleston. *Francis* (1751–1811), a captain in the Continental Army, who served in the defense of Charleston in 1776, and later was lieutenant colonel and quartermaster general of the Southern Department of the Army.

William Hull

• WILLIAM HULL   1753–1825

A valiant junior officer during the Revolutionary War but a dud as a general in the War of 1812, William Hull was born in Derby, Connecticut, on June 24, 1753. After graduation from Yale College at nineteen, he studied law and was admitted to the bar in 1775. With the outbreak of the Revolutionary War, he joined the Connecticut militia as a captain, serving at the siege of Boston. He was commissioned a captain in the Continental Army in January 1776, and fought bravely in the battles of White Plains, Trenton, and Princeton. After the latter battle he was promoted to major. In 1781 as a lieutenant colonel he led a bold raid behind British lines on Morrisania, New York, for which he was praised both by General Washington and by Congress.

After the war Hull practiced law in Newton, Massachusetts, was elected to the state legislature, and became a major general of militia. He was governor of the territory of Michigan from 1805 to 1812, when he was appointed brigadier general in the U.S. Army in command of forces in the Northwest. As such, he suffered several defeats, including the surrender of Detroit and his army of 2,000 troops on August 16, 1812. Upon his release by the British, Hull returned to his law practice in Newton. Then in 1814 he was called before a court-martial in which he was tried on charges of treason, cowardice, and neglect of duty. Found guilty on the last two charges, he was sentenced to be shot and his name stricken from the rolls of the army. President Madison voided the sentence of execution because of Hull's service during the Revolutionary War. Hull spent his remaining years writing a vindication of his conduct. He died in Newton on November 29, 1825.

• CHARLES HUMPHREYS   1714–1786

A Quaker who voted against the Declaration of Independence because of his religion, Charles Humphreys was born in Haverford, Pennsylvania, on September 19, 1714. A miller, he served in the Pennsylvania legislature 1764–1774, and was a delegate to the Continental Congress 1774–76. His opposition to the Declaration of Independence ended his public service. He died in Haverford on March 11, 1786.

• BENJAMIN HUNTINGTON   1736–1800

A delegate to the Continental Congress and one of Connecticut's first representatives to the U.S. Congress, Benjamin

Huntington was born in Norwich, Connecticut, on April 19, 1736. After graduation he studied law and commenced practice in Norwich in 1765. He was elected to the Connecticut legislature 1771–93, serving as speaker of the house 1778–79. He represented Connecticut in the Continental Congress 1780–1784 and 1787–88. He was mayor of Norwich 1784–96, and during the same period was elected to the First U.S. Congress 1789–91. His final public service was as judge of the superior court of Connecticut 1793–98. He died in Rome, New York, on October 16, 1800

- **JEDEDIAH HUNTINGTON   1743–1813**

A Continental Army general during the Revolutionary War, Jedediah Huntington was born in Norwich, Connecticut, on August 4, 1743. After graduation from Harvard College at the age of nineteen, he became active in the Sons of Liberty and joined the militia. A week after the battles of Lexington and Concord in April 1775 he joined the rebel army at Cambridge, Massachusetts, as a colonel in command of the 20th Regiment of Connecticut militia. In July he was commissioned a colonel in the Continental Army, commanding Connecticut regiments during the campaigns in the early years of the war. After being commissioned a brigadier general in May 1777, he joined the Continental Army near Philadelphia. The next year he was a member of the court-martial that tried Gen. Charles Lee, and he sat on the military board that tried the British spy Maj, John André. In 1789 President Washington appointed Huntington as collector of customs at New London, Connecticut, a post he held until his death there on September 25, 1813. His brother, Ebenezer Huntington (1754–1834), served as an officer throughout the Revolutionary War, and commanded an infantry company at the battle of Yorktown.

- **SAMUEL HUNTINGTON   1731–1796**

The seventh President of the Continental Congress and a signer of the Declaration of Independence, Samuel Huntington was born in Windham, Connecticut, on July 3, 1731. After completing an apprenticeship with a cooper to learn to make barrels, Huntington began studying law and commenced practice in Norwich in 1758. He was elected to the colonial assembly 1764–75, and also served as the King's attorney for Connecticut 1765–74. He then was appointed judge of the superior court 1774–84, serving as chief justice in 1784. An outspoken patriot, Huntington represented Connecticut in the Continental Congress 1776–84, where he signed the Declaration of Independence in 1776, the Articles of Confederation in 1778, and served as President from September 28, 1779 to July 6, 1781. Huntington was elected lieutenant governor in 1785. The next year, he was elected governor of Connecticut,

Samuel Huntington

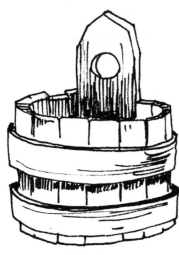

A piggin—
used as a water dipper
—Sketch by Kay Smith

continuing to serve in that office for eleven years until his death in Norwich on January 5, 1796. Huntington was so well liked in Connecticut that in the presidential election of 1789 the state's two electors cast their votes for him rather than for George Washington. His adopted son, Samuel Huntington (1768–1817), served as governor of Ohio 1808–9.

• **RICHARD HUTSON**   **1748–1795**

A South Carolina delegate to the Continental Congress, Richard Hutson was born in Prince William Parish, South Carolina, on July 9, 1748. After graduation from Princeton College at sixteen, he studied law and began practice in Charleston, South Carolina. He was elected to the South Carolina legislature 1776–79, 1781–82, 1785, and 1788. As a delegate to the Continental Congress in 1778–79, Hutson signed the Articles of Confederation. Captured at the fall of Charleston in 1780, he was confined as a prisoner at St. Augustine, Florida, until 1781. After his release, Hutson was elected lieutenant governor in 1782–83. He was appointed to the court of chancery of South Carolina 1784–95, serving the last four years as senior judge of the court. He died in Charleston on April 12, 1795.

• **JARED INGERSOLL**   **1749–1822**

A signer of the United States Constitution, Jared Ingersoll was born in New Haven, Connecticut, on October 24, 1749. After graduation from Yale College at sixteen, he studied law in Philadelphia, extended his legal education at the Middle Temple in London, and then spent a year in Paris. He returned to Philadelphia in 1778 and commenced practice. He was chosen as one of Pennsylvania's delegates to the Continental Congress in 1780–81, and to the federal convention of 1787, where he signed the new U.S. Constitution. He was appointed attorney general of Pennsylvania 1790–99 and served again 1811–17. He was the unsuccessful Federalist candidate for Vice President of the United States in 1812. He was presiding judge of the district court of Philadelphia from 1821 to his death there on October 31, 1822.

• **WILLIAM IRVINE**   **1741–1804**

An unsuccessful Continental Army general, William Irvine was born in Ulster, Ireland, on November 3, 1741. After graduation from Dublin University, he studied medicine and served as surgeon on a British man-of-war 1756–63. After resigning from the English navy, he came to America and settled in Carlisle, Pennsylvania, where he practiced medicine. He was elected a delegate to the revolutionary conventions 1774–76. Commissioned colonel of the 6th Pennsylvania Regiment, he led his troops on the invasion of Canada, where he was captured at the battle of Trois Rivieres on June 8, 1776. He remained a prisoner of war until exchanged May 6, 1778. Appointed brigadier general in 1779, he commanded the 2nd Brigade of General Wayne's army in two unsuccessful actions in 1780. From May 1782 to the end of the war he was in command of Fort Pitt in Pennsylvania. He was elected as one of Pennsylvania's delegates to the Continental Congress 1786–88. During the Whisky Rebellion of 1794, he commanded state troops. Irvine was elected to the Third U.S. Congress 1793–95. He then moved to Philadelphia, where he was superintendent of military stores from 1801 until his death there on July 29, 1804.

• **RALPH IZARD**   **1742–1804**

A diplomat and U.S. Senator, Ralph Izard was born at "The Elms," near Charleston, South Carolina, on January 23, 1742. Educated in England, he was graduated from Christ College at Cambridge. He returned to South Carolina in 1764, but seven years later went back to live in England. With the outbreak of the Revolutionary War, he moved to France in 1776. He was appointed commissioner to the court of Tuscany (Italy) by the Continental Congress on December 30, 1776, but was unable to obtain recognition by Tuscany. He remained in Paris where he meddled in Benjamin Franklin's diplomacy until he was recalled in 1779. He exhibited his patriotism by pledging his large estate in South Carolina for the payment of warships used in the Revolutionary War. He was elected to the Continental Congress in 1782–83, and to the U.S. Senate 1789–95, serving as president pro tempore of the Senate 1794–95. He died on his estate near Charleston, South Carolina, on May 30, 1804.

Ralph Izard

• **DAVID JACKSON**   **c.1730–1801**

A surgeon in the Revolutionary War and a delegate to the Continental Congress, David Jackson was born in Newtown-Limavady, Ireland, about 1730. His family immigrated to America while he was a child, settling in Edenton, Pennsylvania. He graduated from the College of Philadelphia with a medical degree in 1768, and became an apothecary and physician in Philadelphia. During the Revolutionary War he was appointed paymaster of the 2nd Battalion of Philadelphia militia in 1776, and lost an arm at the Battle of Trenton in December. He became quartermaster of militia in the field in 1779 and served as a hospital surgeon in 1780. Jackson was present at the surrender of Lord Cornwallis, at Yorktown, Virginia, on October 19, 1781. He was chosen as a member of the Continental Congress 1785–86. After that he resumed the professions of apothecary and physician. He died in Oxford, Pennsylvania, on September 17,1801.

Sarah VanBrugh Livingston,
wife of John Jay
—From a miniature made in Paris

• JAMES JACKSON   1757–1801

A soldier and politician, James Jackson was born in Moreton-Hampstead, England, September 21, 1757. He came to Savannah, Georgia, at the age of fifteen in 1772. After serving as clerk of the court in 1776–77, he was elected to the first constitutional convention of Georgia in 1777. At twenty-one he was elected governor in 1778 but declined. He served as a captain in the Georgia legion, receiving the keys to Savannah from the British when they surrendered the city on July 12, 1782. As a reward for his services, Jackson was presented with a house in Savannah by the Georgia assembly. He was elected to the First U.S. Congress 1789–91. Defeated for reelection by Gen. Anthony Wayne, he contested the election and the seat was declared vacant by the House on March 21, 1792. Jackson was elected to the U.S. Senate 1793–95, and as governor of Georgia 1798–1801. He then was again elected to the U.S. Senate, serving from 1801 until his death in Washington, D.C., on March 19, 1806.

• JONATHAN JACKSON   1743–1810

A member of the Continental Congress, Jonathan Jackson was born in Boston, Massachusetts, on June 4, 1743. After graduation from Harvard College at eighteen, he became a merchant in Newburyport, Massachusetts. He was elected to the provincial congress in 1775, and to the state house of representatives in 1777. He served in the Continental Congress in 1782. He later was a U.S. marshal 1789–91, and then treasurer of Massachusetts 1802–06. He also became president of the state bank and of the Harvard corporation. Jackson died in Boston on March 5, 1810.

• WILLIAM JASPER   1750–1779

A heroic sergeant who died fighting during the Revolutionary War, William Jasper was born in South Carolina in 1750. Joining a South Carolina regiment at the outbreak of the war, he distinguished himself for bravery at the British attack on Charleston in June 1776, braving enemy fire to replace the flag that had been shot down over Fort Sullivan, later renamed Fort Moultrie. When the governor of South Carolina, John Rutledge, presented Jasper his own sword as a token of respect and offered him a commission, the young man replied that because he could neither read nor write "I'm not fit to keep officers' company; I am but a sergeant." In 1779, during the British assault on Savannah, Georgia, the flag of Jasper's regiment again was shot down. Jasper climbed to the top of the parapet with the colors, but was fatally wounded as he hoisted them into place. He died on October 9, 1779.

• JOHN JAY   1745–1829

President of the Continental Congress and first Chief Justice of the United States, John Jay was born in New York City on December 12, 1745. After graduation from King's College (now Columbia University) in 1764, he studied law and was admitted to the bar in 1768. As a delegate to the Continental Congress 1774–1779, he worked for adoption of the Declaration of Independence but was absent in New York when it was passed and so did not sign it. Jay was appointed chief justice of New York in May 1777 but resigned to become the sixth President of the Continental Congress from December 10, 1778, to September 28, 1779. He was appointed minister to Spain in 1779, but was unable to obtain official recognition. Then in 1781 he was appointed one of the ministers to negotiate peace with England, and as such signed the treaty of Paris ending the Revolutionary War. Returning to New York in 1784, he was appointed secretary of foreign affairs by the Congress 1784–89. During this period his contributions to the Federalist Papers played an important part in winning ratification of the United States Constitution. President Washington appointed Jay as the first Chief Justice of the United States on September 26, 1789. While serving as Chief Justice, Washington sent him to England where he negotiated a treaty to settle controversies still remaining between the two countries. Because of concessions he made, Jay's Treaty became a controversial political issue that helped lead to the decline of the Federalist Party. Upon his return from England in 1795, Jay found he had been elected governor of New York, so he resigned as Chief Justice. After serving two terms as governor 1795–1801, Jay declined re-election and retired to his farm at Bedford in Westchester County, New York, where he died on May 17, 1829.

• THOMAS JEFFERSON   1743–1826

Author of the Declaration of Independence and third President of the United States, Thomas Jefferson was born at Shadwell in Albemarle County, Virginia, on April 13, 1743. After graduation from the College of William and Mary at nineteen, he studied law under George Wythe, who later was one of the signers of the Declaration of Independence. While still a law student, he attended the session of the Virginia house of burgesses to hear Patrick Henry's fiery denunciation of the Stamp Act. In 1767 he was admitted to the bar and began practice in Williamsburg, Virginia. He was elected to the house of burgesses at the age of twenty-six, serving there until the outbreak of the Revolutionary War.

He was ill at the time of the first Continental Congress in 1774, but was elected a member of Virginia's delegation to the second Continental Congress in 1775. His ability as a writer

John Jay

253

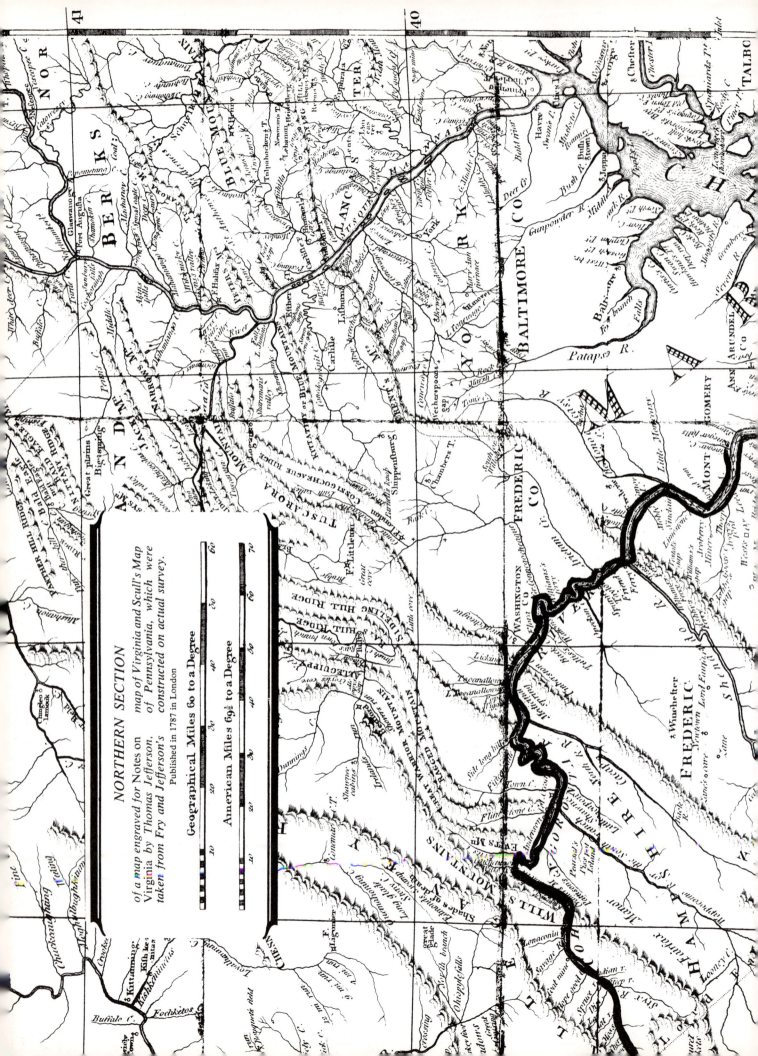

NORTHERN SECTION

of a map engraved for Notes on
Virginia by Thomas Jefferson,
taken from Fry and Jefferson's

map of Virginia and Scull's Map
of Pennsylvania, which were
constructed on actual survey.
Published in 1787 in London

Geographical Miles 60 to a Degree

American Miles 69½ to a Degree

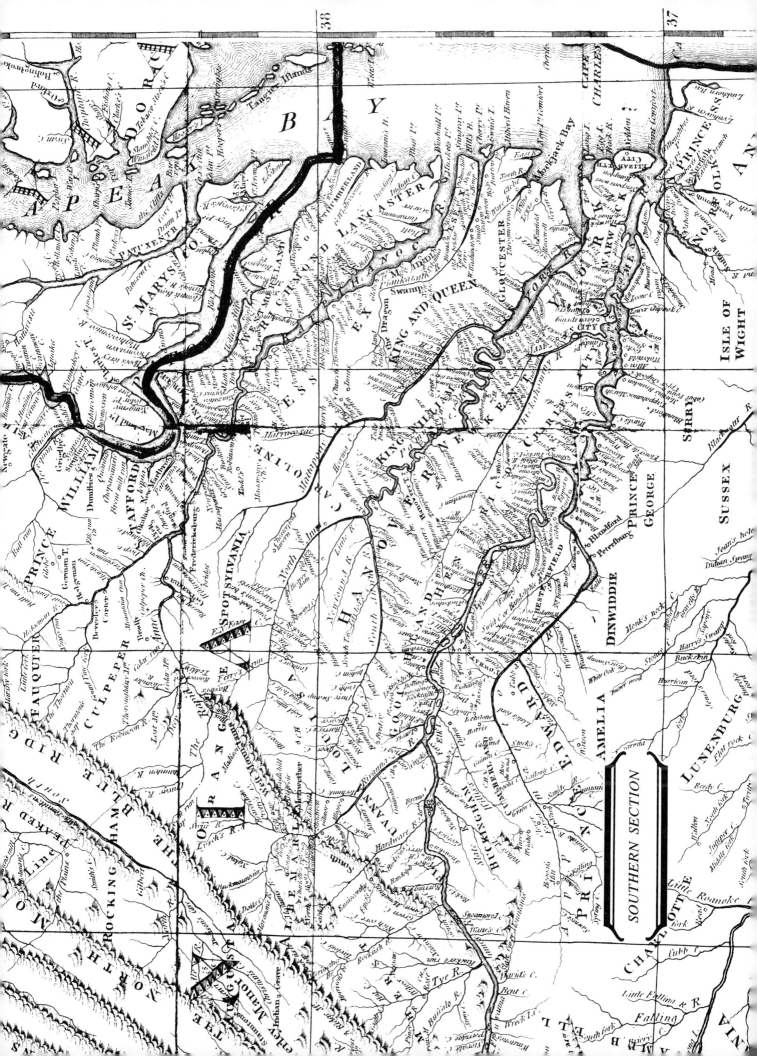

An early sketch of Monticello
(See end papers for a current view in watercolor by Kay Smith.)

was soon recognized, and on June 11, 1776, he was chosen as chairman of the committee to draft the Declaration of Independence. Other members of the committee included Benjamin Franklin and John Adams, but they deferred to the thirty-three-year-old Jefferson in the actual writing of the document. After the Declaration had been approved by Congress and he had signed it, Jefferson resigned, returning to Virginia to help write the laws for the new state. In 1779 the Virginia legislature elected Jefferson as governor, succeeding Patrick Henry. When the British invaded Virginia in 1781, Jefferson felt he was not qualified to command the defense of the state, so he resigned to be succeeded by Gen. Thomas Nelson as governor. In 1783 he again was elected to Congress, where he wrote the draft for the Northwest Ordinance that was adopted four years later.

After the war Jefferson was sent to France in 1784 to aid Benjamin Franklin, and the following year became ambassador to France when Franklin returned home. He was at that post during the time the new United States Constitution was written and ratified. Upon his return from France, Jefferson was appointed by President Washington as the first Secretary of State in the new government, an office Jefferson held from 1790 to 1793. During these years his opposition to the policies of Secretary of the Treasury Alexander Hamilton led to the formation of the American two-party system with Jefferson as head of the Democratic-Republican Party and Hamilton as head of the Federalist Party.

Jefferson's supporters tried to win the presidency for him in 1796, but he came in second to John Adams, and so became the second Vice President of the United States, serving under Adams. Four years later he again ran for President, and this time won. During his eight years as President, from 1801 to 1809, Jefferson's outstanding contribution came in doubling the size of the United States by the purchase from France of the Louisiana Territory at a cost of about $15 million. Jefferson declined to run for a third term as President, instead supporting his friend and Secretary of State, James Madison, for the office.

This octagonal structure in Williamsburg, Virginia, is the ancient Powder Horn built by the order of the House of Burgesses in 1714. Governor Alexander Spotswood drew the plans for the construction with massive walls twenty-two inches thick. There was a wall ten to twelve feet high surrounding the structure. A few months before the battle of Lexington and Concord, Lord Dunmore, then Governor General, very slyly under cover of darkness removed powder from this magazine and put it aboard the schooner Magdalen, *anchored at Burwell's Ferry four miles from Williamsburg. When the mayor and aldermen heard of this, they were outraged and let Dunmore know their feelings in no uncertain terms. The governor said, "I have removed the powder from the magazine where I do not think it secure, and upon my word and honor, whenever it is wanted in an insurrection it shall be delivered in a half hour." The incident caused the greatest excitement and alarm throughout the colony. A company of more than sixty minutemen in Fredericksburg prepared to march to Williamsburg but were dissuaded by Washington and Pendleton, who urged them to wait for Congress to decide the matter. They nevertheless signed a paper pledging themselves to "defend Virginia or any sister colony" and closed with the words "God save the liberties of America." After such a stirring beginning and actual use as a powder arsenal in the Revolutionary War, the old Powder Horn has had a varied background, even including use as an evangelistic church and as a dancing school, reverting again to its original use in 1861 as an arsenal in the Civil War. After that war it became a stable and finally was rescued for future generations by the Association for the Preservation of Virginia Antiquities. Hence, this is one of the truly original old structures in this country.*

FROM A WATERCOLOR SKETCH BY KAY SMITH

The kitchen fireplace and utensils of the Hammond-Harwood house in Annapolis, Maryland, date back to 1774 when the house was built for Matthias Hammond, a patriot who signed the Proclamation of Freemen of Maryland and the Declaration of Rights. The house has been the residence of such prominent Maryland families as Pinkney, Chase, Lockerman, and Harwood, the Harwood family having occupied the house for seventy-five years before it became a museum.

*This charming colonial home in Williamsburg, Virginia, with its festive Christmas decorations,
was formerly the residence of George Wythe, the distinguished professor of law at William
and Mary College who numbered among his students many of the nation's future leaders, including
Thomas Jefferson. He was one of the commissioners to revise the statutes of Virginia in 1776
and a member of the Virginia Convention which ratified the Federal Constitution. This house was used
as headquarters by George Washington in the days immediately preceding the Yorktown campaign.
Legend has it that on moonlight nights the ghost of George Washington appears in the hall.*

Thomas Jefferson

After retiring to his home, Monticello, in Virginia, Jefferson devoted much of his time to writing and to the establishment of the University of Virginia. He died there on July 4, 1826, the 50th anniversary of the adoption of his Declaration of Independence.

• DANIEL OF ST. THOMAS JENIFER   1723–1790

A signer of the United States Constitution, Daniel of St. Thomas Jenifer was born of wealthy parents on a plantation near Port Tobacco, Maryland, in 1723. Although he had been a close adviser of the royal governor of the colony, he joined the patriots, becoming president of the council of safety 1775–77. He was elected president of the state senate 1777–80, and a member of Maryland's delegation to the Continental Congress 1778–82. As a delegate to the federal Constitutional Convention in 1787, Jenifer upheld the Virginia Plan and gladly signed the final draft of the United States Constitution. He was an unsuccessful candidate for governor of Maryland in 1782 and 1785. Jenifer died in Annapolis, Maryland, on November 16, 1790.

• THOMAS JOHNSON   1732–1819

A general of militia and a member of the Continental Congress, Thomas Johnson was born in Calvert County, Maryland, on November 4, 1732. He became a lawyer in Annapolis, Maryland, and was first elected to the colony's assembly in 1762. A delegate to the Continental Congress 1774–77, he helped promote the election of George Washington as commander in chief of the Continental Army in 1775. Johnson served in the Revolutionary War as senior brigadier general of Maryland militia and led the western Maryland forces that went to Washington's relief during his retreat through New Jersey. He was elected the first state governor of Maryland 1777–79. He served as chief judge of the general court of Maryland in 1790–91, and then was appointed by President Washington Associate Justice of the Supreme Court in 1791. He resigned in February 1793, because of illness. He declined nomination by Washington as Secretary of State in 1795, but accepted appointment by President John Adams as chief judge of the District of Columbia in 1801. As a member of the board of commissioners of the Federal City, he assisted in designating sites for public buildings and in naming the capital city "Washington." Johnson died at his estate, "Rose Hill," in Frederick, Maryland, on October 26, 1819.

William Samuel Johnson

• WILLIAM SAMUEL JOHNSON   1727–1819

A signer of the United States Constitution, William Samuel Johnson was born in Stratford, Connecticut, on October 7,

1727. At sixteen he was graduated from Yale College, and at nineteen received master's degrees from both Yale and Harvard. He then studied law and began practice in Stratford in 1749. He was elected to the colonial house of representatives and served as a delegate to the Stamp Act Congress held in New York City in October 1765. The Connecticut assembly sent him as its agent to England 1767–71 to determine the title to Indian lands. Upon his return he served as a member of the governor's council 1771–75, and as judge of the Connecticut supreme court 1772–74. Elected a member of the Continental Congress in 1774, he declined to serve because he opposed independence. He was arrested as a traitor for corresponding with the British in 1779, but was released when he took an oath of allegiance. He was elected a member of the Continental Congress 1784–87, and a delegate to the federal Constitutional Convention in 1787 where he helped edit and signed the final draft of the United States Constitution. He was appointed president of Columbia College in New York in 1787, and two years later was elected as one of Connecticut's first U.S. Senators. He resigned from the Senate in 1791 to devote full time to Columbia. Ill health forced him to resign from Columbia College in 1800, but he lived until the age of ninety-two, when he died at his home in Stratford, Connecticut, on November 14, 1819.

- **SAMUEL JOHNSTON**   **1733–1816**

A member of the Continental Congress, Samuel Johnston was born in Dundee, Scotland, on December 15, 1733. While still a baby, he was brought to America by his parents, who settled in Chowan County, North Carolina, in 1736. Johnston became a lawyer, and was elected to the colonial assembly in 1760. Active in the patriotic movement, he was moderator of the colony's Revolutionary convention in 1775. A member of North Carolina's delegation to the Continental Congress 1780–82, he was elected first president after the Articles of Confederation were signed, but declined to serve. He was elected as a Federalist to the U.S. Senate 1789–93. He later served as judge of the superior court of North Carolina 1800–03. Johnston died near Edenton, North Carolina, on August 18, 1816.

- **ALLEN JONES**   **1739–1798**

A militia general and politician, Allen Jones was born in Edgecombe (now Halifax) County, North Carolina, on December 24, 1739, the elder brother of Willie Jones. After being educated at Eton College in England, he returned to North Carolina. He was elected a member of the colonial assembly 1773–75, and as a delegate to the colony's Revolutionary congress 1774–76. He attained the rank of brigadier general in the

Allen Jones

259

John Paul Jones —From a painting by Cecilia Beaux

Revolutionary War, but saw no notable action. He served in the state senate, and was a delegate to the Continental Congress in 1779–80. Jones died on his plantation, "Mount Gallant," in Northampton County, North Carolina, on November 10, 1798.

• JOHN PAUL JONES   1747–1792

America's greatest naval hero in the Revolutionary War, John Paul (he later adopted the name Jones) was born in Kirkbean, Scotland, on July 6, 1747. Going to sea at the age of twelve, he became commander of a merchant ship by the time he was nineteen. At the outbreak of the Revolutionary War, Jones volunteered his services, and was appointed as a lieutenant in the Continental Navy in December 1775. He was given command of the *Providence* in 1776, and began to establish his reputation as a hard-fighting captain by capturing more than a dozen British ships. In 1777 he was given command of the sloop *Ranger*, which he sailed to Europe. Upon his arrival in France, his ship received from the French the first salute ever given to the American flag by a foreign man-of-war. In April 1778 he made a daring raid on Whitehaven, England, and the following year took a landing party ashore in Scotland in an unsuccessful effort to capture the Earl of Selkirk. In August 1779 Jones sailed from France in command of the *Bonhomme Richard*, a refitted merchant ship that mounted 42 guns.

Jones won a lasting reputation as a naval officer on September 23, 1779, in a night battle with the 44-gun British warship *Serapis*. The two ships became entangled in each other's rigging. When the British captain called to Jones asking if he was ready to surrender, Jones replied with words that became a Navy slogan: "I have not yet begun to fight." For more than two hours Jones and his men fought hand-to-hand with the British seamen in the moonlight. Both ships were on fire, but Jones kept blasting the *Serapis* with his cannon until he shot down its mainmast. The captain of the *Serapis* then surrendered.

Returning to America in February 1781, he was given command of the 76-gun *America*, then being built in Portsmouth, New Hampshire, but, before it could sail, Congress decided to turn the ship over to the French. Jones sailed with the French fleet but saw no outstanding action.

After the end of the Revolutionary War, Jones became an admiral in the Russian Navy, commanding a squadron on the Black Sea in a war with the Turks. Leaving the Russian Navy, he was appointed as U.S. consul to Algiers, but before he could assume the post he died in Paris on July 18, 1792. More than a hundred years later, a U.S. Navy squadron in 1905 brought Jones' body back to the United States from France for entombment at the U.S. Naval Academy in Annapolis, Maryland.

- **JOSEPH JONES**   1727—1805

A member of the Continental Congress, Joseph Jones was born in King George County, Virginia, in 1727. He served on the committee of safety in 1775, and was elected to the state house of delegates in 1776—77, 1780—81, and 1783—85. He was a delegate to the Continental Congress in 1777—78 and 1780—83. Jones was judge of the Virginia general court 1778—79, and from 1789 to his death in Fredericksburg, Virginia, on October 28, 1805. He was an uncle of President James Monroe.

- **NOBLE WYMBERLY JONES**   1723—1805

A doctor and delegate to the Continental Congress, Noble Wymberly Jones was born in Lambeth, England, in 1723. When he was ten, his parents brought him to Savannah, Georgia, where they settled in 1733. Jones studied medicine and began practice in Savannah in 1756. He was elected to the colonial assembly for ten one-year terms before the Revolutionary War, serving as speaker in 1768—69. He was a member of the council of safety in 1775 and was sent as a delegate to the Continental Congress that same year. He moved to Charleston, South Carolina, in 1778, where he was captured by the British in 1780. Jones was imprisoned at St. Augustine, Florida, for a year until he was exchanged in 1781. Upon his release, Jones moved to Philadelphia, where he again represented Georgia in the Continental Congress 1781—82. After the British surrendered Savannah in 1782, Jones returned there and resumed his medical practice. He was president of the state constitutional convention in 1795. Jones died in Savannah on January 9, 1805.

- **WILLIE JONES**   1740—1801

Leader of the patriots in North Carolina, Willie Jones was born in Northampton County, North Carolina, on December 24, 1740, the younger brother of Allen Jones. After being educated at Eton College in England, he returned to North Carolina. In the years before the Revolutionary War he became leader of the colony's patriotic movement. He was president of the North Carolina committee of safety in 1776 and first governor ex officio of the new state. He was said to have written the state's first constitution adopted in 1776. Jones was elected to the state house of commons 1776—78, and was chosen as a member of the North Carolina delegation to the Continental Congress in 1780—81. Elected to the federal Constitutional Convention in 1787, he declined to accept, and led the opposition to ratification of the U.S. Constitution in 1788. When the Constitution was ratified, Jones dropped out of public life. He died at his summer home in Raleigh, North Carolina, on June 18, 1801.

• BARON DE KALB   1721−1780

A major general in the Continental Army who died while fighting, Johann Kalb was born in Huttendorf, Bavaria, on June 29, 1721. Joining the French army, he rose to the rank of brigadier general by 1776. He was engaged by Benjamin Franklin and Silas Deane to serve in the Continental Army and accompanied the Marquis de Lafayette to America in 1777. Appointed a major general by Congress, he served under the immediate command of General Washington until after the evacuation of Philadelphia in 1778, and then in New Jersey and Maryland. In April 1780 he led an army of Continental regiments south to the relief of Charleston, South Carolina, but was unable to get there in time to prevent its capture. He was briefly commander of the Continental Army in the South, but was succeeded by Gen. Horatio Gates. He was fatally wounded at the battle of Camden in South Carolina and died three days later on August 19, 1780.

Baron de Kalb

• JOHN KEAN   1756−1795

A financier and delegate to the Continental Congress, John Kean was born in Charleston, South Carolina, in 1756, where he became a well-to-do merchant. When Charleston was captured by the British in 1780, Kean was taken prisoner and confined aboard a prison ship for several months. At the end of the war Kean was appointed by General Washington a member of the commission to audit accounts of the Revolutionary Army. He served as a member of South Carolina's delegation to the Continental Congress 1785−87. He was appointed by President Washington in 1791 as cashier of the first Bank of the United States in Philadelphia and served in that position until his death in Philadelphia on May 4, 1795.

The Bank of Pennsylvania on South Second Street, Philadelphia, the first bank of the United States, opened in 1780.
—From an engraving by W. Birch & Son

Simon Kenton

• SIMON KENTON   1755–1836

A frontiersman who fought the British and the Indians during the Revolutionary War, Simon Kenton was born in Fauquier County, Virginia, on April 3, 1755. At sixteen he ran away from home believing he had killed another boy in a fist fight over a girl. Using the assumed name of Samuel Butler, he hunted, explored, and fought Indians alongside Daniel Boone and Simon Girty. He was a member of George Rogers Clark's expedition that captured Kaskaskia and Vincennes in 1778–79. In the remaining years of the war, he took part in three more expeditions against the Indians. He was captured by Indians twice—and twice escaped. After the war he learned the boy he believed he had killed was still alive, so he resumed use of his real name. After settling near Maysville, Kentucky, he joined Gen. Anthony Wayne's expedition against the Indians in 1794. During the War of 1812 he served as a brigadier general of militia at the battle of the Thames. Like Daniel Boone, Kenton lost most of the land he had struggled to win because of defective land titles. After years of living in poverty, Congress voted him a small pension in his old age. He died in Logan County, Ohio, on April 29, 1836.

• RUFUS KING   1755—1827

A signer of the U.S. Constitution and unsuccessful candidate for election as President of the United States, Rufus King was born in Scarboro, Maine (then a district of Massachusetts), on March 24, 1755. After graduation from Harvard College in 1777, he served as an aide to Brig. Gen. John Glover in the unsuccessful expedition of 1778 to try to recapture Rhode Island from the British. He studied law in Newburyport, Massachusetts, and commenced practice in 1780. He was a member of the Massachusetts delegation to the Continental Congress 1784–87 and to the federal Constitutional Convention at Philadelphia in 1787. A spokesman for the large states that wanted a strong national government, King happily signed the new U.S. Constitution. King moved to New York City in 1788 and immediately won election to the New York assembly. He then was elected as a Federalist from New York to the U.S. Senate from 1789 to 1796, when he resigned to accept appointment as U.S. minister to Britain. Upon his return to the United States, he ran as the unsuccessful Federalist candidate for Vice President of the United States in 1804 and in 1808. He again served in the U.S. Senate 1813–25, meanwhile running unsuccessfully for governor of New York in 1815 and for President of the United States in 1816. He again was U.S. minister to Britain 1825–26. He died in Jamaica, Long Island, New York, on April 29, 1827.

Mrs. Rufus King

Rufus King
—From a painting by Charles Willson Peale

265

• FRANCIS KINLOCH   1755–1826

A Revolutionary War officer and delegate to the Continental Congress, Francis Kinlock was born in Charleston, South Carolina, on March 7, 1755. After graduation from Eton College in England in 1774, he studied law at Lincoln's Inn, London, and then traveled in Europe with a view to a diplomatic career. Upon his return to the United States in 1777, he was commissioned a lieutenant. He fought in the Battle of Beaufort, in the defense of Charleston, and was wounded in the attack on Savannah in 1779. He was elected to the state house of representatives in 1779 and to the Continental Congress in 1780–81. He retired from public life in 1790 and made two tours of Europe. He died in Charleston, South Carolina, on February 8, 1826.

• JAMES KINSEY   1731–1803

A judge and delegate to the Continental Congress, James Kinsey was born in Philadelphia on March 22, 1731. After studying law, he began practice in Burlington County, New Jersey, in 1753. He was a member of the New Jersey general assembly 1772–75 and of the committee of correspondence for Burlington County in 1774–75. He also was a delegate to the Continental Congress in 1774–75. He served as chief justice of the supreme court of New Jersey from 1789 until his death in Burlington, New Jersey, on January 4, 1803.

• HENRY KNOX   1750–1806

A general in the Continental Army and the first United States Secretary of War, Henry Knox was born in Boston, Massachusetts, on July 25, 1750. He became a bookseller in Boston, owning the London Book-Store. A member of an artillery company at the beginning of the Revolutionary War, he took part in the battle of Bunker Hill. His skill as an artillery officer

Knox drew up a memorandum of the annual cost of living for himself and family for the year 1786. His family included his brother and himself, four or five children, two kinds of women servants, and one girl and two boys who were indentured servants:

Daily cost of food, including breakfast, dinner and supper, averaged at 20 shillings, York currency	365 pounds
House rent and taxes, including 20 pounds rent for stable	215
Expenses of keeping 2 hourses at 4 shillings per day	73
Keeping carriage and harness	15
Wine	180
24 extra dinners annually	120
2 women servants	38.8
2 men (clothing for indentured ones)	38.8
Clothing for myself and family	100
Schooling for my children	50
Furniture, including double bed	60
Charities, fire wood	80
Total	1335.6
Salary	980
Deficit	355.6

General Henry Knox
—From a painting by Gilbert Stuart

was called to the attention of George Washington, and as a colonel he was placed in command of the Continental Army's artillery. In the middle of winter in 1775–76, Knox supervised the removal of about 50 British cannon from captured Fort Ticonderoga and the arduous task of dragging them hundreds of miles to Boston on sledges pulled by oxen. There he set them up and proved their effectiveness in driving the British out of Boston. He and his artillerymen fought in the battle of Long Island in 1776, took part in the retreat to New Jersey, and in the battles of Trenton and Princeton. At the age of twenty-six Knox was appointed brigadier general in the Continental Army. He served loyally throughout the rest of

General Knox was distressed that after the war there was no organized army to help maintain a stable government. He listed what the United States solider drew in 1786 as follows:

1 coat
1 vest
1 pair breeches
1 woolen overalls
1 linen overalls
1 pair shoes
4 shirts
4 pair sox
1 stock and clasp
1 pair shoe buckles
Total value $24.80

267

the war, taking part in the battles of Brandywine, Germantown, Monmouth, and Yorktown. After the latter victory, he was appointed major general.

Upon Washington's retirement from the army in 1783, Knox served as commander in chief of the army for six months during its disbandment. He then was appointed Secretary of War by Congress under the Articles of Confederation in 1785. He continued in that position when Washington became President under the new United States Constitution in 1789. A large man, Knox weighed about 300 pounds, and enjoyed good company, becoming known as "the Philadelphia nabob" because of his generous hospitality. He retired as Secretary of War in 1795. His eating habits caused his death, when he swallowed a chicken bone, dying in Thomaston, Pennsylvania, on October 25, 1806.

• TADEUSZ KOSCIUSZKO   1746−1817

A Polish nobleman who fought for American independence and then tried to win freedom for his homeland from the Russians, Tadeusz Kosciuszko was born in Lithuania, Poland, on February 12, 1746. Serving in the Polish army as a captain at the outbreak of the Revolutionary War, he borrowed money to come to America to help fight against the British, bringing with him a letter of introduction to George Washington from Benjamin Franklin. "What can you do?" Washington is said to have asked, upon meeting him. "Try me," was Kosciuszko's reply.

Appointed as a colonel of engineers in the Continental Army in 1776, the fortifications he built at Saratoga played an important part in winning the victory on that battlefield in 1777. He then designed and built the fortifications at West Point. In the latter part of the Revolutionary War he served in the South under General Greene, both as an engineer and as a cavalry officer. At the end of the war he was brevetted as a brigadier general.

Returning to Poland, he served as a major general in the Polish army, fighting a losing war against a Russian invasion in 1792. Two years later at the head of an army of about 5,000 Poles, he defeated a Russian army at Raclawice on April 4, 1794, and set up a provisional Polish government with himself as its leader. Six months later, surrounded by a combined Prussian and Russian army, he was forced to surrender. After several years of imprisonment in Russia, Kosciuszko was pardoned. He returned to the United States in 1797, where he was awarded a grant of 500 acres of land in Ohio for his services during the Revolutionary War. Returning to France to live, he refused to assist Napoleon in his conquest of Europe because the French emperor would not agree to grant Poland independence. He died in Switzerland on October 15, 1817, when his horse slipped and fell over a cliff.

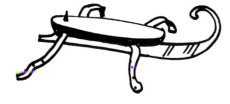

Tadeusz Kosciuszko
—From a print by A. Oleszozynski

A wealthy young Frenchman who became one of Washington's most trusted generals, the Marquis de Lafayette was born in Cavanac, France, on September 6, 1757. Orphaned at thirteen, young Lafayette inherited a huge fortune from his grandfather, as well as his title. He joined the French army at fourteen, and held a commission as captain at the age of eighteen when the Revolutionary War broke out in America.

Caught up with enthusiasm about the American ideas of liberty, he decided to volunteer his services. Outfitting a ship at his own expense, and disobeying orders of the French king who told him not to go, Lafayette sailed for America in 1777, taking with him the Baron de Kalb and several other French officers. Offering to serve without pay, Lafayette was commissioned a major general by Congress in July 1777 while he was still nineteen.

Washington liked the ardent young Frenchman and made him a close friend and adviser. In his first battle at Brandywine, Pennsylvania, in September 1777, Lafayette fought bravely and was wounded, raising him higher in the estimation of his American comrades. After recovering from his wound, Lafayette led 300 troops in a successful skirmish with Hessian soldiers under command of Lord Cornwallis at Gloucester, New Jersey, in November 1777. At Washington's urging, Congress the next month gave Lafayette command of a division of Virginia infantry, and in January 1778 sent him to command a proposed invasion of Canada. When enough troops and supplies could not be gathered for the Canadian expedition, Layfayette recommended calling it off and returned to Washington's headquarters. He narrowly escaped capture by the British in the battle of Barren Hill, Pennsylvania, in May 1778, and then took part in the battle of Monmouth, New Jersey. In the summer of 1778 he commanded two American divisions in the unsuccessful effort to recapture Newport, Rhode Island, from the British.

Realizing that more help was needed from France if the Americans were to win the Revolution, Lafayette returned home in 1779. In France he persuaded the king and his ministers to send money, troops, and ships to help Washington's army.

Arriving back in America in 1780, he was given command of American troops in Virginia, where he skillfully dueled with the British forces of Cornwallis, gradually working that general into the position from which he was unable to escape at the battle of Yorktown. In December 1781 Lafayette sailed back to France to obtain more reinforcements for the American cause, and was there when the war ended in 1783. The following year he again visited the United States, at Washington's invitation, where he received the thanks of the country for his services.

Marie Joseph Paul Yves Roch Gilbert du Motier, marquis de Lafayette

An interview between Lafayette, Marie Antoinette, and Louis XVI —From a painting by C.H. Schmolsze

As commander of the French national guard in 1789, he saved the king and queen of France from the Paris mob. He commanded a French army in a war between France and Austria in 1792, but was relieved as commander by the radical revolutionaries. Fleeing to Belgium to escape being executed with other French nobles, he was taken prisoner by Austrian forces and imprisoned in a dungeon for five years. Freed by Napoleon's troops in 1797, he went home to France, no longer a wealthy man. In 1824, at the invitation of President James Monroe, he again visited the United States for a year-long tour of the nation in which he was honored with parades and celebrations in many cities.

Again commander of the French national guard in 1830, Lafayette led the July Revolution that overthrew the Bourbon ruler of France, Charles X, but he refused to allow himself to be made president of a new French republic. Sacrificing his own desires for a republic, he placed Louis Philippe on the throne in the belief that this was the best course to preserve order in the nation. Four years later the seventy-six-year-old hero of America and France died on May 20, 1834.

General John Lamb

• JOHN LAMB 1735–1800

One of the most active Sons of Liberty agitators in New York City in the years before the Revolutionary War and an artillery officer in the Continental Army throughout the war, John Lamb was born in New York City on January 1, 1735. A successful merchant, he became incensed at the British government over the Stamp Act in 1765, helped organize the Sons of Liberty to oppose it, and then worked for the next ten years to help overthrow British power.

In April 1775, when he received word of the battles of Lexington and Concord, he and fellow-patriot Isaac captured the British custom house and helped prevent British ships from leaving New York. Commissioned as a captain of a New York artillery company in July 1775, he and his men marched to Canada hauling their artillery pieces as part of General Montgomery's army. During the attack on Quebec on New Year's Eve 1775, Lamb was wounded and taken prisoner by the British. Paroled because of his wound, Lamb was unable to resume his military career until 1777, when he was officially exchanged. Promoted to colonel in command of the 2nd Continental Artillery Regiment, he distinguished himself and was wounded while breaking up a British attack at the battle of Campo Hill in Connecticut in April 1778. From 1779 to 1780 he commanded the artillery at West Point. Lamb and his artillerymen marched south with Washington's army to take part in the battle of Yorktown, in which he won praise for his leadership. At the end of the war he was brevetted a brigadier general. In 1789 President Washington appointed Lamb as collector of customs in New York, a post he held until his death on May 31, 1800.

John Langdon
—From a painting by John Sharples

• JOHN LANGDON 1741–1819

A signer of the United States Constitution and first president pro tempore of the U.S. Senate, John Langdon was born in Portsmouth, New Hampshire, on June 25, 1741, the younger brother of Woodbury Langdon. After serving an apprenticeship as a clerk to a merchant, Langdon entered business for himself as a shipbuilder and trader, becoming the wealthiest man in New Hampshire by the time of the Revolutionary War. When the British forbade the export of gunpowder in 1774, Langdon and John Sullivan led 400 patriots on December 13 to Fort William and Mary in Portsmouth harbor, where they overpowered the British soldiers and captured 100 barrels of gunpowder for the patriot cause. He was a member of the Continental Congress in 1775–77, where, because of his shipbuilding experience, he was appointed Navy agent and superintended the construction of several ships of war. He was elected speaker of the New Hampshire house of representatives 1776–81. When word came that British Gen. John Burgoyne was invading New England from Canada in 1777, Langdon used his personal fortune to equip Gen. John Stark's brigade and then joined the troops as a captain, fighting at the Battles of Bennington and Saratoga.

He later served as a colonel in the attempt to recapture Rhode Island from the British in 1778. He was again elected a delegate to the Continental Congress in 1786–87 and to the federal Constitutional Convention in 1787, where he signed the new United States Constitution. He was elected as one of New Hampshire's first U.S. Senators 1789–1801, and was chosen as the first President pro tempore of the U.S. Senate on April 6, 1789, to count the first electoral vote for President and Vice President of the United States. He also was elected

This house in Portsmouth, New Hampshire, constructed in 1758, was a boarding house where John Paul Jones resided in 1779 while the 74-gun ship America *was being fitted. The ship was ultimately given to France. The house was acquired by the Portsmouth Historical Society in 1920.*
—Sketch by Kay Smith

273

president or governor of New Hampshire in 1788–89, 1805–09, and 1810–12. He declined the Democratic nomination as candidate for Vice President in 1812. Langdon died in Portsmouth on September 18, 1819.

- **WOODBURY LANGDON**   1739–1805

A delegate to the Continental Congress, Woodbury Langdon was born in Portsmouth, New Hampshire, in 1739, the elder brother of John Langdon. He also became a wealthy merchant, but was a less ardent patriot than his brother. At the beginning of the Revolutionary War he went to England to protect his financial interests. When he returned to America in 1777, he was captured and imprisoned by the British in New York, but escaped later that year. He served in the state house of representatives in 1778–79, and was a member of the Continental Congress in 1779–80. He then was a member of the State executive council 1781–84, and judge of the state superior court in 1782 and 1786–91. He died in Portsmouth on January 13, 1805.

- **EDWARD LANGWORTHY**   1738–1802

A signer of the Articles of Confederation, Edward Langworthy was born in Savannah, Georgia, in 1738. An orphan, he grew up in the Bethesda Orphan House, and later became an instructor in the institution. He helped organize the Georgia council of safety and became its secretary in 1775. He was chosen as one of Georgia's delegates to the Continental Congress 1777–79, where he signed the Articles of Confederation. After the war he moved to Baltimore, Maryland, where he worked as a newspaper editor 1785–87, and then as a teacher of the classics in Baltimore Academy 1787–91. He then moved to Elkton, Maryland, where he wrote a history of Georgia. He returned to Baltimore in 1795, and was employed as clerk of customs until his death in Baltimore on November 2, 1802.

- **JOHN LAURANCE**   1750–1810

Judge Advocate General of the Continental Army and later a U.S. Senator, John Laurance was born in Cornwall, England, in 1750. At seventeen, he immigrated to New York City, where he studied law and began practice in 1772. Upon the outbreak of the Revolutionary War he was commissioned a lieutenant in the 4th New York Regiment and took part in the invasion of Canada in 1775. General Washington appointed him Judge Advocate General of the army in 1777, and as such he was prosecutor of the cases of Maj. John André and Benedict Arnold. After the war, he returned to his law practice and served as a delegate to the Continental Congress 1785–87.

Henry Laurens
—From a painting by Charles Willson Peale

He was elected as one of New York's U.S. Representatives in the First and Second Congresses 1789–93. He was appointed by President Washington as U.S. judge of the district of New York in 1794, serving until 1796, when he was elected to the U.S. Senate. He served as President pro tempore of the Senate from 1798 until he resigned in 1800. Laurance died in New York City on November 11, 1810.

• **HENRY LAURENS   1724—1792**

The fifth President of the Continental Congress, Henry Laurens was born in Charleston, South Carolina, on March 6, 1724. After a business education in England 1744–47, he returned to Charleston where he became the city's wealthiest merchant in the pre-Revolutionary years. In 1757–61 he served as lieutenant colonel in a campaign against the Cherokee Indians. He was regularly elected to the colony's assembly from 1757 to 1775. Laurens became one of the most influential leaders in South Carolina's patriotic movement, serving as president of the South Carolina Revolutionary congress and the council of safety in 1775–76. He was elected as a delegate to the Continental Congress 1777–80, serving as President from November 1, 1777, to December 9, 1778. Elected minister to Holland by the Continental Congress on October 21, 1779, he sailed for his post early in 1780. The British captured his ship on the voyage and held him a prisoner in the Tower of London for fifteen months, until he was released on December 31, 1781, in exchange for Lord Cornwallis. Laurens was then appointed one of the peace commissioners and signed the preliminary treaty of Paris on November 30, 1782. After his return to the United States in 1784, he retired to his plantation, where he declined all efforts to get him to return to public service. He died on December 8, 1792, at his estate, "Mepkin," on the Cooper River near Charleston.

• JOHN LAURENS   1753–1782

An aide-de-camp to General Washington and a brave officer who was killed in a British ambush during the Revolutionary War, John Laurens was born in Charleston, South Carolina, in 1753, the son of Henry Laurens. After being educated in England, he returned to America shortly after the Revolutionary War began. Volunteering his services to Washington, he became the general's secretary, and because of his fluency in French and German acted as translator in Washington's conversations with his foreign officers. He fought in the battles of Brandywine, Germantown, and Monmouth in 1777 to 1778. In December 1778, when General Charles Lee spoke disparagingly of General Washington, Laurens challenged him to a duel and wounded Lee. In 1779 he was commissioned as a lieutenant colonel. When the British invaded South Carolina, he returned home and joined the militia, fighting at Charleston and Savannah. Captured at the battle of Charleston, he was soon exchanged and released. In 1781, while his father was being held prisoner in the Tower of London, young Laurens was sent by Congress to France to assist Franklin in obtaining more help from the French. Returning to America later that year, he took part in the battle of Yorktown, where he distinguished himself by capturing an artillery battery and receiving the sword of its commander. While trying to round up enemy foragers at Combahee Ferry, South Carolina, on August 27, 1782, Laurens was killed from ambush.

• RICHARD LAW   1733–1806

A judge and delegate to the Continental Congress, Richard Law was born in Milford, Connecticut, on March 7, 1733. After graduation from Yale College at eighteen, he studied law and began practice in Milford in 1755, later moving to New

John Laurens

London, Connecticut. He served as a member of the Connecticut council of safety in 1776, and as a member of the Governor's council 1776–86. He was chosen as a delegate to the Continental Congress in 1778 and 1783–84. For twenty-two years Law was elected and re-elected mayor of New London 1784–1806. He also was judge of the supreme court of Connecticut 1784–89, serving the last four years as chief justice. Law was appointed by President Washington as U.S. district judge for Connecticut in 1789, a position he held until his death in New London on January 26, 1806.

• EBENEZER LEARNED   1721–1801

A general in the Continental Army, Ebenezer Learned was born in Oxford, Massachusetts, in 1721. Having served in the French and Indian War as a captain, he hurried to join the militia at Cambridge, Massachusetts, as soon as he heard of the battles of Lexington and Concord. Commissioned as colonel in the militia, he and his men took part in the battle of Bunker Hill. In 1776 he was made a colonel in the Continental Army, and was given the honor of leading the first American troops into Boston after the British evacuated the city. After being ill for nearly a year, he was promoted to brigadier general in April 1777 and returned to duty. He and his troops took part in the battles of Saratoga in 1777. After spending the winter at Valley Forge, Learned resigned from the army in March 1778 because of his continuing ill health. He died at his home in Oxford on April 1, 1801.

• ARTHUR LEE   1740–1792

A diplomat and delegate to the Continental Congress, Arthur Lee was born at "Stratford," in Westmoreland County, Virginia, on December 20, 1740, a younger brother of Francis Lightfoot Lee and Richard Henry Lee. After attending Eton College in England, he studied medicine at the University of Edinburgh in Scotland, and was graduated in 1765. He then studied law at the Temple Bar in London 1766–70, and practiced law in London 1770–76. He was commissioned as agent of Massachusetts in England and France in 1770, correspondent of Congress in London in 1775, commissioner to France in 1776, and commissioner to Spain in 1777. During this period he wrote many articles supporting the patriotic cause in America, but he also stirred much trouble by his accusations of dishonesty on the part of other American diplomats, including Silas Deane and Benjamin Franklin. Lee returned to Virginia in 1780, where he was elected to the state house of delegates 1781–83 and 1785–86. He was chosen as one of Virginia's delegates to the Continental Congress 1781–84. Lee died on December 12, 1792, at his home, "Lansdowne," in Urbana, Virginia.

Arthur Lee

277

• CHARLES LEE 1731—1782

A Continental Army general—third in command to George Washington—whose conduct did more to help the British than the Americans, Charles Lee was born in Dernhall, England, in 1731, the son of an army officer. Joining his father's regiment as a boy, Lee was commissioned an ensign at sixteen and a lieutenant at twenty. During the French and Indian War in 1754 he was sent to America with his regiment, taking part in General Edward Braddock's defeat at Fort Duquesne (Pittsburgh) in 1755. Going north to the Mohawk Valley with the remnants of his regiment, he bought a commission as captain and married the daughter of an Indian chief. With his regiment he fought at Ticonderoga, Niagara, and Montreal. Returning to England in 1760, he was promoted to major and then served in Portugal. When his regiment was disbanded at the end of the war in 1763, Lee retired at half-pay. He then became a major general in the Polish army, served briefly in the Russian army, and finally returned to America in 1773. After purchasing an estate in Virginia, Lee became an outspoken revolutionary, urging the training of an American army in preparation for war against the British.

Upon the outbreak of the Revolutionary War, Congress offered him a commission as major general in the Continental Army, ranking third after Washington and Artemas Ward. Lee, however, refused to accept the commission until Congress paid him $30,000 for loss of property and loss of his retirement pension as a British officer. After receiving the payment, Lee proceeded to Boston, where he took part in the siege. Contemptuous of the ill-trained American soldiers and jealous of Washington, Lee did little to further the war effort. In December 1776 the British captured Lee at a tavern in Basking Ridge, New Jersey. Although it did not become known until many years after Lee's death, during his captivity by the British in New York City he tried to interest his jailers in plans to break the American rebellion by capturing Pennsylvania, Virginia, and Maryland, a plan later adopted by the British.

Upon Lee's exchange as a prisoner in 1778, he rejoined the Continental Army and was given field command of the army with which Washington hoped to destroy the British as they evacuated Philadelphia. In the ensuing battle of Monmouth in New Jersey on June 28, 1778, Lee ordered a retreat rather than an attack. Learning of the debacle, Washington galloped to the scene, roundly cursed out Lee for disobeying orders, and relieved him of his command. A week after the battle Lee was brought before a court-martial, and after a trial that lasted a month was found guilty of disobedience, misbehavior, and disrespect to Washington. He was sentenced to a year's suspension from command. When Lee continued to speak and publish aspersions about Washington, the general's aide-de-

*A highboy
of the colonial period*
—Sketch by Kay Smith

camp, Colonel John Laurens, challenged Lee to a duel and wounded him. Lee retired to his Virginia estate in 1779 and the following year was dismissed from the army by Congress. On a visit to Philadelphia in 1782 he became ill with a fever and died on October 2.

- ## FRANCIS LIGHTFOOT LEE   1734–1797

A signer of the Declaration of Independence, Francis Light-foot Lee was born at "Stratford," in Westmoreland County, Virginia, on October 14, 1734, a brother of Arthur Lee and Richard Henry Lee. After receiving an education from private tutors, he served as a member of Virginia's house of burgesses for eighteen years 1758–75. As one of Virginia's delegates to the Continental Congress 1775–80, he signed the Declaration of Independence. Lee then served in the Virginia state senate 1778–82. Lee died at his home, "Menoken," in Richmond County, Virginia, on January 11, 1797.

- ## HENRY "LIGHT-HORSE HARRY" LEE   1756–1818

Cavalry leader, governor, and member of Congress, Henry Lee was born at "Leesylvania," in Prince William County, Virginia, on January 29, 1756, an older brother of Richard Bland Lee. At seventeen Lee was graduated from Princeton College, and at twenty he was commissioned captain of a company of Virginia Dragoons in 1776. Lee distinguished himself with defense of the Spread Eagle Tavern near Valley Forge, Pennsylvania, in January 1778. A special act of Congress in April promoted him to major in command of a separate cavalry corps that later became known as "Lee's Legion." His raid on Paulus Hook, New Jersey, on August 19, 1779, captured over 150 British soldiers and officers, and won him one of the eight gold medals awarded by Congress during the Revolutionary War. At twenty-four he was promoted to lieutenant colonel in 1780. During the next year "Light-Horse Harry," as he was called, led his cavalry brilliantly in a series of battles in Gen. Nathanael Greene's Southern campaign. With the end of the fighting in 1782, Lee retired from the army. He was chosen as one of Virginia's delegates to the Continental Congress 1785–88, and was elected governor of Virginia 1791–94. When an invasion by France was feared in 1798, he was commissioned as a major general in the new U.S. Army. Elected as a Federalist to the Sixth U.S. Congress 1799–1801, he delivered a eulogy upon the death of George Washington in 1799 before both branches of Congress, in which he described his former commander as "first in war, first in peace, and first in the hearts of his countrymen." Living beyond his means, Lee was imprisoned for debt in 1808–9. He then lived in the West Indies for several years. He died on

Henry Lee

279

Cumberland Island, Georgia, on March 25, 1818. His son, Robert E. Lee, was commander of the Confederate Army in the Civil War.

• **RICHARD BLAND LEE**   **1761–1827**

One of Virginia's first representatives in the U.S. Congress, Richard Bland Lee was born at "Leesylvania," in Prince William County, Virginia, on January 20, 1761, a younger brother of Henry Lee. After attending William and Mary College, he was elected to the state house of delegates 1784–88, and then was elected to the First, Second, and Third U.S. Congresses 1789–95 where he was instrumental in selection of the site for Washington, D.C. He was again a member of the state house of delegates 1796 and 1799–1806. He was appointed by President Madison in 1816 as commissioner to adjudicate claims arising out of the loss or destruction of property during the War of 1812. In 1819 he was appointed by President Monroe as judge of the Orphans' Court of the District of Columbia, serving in this position until his death in Washington, D.C., on March 12, 1827.

• **RICHARD HENRY LEE**   **1732–1794**

A signer of the Declaration of Independence and the twelfth President of the Continental Congress, Richard Henry Lee was born at "Stratford," in Westmoreland County, Virginia, on January 20, 1732, an older brother of Arthur Lee and Francis Lightfoot Lee. After being educated at Wakefield Academy in England, Lee returned to Virginia in 1751. His seventeen years of service in Virginia's house of burgesses 1758–75 made him one of the colony's most influential leaders. In 1773 Lee organized Virginia's committee of correspondence to pass information on patriotic activities from colony to colony.

As a member of the Continental Congress 1774–80, Lee introduced the resolution of June 7, 1776, that led to adoption of the Declaration of Independence, which he signed. Lee also was author of the first national Thanksgiving Day proclamation issued by Congress at York, Pennsylvania, on October 31, 1777, after the capture of Burgoyne's army at Saratoga, New York. As colonel of the Westmoreland County militia, Lee fought off the British at Stratford Landing on April 9, 1781. He again was a member of the Continental Congress 1784–87 and was elected as the twelfth President of the Congress from November 30, 1784 to November 23, 1785. Lee opposed ratification of the United States Constitution, but accepted election as one of Virginia's first U.S. Senators 1789–92. Lee died at his home, "Chantilly," in Westmoreland County, Virginia, on June 19, 1794.

Richard Henry Lee

• THOMAS SIM LEE   1745–1819

A delegate to the Continental Congress and governor of Maryland, Thomas Sim Lee was born near Upper Marlboro, Maryland, on October 29, 1745. After holding several lesser offices, he was elected governor of Maryland 1779–83, and then served as a member of the Continental Congress in 1783–84. He again was elected governor in 1792–94. But when he was elected governor for a third time in 1798, he declined to serve. Lee died at his plantation, "Needwood," in Frederick County, Maryland, on October 9, 1819.

Pierre L'Enfant

• PIERRE L'ENFANT   1755–1825

An officer in the Continental Army during the Revolutionary War and later designer of the capital city of Washington, D.C., Pierre L'Enfant was born in Paris in 1755, the son of an artist. He came to America with Lafayette in 1777 and became a lieutenant of engineers. Serving under the command of Colonel John Laurens in the South, he was wounded at the battle of Savannah in 1779 and was captured at the fall of Charleston in 1780. Held prisoner by the British for two years, he finally was exchanged in 1782. At the end of the war he was brevetted as a major. Turning to art and architecture, he supervised the conversion of New York's city hall into Federal

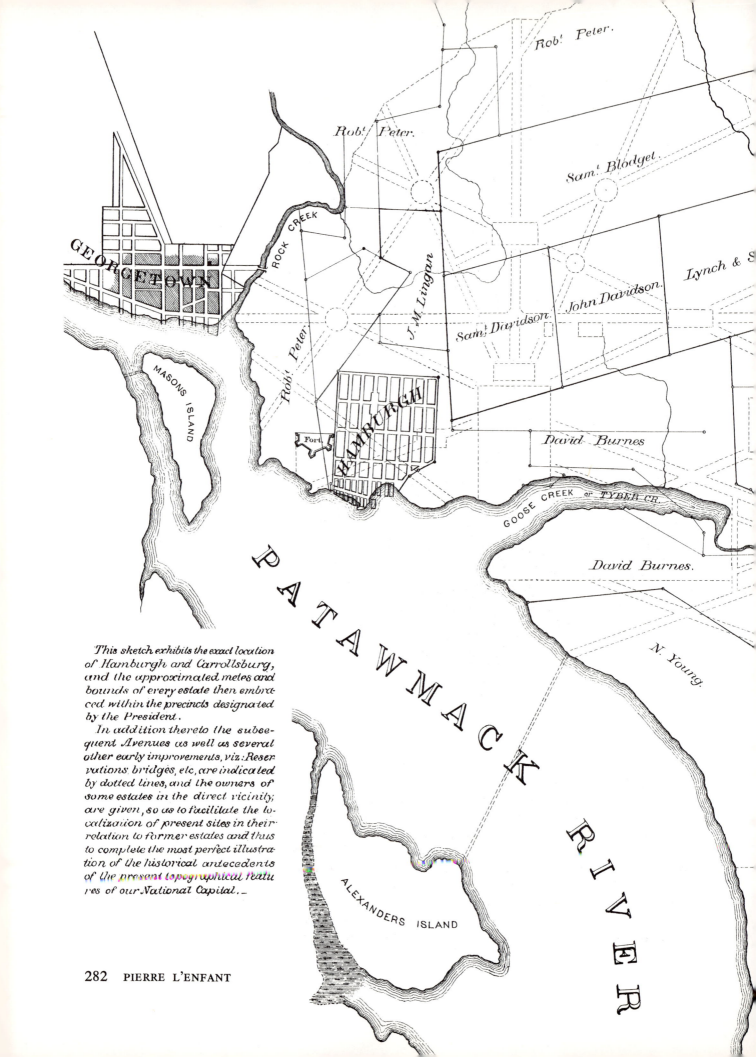

Rob.ᵗ Peter.

Rob.ᵗ Peter.

Sam.ᵗ Blodget.

ROCK CREEK

GEORGETOWN

J. M. Lingan

Rob.ᵗ Peter.

John Davidson.

Lynch & S

Sam.ᵗ Davidson.

MASONS ISLAND

HAMBURGH

Fort

David Burnes

GOOSE CREEK or TYBER CR.

David Burnes.

This sketch exhibits the exact location of Hamburgh and Carrollsburg, and the approximated metes and bounds of every estate then embraced within the precincts designated by the President.

In addition thereto the subsequent Avenues as well as several other early improvements, viz: Reservations, bridges, etc, are indicated by dotted lines, and the owners of some estates in the direct vicinity, are given, so as to facilitate the localization of present sites in their relation to former estates and thus to complete the most perfect illustration of the historical antecedents of the present topographical features of our National Capital.—

P A T A W M A C K   R I V E R

N. Young.

ALEXANDERS ISLAND

282   PIERRE L'ENFANT

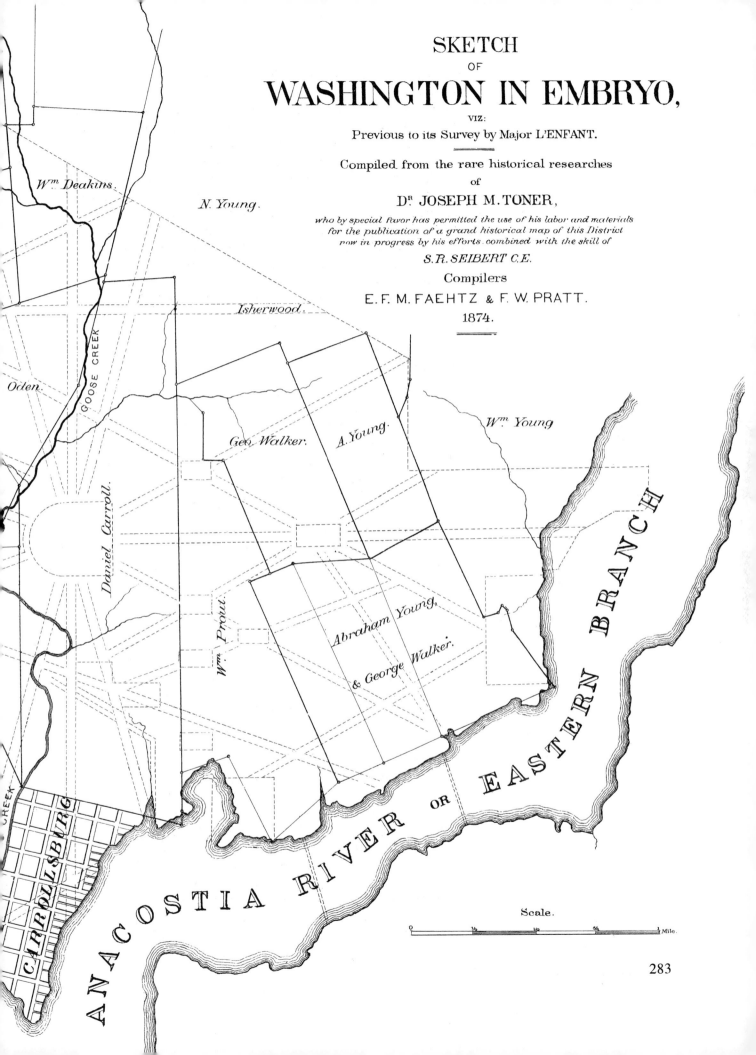

SKETCH

OF

WASHINGTON IN EMBRYO,

VIZ:

Previous to its Survey by Major L'ENFANT.

Compiled from the rare historical researches

of

DR. JOSEPH M. TONER,

who by special favor has permitted the use of his labor and materials
for the publication of a grand historical map of this District
now in progress by his efforts combined with the skill of

S. R. SEIBERT C.E.

Compilers

E. F. M. FAEHTZ & F. W. PRATT.

1874.

Wm. Deakins.

N. Young.

Isherwood.

Oden.

GOOSE CREEK

Geo. Walker.

A. Young.

Wm. Young

Daniel Carroll.

Wm. Prout.

Abraham Young,

& George Walker.

CARROLLSBURG

CREEK

ANACOSTIA RIVER OR EASTERN BRANCH

Scale.

0   ¼   ½   ¾   1 Mile.

283

Hall when Congress moved the capital to that city from Philadelphia in 1785.

When Congress decided to build a new federal city in the District of Columbia, L'Enfant in 1791 laid out a plan, at least a century ahead of his time, in which the streets were laid out in a rectangular checkerboard, but with broad avenues radiating diagonally across the design to carry traffic quickly to and from the main government buildings at the center of the city. Because he was argumentative with officials who wished to change his plan, L'Enfant was dismissed from supervising the actual construction of his plan. During the last years of his life, L'Enfant repeatedly petitioned Congress for commissions that he believed were owed him for his design. He died in poverty in Prince George's County, Maryland, on June 14, 1825.

• GEORGE LEONARD   1729–1819

One of Massachusetts' first Representatives in the U.S. Congress, George Leonard was born in Norton, Massachusetts, on July 4, 1729. After graduation from Harvard College in 1748, he studied law and commenced practice in Norton in 1750. He was a member of the colonial assembly 1764–66 and an executive councillor 1770–75. He was appointed judge of the probate court 1784–90 and judge of the common pleas court 1785–98. He was elected to the First U.S. Congress 1789–91, and to the Fourth U.S. Congress 1795–97. He served as chief justice of the court of common pleas 1798–1804. Leonard died in Raynham, Massachusetts, on July 26, 1819.

• ANDREW LEWIS   1730–1781

A general in the Continental Army, Andrew Lewis was born in Donegal, Ireland, in 1730. As a baby, he was brought to America by his parents in 1732 and grew up at Staunton, Virginia. During the French and Indian War he served as a major of Virginia militia during General Edward Braddock's defeat at Fort Duquesne (Pittsburgh) in 1755. He later was taken prisoner by the French and imprisoned in Montreal. As a brigadier general of Virginia militia, he commanded a force of about 1,200 troops in defeating an Indian army under the Shawnee chief Cornstalk in the battle of Point Pleasant in what is now West Virginia, on October 10, 1774. Lewis was appointed a brigadier general in the Continental Army in 1776, and commanded the troops that drove the British governor, Lord Dunmore, out of Virginia. When Congress failed to promote him to major general in 1777, Lewis resigned from the army, claiming ill health. He died in Bedford County, Virginia, on September 26, 1781.

• FRANCIS LEWIS   1713–1803

A signer of the Declaration of Independence, Francis Lewis was born in Llandaff, Wales, in March 1713. After apprenticeship in a London counting house, he immigrated to America in 1735. He established stores in New York and Philadelphia, and became a wealthy man after obtaining a contract to clothe the British Army in America in 1753. Lewis fought in the French and Indian War, and was captured at Fort Oswego, New York, in 1756. He was held prisoner in France for several years. On his return the colonial government gave him 5,000 acres of land in recognition of his services. He was elected as one of New York's delegates to the Stamp Act Congress that met in New York City in 1765. He was chosen as a member of the Continental Congress 1774–79, where he signed the Declaration of Independence. In 1776 British cavalry destroyed his home on Long Island, New York, near the present site of the Whitestone bridge, and carried off his wife, who was mistreated and held prisoner for nearly two years. He died in New York City on December 30, 1803. His son, Morgan Lewis (1754–1844), was an officer in the Continental Army and governor of New York 1804–07.

Francis Lewis

• EZRA L'HOMMEDIEU   1734–1811

A member of the Continental Congress, Ezra L'Hommedieu was born in Southold, Long Island, New York, on August 30, 1734. After graduation from Yale College in 1754, he studied law and practiced in Southold. He was elected to New York's Revolutionary congress 1775–77 and to the state assembly 1777–83. He was chosen as a delegate to the Continental Congress 1779–83 and 1787–88. He was elected to the state senate 1784–92 and 1794–1809. For twenty-seven years, from 1784 to his death, L'Hommedieu was clerk of Suffolk County. He died in Southold on September 27, 1811.

• BENJAMIN LINCOLN   1733–1810

A major general in the Continental Army who received the surrender of the British in the major victory at Yorktown, Benjamin Lincoln was born in Hingham, Massachusetts on January 24, 1733. A farmer, he was a lieutenant colonel of militia at the beginning of the Revolutionary War and hurried to Cambridge, Massachusetts, with other Minutemen at the outbreak of fighting. A good officer, he was steadily promoted, advancing to major general in the Massachusetts militia in 1776. Given command of the Massachusetts troops sent to reinforce New York City in September 1776, he impressed General Washington with his ability. He was appointed a major general in the Continental Army in February 1777. He commanded the New England militia in the defeat of British

General Benjamin Lincoln

285

General John Burgoyne at the battles of Saratoga in 1777, where he received a leg wound that put him out of action for nearly a year and left him with a severe limp for the rest of his life. Returning to service, Lincoln was placed in command of American troops in the South in September 1778. He arrived in Georgia too late to prevent the British capture of Savannah in December. Although he fought against the superior British forces with determination during the next months, the British finally forced him to surrender his army at Charleston, South Carolina, in May 1780.

Freed by a prisoner exchange several months later, Lincoln was given command of the American divisions that engaged in the battle of Yorktown. General Washington designated Lincoln to accept the formal British surrender in the conclusive victory that followed. Two weeks after the Yorktown victory, Congress appointed Lincoln as Secretary of War on October 30, 1781, a position he held for two years, until the end of the Revolutionary War. In 1787 he commanded the Massachusetts troops that suppressed Shays' Rebellion, and that same year was elected lieutenant governor of Massachusetts. When he was defeated for re-election in 1789, President Washington appointed him as collector of the port of Boston, a position he held for the next twenty years. Lincoln died in Hingham on May 9, 1810.

- ## SAMUEL LIVERMORE   1732–1803

A delegate to the Continental Congress and U.S. Senator, Samuel Livermore was born in Waltham, Massachusetts, on May 14, 1732. After graduation from Princeton College in 1752, he studied law and commenced practice in Waltham in 1756. He moved to New Hampshire in 1758. He was elected a member of New Hampshire's delegation to the Continental Congress 1780–83 and 1785–86. He served as chief justice of the New Hampshire supreme court 1782–89. Livermore was elected as one of the state's first Representatives to the U.S. Congress 1789–93, and then to the U.S. Senate 1793–1801. He died in Holderness, New Hampshire, on May 18, 1803.

- ## PHILIP LIVINGSTON   1716–1778

A signer of the Declaration of Independence, Philip Livingston was born in Albany, New York, on January 15, 1716. After graduation from Yale College in 1737, he became a wealthy merchant in New York City. He was a New York City alderman 1754–62, and a member of the colonial legislature 1763–69, serving as speaker of the house in 1768–69. He was chosen as one of New York's delegates to the Stamp Act Congress in October 1765. As leader of New York's conservative patriots, he was a delegate to the Continental Congress 1774–78, where he signed the Declaration of Independ-

Philip Livingston

ence. Livingston died while attending the sixth session of the Continental Congress in York, Pennsylvania, on June 12, 1778. He was a brother of William Livingston, uncle of Robert R. Livingston, and father of Walter Livingston.

• ROBERT R. LIVINGSTON 1746–1813

A delegate to the Continental Congress and first Secretary of Foreign Affairs, Robert R. Livingston was born in New York City on November 27, 1746. After graduation at eighteen from King's College (now Columbia University), he studied law and commenced practice in New York in 1773. He was a member of New York's Revolutionary convention of 1775. A New York delegate to the Continental Congress 1775–77 and 1779–81, he was one of the committee of five appointed to draw up the Declaration of Independence but was opposed to immediate independence and returned to duties in the New York assembly before the Declaration was signed.

He was chosen by Congress as Secretary of Foreign Affairs from August 1781 to August 1783, during the period peace was negotiated with Britain. He served twenty-five years as chancellor (chief judge) of New York state 1777–1801 and administered the oath of office to President Washington on April 30, 1789. President Jefferson appointed him as minister to France 1801–1804, during which time he negotiated the Louisiana Purchase from Napoleon. He was a partner of Robert Fulton in constructing the first practical steamboat, the *Clermont*, in 1807. He died on his estate "Clermont," near Clermont, New York, on February 26, 1813. His son, Henry Beekman Livingston (1750–1831), fought as an officer in the Revolutionary War. Robert R. Livingston was a nephew of Philip Livingston and William Livingston.

• WALTER LIVINGSTON 1740–1797

A member of the Continental Congress, Walter Livingston was born in New York City on November 27, 1740, the son of Philip Livingston. He was a delegate to the Revolutionary convention and congress in New York in 1775. Livingston aided the Continental Army as commissary of stores and provisions for the department of New York 1775–76 and as deputy commissary general of the northern department in the same period. He was elected to the state assembly 1777–79, serving as speaker in 1778–79. He was chosen as a member of New York's delegation to the Continental Congress in 1784–85. Livingston died in New York City on May 14, 1797.

• WILLIAM LIVINGSTON 1723–1790

The first state governor of New Jersey and a signer of the United States Constitution, William Livingston was born in

Robert Livingston

287

Liberty Hall, the residence of William Livingston

William Livingston

Albany, New York, on November 30, 1723. After graduation from Yale College at seventeen, he studied law and commenced practice in New York City in 1748. A Presbyterian, he established and edited the *Independent Reflector* 1752–53, in which he attacked the Church of England. He was active in organizing the Sons of Liberty during the Stamp Act crisis in 1765. Having become wealthy from his law practice, Livingston decided at the age of forty-nine to retire to an estate, "Liberty Hall," that he owned in New Jersey, near Elizabethtown (now Elizabeth). He was a member of the Continental Congress in 1774–76, but left the Congress before the Declaration of Independence was adopted, having been given command of New Jersey's militia as a brigadier general.

On August 31, 1776, he was elected as New Jersey's first state governor, an office he held for the next fourteen years until his death. He was one of New Jersey's delegates to the federal Constitutional Convention in Philadelphia in 1787 and was one of the signers of the new United States Constitution. Livingston died in Elizabethtown on July 25, 1790. His son, Henry Brockholst Livingston (1757–1823), fought as an officer in the Revolutionary War and became an associate justice of the U.S. Supreme Court. William Livingston was a brother of Philip Livingston and uncle of Robert T. Livingston.

FROM A WATERCOLOR PAINTING BY KAY SMITH

This stone structure in Newburgh, New York, served as Washington's headquarters from April 1, 1782 until August 18, 1783. The building was started in 1725 and enlarged about 1750 by Jonathan Hasbrouck. In 1770 there was another remodeling and enlargement to its present size and appearance. It was in this building that the Order of the Purple Heart was established and it was here that Washington wrote his famous letter rejecting the suggestion that he become king with surprise and astonishment, "viewed with abhorrence and reprimanded with severity." The headquarters were always overcrowded, and when a visitor remained overnight he had to arise early so that his cot might be made up and the room turned over to the General as an office. Martha Washington spent a number of months here as hostess to officers and their wives. Here also, on April 10, 1783, Washington announced the cessation of hostilities.

Fort Putnam at West Point,
New York, 451 feet above the
Hudson River overlooking
the plains of West Point,
helped defend the lower forts,
which were strategically
placed close enough to the
Hudson River to prevent
enemy ships from penetrating
the interior of New York
and New England to the north.
The river was an important
communication and supply link
between New York and the
interior, so it had to be
kept secure at all costs.
Construction of the fort
during the Revolutionary War
was an engineering feat
necessitating the transportation
of huge boulders and mortar
to the top of the steep hills
that line both shores of the
Hudson River at this point.
It was this fort and others
that Benedict Arnold intended
to deliver to the British
in the most treasonous act
in American history.

FROM A WATERCOLOR PAINTING BY KAY SMITH

Near Newburgh, New York, this is known as the John Ellison House, which served as headquarters of Generals Knox and Gates during the Revolutionary War. Construction was begun in 1734—with an addition in 1754—and was completed in 1782. Today, furnished with period furniture, the house is open to the public and is one of the best examples of colonial architecture.

• **EDWARD LLOYD**   **1744–1796**

A member of the Continental Congress, Edward Lloyd was born at "Wye House" in Talbot County, Maryland, on December 15, 1744. He was elected to the Maryland general assembly in 1771–74, was a member of the committee of safety in 1775, and was a delegate to the colony's Revolutionary convention in 1776. He served on the governor's executive council 1777–79, and then in the state senate. He was chosen as one of Maryland's delegates to the Continental Congress 1783–84. Lloyd died at "Wye House" on July 8, 1796.

• **PIERCE LONG**   **1739–1789**

A Revolutionary War officer and delegate to the Continental Congress, Pierce Long was born in Portsmouth, New Hampshire, in 1739. As colonel of the 1st New Hamphire Regiment, he took part in the battles of Ticonderoga at Saratoga. At the end of the war he was brevetted a brigadier general. Long served as a New Hampshire delegate to the Continental Congress 1784–86, and as a member of the governor's council 1786–89. He died in Portsmouth on April 13, 1789.

• **JAMES LOVELL**   **1737–1814**

A delegate to the Continental Congress, James Lovell was born in Boston on October 31, 1737. He was the son of John Lovell (1728–78), who for forty-one years was headmaster of the Boston Latin School where many of the leaders of the Revolution received their early education. James Lovell was graduated from the Boston Latin School in 1752 and from Harvard College in 1756. He continued on at Harvard in graduate studies until 1759. He then taught under his father at the Boston Latin School for eighteen years, 1757–75.

Noted as an orator, he became aligned with the patriotic cause after making a commemorative address in 1771 on the Boston Massacre. During the British occupation of Boston, Lovell was arrested as a spy and taken by the British to Halifax when they evacuated Boston in 1776. Lovell's father, a Loyalist, also went with the British. Lovell was released in a prisoner exchange in November 1776 and returned to Boston. He was chosen as a delegate to the Continental Congress 1777–82, where he took an active role on the foreign affairs committee. Because of his skill in the French language, he acted as translator or as spokesman in Congress' dealings with the Marquis de Lafayette and other French officers. After his service in Congress, Lovell became a tax collector 1784–88, and then collector of customs at Boston 1788–89. He served as naval officer of the port of Boston from 1789 until his death in Windham, Maine, on July 14, 1814.

• ISAAC LOW   1735–1791

A member of the Continental Congress who abandoned the patriotic cause, Isaac Low was born at Raritan Landing, near New Brunswick, New Jersey, on April 13, 1735. He became a wealthy merchant in New York City and was a founder and president of the New York Chamber of Commerce. In 1765 Low was one of New York's delegates to the Stamp Act Congress. He represented New York in the Continental Congress 1774–75, where he opposed independence. Low was arrested for treason in 1776 and his property was ordered confiscated in 1779. When the British left New York at the end of the war, Low went with them to England, where he died in Cowes, Isle of Wight, on July 25, 1791.

• JOHN LOWELL   1743–1802

A member of the Continental Congress, John Lowell was born in Newburyport, Massachusetts, on June 17, 1743. After graduation from Harvard at seventeen, he studied law and commenced practice in Newburyport in 1762. He was elected to the state legislature in 1778 and 1780–82, and was a delegate to the Continental Congress 1782–83. He served as judge of the Massachusetts court of appeals 1784–89, and then as a U.S. district judge from 1789 until his death in Roxbury, Massachusetts, on May 6, 1802.

• THOMAS LYNCH   1727–1776

A delegate to the Continental Congress, Thomas Lynch was born in St. James' Parish, South Carolina, in 1727. One of the wealthiest planters in the colony, Lynch also was an influential politician, serving more than a dozen years in the colonial legislature. He was a representative to South Carolina's Revolutionary congress in 1774–75. He was chosen as a delegate to the Continental Congress 1774–76, but suffered a stroke of paralysis in Philadelphia. While being taken home by his son, Lynch died in Annapolis, Maryland, in December 1776.

• THOMAS LYNCH JR.   1749–1779

A signer of the Declaration of Independence, Thomas Lynch, Jr. was born in Prince George's Parish, South Carolina, on August 5, 1749, the son of a wealthy planter, Thomas Lynch. After an education at Eton College and Cambridge University in England, he studied law at the Middle Temple in London. Upon his return to South Carolina in 1772, he became a planter on the North Santee River. He was commissioned a captain in the militia in 1775, and shortly after received word his father had suffered a stroke in Philadelphia. When his commanding officer would not give him leave to go to his father's

Thomas Lynch, Jr.

side, Lynch's political friends got him named as a delegate to the Continental Congress on February 1, 1776. When young Lynch arrived in Philadelphia, he took part in the debate on the Declaration of Independence and signed it. His father's death, while they were on the way home later that year, and his own poor health caused him to drop out of public affairs. He and his wife sailed for the West Indies in 1779, hoping to find a cure for his illness, and were never heard from again. Their ship was believed to have been lost at sea with all hands.

• **WILLIAM MACLAY   1737–1804**

One of Pennsylvania's first U.S. Senators, William Maclay was born in New Garden, Pennsylvania, on July 20, 1737. During the French and Indian Wars he was a lieutenant in Gen. John Forbes' expedition to Fort Duquesne in 1758. After studying law, he was admitted to the bar in 1760. During the Revolutionary War, Maclay served as a commissary for the Continental Army. He was elected to the U.S. Senate 1789–91. He was elected to the state legislature in 1796 and 1803–04, and was a county judge 1801–03. Maclay died in Harrisburg, Pennsylvania, on April 16, 1804.

• **JAMES MADISON   1751–1836**

The Father of the Constitution and the fourth President of the United States, James Madison was born at Port Conway, Vir-

James Madison

ginia, on March 16, 1751. After graduation from the College of New Jersey (now Princeton University) at the age of twenty in 1771, he returned to Virginia to take an active role in pre-Revolutionary politics. Elected as a delegate to the Virginia revolutionary convention of 1776, he helped draft the state's first constitution and bill of rights. The next year he was elected to the state legislature, where he became a friend of Thomas Jefferson, who had returned to Virginia after writing the Declaration of Independence. He then served as a member of the governor's advisory council under both Patrick Henry and Jefferson. At the age of twenty-eight Madison was chosen as a member of Virginia's delegation to the Continental Congress, serving in that body 1780–83 and 1786–88. He represented Virginia at the Annapolis Convention in 1786, where he and Alexander Hamilton worked together to get the states to agree to a convention to establish a new national government, and the following year was made a member of the state's delegation to the Constitutional Convention in Philadelphia.

Madison played a major role throughout the convention in winning agreement between the contending forces on the contents of the new Constitution. He made more speeches than any other delegate, and at the same time kept the most comprehensive notes on the proceedings. After signing the final draft of the United States Constitution with the other delegates in 1787, Madison worked for the next several months with Alexander Hamilton and John Jay in writing the series of essays defending and explaining the Constitution that became known as *The Federalist*. He helped win Virginia's ratification of the Constitution by promising that a Bill of Rights would be drafted and attached. He won election to the First United States Congress, defeating James Monroe, and then won re-election to three succeeding Congresses, serving from 1789 to 1797. He declined President Washington's offer to appoint him Secretary of State in 1794, but seven years later accepted President Jefferson's appointment to that position.

After serving eight years as Secretary of State, Madison was elected President. During his administration 1809–17, the War of 1812 with Britain was fought and the movement of settlers to the American frontier accelerated. After retiring from the White House, Madison lived at his estate, "Montpelier," in Virginia until his death there at the age of eighty-five on June 28, 1836—the last of the signers of the United States Constitution to die.

Dolley Madison,
wife of James Madison

• **JOHN MANLEY   1734–1793**

The third ranking officer in the Continental Navy, John Manley was born in Torquay, England, in 1734. After becoming a seaman as a boy, he rose to command of merchant ships and settled in Marblehead, Massachusetts. During the siege of the

British in Boston in 1775, Washington commissioned him as captain of the armed schooner *Lee*, with which he captured three British ships laden with guns, mortars, and other military supplies desperately needed by Washington's troops. In 1776 Manley was commissioned as a captain in the new Continental Navy and given command of the 32-gun frigate *Hancock*. He captured the 28-gun British frigate *Fox* in June 1777, but a month later he was forced to surrender both the *Hancock* and the *Fox* in an action with the 44-gun British warship *Rainbow*. After being held in captivity aboard a prison ship at New York for nearly eight months, Manley was exchanged in 1778. A court-martial acquitted him of all charges in connection with the loss of his ship. During the next several months he sailed as captain of a privateer, but was captured again by the British in February 1779 and imprisoned in Barbados. After escaping from this prison, he served again as a privateer as captain of the *Jason*. Captured by the British a third time, he was sent to prison in England, where he remained for two years until being exchanged in 1782. Upon his return to the United States he was given command of the frigate *Hague*, with which he took the British ship *Baille* in January 1783 in the last naval action of the war. Manley died in Boston on February 12, 1793.

• **JAMES MANNING** 1738–1791

A Baptist minister and delegate to the Continental Congress, James Manning was born in Elizabethtown (now Elizabeth), New Jersey, on October 22, 1738. After graduation from the College of New Jersey (now Princeton University) in 1762, he studied theology and became a Baptist minister in 1763. Moving to Warren, Rhode Island, in 1764, he was one of the founders and the first president of Rhode Island College (now Brown University). He moved to Providence with the college in 1770, and served as pastor of the First Baptist Church of Providence for twenty years in 1771–91. He was chosen as a member of Rhode Island's delegation to the Continental Congress in 1785–86. Manning died in Providence on July 29, 1791.

• **HENRY MARCHANT** 1741–1796

A signer of the Articles of Confederation, Henry Marchant was born in Martha's Vineyard, Massachusetts, on April 9, 1741. After graduation from the College of Philadelphia in 1762, he studied law and commenced practice in 1767 in Newport, Rhode Island. He was appointed attorney general of Rhode Island 1771–77. As a member of the Continental Congress 1777–80 and 1783–84, he was one of the signers of the Articles of Confederation. He served as U.S. District judge for Rhode Island from 1790 until his death in Newport on August 30, 1796.

• FRANCIS MARION   1732−1795

A Southern guerrilla general known as "the Swamp Fox,"
Francis Marion was born in Georgetown, South Carolina, in
1732. Going to sea at sixteen, his ship sank on a cruise to the
West Indies. He and other crewmen drifted for weeks in an
open boat, several of them dying of starvation before Marion
was rescued by a passing ship. After that he gave up the sea
and became a farmer. As a captain of militia in the French and

*General Francis Marion—his portrait, his residence,
and an artist's concept of Marion in battle action*

Indian War, he led the forlorn hope—the advance guard—at the battle against the Cherokee Indians at Echoe, near present-day Franklin, North Carolina, in 1761, and was one of the few men in his detachment of thirty to survive.

On the outbreak of the Revolutionary War he was elected to the South Carolina Revolutionary congress and became an officer in the militia. In June 1776 he took part in the defense of Charleston's Fort Sullivan. As commander of the 2nd South Carolina Regiment with the rank of lieutenant colonel, Marion led the unsuccessful allied attempt to recapture Savannah from the British in October 1779. After the British ended organized American resistance in the South with the capture of Charleston, Marion was appointed a brigadier general of militia. He organized a small band of about thirty to fifty guerrillas and harassed the British and their Loyalist sympathizers, slipping away into the swamps of the Santee River before they could be caught. The British cavalry officer Banastre Tarleton, who repeatedly tried to capture Marion, said of him: "As for this damned old fox, the devil himself could not catch him." Other British officers complained that Marion "would not fight like a gentleman or a Christian." In 1781 Marion recruited and trained about 2,500 militia that became known as Marion's Brigade. He led his men with distinction in the battle of Eutaw Springs, South Carolina, in September 1781, the last major battle in the Deep South during the war. After the war, Marion was elected to the state senate. He died at his plantation near Nelson's Ferry, South Carolina, on February 27, 1795.

• **JOHN MARSHALL   1755–1835**

A Revolutionary War officer and fourth Chief Justice of the United States, John Marshall was born in Germantown, Virginia, on September 24, 1755. At the age of twenty he interrupted his law studies to join the Culpeper Minute Men as a lieutenant, fighting with them in the first battles in Virginia at Great Bridge on December 9, 1775, and at Norfolk on January 1, 1776. Marshall was promoted to captain and in the succeeding years took part in the battles of Brandywine, Germantown, Monmouth, and Stony Point. In 1779 he was ordered to Virginia to help train the militia. He resumed his law studies at William and Mary College, and was admitted to the bar in 1780. He then returned to the command of his company, joining the forces of Baron von Steuben in the defense of Virginia.

After the war, Marshall settled in Richmond, Virginia, where he practiced law. He was elected to the Virginia legislature 1782–91 and 1795–97. He was a delegate to the state convention in 1788 in which he helped lead the fight for ratification of the new United States Constitution. He went to France in 1797–98 as one of the special commissioners to settle the undeclared war with France. Upon his return, he

The residence of John Marshall in Richmond, Virginia

resumed the practice of law in Virginia, declining appointment as Associate Justice of the Supreme Court offered by President Adams.

Marshall was elected as a Representative in the U.S. Congress, serving as a Federalist from 1799 until he resigned in 1800 to become Secretary of State under President John Adams. The following year President Adams appointed Marshall as Chief Justice. He took the oath of office as Chief Justice on February 4, 1801, but also continued to serve as Secretary of State until March 4, 1801.

During the next thirty-four years, Chief Justice Marshall established the power of the Supreme Court to determine the constitutionality of laws and to interpret the Constitution. He was still Chief Justice at the time of his death at the age of seventy-nine on July 6, 1835, in Philadelphia.

- **LUTHER MARTIN   1744–1826**

A member of the Continental Congress and one of the most prominent lawyers of his time, Luther Martin was born in New Brunswick, New Jersey, on February 9, 1744. After graduation from Princeton College in 1766, he taught school in Queenstown, Maryland, 1766–71. He then began studying law and commenced practice in Accomack County, Virginia, in 1771. From 1778, Martin served for twenty-seven years as attorney general of Maryland. He was a delegate to the Continental Congress in 1784–85, and to the federal Constitutional Convention in 1787 but refused to sign the new United States Constitution because he did not like the two-house Congress it embodied.

After resigning as Maryland's attorney general in 1805, Martin was defense counsel and obtained acquittal for Supreme Court Justice Samuel Chase at his impeachment trial before the U.S. Senate, which was presided over by Vice President Aaron Burr. Three years later, in 1807, Martin was defense counsel for Burr at his treason trial and won him a not-guilty verdict. Martin again became attorney general of Maryland in 1818, but was forced to resign in 1820 because of

John Marshall

297

a stroke of paralysis. To help him, the Maryland Legislature passed an act requiring every lawyer in the state to pay an annual license tax of $5 to be turned over to trustees for his use. Martin passed his last years with Aaron Burr in New York City, where he died on July 10, 1826.

George Mason

- GEORGE MASON   1725–1792

Author of Virginia's declaration of rights and its first state constitution, George Mason was born in Fairfax County, Virginia, in 1725. A neighbor and personal friend of George Washington, Mason took an active role in the patriotic movement in Virginia. In 1769 he drew up the non-importation resolutions that Washington presented to and that were adopted by the rebellious Virginia assembly. He was a member of Virginia's committee of safety in 1775, and the following year wrote the declaration of rights and the state constitution which were adopted by the Virginia Revolutionary convention. As one of Virginia's delegates to the Constitutional Convention in Philadelphia in 1787, he took an important part in writing the United States Constitution. However, when the document was completed, he was one of the three delegates who refused to sign it, because he believed that it should have provided for the end of slavery and should have contained a bill of rights. He joined with Patrick Henry in opposing Virginia's ratification of the Constitution, and then declined election as one of the state's first U.S. Senators.

Jefferson wrote of Mason: "He was a man of the first order of wisdom, of expansive mind, profound judgment, cogent in argument, learned in the lore of our form of constitution, and earnest for the republican change on democratic principles." He died at his estate, "Gunston Hall," in Fairfax County, Virginia, on October 7, 1792.

- GEORGE MATHEWS   1739–1812

A Revolutionary War officer, governor of Georgia, and Congressman, George Mathews was born in Augusta County, Virginia, on August 30, 1739. He commanded a volunteer company against the Indians in 1757, and fought at the battle of Point Pleasant against the Shawnee Indians in Lord Dunmore's War in 1774. Commissioned colonel of the 9th Virginia Regiment in the Revolutionary War, he fought in 1777 at Brandywine, and then at Germantown, where he was wounded and captured. After four years imprisonment, he was exchanged in December 1781 and joined General Greene's army as colonel of the 3rd Virginia Regiment. He moved to Georgia in 1785, and was elected governor of Georgia in 1787. He then was elected as one of Georgia's Representatives to the First U.S. Congress 1789–91. He again was elected governor of Georgia 1793–96. As a brigadier general of militia he led a troop of volunteers into Florida in 1812 and took possession of that territory from Spain in the name of the United States. However, President Monroe repudiated Mathews' action. Mathews died in Augusta, Georgia, on August 30, 1812.

• JOHN MATHEWS   1744–1802

Member of the Continental Congress and governor of South Carolina, John Mathews was born in Charleston, South Carolina, in 1744. He served as a lieutenant at the age of sixteen in the South Carolina militia in the expedition against the Cherokee Indians in 1760. He studied law at the Middle Temple in London, England, being admitted to the bar in 1764. After returning to South Carolina, he was elected to the colonial house of assembly in 1772. In the Revolutionary convention of 1774, Mathews was appointed a member of the "general committee of ninety-nine." He then was elected to the provincial congresses of South Carolina in 1775–76. During the Revolutionary War he was a captain of the Colleton County militia. Elected to the state house of representatives 1776–80, he was speaker in 1777–78. He became a delegate to the Continental Congress in 1778–82, and then was elected governor of South Carolina in 1782–83. He was elected judge of the court of equity in 1791 and served until 1797, when he resigned. Mathews died in Charleston on November 17, 1802.

• TIMOTHY MATLACK   1730–1829

A member of the Continental Congress who lived to the age of ninety-nine, Timothy Matlack was born in Haddonfield, New Jersey, in 1730. After attending Quaker schools in Haddonfield and Philadelphia, he became a merchant in Philadelphia. Matlack was a delegate to Pennsylvania's Revolutionary conventions of 1775–76, and was appointed secretary of state. As commander of a battalion of "Associators," he fought at the battle of Princeton in 1777. Matlack was a delegate to the Continental Congress in 1780–81. After he reached the age of eighty, he was elected to the Philadelphia board of aldermen 1813–18. Matlack died at Holmesburg, Pennsylvania, near Philadelphia, on April 14, 1829.

• JAMES McCLENE   1730–1806

A member of the Continental Congress from Pennsylvania, James McClene was born in New London, Pennsylvania, on October 11, 1730. He was elected to the state house of representatives in 1776–77, and to the state executive council in 1778–79. McClene was a delegate to the Continental Congress in 1779–80. He again was elected to the state house of representatives in 1790–91 and 1793–94. McClene died in Antrim Township, Pennsylvania, on March 13, 1806.

A wooden funnel

• ALEXANDER McDOUGALL 1731–1786

A general in the Continental Army and a delegate to the Continental Congress, Alexander McDougall was born in the Parish of Kildalton, on the island of Islay, Scotland, in 1731. When he was nine, he was brought to America by his parents, who settled in New York. Having shipped out to sea at an early age, by the time he was twenty-four he was in command of two privateers in the French and Indian War. He then became a successful merchant in New York City. The royal government jailed him for over a year in 1770–71 for writing a pamphlet called *A Son of Liberty to the Betrayed Inhabitants of the City and Colony of New York*, and thereafter he became known as "the first martyr in the patriot cause."

As a brigadier general in the Continental Army, McDougall commanded the main battle line in the battle of White Plains, New York, in October 1776, and fought at Germantown, Pennsylvania, in October 1777. Shortly after the latter battle he was promoted to major general and placed in command of forces in the Hudson Highlands north of New York City. In 1780 he succeeded Benedict Arnold as commander of West Point, New York. McDougall was a member of New York's delegation to the Continental Congress in 1781–82 and 1784–85. After the war he was elected to the state senate from 1783 until he died in New York City on June 9, 1786.

• JAMES McHENRY 1753–1816

A surgeon and aide to General Washington in the Revolutionary War and later a signer of the United States Constitution and U.S. Secretary of War, James McHenry was born in Ballymena, County Antrim, Ireland, on November 16, 1753. At eighteen he came to America and settled in Philadelphia, where he studied medicine under Dr. Benjamin Rush.

At the outbreak of the Revolutionary War, the twenty-one-year-old McHenry hurried to Massachusetts in July, 1775, and joined the patriots as a volunteer surgeon. He then was assigned as surgeon with the 5th Pennsylvania Battalion at Fort Washington, New York. When the fort surrendered in November 1776, McHenry was captured with about 2,000 other American troops. As a prisoner he tended sick and wounded for about two months until he was paroled in January 1777. He was freed from parole in a prisoner exchange in March 1778, resuming his military service as a surgeon with the Continental Army at Valley Forge, Pennsylvania. General Washington appointed McHenry as his personal secretary in June 1778, a position he held for more than two years until he was transferred to become aide to the Marquis de Lafayette. While he was serving at the siege of Yorktown in 1781, McHenry was elected to the Maryland state senate.

After the British surrendered at Yorktown, he resigned from

the army and went to Annapolis, Maryland, where he served in the state senate 1781–86. He was chosen as one of Maryland's delegates to the Continental Congress 1783–86, and to the federal Constitutional Convention in Philadelphia in 1787, where he signed the new United States Constitution. He again served in the Maryland legislature in 1789–96. McHenry was appointed Secretary of War in the Cabinets of President Washington and President John Adams 1796–1800, during which time he organized the new United States Army and United States Navy. At the age of forty-six, McHenry retired from public life to "Fayetteville," his country estate, near Baltimore, Maryland, where he died on May 3, 1816.

• LACHLAN McINTOSH   1725–1806

A general in the Revolutionary War, Lachlan McIntosh was born near Raits, in Badenoch, Scotland, on March 17, 1725. When he was eleven, he was brought to America by his parents, who helped establish the settlement of New Inverness, Georgia. He became a surveyor, a clerk, and then a businessman. In 1775 he was elected as a delegate to the provincial congress in Savannah. In 1776 he was commissioned colonel in the Georgia militia, and later that year was promoted to brigadier general in the Continental Army.

In May 1777 he killed Button Gwinnett, a signer of the Declaration of Independence, in a duel growing out of a dispute as to which of them was in command of military forces in Georgia. Although McIntosh was acquitted of any crime in a trial that followed Gwinnett's death, he asked to be transferred out of Georgia because of ill will against him there. He was made commander of the Western frontier of Pennsylvania in 1778, where he built several forts to withstand Indian attacks. In 1779 he was ordered back to the South, where he took part in the unsuccessful attempt to recapture Savannah, Georgia, from the British in October. In 1780 McIntosh was captured by the British at the surrender of Charleston, South Carolina, and was not exchanged until the fighting was over in 1782.

He was elected a delegate to the Continental Congress in 1784, but did not serve because he could not afford to go. McIntosh died in Savannah, Georgia, on February 20, 1806. He was an uncle of John McIntosh (1755–1826), a lieutenant colonel known by the nickname of "Come and take it," because that was the message he sent to the British when they demanded that he surrender Fort Morris, Georgia, in November 1778.

• THOMAS McKEAN   1734–1817

A signer of the Declaration of Independence, the eighth President of the Continental Congress, and the governor of two states, Thomas McKean was born in New London, Pennsyl-

Lachlan McIntosh

Thomas McKean

vania, on March 19, 1734. He studied law and began practice in New Castle, Delaware, in 1755. Beginning in 1762, he was regularly elected to the Delaware legislature for seventeen years, serving as speaker in 1772–73. He was a delegate to the Stamp Act Congress in New York in 1765. Chosen as a delegate from Delaware to the Continental Congress in 1774, he was the only member of the Congress to serve continuously throughout the Revolutionary War to 1783. In Congress McKean signed both the Declaration of Independence and the Articles of Confederation. He served as President of the Congress from July 10, 1781, to November 5, 1781. Simultaneously with his Congressional duties, McKean was president of the state of Delaware in 1777, and was chief justice of Pennsylvania for twenty-two years—1777–1799. He resigned as chief justice upon his election as governor of Pennsylvania in 1799, an office he held for three terms until he retired in 1808. McKean died in Philadelphia on June 24, 1817.

• RETURN JONATHAN MEIGS   1734–1823

A courageous Revolutionary War officer and the founder of the city of Marietta, Ohio, Return Jonathan Meigs was born in Middletown, Connecticut, on December 17, 1734. He supposedly received his unusual name because of a lover's quarrel during his grandfather's courtship of his grandmother in which his grandfather was preparing to ride away after a spat and his grandmother, relenting, called, "Return, Jonathan!"

A captain in the militia at the beginning of the Revolutionary War, Meigs accompanied Benedict Arnold's expedition to Quebec and was captured there on New Year's Eve 1775. A year later he was exchanged in 1777 and returned to duty as a lieutenant colonel. His most famous exploit of the war was a raid he carried out in May 1777 on a Loyalist foraging party at Sag Harbor on Long Island, New York. At night he led a small flotilla of a dozen whaleboats across Long Island Sound from Connecticut, killed six Loyalists, captured more than sixty, burned a dozen British vessels, and then escaped back to Connecticut with his prisoners. In recognition of his exploit, Congress voted Meigs an "elegant sword." Meigs fought bravely at the battles of Stony Point, New York. After the war he led a band of settlers to the Ohio Valley, founding the city of Marietta, Ohio. In 1801 he was appointed Indian Agent for the Cherokee tribe. He died at the Cherokee agency in Georgia on January 28, 1823. His son, Return Jonathan Meigs (1765–1825), was governor of Ohio in 1810–14.

• HUGH MERCER   c.1720–1777

A heroic Continental Army general who was fatally wounded at the battle of Princeton, Hugh Mercer was born in Aberdeen, Scotland, about 1720. After receiving a medical degree

General Hugh Mercer

The Battle of Princeton where General Mercer was killed.

at the University of Aberdeen, he served as a surgeon at the battle of Culloden on the side of the Young Pretender. Forced to flee the country, he came to America, settling in Mercersburg, Pennsylvania, about 1747, where he practiced medicine. Serving as a captain in the Pennsylvania militia, he was severely wounded in the French and Indian War during General Edward Braddock's expedition against Fort Duquesne (Pittsburgh). Promoted to lieutenant colonel, he took part in General John Forbes' successful attack on Fort Duquesne in 1758, and afterward was made colonel in command of the fort, renamed Fort Pitt. Having become a good friend of George Washington, who commanded Virginia troops during the Forbes expedition, he moved to Fredericksburg, Virginia, after the war. In 1776 he was commissioned a brigadier general in the Continental Army and given command of the Flying Camp, a strategic reserve force of about 2,000 militia troops. On December 26, 1776, Mercer led an attack column in Washington's victory at Trenton. Eight days later Mercer was fatally wounded at the battle of Princeton, dying on January 11, 1777.

• JAMES MERCER   1736–1793

A Virginia delegate to the Continental Congress, James Mercer was born at "Marlborough" in Stafford County, Virginia, on February 26, 1736, an older brother of John Francis Mercer. After graduation from William and Mary College, he served as a captain in the French and Indian War, commanding Fort Loudoun in Winchester, Virginia, in 1756. He then became a lawyer and was elected for fourteen years to the Virginia house of burgesses 1762–76. Active in the patriotic movement, he was a member of the Virginia Revolutionary conventions 1774–76 and of the committee of public safety in 1775–76. He was chosen a delegate to the Continental Congress 1779–80. Mercer served as a judge of the general court of Virginia 1779–89, and then as judge of the first Virginia court of appeals from 1789 until his death in Richmond, Virginia, on October 31, 1793.

• JOHN FRANCIS MERCER   1759–1821

A Revolutionary War officer, delegate to the Continental Congress from Virginia, and governor of Maryland, John Francis Mercer was born at "Marlborough" in Stafford County, Virginia, on May 17, 1759, a younger brother of James Mercer. After graduation from William and Mary College at sixteen, he joined the 3rd Virginia Regiment with a commission as lieutenant. He was wounded at the battle of Brandywine in 1777 and was promoted to captain at the age of eighteen. Mercer served as aide-de-camp to Gen. Charles Lee in 1778–79, and then was promoted to lieutenant colonel of Virginia cavalry. With the end of fighting, he resigned from the army, studied law, and began practice in Williamsburg, Virginia. He was chosen as a member of Virginia's delegation to the Continental Congress 1782–85. He then moved to West River, Anne Arundel County, Maryland. He was elected to the Maryland legislature 1788–89 and 1791–92. Then he was elected as a Democrat to the U.S. Congress 1792–94. Mercer won election as governor of Maryland 1801–03, and then served again in the state legislature 1803–06. He died in Philadelphia on August 30, 1821.

• SAMUEL MEREDITH   1741–1817

A Revolutionary War militia general, delegate to the Continental Congress, and first Treasurer of the United States, Samuel Meredith was born in Philadelphia in 1741. He became a successful merchant in Philadelphia in the years before the Revolutionary War. At the beginning of the war in 1776 he served as major and then lieutenant colonel of the 3rd Battalion of Associators. He was promoted to brigadier general of Pennsylvania militia in 1777 "for gallant services in the battles of Brandywine and Germantown." He became a Pennsylvania delegate to the Continental Congress in 1787–88. President Washington appointed him the first Treasurer of the United States, an office he held for twelve years 1789–1801. Meredith died at his country home, "Belmont Manor," near Pleasant Mount, Pennsylvania, on February 10, 1817.

• ARTHUR MIDDLETON   1742–1787

A signer of the Declaration of Independence, Arthur Middleton was born at "Middleton Place" on the Ashley River near

Arthur Middleton

Charleston, South Carolina, on June 26, 1742, the eldest son of the wealthy planter and political leader Henry Middleton. After graduation from St. John's College of Cambridge University in England, he studied law at the Temple in London and toured Europe. Returning to South Carolina in 1763, he helped manage his father's plantations and was elected to the colonial legislature in 1765–68. He and his wife traveled extensively in Europe 1768–71. He again was a member of the colonial legislature in 1772–75. He took an active part in the South Carolina Revolutionary conventions in 1774–75, and was a member of the council of safety in 1775–76. He was elected a delegate to the Continental Congress 1776–78, and signed the Declaration of Independence. He was captured by the British at Charleston, South Carolina, in May 1780 and imprisoned in St. Augustine, Florida, until July 1781 when he was exchanged. Upon his release he again served in the Continental Congress 1781–83. After the war he was elected to the state legislature. At the age of forty-four, he died at "The Oaks," near Charleston, South Carolina, on January 1, 1787.

• HENRY MIDDLETON   1717–1784

The second President of the Continental Congress, Henry Middleton was born at "The Oaks" near Charleston, South Carolina, in 1717. After an education in England, he returned to South Carolina where he became a wealthy planter. He was a member of the colonial house of commons 1742–55, serving as speaker 1745–47 and 1754–55. He then was a member of the royal governor's council from 1755 until his resignation in September 1770. A leader in the patriotic movement, he was a member of the South Carolina Revolutionary convention of 1774, and president of the South Carolina congress of 1775–76. He was sent as a delegate to the Continental Congress 1774–76, and was elected as the second President of the Congress from October 22, 1774, to May 10, 1775. He played an active part in state affairs as a member of the South Carolina senate until 1780. When the British invaded the state in 1780, Middleton decided the patriotic cause was lost and went to them to ask for protection. He died in Charleston on June 13, 1784. He was the father of Arthur Middleton, the signer of the Declaration of Independence.

Henry Middleton

• THOMAS MIFFLIN   1744–1800

A Revolutionary War general, the eleventh President of the Continental Congress, and a signer of the United States Constitution, Thomas Mifflin was born in Philadelphia on January 10, 1744. After graduation from the College of Philadelphia at sixteen, he served an apprenticeship as a clerk and then opened a store with his brother George. He was elected to the

Thomas Mifflin

colonial legislature 1772–74 and to the Pennsylvania Revolutionary conventions of 1774–75. He was a member of the Continental Congress 1774–76, but left it on July 4, 1775, to become major and chief aide-de-camp to General Washington. Because of his experience as a merchant, a month later he was appointed Quartermaster General of the Continental Army. In this position he rose to the rank of major general by February 1777.

After the British captured Philadelphia in September 1777, Mifflin resigned as Quartermaster General, and was appointed by Congress as a member of the board of war. After questions were raised about his accounts while he was Quartermaster General, he resigned his commission as major general in February 1779.

Returning to politics, Mifflin was elected to the state legislature 1778–81, and then was named a member of Pennsylvania's delegation to the Continental Congress 1782–84, where he was elected its eleventh President from November 3, 1783, to November 30, 1784. He next served as speaker of the Pennsylvania house of representatives 1785–88. Mifflin was chosen as a delegate to the federal Constitutional Convention in 1787, where he signed the new United States Constitution. He succeeded Benjamin Franklin as president of Pennsylvania 1788–90. He presided over the state constitutional convention in 1790, and then was elected as the first state governor of Pennsylvania 1790–99. He died a month after retiring as governor in Lancaster, Pennsylvania, on January 20, 1800.

• **NATHAN MILLER   1743–1790**

A Rhode Island delegate to the Continental Congress, Nathan Miller was born in Warren, Rhode Island, on March 20, 1743. A merchant and shipbuilder, he served as a brigadier general of Rhode Island militia during the Revolutionary War. He was elected to the Rhode Island general assembly 1772–74, 1780, and 1782–83. Miller was chosen as one of Rhode Island's delegates to the Continental Congress in 1786. He again was a member of the Rhode Island legislature when he died in Warren on May 20, 1790.

• **NATHANIEL MITCHELL   1753–1814**

A Revolutionary War officer and governor of Delaware, Nathaniel Mitchell was born near Laurel, Delaware, in 1753. A farmer, he served in the Revolutionary War, rising to the rank of brigade major under Gen. Peter Muhlenberg. He was a delegate to the Continental Congress 1786–88. A Federalist, he was elected governor of Delaware 1805–08. After serving in the state senate 1810–12, Mitchell died in Laurel on February 21, 1814.

James Monroe

• **JAMES MONROE   1758–1831**

A Revolutionary War officer and fifth President of the United States, James Monroe was born in Westmoreland County, Virginia, on April 28, 1758. At seventeen he dropped out of William and Mary College in 1775 to join the Continental Army as a lieutenant in the 3rd Virginia Regiment. In 1776 he was wounded in the battle of Harlem Heights and led the advance guard in the battle of Trenton, where Washington promoted him to captain for his bravery. Fighting in the battles of Brandywine, Germantown, and Monmouth, he advanced to the rank of lieutenant colonel.

After the war he studied law under Thomas Jefferson, and with Jefferson was chosen as a delegate to the Continental Congress 1783–86, where he helped draft the Northwest Ordinance. He was elected to the Virginia legislature 1786–90,

307

and then to the U.S. Senate 1790–94. President Washington appointed Monroe ambassador to France 1794–96. Returning to America, he was elected governor of Virginia 1799–1802. President Jefferson appointed him ambassador to France in 1803, and then to England 1803–07. He was again elected to the Virginia assembly 1810–11, and again as governor of Virginia in 1811.

Monroe was appointed Secretary of State in the Cabinet of President Madison in 1811–1817, throughout the period of the War of 1812. As the Democratic-Republican presidential candidate in 1816, Monroe defeated Federalist U.S. Senator Rufus King of New York with an electoral vote of 183–34. His declaration of the Monroe Doctrine in 1823 is generally regarded as his outstanding achievement. After completing a second term as President in 1825, Monroe retired to his farm in Virginia. Impoverished in his old age, Monroe was forced to sell his Virginia farm and go to live with a married daughter in New York City, where he died on July 4, 1831.

Richard Montgomery

- **JOSEPH MONTGOMERY   1733–1794**

A minister and a Pennsylvania delegate to the Continental Congress, Joseph Montgomery was born in Paxtang, Pennsylvania, on September 23, 1733. After graduation from Princeton College in 1755, he studied for the ministry and was ordained in 1761. He held several pastorates 1761–77, and then served as a chaplain in Col. Smallwood's Maryland Regiment of the Continental Army 1777–80. Montgomery was elected to the general assembly of Pennsylvania 1780–82 and during the same period served as a delegate to the Continental Congress. From 1786 he was justice of the court of common pleas of Dauphin County to his death in Harrisburg, Pennsylvania, on October 14, 1794.

- **RICHARD MONTGOMERY   1738–1775**

A Continental Army general who died trying to capture the city of Quebec, Richard Mongomery was born in Dublin, Ireland, on December 2, 1738. After attending Trinity and St. Andrews colleges in Dublin, he joined the British army at eighteen with the commission of ensign. During the French and Indian War he was sent to America with his regiment. He took part in the siege of Louisbourg in 1758, and then was promoted to lieutenant, fighting in the battles of Ticonderoga, Crown Point, and Montreal. Next, he fought in the capture of Havana and Martinique in the West Indies in 1762, winning promotion to captain. Ten years later Mongomery decided to retire from the British army and return to America. In 1773 he bought a farm at Rhinebeck, New York, on the Hudson River. He was elected to the New York revolutionary convention in 1775 and in June of that year was commissioned as one of the first eight brigadier generals of the Continental Army. He was placed as second in command to General Philip Schuyler to plan and carry out an invasion of Canada.

In August 1775 Montgomery started north with about 1,200 men, commanding the operation because Schuyler had fallen ill. After a two-month siege he captured a force of about 600 British troops at St John's on November 2. He then marched on Montreal, which surrendered without a fight on November 13. Pressing on to Quebec with about 300 men, Montgomery joined Benedict Arnold who had reached Quebec with about 700 men on the same day Montgomery took Montreal. Throughout a bitterly cold December the Americans besieged the city, then Montgomery developed a plan to capture Quebec with a surprise assault on New Year's Eve. While rushing a blockhouse, Montgomery and two of his officers were killed. Arnold, attacking the city from another quarter, was severely wounded. After Montgomery's death on December 31, the American army continued the siege throughout the winter, finally being forced to retreat in May when British reinforcements arrived.

• WILLIAM MONTGOMERY   1736–1816

A colonel in the Revolutionary War and a delegate to the Continental Congress, William Montgomery was born in Londonderry Township, Chester County, Pennsylvania, on August 3, 1736. He served in the Revolutionary War as colonel of the 4th Battalion of the Chester County militia. After the battle of Long Island his regiment became known as the Flying Camp. In 1779 he was elected to the Pennsylvania assembly and was repeatedly re-elected. He was chosen as a delegate to the Continental Congress 1784–85, resigning to accept appointment as judge of Northumberland and Luzerne Counties in 1785. Montgomery, a Democratic-Republican, was elected to the Third U.S. Congress 1793–95. He was commissioned major general of Pennsylvania militia in 1793, a rank he held for fourteen years. Upon the establishment of a post office at Danville, Pennsylvania, he was made its first postmaster 1801–03. Montgomery died in Danville on May 1, 1816.

• ANDREW MOORE   1752–1821

A Revolutionary War officer and member of the First U.S. Congress, Andrew Moore was born at "Cannicello," near Fairfield, Virginia, in 1752. After attending Augusta Academy (now Washington and Lee University), he studied law and began practice in 1774. Joining the Continental Army, he served as a lieutenant in the battle of Saratoga, being present at the surrender of Burgoyne. He resigned in 1779 with the rank of captain, and then was commissioned brigadier general of Virginia militia. He was elected to the Virginia house of delegates

1780–83 and 1785–88. Moore won election to the first and to the three succeeding U.S. Congresses 1789–97. He again was elected to the Eighth U.S. Congress in 1804, resigning in August to accept appointment to the U.S. Senate, where he served 1804–09. Moore died in Lexington, Virginia, on April 14, 1821.

• DANIEL MORGAN   1736–1802

Daniel Morgan

A frontiersman, general in the Revolutionary War, and U.S. Congressman, Daniel Morgan was born near Junction, New Jersey, in 1736, a cousin of Daniel Boone. At nineteen he served with Boone as a teamster in Gen. Edward Braddock's unsuccessful expedition against Fort Duquesne in the French and Indian War. When he hit a British officer who had slapped him with the flat of his sword, Morgan was given a punishment of 500 lashes across his back. In 1758 an Indian bullet knocked out half his teeth. He also took part in Pontiac's War in 1763 and Dunmore's War in 1774.

At the beginning of the Revolutionary War, he was commissioned captain of a company of Virginia riflemen in July 1775. After fighting heroically, he was taken prisoner at the battle of Quebec on December 31, 1775. After being exchanged, Morgan was made colonel of the 11th Virginia Regiment on November 12, 1776. He and his riflemen played an important part in winning the two battles of Saratoga in 1777. Commissioned a brigadier general in 1780, he distinguished himself with the strategy he devised to beat the British at the battle of Cowpens, South Carolina, in January 1781, being given one of the eight medals awarded by Congress during the war.

At the close of the war Morgan returned to the frontier, where he accumulated a quarter of a million acres of land in what is now West Virginia. In 1794 he commanded the Virginia militia ordered out by President Washington to suppress the Whisky Insurrection in Pennsylvania. Morgan was elected to the Fifth U.S. Congress 1797–98, but declined to be a candidate for renomination. He died at his estate, "Saratoga," near Winchester, Virginia, on July 6, 1802.

• CADWALADER MORRIS   1741–1795

A Pennsylvania delegate to the Continental Congress, Cadwalader Morris was born in Philadelphia on February 19, 1741. A successful businessman, he served during the early part of the Revolutionary War as a member of the Philadelphia Troop of Light Horse. In 1781 he was one of the founders and a director of the Bank of North America. He was chosen as a delegate to the Continental Congress 1783–84, and declined election for another term. After the war he operated an iron furnace in Birdsborough, Pennsylvania, but subsequently returned to Philadelphia, where he died on January 25, 1795.

Gouverneur Morris

• GOUVERNEUR MORRIS   1752–1816

The man who wrote the final version of the United States
Constitution, Gouverneur Morris was born on the manor of
Morrisania (now a part of the borough of the Bronx of New
York City) on January 31, 1752, the half brother of Lewis
Morris. After graduation from King's College (now Columbia
University) at sixteen, he studied law and commenced practice
in New York City in 1771.

Morris was elected to the New York Revolutionary provincial congress 1775–77 and to the state's first legislature
1777–78. He was unable to serve in the army in the Revolutionary War because he had lost a leg in his twenties, and
wore a wooden peg leg the rest of his life. He was chosen as
one of New York's delegates to the Continental Congress in
1777–78, where he was a signer of the Articles of Confederation. He remained in Philadelphia, where he was appointed
assistant minister of finance in 1781. He was chosen as one of
Pennsylvania's delegates to the federal convention that framed
the Constitution of the United States in 1787. As a member of

Morgan's Virginia rifleman

311

the convention's committee on style, he drafted the final version of the Constitution, and is particularly credited with the wording of its preamble, and was one of the signers of the Constitution.

President Washington appointed him as special commissioner to England in 1789–91, and as ambassador to France in 1792–94. Upon the death of his brother, Lewis Morris, he returned to New York as lord of the manor of Morrisania. He was elected as a Federalist to the U.S. Senate 1800–03. In his latter years he devoted much time to the building of the Erie Canal as chairman of the Erie Canal Commission 1810–13. Morris died at Morrisania, on November 6, 1816.

Lewis Morris

● **LEWIS MORRIS** 1726–1798

A signer of the Declaration of Independence and a wealthy New York landowner, Lewis Morris was born at Morrisania (now part of the borough of the Bronx of New York City) on April 8, 1726, the elder half brother of Gouverneur Morris. After graduation from Yale College in 1746 he helped manage the family estates. He was appointed by the crown a judge of the Court of Admiralty in 1760, but resigned fourteen years later in 1774. He was a member of New York's delegation to the Continental Congress 1775–77, where he signed the Declaration of Independence. During the Revolutionary War he rose from brigadier general to major general in the New York militia, concerning himself mostly with gathering supplies. He also was elected to the state senate 1777–81 and 1784–88. He was a member of the first board of regents of the University of New York, serving from 1784 until his death at Morrisania on January 22, 1798.

● **ROBERT MORRIS** 1734–1806

A signer of the Declaration of Independence, the Articles of Confederation, and the United States Constitution, Robert Morris was born in Liverpool, England, on January 20, 1734. At thirteen he immigrated to America in 1747 to join his father who had established a tobacco business in Oxford, Maryland. Left an orphan at fifteen, Morris became an apprentice to a merchant in Philadelphia. By the time of the Revolutionary War, Morris had become one of Philadelphia's wealthiest merchants.

Morris was chosen as one of Pennsylvania's delegates to the Continental Congress 1776–78, where he opposed adoption of the Declaration of Independence, but signed it after the other delegates approved it. In 1776 he pledged his personal credit to provide Washington's army with the supplies needed for the battles of Trenton and Princeton. By many, Morris is regarded as second only to George Washington in importance for his contributions in winning the struggle for independence.

He became known as the "Financier of the American Revolution" for his continued efforts in raising money and supplies for the Continental Army.

After the ratification of the Articles of Confederation, which Morris had signed in 1778, Congress appointed him as superintendent of finance 1781–84. Morris helped found the Bank of North America in 1781. He was chosen as one of Pennsylvania's delegates to the federal Constitutional Convention of 1787, where he signed the new United States Constitution. He then was elected to the U.S. Senate, serving from 1789 to 1795. He declined President Washington's offer of the post of Secretary of the Treasury. In the late 1790s he became involved in unsuccessful land speculations, which caused him to be imprisoned for debt from 1798 to 1801. During this period, Washington had dinner in prison with his old friend on a visit to Philadelphia after leaving the presidency. After his release from prison he lived in poverty until his death in Philadelphia on May 8, 1806.

Robert Morris

Mrs. Robert Morris

• JOHN MORTON   1724–1777

A signer of the Declaration of Independence, John Morton was born near the old Morris Ferry (now the Darby Creek Bridge) in Ridley Township, Delaware County, Pennsylvania, in 1724. Although he had only three months of formal schooling, his stepfather taught him surveying, an occupation he followed for many years. He was elected a member of Pennsylvania's colonial assembly 1756–66 and 1769–75, serving as speaker 1771–75. As a member of the Continental Congress 1774–77, Morton cast the deciding vote of the Pennsylvania delegation on the adoption of the Declaration of Independence and was a signer thereof. Criticism that he received from conservatives who opposed adoption of the Declaration was believed to have hastened his death, which came in Ridley Park, Pennsylvania, in April 1777, only nine months after he had voted for independence.

• ISAAC MOTTE   1738–1795

An officer in the Continental Army and a delegate to the Continental Congress, Isaac Motte was born in Charleston, South

John Morton

The defense of Fort Moultrie—the heroism of Sergeant Jasper —From a painting by J. A. Oertel

Carolina, on December 8, 1738. At eighteen he joined in the French and Indian War as an ensign in the British 60th Royal American Regiment, and was promoted to lieutenant in 1759. He resigned from the army in 1766 and returned to Charleston. He was elected to the colonial house of commons in 1772, and to the South Carolina Revolutionary congresses of 1774–76. During the Revolution he served as a lieutenant colonel of the 2nd South Carolina Regiment in the defense of Fort Moultrie in 1776, and was promoted to colonel the next year. He resigned from the army in 1779 after being elected to the state legislature. He was selected as a member of South Carolina's delegation to the Continental Congress 1780–82. After adoption of the United States Constitution, Motte was appointed naval officer for the port of Charleston by President Washington, a post he held until his death in Charleston on May 8, 1795.

General William Moultrie

- **WILLIAM MOULTRIE   1730–1805**

A general in the Continental Army, William Moultrie was born in South Carolina in 1730. He served as a militia captain in the fighting against the Cherokee Indians in 1761. Commissioned a colonel in the Continental Army in 1775, Moultrie became a national hero for his defense of Fort Sullivan in Charleston Harbor on June 28, 1776, that beat off an attack by the British fleet with heavy British losses. The fort was renamed in Moultrie's honor. Three months later he was promoted to brigadier general in the Continental Army. In 1779 Moultrie defeated a force of about 200 British troops in the battle of Beaufort, South Carolina. The next year he was captured by the British at the surrender of Charleston. Moultrie was imprisoned for nearly two years until he was exchanged for General John Burgoyne in February 1782. Eight months later he was promoted to major general, but by that time the fighting was over. Moultrie was elected governor of South Carolina in 1785–86 and 1794–96. He died in Charleston on September 27, 1805.

- **DANIEL MOWRY, Jr.   1729–1806**

A Rhode Island delegate to the Continental Congress, Daniel Mowry, Jr., was born in Smithfield, Rhode Island, on August 17, 1729. After serving an apprenticeship, he became a barrelmaker. He was elected to the Rhode Island general assembly 1766–76, and then was appointed judge of the court of common pleas 1776–81. He was a member of Rhode Island's delegation to the Continental Congress 1780–82, but declined to be a candidate for renomination. After the Revolutionary War he became a farmer. He died in Smithfield on July 6, 1806.

315

• FREDERICK MUHLENBERG   1750–1801

A Lutheran minister, delegate to the Continental Congress, and one of Pennsylvania's first U.S. Congressmen, Frederick Augustus Conrad Muhlenberg was born in Trappe, Pennsylvania, on January 1, 1750, a brother of Peter Muhlenberg. After attending the University of Halle in Germany, he studied theology and was ordained a minister of the Lutheran Church at the age of twenty in 1770. He preached in Stouchsburg and Lebanon, Pennsylvania, 1770–74, and in New York City 1774–76. When the British army entered New York in 1776, he returned to Pennsylvania. He served as a pastor in New Hanover, Oley, and New Goshenhoppen 1776–79. He was chosen as a member of Pennsylvania's delegation to the Continental Congress in 1779–80. He was elected to the state house of representatives 1780–83, where he served as speaker. Both he and his brother Peter were elected as Representatives to the First U.S. Congress in 1789. He served in Congress until 1797, being elected the first Speaker of the House of Representatives in the First U.S. Congress and again in the Third U.S. Congress. He was appointed receiver general of the Pennsylvania land office in 1800, an office he held until his death in Lancaster, Pennsylvania, on June 5, 1801.

• PETER MUHLENBERG   1746–1807

A Lutheran minister, general in the Continental Congress, U.S. Congressman, and U.S. Senator, John Peter Gabriel Muhlenberg was born in Trappe, Pennsylvania, on October 1, 1746, an older brother of Frederick Muhlenberg. After attending the College of Philadelphia, he was sent at fourteen to study at the University of Halle in Germany. Leaving school, he was apprenticed to a grocer. He then ran away and at sixteen joined a German regiment of dragoons, the 60th British Royal Americans, who had been recruited to fight in the French and Indian War.

Discharged from the army in 1767, he studied theology, was ordained, and became a pastor of Lutheran churches in New Germantown and Bedminster, New Jersey, in 1768. He moved to Woodstock, Virginia, in 1772, and later that year visited England where he was ordained a priest in the Episcopal Church by the Bishop of London. He was elected to the Virginia house of burgesses in 1774, where he became a friend of George Washington. In 1775 he was commissioned colonel of the 8th Virginia (German) Regiment. He told his congregation: "There is a time for all things—a time to preach and a time to pray; but there is also a time to fight, and that time has now come." In 1777 he was promoted to brigadier general of the Continental Army, leading his brigade in the battles of Brandywine and Germantown. The next year he fought in the

General John Peter Gabriel Muhlenberg

battle of Monmouth, and then was sent to Virginia where he was second in command to Gen. Friedrich von Steuben. In 1781 he led his brigade in the assault on Redoubt No. 10 in the battle of Yorktown.

After the war he returned to Pennsylvania where he served as vice president of the state under Benjamin Franklin in 1785–88. He was elected to the First U.S. Congress 1789–91, the Third U.S. Congress 1793–95, and the Sixth U.S. Congress 1799–1801. As a Democratic-Republican he was elected to the U.S. Senate in 1801, but resigned to accept President Jefferson's appointment as supervisor of revenue for Pennsylvania in June 1801. The next year he was appointed collector of customs at Philadelphia, an office he held until his death at his estate, "Providence," near Philadelphia, on October 1, 1807.

- ### ABNER NASH   1740–1786

A governor of North Carolina and delegate to the Continental Congress, Abner Nash was born at Templeton Manor on the Appomattox River near Farmville, Virginia, on August 8, 1740. In 1762 he moved to North Carolina, where he married the young widow of Gov. Arthur Dobbs. He became one of the most prominent leaders in the pre-Revolutionary movement in the colony. He was elected to the North Carolina house of commons in 1777–78 and 1782, serving as speaker in 1777. He then became a state senator in 1779–80, and was president of the state senate in 1779. He was elected governor of North Carolina in 1780–81, while the state was the scene of fighting during the Revolutionary War. He served in the Continental Congress from 1782 until his death in New York City on December 2, 1786, while attending a session.

- ### FRANCIS NASH   1720–1777

A Continental Army general who was fatally wounded in the battle of Germantown, Francis Nash was born on May 10, 1720, in Prince Edward County, Virginia, an older brother of Abner Nash. Having moved to North Carolina, he was elected to the colonial legislature there in the 1760s and early 1770s. As a captain in the militia he served under Governor William Tryon in defeating the Regulators at the battle of Alamance in 1771. He was elected to the North Carolina revolutionary conventions in 1775, and that same year was commissioned a lieutenant colonel in the Continental Army. He was promoted to colonel in 1776, and the following year to brigadier general. Ordered to march his troops north for the defense of Philadelphia in 1777, he took part in the battle of Brandywine on September 11. The next month, while leading his troops at Germantown, he was struck by a cannon ball. Three days later he died on October 7, 1777.

317

Thomas Nelson

- **THOMAS NELSON**   **1738–1789**

A signer of the Declaration of Independence and governor of
Virginia, Thomas Nelson was born in Yorktown, Virginia, on
December 26, 1738. After graduation from Trinity College,
Cambridge, England, in 1761, he was elected a member of the
Virginia house of burgesses while on his way home from England. He regularly was re-elected to the house of burgesses
until it was dissolved by the royal governor in 1774. He was
chosen as one of Virginia's delegates to the Continental Congress 1775–77, where he signed the Declaration of Independence. In 1777 he was appointed brigadier general and commander of the Virginia state militia, organizing the defenses of
the state against British attack. Elected governor of Virginia in
1781, he pledged his personal fortune and estates to raise supplies for Washington's Army. At the battle of Yorktown, he
directed the artillery to destroy his own home, which was being used as Cornwallis' headquarters. Ruined by his losses
during the war, Nelson retired to a small farm he still owned in
Hanover County, Virginia, where he died on January 4, 1789.

- **JOHN NIXON**   **1725–1815**

A general in the Continental Army, John Nixon was born in
Framingham, Massachusetts, on March 4, 1725. At eighteen

he joined the army to fight in King George's War, taking part in the capture of Louisbourg in 1745. Ten years later he rejoined the army to serve in the French and Indian War as a captain, fighting at Crown Point and Ticonderoga. On the first day of fighting in the Revolutionary War, April 19, 1775, Nixon marched a company of Minutemen from Sudbury to the defense of Concord. Five days later he was appointed a colonel. On June 17 he was wounded while taking part in the battle of Bunker Hill. The following year Nixon was appointed to brigadier general in the Continental Army. At the battle of Harlem Heights in September 1776 he and his brigade performed bravely in the front line of attack. In 1777 Nixon and his men took part in the battles of Saratoga, where an eye and ear were permanently injured when a cannon ball narrowly missed blowing his head off. He went on sick leave after this action, and resigned from the army in 1780. He died in Middlebury, Vermont, on March 24, 1815.

• JEREMIAH O'BRIEN   1740–1818

Leader of the first successful American naval action of the Revolutionary War, Jeremiah O'Brien was born in 1740 in Scarboro, now in Maine. Upon hearing of the battles of Lexington and Concord, O'Brien with four of his brothers and several volunteers captured the British armed schooner *Margaretta* and two supply sloops in Machias Bay on June 12, 1775, to prevent their taking lumber and naval stores back to British forces in Boston. O'Brien then fought as a privateer, commanding the *Resolution* in 1777 which took the British ship *Scarborough*. As captain of the *Hannibal* in 1780 he was captured by the British. He was imprisoned for a time in the prison ship *Jersey* in New York and then taken to England. He escaped from prison there and again commanded privateers for the rest of the war. After the war he served for many years as collector of customs at Machias. He died there on October 5, 1818.

His brother, Richard O'Brien (1758–1824), also commanded a privateer in the Revolutionary War and then served as a naval officer aboard the brig *Jefferson* in 1781. Captured by the Dey of Algiers, Richard O'Brien was enslaved and forced to wear a ball and chain until the United States government finally obtained his release in 1797.

• SAMUEL OSGOOD   1748–1813

A Revolutionary War officer and first Postmaster General of the United States, Samuel Osgood was born in Andover, Massachusetts, on February 3, 1748. After graduation from Harvard College in 1770, he became a merchant. At the beginning of the Revolutionary Army he was commissioned a

Colonel John Nixon

319

captain and later was promoted to colonel and assistant quartermaster. He was chosen as one of Massachusetts' delegates to the Continental Congress 1780–84. President Washington appointed him as his first Postmaster General 1789–91. Having moved to New York City, Osgood was elected a member of the state assembly 1800–03. He was appointed naval officer at the port of New York in 1803, an office he held until his death on August 12, 1813.

• JAMES OTIS   1725−1783

James Otis

One of Boston's most prominent lawyers, whose writings and speeches about the rights of the American colonists set the stage for the Revolutionary War, James Otis was born in West Barnstable, Massachusetts, on February 5, 1725. After graduation at eighteen from Harvard College, where he was a schoolmate of Samuel Adams, Otis studied law and began practice in Plymouth, Massachusetts, in 1748. Otis came to prominence when he resigned as king's attorney for the colony's court of admiralty in 1760 on the grounds that he refused to aid the royal government in its use of writs of assistance, a kind of search warrant used by customs officials to search for smuggled goods. In a hearing before the chief justice of Massachusetts in 1761, Otis won a ruling that the writs were not legal. John Adams, then a young lawyer, attended the hearing and described what he heard: "Otis was a flame of fire! . . . American independence was then and there born; the seeds of patriots and heroes were then and there sown. . . . Every man of a crowded audience appeared to me to go away, as I did, ready to take arms against writs of assistance."

In the years that followed Otis published several pamphlets dealing with the right of the colonial legislature to determine what taxes should be levied and other rights of the colonists. In 1765 he headed the Massachusetts delegation to the Stamp Act Congress in New York. The following year he was elected speaker of the Massachusetts legislature, but his election was vetoed by the royal governor because of Otis' outspoken opposition to royal policies. Otis and Sam Adams wrote a circular letter to the other colonies suggesting united opposition to the Townshend Acts. After the British quartered troops in Boston, Otis made speech after speech denouncing the action as military occupation.

When Otis published an advertisement in 1769 accusing the governor and customs collectors of sending false reports about him to London, one of the customs collectors approached him in a coffee shop and struck him with a heavy cane or the flat of a sword. The wound damaged Otis' brain, and he no longer was able to assist the patriotic cause. He lived the rest of his life on a farm near Andover, Massachusetts, dying on May 23, 1783, when he was struck by a bolt of lightning.

FROM A WATERCOLOR PAINTING BY KAY SMITH

The William Paca house and garden, Annapolis, Maryland, which is being restored. This lovely house and garden in the center of Annapolis, Maryland, was developed in 1765 by William Paca, a signer of the Declaration of Independence who also served as Governor of Maryland during the Revolutionary period. In the ensuing years the house had become part of Carvel Hall, a hotel, and the gardens had undergone many changes in the conversion from a colonial estate to commercial use. Through the alert and dedicated work of individuals and Historic Annapolis, Inc., the house and gardens will be completely restored by 1976 for the observance of the Bicentennial.

FROM A WATERCOLOR PAINTING BY KAY SMITH

In this historic and graceful
structure, the State House,
Annapolis, Maryland, every session
of the Maryland legislature
since 1775 has been held, with
the exception of 1861, when they
met in Frederick, Maryland,
due to the strong confederate
sentiment of the southern
Maryland residents. In the old
state Senate chamber, which was
the Capitol of the United States
from November 1783 to June 1784,
George Washington resigned his
commission as Commander in Chief
on December 23, 1783.
On January 14, 1784, the Treaty
of Paris, officially ending the
Revolutionary War, was ratified
here. In 1786 the Annapolis
Convention was held here,
which meeting led to the
Constitutional Convention in
Philadelphia in 1787.

FROM A WATERCOLOR PAINTING BY KAY SMITH

Living in an aristocratic manner befitting their wealth and ancestry, the Carroll family traced their lineage to the ancient kings of Ireland. It was in this Annapolis, Maryland townhouse of his father, Charles Carroll of Annapolis, that Charles Carroll of Carrollton spent most of his time after completing his education in France and England. The only Roman Catholic to sign the Declaration of Independence and one of the three wealthiest men in America—the others being George Washington and Henry Middleton—he risked his life and fortune for the cause of liberty and religious freedom.

- **SAMUEL ALLYNE OTIS   1740–1814**

A delegate to the Continental Congress and first Secretary of the U.S. Senate, Samuel Allyne Otis was born in Barnstable, Massachusetts, on November 24, 1740. After graduation from Harvard College in 1759, he became a merchant in Boston. He was elected to the state house of representatives in 1776 and 1784–87, becoming speaker of the house in 1784. He was a member of Massachusetts' delegation to the Continental Congress in 1787–88. Otis was elected Secretary of the U.S. Senate on April 8, 1789, an office he held until his death in Washington, D.C., on April 22, 1814.

- **WILLIAM PACA   1740–1799**

A signer of the Declaration of Independence and governor of Maryland, William Paca was born at "Wye Hall," near Abingdon, Maryland, on October 31, 1740. After graduation from the College of Philadelphia at nineteen, he studied law in the Middle Temple in London, England, and commenced practice in Annapolis in 1764. He was a close associate of Samuel Chase in the pre-Revolutionary activities of the Sons of Liberty in Maryland. He was elected to the colonial assembly in 1768–74. Paca was chosen as one of Maryland's delegates to the Continental Congress 1774–79, where he signed the Declaration of Independence. Paca was appointed chief judge of the superior court of Maryland 1778–80, and then chief justice of the court of appeals in prize and admiralty cases 1780–82. He was elected governor of Maryland 1782–85. Although Paca opposed ratification of the new United States Constitution, he was appointed by President Washington as judge of the U.S. district court for Maryland, serving from 1789 until his death at "Wye Hall" on October 23, 1799.

William Paca

- **JOHN PAGE   1744–1808**

A militia officer in the Revolutionary War and one of Virginia's first U.S. Congressmen, John Page was born at "Rosewell" in Gloucester County, Virginia, on April 17, 1744, the older brother of Mann Page. After graduation from William and Mary College at nineteen, he served under George Washington in an expedition in the French and Indian War. Page was lieutenant governor of Virginia under Gov. Patrick Henry at the beginning of the Revolutionary War. As a colonel of militia he recruited and trained a regiment from Gloucester County. Page was elected to the Virginia house of delegates 1781–83 and 1785–88. He won election as a Democrat to the first and three succeeding U.S. Congresses 1789–97. After again serving in the state house of delegates in 1797–98 and 1800–01, Page was elected governor of Virginia in 1802–05. He then was appointed U.S. commissioner of loans for Virginia, holding that office until his death in Richmond, Virginia, on October 11, 1808.

• MANN PAGE   1749–1781

A Virginia delegate to the Continental Congress, Mann Page was born at "Rosewell" in Gloucester County, Virginia, in 1749, a younger brother of John Page. After graduation from the College of William and Mary, he became a lawyer and was elected to the Virginia house of burgesses. He was chosen as one of Virginia's delegates to the Continental Congress in 1777. Page died on his estate, "Mansfield," near Fredericksburg, Virginia, in 1781.

• EPHRAIM PAINE   1730–1785

A physician and a New York delegate to the Continental Congress, Ephraim Paine was born in Canterbury, Connecticut, on August 19, 1730. After studying medicine, he began practice in Amenia, New York. He was elected as a delegate to the Revolutionary New York provincial congress in 1775. Paine was appointed judge of Dutchess County 1778–81, and was elected to the state senate 1780–84. He was chosen as a member of New York's delegation to the Continental Congress in 1784–85. Paine died in Amenia on August 10, 1785.

• ROBERT TREAT PAINE   1731–1814

A signer of the Declaration of Independence, Robert Treat Paine was born in Boston, Massachusetts, on March 11, 1731. After graduation from Harvard College at eighteen, he studied theology and was chaplain of New England troops in the French and Indian War on the Crown Point expedition in 1755. He then studied law and began practice in 1759. Having become one of the leading lawyers of Massachusetts, he was chosen as special prosecutor for the trial of British soldiers in the Boston Massacre of 1771, while John Adams opposed him, serving for the defense. Paine was elected to the Massachusetts colonial legislature 1773–75, and with Adams was chosen as a member of Massachusetts' delegation to the Continental Congress in 1774–78, where he signed the Declaration of Independence. Paine was appointed as the first attorney general of the state of Massachusetts 1777–90. He then served as a judge of the Massachusetts supreme court 1790–1804. Paine died in Boston on May 12, 1814.

• THOMAS PAINE   1737–1809

A patriotic writer whose words helped urge America on to win the Revolutionary War, Thomas Paine was born in Thetford,

Robert Treat Paine

Thomas Paine —From a painting by Auguste Milliere

England, on January 29, 1737. The son of a poor Quaker corset maker, Paine spent his boyhood learning his father's trade. At nineteen he ran away from home to spend a year as a seaman aboard a privateer, but when the cruise was over he returned home to the corset business to help support his family. In the years that followed he educated himself by reading while working at a variety of occupations. After obtaining an appointment as a tax collector, he was chosen by his fellow tax collectors to go before parliament in 1772 to ask for a raise. For his efforts, Paine was dismissed from his post. Benjamin Franklin, then in London as the representative of the Massachusetts colony, met Paine and suggested that he go to America. Paine, then thirty-seven, followed Franklin's advice and arrived in Philadelphia in November 1774.

With letters of introduction from Franklin, Paine found work as a free-lance writer. He met Dr. Benjamin Rush, and that future signer of the Declaration of Independence suggested to Paine that he write a short pamphlet urging the people to seek independence from Britain, a subject that was extremely controversial in the winter of 1775–76, when the Continental Congress had not yet made up its mind on the issue. Rush suggested that the pamphlet be called *Common Sense*. Paine wrote the booklet, publishing it anonymously in January 1776. Until that time most of the pamphlets and essays written

TWENTY FOUR SHILLINGS

Iſſued in defence of American Liberty

Enſe petit placidam, ſub Libertate Quietem

MAGNA CHARTA

Augt 18. 1775.

about the issues had been by lawyers, such as John Dickinson or James Otis, and were couched in legalistic phrases that had little appeal to the layman. On the other hand, Paine's pamphlet minced no words. Of the monarchy he said:

"One of the strongest natural proofs of the folly of hereditary right in kings is that nature disapproves it; otherwise she would not so frequently turn it into ridicule by giving mankind *an ass for a lion.*"

As for independence, Paine's pamphlet said:

"Everything that is right or reasonable pleads for separation. The blood of the slain, the weeping voice of nature cries, *'Tis time to part.*"

Paine's *Common Sense* became a best seller with more than 100,000 copies sold during the next few months. More importantly, it had the effect Rush had hoped for. Less than six months after its publication the Continental Congress adopted the Declaration of Independence.

Paine enlisted in the army in 1776, serving as aide to General Nathanael Greene. After Washington's defeat in the battle of Long Island and his subsequent loss of New York to the British, many Americans began to waver in their determination. So Paine began writing a series of essays called *The Crisis*, the first of which appeared in the *Pennsylvania Journal* in December 1776, beginning with these words:

"These are the times that try men's souls. The summer soldier and the sunshine patriot will, in this crisis, shrink from the service of their country; but he that stands it *now*, deserves the love and thanks of man and woman. Tyranny, like hell, is not easily conquered; yet we have this consolation with us, that the harder the conflict, the more glorious the triumph."

To help Paine support himself while continuing to write his pamphlets, Congress appointed him to the paid position of secretary to the committee on foreign affairs in April 1777. But within eighteen months Paine got himself involved in a controversy over Silas Deane and was forced to resign from his post. The Pennsylvania legislature came to Paine's financial rescue by hiring him as a clerk. Throughout the war Paine continued to publish new essays in his *The Crisis* series.

When the war was over, the state of New York gave Paine as a reward the former estate of a loyalist at New Rochelle, New York, and the Pennsylvania legislature voted him a bonus of $2,500. Paine went to Europe in 1787, where he was feted in London and Paris. He invented the first iron bridge in the world and supervised its construction over the Wear River at Sunderland, England. In 1791 he wrote the first half of his book *The Rights of Man*. The following year he went to France, where he was elected to the French national assembly as a hero, while the British government indicted him for treason *in absentia*. He published the second half of *The Rights of Man* in 1792, and its sales zoomed past those of his earlier *Common Sense*.

Falling into disfavor with the French revolutionists, Paine was jailed in 1793. He used his time in prison to write *The Age of Reason*, a long diatribe against organized religion. Released from prison by the French at the urging of U.S. ambassador to France James Monroe, Paine published a long "letter" to George Washington in 1796 criticizing his Federalist policies.

Returning to the United States in 1802, Paine lived out the rest of his life on his farm at New Rochelle, New York, dying there on June 8, 1809.

• JOHN PARKER   1759–1832

A South Carolina delegate to the Continental Congress, John Parker was born in Charleston, South Carolina, on June 24, 1759. After studying law at the Middle Temple in London, England, he began practice in Charleston, South Carolina, in 1785. He was chosen as one of South Carolina's delegates to the Continental Congress 1786–88. He then turned his attention to managing his large rice plantations, "Hayes" and "Cedar Grove." He died at "Hayes" near Charleston on April 20, 1832.

• JOSIAH PARKER   1751–1810

An officer in the Revolutionary War and one of Virginia's first U.S. Congressmen, Josiah Parker was born at "Macclesfield" in Isle of Wight County, Virginia, on May 11, 1751. Active in the pre-Revolutionary movement, he was a member of the local committee of safety in 1775 and of the Virginia Revolutionary convention of that year. Commissioned major in the 5th Virginia Regiment in 1776, he served with distinction at the battles of Trenton, Princeton, and the Brandywine. After having been promoted to colonel, he resigned from the army in 1778. Parker was elected to the Virginia house of delegates in 1780–81. He was elected to the first and five succeeding U.S. Congresses 1789–1801. He then retired to "Macclesfield," where he died on March 18, 1810.

• GEORGE PARTRIDGE   1740–1828

A delegate from Massachusetts to the Continental Congress and one of the state's first U.S. Congressmen, George Partridge was born in Duxbury, Massachusetts, on February 8, 1740. After graduation from Harvard College in 1762, he taught school in Kingston, Massachusetts. Partridge was elected to the Massachusetts legislature 1775–79. For twenty-five years he served as sheriff of Plymouth County 1777–1812. He was chosen as a delegate to the Continental Congress 1779–85, and then was elected to the First U.S. Congress 1789–90. He died in Duxbury on July 7, 1828.

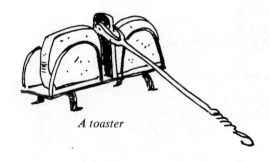

A toaster

• JOHN PATERSON   1744–1808

A general in the Revolutionary War and a U.S. Congressman, John Paterson was born in New Britain, Connecticut, in 1744. After graduation from Yale College at eighteen, he studied law and began practice in Lenox, Massachusetts. When news came of the battles of Lexington and Concord in 1775, he raised a regiment of militia and marched to Boston as their colonel. His regiment became the 15th Continental Infantry on January 1, 1776. He led his men to Canada and then took part in the battles of Trenton and Princeton. Promoted to brigadier general in 1777, he had a horse shot out from under him in the campaign at Saratoga. After taking part in the battle of Monmouth in 1778, he spent the rest of the war with his regiment in the Hudson Highlands.

At the end of the war he was brevetted a major general, and then returned to his law practice in Lenox. Paterson commanded Massachusetts militia in putting down Shays' Rebellion in 1786. Four years later he moved to Broome County, New York, where he was elected to the state assembly in 1792–93. He then served as county judge of Broome County 1798–1806. Paterson was elected to the Eighth U.S. Congress 1803–05. He died in what is now Whitney Point, New York, on July 19, 1808.

• WILLIAM PATERSON   1745–1806

A signer of the United States Constitution, a U.S. Senator and governor of New Jersey, and an associate justice of the U.S. Supreme Court, William Paterson was born in Antrim, Ireland, on December 24, 1745. While still a baby, he was brought to America in 1747 by his parents. After graduation from the College of New Jersey in 1763, he studied law and commenced practice in New Bromley, New Jersey, in 1769. He was active in the pre-Revolutionary movement, and was one of a four-man committee who arrested the royal governor in 1776. He then became attorney general of New Jersey 1776–83. He was a member of New Jersey's delegation to the federal Constitutional Convention in Philadelphia in 1787. He put foward the "New Jersey Plan" for the new government, but when it was rejected signed the new United States Constitution.

He was elected as one of New Jersey's first U.S. Senators in 1789, but resigned in 1790, having been elected governor of New Jersey 1790–93. He then resigned as governor to accept appointment by President Washington as an associate justice of the Supreme Court of the United States, a position he held for thirteen years until his death at the home of a daughter in Albany, New York, on September 9, 1806. The city of Paterson, New Jersey, founded in 1792 while he was governor, was named for him.

William Paterson

- **JOHN PATTEN**   1746–1800

A Revolutionary War officer and delegate to the Continental Congress, John Patten was born in Kent County, Delaware, on April 26, 1746. At twenty he joined the Continental Army as a lieutenant. Serving in many battles from Long Island to Camden, he advanced to the rank of major by the end of the war. He was chosen as a delegate from Delaware to the Continental Congress in 1785–86. Patten was elected to the U.S. Congress 1793–97, and then retired to his farm, "Tynhead Court," near Dover, Delaware, where he died on December 26, 1800.

- **NATHANIEL PEABODY**   1741–1823

A physician, militia general, and delegate to the Continental Congress, Nathaniel Peabody was born in Topsfield, Massachusetts, on March 1, 1741. After studying medicine, he commenced practice at the age of twenty in Plaistow, New Hampshire, in 1761. He took part in the capture of Fort William and Mary, New Castle, New Hampshire, in 1774, and was a member of the committee of safety, serving as its chairman in 1776. During the Revolutionary War he was adjutant general of the New Hampshire militia, commanding a brigade in Rhode Island in 1779. From 1776 to 1793 he was elected to the state legislature, serving alternately in the house and the senate. Peabody was chosen as a delegate to the Continental Congress in 1779–80. From 1793–98 he was major general of New Hampshire militia. Falling into debt, Peabody was imprisoned as a debtor for about twenty years. He died in Exeter, New Hampshire, on June 27, 1823.

- **WILLIAM PEERY**   ?–1800

A militia officer in the Revolutionary War and a delegate to the Continental Congress, William Peery grew up near Lewes, Delaware, where his father was a farmer. In the Revolutionary War, Peery raised and equipped an independent company at his own expense and was commissioned its captain in 1777. After the war, he studied law and commenced practice in Sussex County, Delaware, in 1785. Elected to the state legislature, he was chosen as a delegate to the Continental Congress in 1785–86. He died at Cool Spring, Delaware, on December 17, 1800.

- **EDMUND PENDLETON**   1721–1803

First head of the Revolutionary government in Virginia and a delegate to the Continental Congress, Edmund Pendleton was born in Caroline County, Virginia, on September 9, 1721. After studying law, he began practice at the age of twenty. He became one of Virginia's leading statesmen, serving in the house of burgesses for twenty-two years 1752–74. As president of the committee of safety, he was the first head of Virginia's government at the beginning of the Revolutionary War in 1774–76. He was chosen as one of Virginia's delegates to the first two sessions of the Continental Congress in 1774–75. He was appointed judge of the general court and the court of chancery in 1777, and presiding judge of the court of appeals in 1779. He died in Richmond, Virginia, on October 23, 1803.

John Penn

• **JOHN PENN   1741–1788**

A signer of the Declaration of Independence and of the Articles of Confederation, John Penn was born near Port Royal, Virginia, on May 17, 1741. After studying law, he began practice in Bowling Green, Virginia, in 1762. He moved to Granville County, North Carolina, in 1774, where he took an active part in the pre-Revolutionary movement. He was chosen as one of North Carolina's delegates to the Continental Congress 1775–80, where he signed both the Declaration of Independence, and the Articles of Confederation. After the War, he resumed the practice of law. He died at his home near Stovall, North Carolina, on September 14, 1788.

• **RICHARD PETERS, JR.   1743–1828**

A Revolutionary War officer and delegate to the Continental Congress, Richard Peters, Jr., was born near Philadelphia on June 22, 1743. After graduation from the College of Philadelphia at seventeen, he studied law and commenced practice in Philadelphia. At the beginning of the Revolutionary War, he was commissioned a captain and served as secretary of the

Continental Board of War from 1776 to 1781. He was chosen as one of Pennsylvania's delegates to the Continental Congress in 1782–83. Peters was elected to the state assembly 1787–90, serving as speaker. He was appointed judge of the U.S. district court of Pennsylvania in 1792, a position he held for thirty-six years, until his death in Philadelphia on August 22, 1828.

• **CHARLES PETTIT   1736–1806**

An officer in the Continental Army and a delegate to the Continental Congress, Charles Pettit was born near Amwell, New Jersey, in 1736. After studying law in England, Pettit returned to America where he served in several legal offices for the colonial government of New Jersey, and in 1771 became aide-de-camp to the royal governor, William Franklin. After Franklin was arrested by the patriots in 1776, Pettit became secretary of state of New Jersey and aide to Gov. William Livingston. In 1778 he joined the Continental Army as assistant adjutant general on the staff of Gen. Nathanael Greene, declining promotion to quartermaster general. After the war he was elected to the Pennsylvania house of representatives in 1783–84, and was chosen as a delegate to the Continental Congress in 1785–87. He became a successful merchant in Philadelphia, where he died on September 4, 1806.

• **ANDREW PICKENS   1739–1817**

A general of guerrillas in the South in the Revolutionary War and later a U.S. Congressman, Andrew Pickens was born in Paxton, Pennsylvania, on September 13, 1739. He moved with his parents to the Waxhaw settlement in South Carolina in 1752. At twenty-one, Pickens served in the militia in the campaign against the Cherokee Indians in 1760–61. As a captain of militia he fought in the battle of Ninety-Six, South Carolina, in 1775. Promoted to colonel, Pickens won an important battle against a large group of marauding Tories at Kettle Creek, Georgia, in February 1779, and received a sword from Congress for his conduct at the Battle of Cowpens in 1781. Promoted to brigadier general, he organized a large guerrilla army, paid with plunder they took from Loyalists. In June 1781 Pickens and his men helped capture Augusta, Georgia. Pickens was wounded at the battle of Eutaw Springs in September 1781. Pickens then commanded an expedition against an uprising of the Cherokee Indians in 1782. He was elected to the South Carolina house of representatives 1781–94, and then to the Third U.S. Congress 1793–95. He again was elected to the state legislature in 1800–12. Pickens died in Tamassee, South Carolina, on August 11, 1817. His son, Andrew Pickens, Jr., (1779–1838) was elected governor of South Carolina in 1816–18.

General Andrew Pickens

Timothy Pickering
—By William Veckett after Gilbert Stuart

• TIMOTHY PICKERING   1745–1829

An officer in the Revolutionary War and a Cabinet member under President Washington and President Adams, Timothy Pickering was born in Salem, Massachusetts, on July 17, 1745. After graduation from Harvard College at seventeen, he studied law and commenced practice in Salem in 1768. Active in the pre-Revolutionary patriotic movement, he was a member of the committee of correspondence and safety in 1774–75. He was commissioned a colonel in the militia in 1774 and served in the battles in New York and New Jersey in 1776–77. He was appointed adjutant general of the Continental Army on May 24, 1777. Six months later the Continental Congress elected him as a member of the Board of War. He then became Quartermaster General of the army on August 5, 1780. President Washington appointed Pickering as Postmaster General on August 12, 1791, as Secretary of War on January 2, 1795, and as Secretary of State on December 10, 1795. He continued to serve as Secretary of State under President Adams until May 10, 1800. He then returned to Massachusetts, where he was appointed chief justice of the court of common pleas in 1802. As a Federalist he was elected and reelected to the U.S. Senate 1803–11, and then as a U.S. Representative to Congress 1813–17. He died in Salem on January 29, 1829.

• WILLIAM PIERCE   1740–1789

An officer of the Revolutionary War and a delegate to the Continental Congress, William Pierce was born in Georgia in 1740. He served in the Continental Army during the Revolutionary War as aide-de-camp to Gen. Nathanael Greene. Pierce was complimented by Congress and presented with a sword for his meritorious conduct at the battle of Eutaw Springs in 1781. After the war he became a merchant in Savannah, Georgia. He was elected to the state house of representatives in 1786. Then he was chosen as a member of the Continental Congress in 1787, and as a delegate to the federal Constitutional Convention at Philadelphia in 1787, but left before the United States Constitution was signed. He died in Savannah on December 10, 1789.

• CHARLES PINCKNEY   1757–1824

The youngest man to sign the United States Constitution, Charles Pinckney was born in Charleston, South Carolina, on October 26, 1757, a cousin of Charles Cotesworth Pinckney and Thomas Pinckney. An unusually precocious boy, after preparatory education in England he was admitted to study law in the Middle Temple in London when he was fifteen. Returning to South Carolina at the outbreak of the Revolutionary War, he immediately took an active part in patriotic political activities, helped by his father, Col. Charles Pinckney, who was chairman of the colony's committee of safety and president of South Carolina's Revolutionary congresses. When his father decided to retire from public life because he felt he could not support independence from Britain, eighteen-year-old Charles stepped into his father's shoes. He became a member of the three-man executive council that governed South Carolina in 1775–76 and helped draft the first state constitution. At the age of nineteen he was chosen to represent the state in the Continental Congress 1777–78. He then returned to South Carolina, was elected to the state legislature, and began practicing law.

As a captain of militia he helped in the defense of Charleston, but was taken prisoner by the British when the city surrendered in 1780. With other "dangerous rebels" he was imprisoned at St. Augustine, Florida, until released in a prisoner exchange the following year.

Pinckney again was sent to represent South Carolina in the Congress in 1784–87, and was a member of the delegation to the Constitutional Convention in Philadelphia in 1787. He presented what was called the "Pinckney Plan" to the Constitutional Convention on the fifth day of its sessions. Although the original copy of this plan has been lost, many of its points were adopted into the final draft of the United States Constitution, which the twenty-nine-year-old Pinckney signed with other delegates.

Pinckney served in public office continuously for most of the rest of his life. He was governor of the state three times in 1789–92, 1796–98, and 1806–08. As a Democratic-Republican and supporter of Thomas Jefferson, he was U.S. Senator 1798–1801 and U.S. minister to Spain 1801–05. In between these offices, he sat in the state legislature. Pinckney closed his political career by serving as a U.S. Representative in Congress 1819–21, where he opposed the Missouri Compromise. He died in Charleston on October 29, 1824.

• CHARLES COTESWORTH PINCKNEY   1746–1825

An officer in the Revolutionary War, signer of the United States Constitution, and unsuccessful Federalist candidate for President, Charles Cotesworth Pinckney was born in Charleston, South Carolina, on February 25, 1746, an older brother of Thomas Pinckney and a cousin of Charles Pinckney. As a boy he received sixteen years of education in England and France, graduating from Oxford University, where he studied law under Sir William Blackstone, learning the practice of law at the Temple in London, and then receiving military training at the Royal Military Academy of Caen in France. At the age of twenty-three he returned to South Carolina and began law

Charles Cotesworth Pinckney

practice in 1770. Three years later he was appointed deputy to the colony's royal attorney general.

As a lieutenant colonel of militia he served under Colonel William Moultrie in successfully beating off a British attack on Charleston's Fort Sullivan in June 1776. He served as an aide to General Washington at the battles of Brandywine and Germantown in 1777. As a colonel of militia he then led his regiment in the unsuccessful invasion of Florida in 1778. When the British captured Charleston in 1780, Pinckney was taken prisoner, and was not exchanged until February 1782,

The Pink House in Charleston, South Carolina, which dates back to the eighteenth century, once served as a tavern inside the original walled city of Charles Towne.
                                                    —Sketch by Kay Smith

preventing his taking part in any further fighting. At the end of the war he was brevetted as a brigadier general.

Pinckney was chosen as a delegate to the Constitutional Convention in Philadelphia in 1787, where he was a defender of states' rights and helped prevent attempts to outlaw slavery in the Constitution. When the draft of the United States Constitution was completed, he signed it with other delegates. Pinckney refused several offers by President Washington to become a Cabinet officer in the new government. In 1796 he accepted appointment as ambassador to France, but when he got there the revolutionary government then in power refused to accept him as an envoy. The next year French officials identified only as X, Y, and Z demanded bribes and a large loan from the United States in order to smooth diplomatic relations between the nations. Pinckney became famous for his reply: "It is no, no! Not a sixpence."

As the United States prepared for war with France over the issue, Pinckney was appointed major general of the new U.S. Army, third in command after George Washington and Alexander Hamilton. Pinckney returned from France in 1798 to assist in recruiting and training the new army.

In 1800 Pinckney was President John Adams' running mate as the Federalist candidate for Vice President in the presidential election, but he and Adams were defeated by the Democratic-Republican candidates Thomas Jefferson and Aaron Burr. In 1804 and in 1808 Pinckney ran as the Federalist candidate for President against James Madison, but both times lost the election. From 1805 to the end of his life Pinckney was president of the Society of the Cincinnati, the association of officers who had served in the Revolutionary War. He died in Charleston on August 1, 1825.

• **THOMAS PINCKNEY   1750–1828**

An officer in the Revolutionary War and later a United States diplomat, Thomas Pinckney was born in Charleston, South Carolina, on October 23, 1750, a younger brother of Charles Cotesworth Pinckney and a cousin of Charles Pinckney. After receiving an education in England, he returned to South Carolina shortly before the outbreak of the Revolutionary War. As a captain in the 1st South Carolina Regiment, he served in the defense of Charleston in 1776, and then spent the next two years in command of Fort Moultrie (formerly Fort Sullivan) in Charleston. Promoted to major in 1778, he accompanied his brother on the unsuccessful invasion of Florida that year. He served as aide-de-camp to General Lincoln at the battle of Stono Ferry in June 1779 and to the French admiral, the Comte d'Estaing, in the unsuccessful allied attempt to recapture Savannah in October 1779. He escaped capture at the siege of Charleston in 1780, because shortly before the city's surrender he had been sent out with a message to carry to

Thomas Pinckney

General Washington. As aide-de-camp to General Gates, Pinckney was wounded and captured at the battle of Camden in August 1780, but was released in a prisoner exchange four months later. Pinckney then served under the command of the Marquis de Lafayette at the battle of Yorktown.

After the war he was elected governor of South Carolina 1787–89. President Washington appointed him as U.S. ambassador to England in 1792–96, and during this time he was given a special diplomatic mission to Spain, where he arranged what became known as "Pinckney's Treaty," opening the Mississippi River to United States' navigation.

The Federalists nominated Pinckney as John Adams' running mate for Vice President in the election of 1796, but Alexander Hamilton's inept efforts to have Pinckney elected President instead of Adams resulted in Pinckney losing the vice presidency to Thomas Jefferson. Pinckney next was elected as one of South Carolina's representatives in the U.S. Congress, where he served 1797–1801.

During the War of 1812 he was commissioned a major general, commanding the Southern military district where there was no military action. After General Andrew Jackson defeated the Creek Indians in the battle of Horseshoe Bend in 1814, Pinckney negotiated a treaty with the Creek nation. Retiring from public life after the war, Pinckney devoted himself to agricultural experiments. He died in Charleston on November 2, 1828.

• MOLLY PITCHER   1754–1832

A heroine of the Revolutionary War who kept her husband's cannon firing after he had fallen during the battle of Monmouth, Molly Pitcher, whose real name was Mary Ludwig, was born near Trenton, New Jersey, in 1754. At sixteen she married John Caspar Hays, a barber, and lived in Carlisle, Pennsylvania. At the beginning of the Revolutionary War, her husband joined the 1st Pennsylvania Artillery. Like many other soldiers' wives, she followed her husband when he went off to war, doing his cooking and washing in camp. In battle she carried water in a pitcher for her husband and other soldiers, gaining the nickname "Molly Pitcher."

At the battle of Monmouth, New Jersey, on June 28, 1778, her husband fell of heat prostration while manning his gun. Molly Pitcher picked up her husband's ramrod and took his place at the cannon, keeping the gun firing for the remainder of the battle.

After the war Hays died in 1789. Molly married another Revolutionary War veteran, George McCauley, but she left him when he proved to be shiftless. In her old age tobacco-chewing Molly was voted a $40-a-year pension by the Pennsylvania legislature in recognition of her services. She died in Pennsylvania at the age of seventy-eight in 1832.

Molly Pitcher at Monmouth

Gateway to Trenton, New Jersey in 1776.
　—from a sketch of a sketch by Kay Smith

gateway to Trenton. 1776

The French Arms Tavern in Trenton, New Jersey which served briefly as the meeting place of Congress from November 1, 1784 until December 24, 1784.

—from a sketch by Kay Smith

• GEORGE PLATER 1735–1792

A delegate to the Continental Congress and governor of Maryland, George Plater was born at "Sotterly," near Leonardtown, Maryland, on November 8, 1735. After graduation from William and Mary College at seventeen, he studied law and commenced practice in Annapolis, Maryland. He was elected to the Maryland colonial assembly in 1758, was naval officer at Patuxent 1767–71, and then was appointed judge of the Colony's court 1771–73. Plater was chosen as a member of Maryland's delegation to the Continental Congress 1778–81. He was president of the state constitutional convention in 1788 that ratified the United States Constitution. Elected governor of Maryland in 1791, he died in that office in Annapolis, Maryland, on February 10, 1792.

• ZEPHANIAH PLATT 1735–1807

A delegate to the Continental Congress from New York, Zephaniah Platt was born in Huntington, Long Island, New York, on May 27, 1735. After being educated in England, he studied law and commenced practice in Poughkeepsie, New York. He was elected to New York's Revolutionary congress 1775–77, and then to the state senate 1777–83. He was sent as a delegate to the Continental Congress in 1784–86. He founded the town of Plattsburg, New York, in 1784, and died there on September 12, 1807.

• SETH POMEROY 1706–1777

The oldest general to see action in the Revolutionary War, Seth Pomeroy was born in Northampton, Massachusetts, on May 20, 1706. As a militia major, he served in King George's War at the battle of Louisbourg in 1745. Ten years later he fought as a lieutenant colonel of militia in the French and Indian War, becoming a hero when he captured the French commander in the battle of Lake George, New York, on September 8, 1755. He took an active part in the patriotic movement as a member of the local committee of safety in Northampton and as a delegate to the Massachusetts Revolutionary congresses in 1774–75. As a brigadier general of militia he helped recruit and train the Minutemen before the outbreak of hostilities.

At the battle of Bunker Hill on June 17, 1775, the sixty-nine-year-old Pomeroy inspired the troops by taking his place as an infantryman in the front line of the fighting, carrying with him a musket that he himself had made and had used at Louisbourg thirty years earlier. When the Americans were forced to retreat in the face of heavy British fire, Pomeroy walked backward, continuing to face the enemy, while holding the musket, whose stock had been shattered in the action. Appointed a major general of militia a few days after the battle, Pomeroy declined Congress' offer to commission him at the lesser rank of senior brigadier general in the Continental Army. In February 1777, in response to a call by General Washington for more Massachusetts troops to help defend Philadelphia, Pomeroy, now seventy, marched at the head of his troops to Peekskill, New York. But the cold brought on an attack of pleurisy, causing his death in Peekskill on February 19, 1777.

• ENOCH POOR 1736–1780

A Continental Army general who died during the Revolutionary War, Enoch Poor was born in Andover, Massachusetts, on June 21, 1736. After serving in the army in the French and Indian War in 1755, he moved to Exeter, New Hampshire, where he became a merchant. In 1775 he was appointed colonel in command of the 2nd New Hampshire Regiment, and led his troops to the siege of Boston. In 1776 he and his regiment went to upper New York state to reinforce the American troops retreating from the invasion of Canada. In February 1777 Poor was promoted to brigadier general. Eight months later he led his brigade of about 800 men in the advance on the right side of the battle line in the victory at Saratoga, New York, in October 1777. After spending the winter at Valley Forge, Poor and his troops took part in the battles of Barren Hill, Pennsylvania, in May 1778 and Monmouth, New Jersey, in June 1778. The following year he accompanied General Sullivan's expedition against the Iroquois Indians, winning a victory at the battle of Newtown, near present-day Elmira, New York, in August 1779. Poor died near Hackensack, New Jersey, on September 8, 1780. Conflicting sources say he died either of typhus fever or as the result of a duel with a French officer.

William Prescott

William Prescott at Bunker Hill where his instructions, "Don't fire until you see the whites of their eyes," became a lasting symbol of the American spirit.

• **RICHARD POTTS   1753–1808**

A delegate to the Continental Congress, judge, and U.S. Senator, Richard Potts was born in Upper Marlboro, Maryland, on July 19, 1753. After studying law, he commenced practice in Frederick County, Maryland, in 1775. During the Revolutionary War he served as aide to Gov. Thomas Johnson in the Flying Camp. Potts was elected to the Maryland house of delegates in 1779–80, and was chosen as a member of Maryland's delegation to the Continental Congress in 1781–82. He again served in the Maryland legislature in 1787–88. He was appointed by President Washington as U.S. district attorney for Maryland 1789–91, and then as chief judge of the U.S. circuit court of Maryland 1791–93. Potts was elected as a Federalist to the U.S. Senate 1793–96, and then was again appointed chief judge of the U.S. circuit court of Maryland 1796–1801. He became associate justice of the Maryland court of appeals 1801–04. Potts died in Frederick, Maryland, on November 26, 1808.

• **WILLIAM PRESCOTT   1726–1795**

One of the heroes of the battle of Bunker Hill, William Prescott was born in Groton, Massachusetts, on February 20, 1726. As a teen-ager he took part in King George's War in the 1740s, and as a militia officer he fought in Canada in the French and Indian War in the 1750s. A militia colonel at the outbreak of the Revolutionary War, he hurried his Minutemen to Concord when he learned of the fighting there, but arrived too late to take part in the action. He became a member of the Massachusetts council of war. At the battle of Bunker Hill in June 1775, he supervised the construction of fortifications on Breed's Hill and then commanded the militia in defending it against the fierce British assault. As the British regulars approached up the hill, he is said to have told his men, "Don't fire until you see the whites of their eyes. Then aim at their waistbands; and be sure to pick off the commanders, known by their handsome coats." The patriots fired until their ammunition ran out. Then, as the British rushed into the fortification, Prescott and his men fought their way out, using the stocks of their muskets as clubs against the bayonets of the redcoats. Prescott took part in the battles in New York in 1776, and served as a volunteer at the battles of Saratoga in 1777. He then resigned his commission and retired to his farm. After the war he was elected to the Massachusetts legislature. He died in Pepperell, Massachusetts, on October 13, 1795.

His brother, Oliver Prescott (1731–1804), was a major general of Massachusetts militia during the Revolutionary War, but saw no significant action. A cousin, Dr. Samuel Prescott (1751–c.1777), carried the warning that the British were coming to Concord after Paul Revere and William Dawes had been stopped, and later died aboard a British prison ship after having been captured while serving aboard a privateer.

• COUNT CASIMIR PULASKI   1748–1779

A Polish nobleman who was fatally wounded leading a cavalry charge at Savannah, Georgia, during the Revolutionary War, Count Casimir Pulaski was born in Podolia, Poland, on March 4, 1748. When his father, who had been a leader of the resistance to Russian rule, died in a Russian prison, the twenty-two-year-old count was elected commander-in-chief by his father's troops. The following year Pulaski with a group of about forty of his men disguised as peasants kidnaped King Stanislaus from Warsaw, but were pursued by superior forces and forced to give him up. Soon after, his army was defeated. Condemned to death as an outlaw, Pulaski fled to Turkey, continuing his fight against Russia by joining the Turkish army. Later, having gone to France, he met Benjamin Franklin and volunteered to fight for the American cause.

Arriving in America in 1777, he joined General Washington in Pennsylvania, fighting as a volunteer at the battle of Brandywine in September. At Washington's suggestion, Congress commissioned Pulaski as commander of cavalry with the rank of brigadier general. Pulaski fought in the battle of Germantown in October 1777. While the army was in winter quarters at Valley Forge, Pulaski fell into disputes with the American cavalry officers he was supposed to command. Communication was difficult since he did not understand or speak English. In March 1778 he resigned as commander of the cavalry and received permission to recruit his own corps of cavalry and light infantry, which became known as Pulaski's Legion. In October 1778 while Pulaski's men were camped on Minnock

Count Casimir Pulaski

Island at Little Egg Harbor, near present-day Atlantic City, New Jersey, the British made a surprise night raid. The raiders killed about fifty of Pulaski's officers and soldiers before Pulaski arrived with his cavalry and drove them off. After rebuilding the strength of his corps during the next several months, Pulaski led his men to the Southern theater of operations in February 1779. In May he suffered defeat in a skirmish near Charleston, South Carolina, with British soldiers led by General Augustine Prevost. Five months later Pulaski's Legion took part in the unsuccessful attempt to drive the British out of Savannah, Georgia. In a cavalry charge on the British fortifications, Pulaski was fatally wounded by a round of grapeshot. Taken aboard the U.S. brig *Wasp*, he died two days later, on October 11, 1779.

• ISRAEL PUTNAM   1718–1790

A major general in the Continental Army, Israel Putnam was born in Old Salem (now Danvers), Massachusetts, on January 7, 1718. When he was twenty-one he settled in Pomfret, Connecticut, where he became a farmer. As a militia lieutenant, he joined Rogers' Rangers in the French and Indian War in 1755. During the seven years of that war he rose to the rank of lieutenant colonel, and had two narrow escapes. In 1758 he was captured by Indians and was about to be burned alive at the stake when a French officer dashed through the yelling Indians, scattered the burning wood, and cut Putnam loose. In 1762, while on an expedition to capture Havana, his ship was wrecked and he was one of a handful of survivors. He next fought in Pontiac's War in 1764, leading Connecticut troops on a march to Detroit. In 1772 to 1774 he made a voyage up the Mississippi to survey land that had been granted to veterans of the Havana expedition. Having returned to Connecticut before the Revolutionary War, he resumed farming and opened a tavern, called "The General Wolfe." He took an active part in the patriotic movement as a member of the Sons of Liberty. When the British closed the port of Boston in 1774, Putnam drove a herd of sheep from Connecticut to Boston to help feed the people.

The birthplace of Israel Putnam

Legend has it that Putnam was plowing in his field when he received word of the battles of Lexington and Concord, and that he immediately unhitched the plow, jumped on the horse, and rode the 100 miles to Cambridge, Massachusetts, in eighteen hours.

As a brigadier general of Connecticut militia, Putnam shared command with Colonel William Prescott at the battle of Bunker Hill in June 1775. A few days after the battle Putnam received word that he had been appointed by Congress as a major general of the Continental Army. In 1776 he was in overall field command of American forces in their defeat at the battle of Long Island in August. Having lost Washington's

(Above) Israel Putnam, major general of the Connecticut forces. (At right) Putnam escaping capture by the British by driving his horse down a rocky cliff.

confidence in him, he was given less critical commands for the rest of his service in the war. Legend gives him credit for one more daring act. While commanding troops in Connecticut in 1779, he is said to have ridden his horse at a gallop down a rocky cliff near Stamford to escape capture by the British. Later that year he suffered a paralytic stroke and was forced to retire from the army. His cousin, Rufus Putnam (1738–1824), served as a colonel of engineers during the Revolutionary War and was appointed a brigadier general in the last year of the war.

• **DAVID RAMSAY**   **1749–1815**

A military surgeon in the Revolutionary War and delegate to the Continental Congress from South Carolina, David Ramsay was born in Dunmore, Pennsylvania, on April 2, 1749, a younger brother of Nathaniel Ramsay. After graduation from the College of New Jersey at sixteen, he received a medical degree from the College of Philadelphia in 1772 and began practice in Charleston, South Carolina, the next year. Beginning in 1776, he was elected to the state house of representatives each year until 1790. Ramsay served in the Revolutionary War as surgeon of the Charleston militia. He was captured at the fall of Charleston in May 1780 and imprisoned by the British at St. Augustine, Florida, for eleven months. He was chosen as a member of South Carolina's delegation to the Continental Congress 1782–86, and served as president pro tempore of the Congress in 1785–86. Elected to the state senate in 1792, he served as president of that body for seven years. In his latter years he wrote several historical works on the Revolutionary War and on South Carolina. Ramsay was fatally wounded by a maniac he had testified against in a court suit, and died in Charleston on May 8, 1815.

• **NATHANIEL RAMSAY**   **1741–1817**

A Revolutionary War officer and delegate to the Continental Congress, Nathaniel Ramsay was born in Lancaster County, Pennsylvania, on May 1, 1741, an older brother of David Ramsay. After graduation from the College of New Jersey in 1767, he studied law and began practice in Cecil County, Maryland. In January 1776 he was appointed captain in Smallwood's Maryland Regiment, which fought with distinction at the battle of Long Island in August 1776. When the regiment was absorbed into the Continental Army as the 3rd Maryland Regiment in December 1776, Ramsay was promoted to lieutenant colonel. He was with the army at Valley Forge during the winter of 1777–78, and then was wounded and taken prisoner while commanding the regiment in an effort to check the advance of the British during the retreat of Gen. Charles Lee at the Battle of Monmouth on June 28, 1778. After being exchanged in December 1780, he retired from the army. Ramsay was one of Maryland's delegates to the Continental Congress in 1785–87, at the time his brother was serving as president pro tempore of the Congress. He was appointed U.S. marshal for Maryland by President Washington, serving 1790–98. Ramsay's last public service was as naval officer of the port of Baltimore, a position he held from 1794 until his death in Baltimore on October 23, 1817.

Wind vane from mill in which William Penn was a partner.

Edmund Jennings Randolph

• EDMUND JENNINGS RANDOLPH   1753–1813

An officer in the Revolutionary War, a member of the Continental Congress, and first Attorney General of the United States, Edmund Jennings Randolph was born in Williamsburg, Virginia, on August 10, 1753. After graduation from William and Mary College, he studied law and commenced practice in Williamsburg. At twenty-two he was appointed aide-de-camp to General Washington in 1775. Upon the death of his uncle, Peyton Randolph, in October 1775, he returned to Virginia to help settle the family's affairs, his own father having left Virginia with other Loyalists.

The next year he was appointed Virginia's first attorney general. He represented Virginia in the Continental Congress in 1779–82. Randolph was elected governor of Virginia in 1786 but resigned in 1788 to serve in the state house of delegates so he could participate in the codification of the laws of Virginia in 1788–89. As governor, he led Virginia's delegation to the federal Constitutional Convention of 1787, where he presented the Virginia plan that laid the basis for discussions at the convention. When the United States Constitution finally was drafted, he refused to sign it, but later reversed himself to support its ratification by Virginia.

In 1789 Randolph was appointed the first Attorney General of the United States, in the Cabinet of President Washington. After Thomas Jefferson resigned from the Cabinet, Randolph was appointed Secretary of State on January 2, 1794, and served until August 19, 1795, when he was requested to resign following charges (subsequently found to be false) that he had been bribed by the French ambassador. Randolph was the chief defense counsel for Aaron Burr when the latter was tried and acquitted of treason in 1807. In his fifties, Randolph suffered a stroke of paralysis and was bedridden for several years until his death in Clarke County, Virginia, on September 12, 1813.

• PEYTON RANDOLPH   1721–1775

The first and third President of the Continental Congress and the most prominent pre-Revolutionary Virginia leader, Peyton Randolph was born at "Tazewell Hall," Williamsburg, Virginia, in September 1721. After graduation from William and Mary College, he studied law at the Inner Temple in London, England, returning to practice law in Williamsburg in 1744. From 1748 he served as King's attorney for Virginia for eighteen years. He also was elected as a member of the Virginia house of burgesses for thirty-seven years, serving as speaker from 1766. He became chairman of the patriots' committee of correspondence in 1773, and president of the Virginia Revolutionary conventions of 1774–75. He headed Virginia's delegation to the first Continental Congress in Philadelphia, and was elected its President on September 5, 1774, but resigned on October 22, 1774, to attend the Virginia legislature where he was speaker. He was re-elected as President of the second Continental Congress on May 10, 1775, but was forced to resign two weeks later on account of ill health. After five months illness, he died in Philadelphia on October 22, 1775.

• GEORGE READ   1733–1798

A signer of both the Declaration of Independence and the United States Constitution, George Read was born on his father's plantation near North East, Maryland, on September 18, 1733. After studying law, he began practice in New Castle, Delaware, at the age of twenty. In 1763 Read was appointed attorney general for Pennsylvania and Delaware, an office he held until the Revolutionary War. In 1765 he was elected to the Delaware legislature and was regularly re-elected for the next fifteen years. He was chosen a delegate from

George Read

Delaware to the Continental Congress 1774–77, where he opposed but later signed the Declaration of Independence. Read was president of the Delaware constitutional convention in 1776, and then served as the state's acting president in 1777–78. Read was appointed by Congress to the court of appeals in admiralty cases 1782–89. He was chosen as a delegate from Delaware to the federal Constitutional Convention where he helped design and then signed the new United States Constitution. He was elected to the U.S. Senate in 1789, serving until September 18, 1793, when he resigned to accept appointment as chief justice of Delaware, a position he held until his death in New Castle on September 21, 1798. His brother Thomas Read (1740–1788) was appointed as the eighth ranking captain in the Continental Navy in 1776, and his brother James Read (1743–1822) served as an officer in the Revolutionary War, fighting in the battles of Trenton, Princeton, Brandywine, and Germantown.

• **JACOB READ**　1751–1816

A Revolutionary War officer and U.S. Senator from South Carolina, Jacob Read was born on the Hobcaw plantation, in Christ Church Parish, near Charleston, South Carolina, in 1751. After studying law in England, Read returned to South Carolina and served as an officer in the Revolutionary War. He was captured by the British at the fall of Charleston in 1780 and sent as a prisoner to St. Augustine. Upon his release, Read was elected to the state house of representatives in 1781–82. He was chosen as a delegate to the Continental Congress in 1783–85, and then resumed his seat in the legislature, serving as speaker of the house 1789–94. Read was elected as a Federalist to the U.S. Senate in 1795–1801. From 1801 until his death he was judge of the U.S. court for the district of South Carolina. In addition, he served as a brigadier general of South Carolina militia in 1810–16 including the period of the War of 1812. Read died in Charleston on July 17, 1816.

• JOSEPH REED   1741–1785

A military officer in the Revolutionary War, signer of the Articles of Confederation, and head of the government of Pennsylvania after the end of British occupation, Joseph Reed was born in Trenton, New Jersey, on August 27, 1741. After graduation from the College of New Jersey at fifteen, he studied law at the Temple in London, commenced practice in Trenton, New Jersey, in 1767, and then moved to Philadelphia in 1770. He took an active part in pre-Revolutionary affairs, becoming a member of the committee of correspondence in 1774 and president of the Pennsylvania Revolutionary convention in 1775. When George Washington was appointed commander-in-chief of the Continental Army, Reed accompanied him to Cambridge in July 1775 as his aide-de-camp and military secretary with the rank of lieutenant colonel. He then served during the campaign of 1776 as adjutant general of the Continental Army, rendering especially valuable service by helping plan the battles of Trenton and Princeton and gathering secret intelligence about the disposition of the British forces in the area. Resigning from the army in 1777, he was a Pennsylvania delegate to the Continental Congress in 1777–78, where he signed the Articles of Confederation. He then was elected head of the Pennsylvania government as president of the supreme executive council 1778–81. After the war he visited England in 1784, and died shortly after his return in Philadelphia on March 5, 1785.

• JAMES RANDOLPH REID   1750–1789

An officer in the Revolutionary War and a delegate to the Continental Congress, James Randolph Reid was born in what is now Adams County, Pennsylvania, on August 11, 1750. After graduation from the College of New Jersey, he served in the Revolutionary War. As a lieutenant he took part in the battles of Three Rivers and Ticonderoga in 1776 with Anthony Wayne's 4th Pennsylvania Regiment. He later was promoted to major in "Congress' Own" Regiment. He was a member of Pennsylvania's delegation to the Continental Congress in 1787–89. He died in Middlesex, Pennsylvania, on January 25, 1789.

Paul Revere's ride

Sauce pan

• PAUL REVERE   1735—1818

Famous for all time for his midnight ride that sounded the alarm "the British are coming" to the Minutemen of Lexington, Paul Revere was born on January 1, 1735, in Boston, one of a family of thirteen children. As a boy he learned his father's trade of silversmithing. In his twenties he served in the French and Indian War as a lieutenant of artillery at Fort Edward on the upper Hudson River. Upon his return to Boston he established himself as a silversmith and in addition taught himself the art of copper-plate engraving. In the mid-1700s he was one of only four engravers in America. Taking an increasingly active part in the growing patriotic movement, he became a friend of Samuel Adams, John Hancock, Joseph Warren, and other leaders. He put his art as an engraver to use for propaganda purposes, pictorializing the repeal of the Stamp Act in 1766 and of the Boston Massacre in 1770. He was one of the inner circle of Sons of Liberty who planned and carried out the Boston Tea party in 1773 while disguised as Indians. Throughout the period he was used more and more frequently as a confidential courier to carry letters and dispatches from Boston to the committees of correspondence in the other colonies.

On Sunday evening April 16, 1775, Warren, who was head of the Boston committee of safety, sent Revere on a secret mission to Lexington to warn Samuel Adams and John Hancock, who were there, that he had heard rumors that the British might send soldiers to arrest them, and that they should leave as soon as possible for the meeting of the Continental Congress in Philadelphia. Upon Revere's return from carrying this message, he arranged with patriots in nearby Charleston to watch for British troop movements and put a signal in the church tower: "one if by land" and "two if by sea." Late on Tuesday night April 18, Warren sent for Revere and William Dawes to carry the alarm that the British were marching that night. Each was sent by a different route. Revere carried the warning to the Minutemen of Medford and then raced on to Lexington, giving the message to Adams, Hancock, and Captain John Parker, who was in charge of the local company of Minutemen.

Dawes arrived while Revere was still in Lexington, and the two proceeded together toward Concord, accompanied by Dr. Samuel Prescott. En route they ran into a British patrol. Revere was caught. Prescott hurried on to Concord with the alarm and Dawes escaped on the road back to Lexington. After taking Revere's horse, the British let him go and he made his way on foot to Lexington. His news of the nearby British patrol convinced Hancock and Adams to leave at once. Revere saw them on their way, and then returned to Lexington to watch the clash that began the Revolutionary War.

In the months that followed, Revere learned how to make gunpowder, setting up a factory at Canton, Massachusetts. He engraved and printed new paper money both for Massachusetts and for the Continental Congress.

As a lieutenant colonel in the militia he commanded Castle William, the fortress in Boston Harbor, in 1778–79. He commanded the artillery in an attack that Massachusetts authorities launched in 1779 on a British base at Penobscot, Maine. The assault was a disaster, with about a fourth of the 2,000 American troops involved lost during the battle. Revere and several other officers were court-martialed for their conduct in the affair, but he was acquitted.

After the war Revere expanded his business, making church bells and casting cannon. He founded the Revere Copper Company at Canton, Massachusetts, where he was the first in the United States to smelt copper ore and roll the copper into sheets. He died in Boston at the age of eighty-three on May 10, 1818.

Paul Revere

• **SAMUEL RHOADS**   1711–1784

A delegate to the Continental Congress, Samuel Rhoads was born in Philadelphia in 1711. He received a limited schooling and became a carpenter and builder. He was elected to the city council in 1741, and to the colonial assembly 1761–64 and 1771–74. He became mayor of Philadelphia in 1774. He was one of Pennsylvania's delegates to the Continental Congress in 1774–75. Rhoads died in Philadelphia on April 7, 1784.

• **RICHARD RIDGELY**   1755–1824

A delegate to the Continental Congress, Richard Ridgely was born in Queen Caroline Parish, Anne Arundel County, Maryland, on August 3, 1755. After attending St. John's College in Annapolis, Maryland, he studied law and commenced practice in Baltimore in 1780. He was chosen as a member of Maryland's delegation to the Continental Congress in 1785–86. He then served in the state senate 1786–91. Ridgely was appointed judge of the county court in 1811, a position he held until his death at his "Dorsey Hall" estate near Columbia, Maryland, on February 25, 1824.

• **DANIEL ROBERDEAU**   1727–1795

A militia general and delegate to the Continental Congress, Daniel Roberdeau was born on the island of St. Christopher in the West Indies in 1727. He came to Philadelphia as a boy, and developed a lumber business. He became manager of the Pennsylvania Hospital 1756–58 and 1766–76. He was commissioned first brigadier general of Pennsylvania militia in 1776. Roberdeau was one of Pennsylvania's delegates to the Continental Congress in 1777–79, where he signed the Articles of Confederation. He moved to Virginia in 1785, and died ten years later in Winchester, Virginia, on January 5, 1795.

• **CAESAR RODNEY**   1728–1784

A delegate to the Continental Congress who rode seventy miles day and night to ensure that the vote for the Declaration of Independence would be unanimous, Caesar Rodney was born in Dover, Delaware, on October 7, 1728, a brother of Thomas Rodney. A wealthy planter, he was elected high sheriff of Kent County in 1755–58. He was elected to the Delaware colonial legislature 1761–76, and was one of the colony's delegates to the Stamp Act Congress in New York City in 1765. He was chosen as one of Maryland's delegates to the Continental Congress 1774–78 and 1782–84. He was appointed brigadier general in command of Delaware's militia in 1775.

He was occupied with his military duties in 1776 when he received a message that his vote was needed to break a tie in the Delaware delegation on the vote for the Declaration of Independence. So he rode the seventy miles through a summer storm without stopping until he got to Philadelphia and cast his tie-breaking vote. He later signed the Declaration with the other delegates on August 2, 1776, and then returned to his militiamen. He served with his troops in the winter fighting of 1776–77. He put down a Loyalist uprising in Sussex County, Delaware, in 1777, and in September of that year was commissioned as a major general.

The state legislature elected Rodney president of Delaware in 1778, a position he held until 1781. Throughout the Revolutionary War he had suffered from a growing cancer on his face, wearing a green silk scarf to cover the tumor. Because of the disease he was unable to attend meetings of Congress in 1782–84, and he died on June 29, 1784, at his plantation "Byfield," near Dover.

Caesar Rodney

• **THOMAS RODNEY   1744–1811**

A Revolutionary War officer and delegate to the Continental Congress, Thomas Rodney was born near Dover, Delaware, on June 4, 1744, a brother of Caesar Rodney. He served as a captain of militia in the battles of Trenton and Princeton in 1776–77, and then joined his brother as adjutant in defending Delaware from the invasion of British troops. He represented Maryland in the Continental Congress 1781–83 and 1785–87. He was elected speaker of the state assembly in 1787. Rodney became an associate justice of the supreme court of Delaware in 1802, and then resigned in 1803 to accept appointment as U.S. judge for the Mississippi Territory. He died in Natchez, Mississippi, on January 2, 1811.

• **JOHN ROGERS   1723–1789**

A delegate from Maryland to the Continental Congress, John Rogers was born in Annapolis, Maryland, in 1723. A lawyer, he took an active part in the pre-Revolutionary movement as a member of the committee of safety in 1774–75 and of the Maryland Revolutionary conventions in 1774–76. He also served as a major of the Prince Georges County militia. Rogers was a delegate to the Continental Congress in 1775–76. He was appointed judge of the court of admiralty in 1776. He then served as chancellor of Maryland from 1778 until his death in Upper Marlboro, Maryland, on September 23, 1789.

• **JESSE ROOT   1736–1822**

A minister, lawyer, judge, and delegate to the Continental Congress, Jesse Root was born in Coventry, Connecticut, on

December 28, 1736. After graduation from the College of New Jersey in 1756, he studied theology and was ordained a minister, preaching from 1758 to 1763. He then took up the study of law and commenced practice in Hartford, Connecticut, in 1763. During the Revolutionary War, he served in the militia, advancing from captain to lieutenant colonel. He was one of Connecticut's delegates to the Continental Congress 1778–83. He served as attorney for the state of Connecticut 1785–89, as judge of the superior court 1789–96, and as chief justice 1796–1807. He was elected to the Connecticut house of representatives 1807–09, and to the state constitutional convention in 1818. Root died in Coventry on March 29, 1822.

• **BETSY ROSS   1752–1836**

Said to have made the first Flag of the United States following a design sketched by George Washington, Elizabeth "Betsy" Griscom was born in Philadelphia on January 1, 1752. At twenty-one she married John Ross, the son of an Episcopalian clergyman, who had established himself in business as an upholsterer. At the outbreak of the Revolutionary War her husband joined the militia. He was fatally injured when a cargo of gunpowder that he was guarding exploded in January 1776. After his death Betsy Ross carried on his business.

According to an otherwise undocumented story first told by her grandson William Canby in 1870, Betsy Ross was asked by a committee of the Continental Congress made up of George Washington, Robert Morris, and George Ross, who was her husband's uncle, to sew the first flag in June 1776. Canby said that when he was eleven, his eighty-four-year-old grandmother told him how she had met with the committee in her back parlor. She said that the committee gave her a rough sketch for the flag, which Washington redrafted in her presence. She said she had argued him out of using six-pointed stars in favor of five-pointed ones. Although historians have been unable to find any documentary proof that the story is true, neither have they been able to find any evidence that it is false. And it is a fact that as a seamstress Betsy Ross made many flags during the Revolutionary War for the Pennsylvania Navy. The design which Betsy Ross may have been the first to sew was officially adopted by Congress a year later, on motion of John Adams, on June 14, 1777.

The day after Congress officially adopted the flag of thirteen stripes and thirteen stars, Betsy Ross remarried, this time to Joseph Ashburn. Her second marriage also ended in tragedy when Ashburn was captured at sea by the British in 1780 and imprisoned in Old Mill Prison in England, where he died in 1782. John Claypoole, a friend of Ashburn who had been a fellow prisoner, brought Betsy news of her husband's death and his last words to her in August 1782. The following May she and Claypoole were married. Her business as a flag-maker

A painting of Betsy Ross which is probably an artist's concept of what she looked like rather than a true likeness.

continued to prosper and was carried on after her death by her daughter. She died in Philadelphia on January 30, 1836. The 200th anniversary of her birth was celebrated by the United States government by the issue of a commemorative postage stamp in 1952.

• **DAVID ROSS   1755–1800**

An officer in the Revolutionary War and a delegate to the Continental Congress, David Ross was born in Prince Georges County, Maryland, on February 12, 1755. At twenty-one he was commissioned a major of Grayson's Continental Army Regiment. He resigned in December 1777 upon the death of his father, and devoted his time to the management of his family's large estate. After studying law, he commenced practice in Frederick County, Maryland, in 1783. Ross served as a delegate to the Continental Congress in 1786–88. He died in Frederick County in 1800.

George Ross

- **GEORGE ROSS**   **1730–1779**

A signer of the Declaration of Independence, George Ross was born in New Castle, Delaware, on May 10, 1730. After studying law, he commenced practice in 1750 in Lancaster, Pennsylvania, then on the western frontier. He was elected to the Pennsylvania assembly 1768–76, and was chosen as a delegate to the Continental Congress 1774–77, where he signed the Declaration of Independence. He was appointed judge of the court of admiralty for Pennsylvania in April 1779, but died of gout three months later in Philadelphia on July 14, 1779.

- **BENJAMIN RUMSEY**   **1734–1808**

A delegate to the Continental Congress, Benjamin Rumsey was born in Bohemia Manor, Maryland, on October 6, 1734. A graduate of the College of New Jersey, Rumsey was commissioned a colonel of militia in 1776 and was a member of the council of safety in 1776. He represented Maryland in the Continental Congress 1776–78, and then was chief justice of the Maryland court of appeals 1778–1805. He died in Joppa, Maryland, on March 7, 1808.

- **BENJAMIN RUSH**   **1745–1813**

A signer of the Declaration of Independence and the leading American physician of his time, Benjamin Rush was born in Byberry Township, near Philadelphia, on December 24, 1745. After graduation from the College of New Jersey at fourteen, he studied medicine for six years as an apprentice to a physician in Philadelphia. He then went to Europe, where he received an M.D. from the University of Edinburgh in 1768, and then visited hospitals in London and Paris before returning to Philadelphia in August 1769. At twenty-three he became the first professor of chemistry at the College of Philadelphia. As a member of the Continental Congress in 1776–77, Rush signed the Declaration of Independence. He was appointed surgeon general of the Middle Department of the Continental Army in April 1777, and was made physician general in July 1777. He resigned in February 1778 when General Washington confronted him with a letter Rush had written to Patrick Henry recommending that Washington be replaced as commander in chief.

Resuming the private practice of medicine, Rush helped found the Pennsylvania Hospital in Philadelphia, became president of the Philadelphia medical society, established the first free medical clinic for the poor in 1786, and continued to teach medicine at the University of Pennsylvania. He became world famous by his dedication to duty during Philadelphia's two great yellow fever epidemics in 1793 and 1798 that killed about 8,000 persons. He was honored for his contributions to medical science by medals and presents from the King of Prussia, the Queen of Etruria (Italy), and the Czar of Russia. President John Adams appointed Rush as Treasurer of the United States Mint at Philadelphia in 1799, an office he held until his death in Philadelphia on April 19, 1813.

Dr. Benjamin Rush

Edward Rutledge

- **EDWARD RUTLEDGE**   **1749–1800**

The youngest signer of the Declaration of Independence, Edward Rutledge was born in Charleston, South Carolina, on November 23, 1749, a younger brother of John Rutledge. After studying law at the Middle Temple in London, England, he began practice in Charleston in 1773. At twenty-four he was chosen as a delegate to the Continental Congress, where he served 1774–77, signing the Declaration of Independence at the age of twenty-six. While serving as a captain of militia, Rutledge was taken prisoner when the British captured Charleston in 1780. After being imprisoned at St. Augustine, Florida, more than a year, he was exchanged. He was elected to the South Carolina legislature 1782–98, and then was elected governor of South Carolina, an office he held from 1798 until his death in Charleston on January 23, 1800.

- **JOHN RUTLEDGE**   **1739–1800**

Head of the government of South Carolina during most of the Revolutionary War and a signer of the United States Constitution, John Rutledge was born in Charleston, South Carolina, in September 1739, the older brother of Edward Rutledge. After studying law at the Middle Temple in London, England, he returned to Charleston and commenced practice in 1761. He was elected and re-elected to the South Carolina legislature for sixteen years 1761–76. At twenty-four he was appointed attorney general of South Carolina. The next year at twenty-five he was the youngest delegate to attend the Stamp Act Congress at New York City in 1765, where he was made chairman of the committee that drafted the memorial and peti-

John Rutledge

The village blacksmith, possessing a wide variety of skills in addition to the shoeing of horses, was an essential member of every colonial community.

—Sketch by Kay Smith

357

tion to the English House of Lords. He and his brother both were delegates to the Continental Congress in 1774–77, but he did not sign the Declaration of Independence because he had been called back to South Carolina by the press of duties there. He wrote South Carolina's first state constitution in 1775, and was elected as the state's first chief executive in March 1776.

Rutledge served as president and commander in chief of South Carolina 1776–78 and as the state's first governor 1779–82. During this period he organized the defense of the state in the face of the British invasion, earning the nickname "Dictator John." He was again a delegate to the Continental Congress in 1782–83, and then served seven years as judge of the state's court of chancery 1784–89. At forty-eight he was a member of South Carolina's delegation to the federal Constitutional Convention of 1787, where he played a major role in drafting the new United States Constitution. After signing it, he helped win South Carolina's ratification of the document.

President Washington appointed Rutledge as one of the first associate justices of the United States Supreme Court 1789–91. He resigned to become chief justice of South Carolina 1791–95, and then was appointed acting Chief Justice of the United States in 1795 and presided at the August term. However, the U.S. Senate on December 15, 1795, refused to confirm him because of remarks he had made opposing the recently negotiated Jay Treaty with Britain. He died in Charleston on July 18, 1800.

• ARTHUR ST. CLAIR   1734–1818

A major general in the Revolutionary War and the fifteenth President of the Continental Congress, Arthur St. Clair was born in Thurso, Caithness, Scotland, on March 23, 1734 (old style). After attending the University of Edinburgh and studying medicine in London, he purchased a commission as ensign in the 60th Royal American Foot Regiment in 1757, and came to America to fight in the French and Indian War. He served under General Amherst at the capture of Louisbourg on July 26, 1758, and under Gen. James Wolfe at Quebec in September 1758. After resigning in 1762, St. Clair settled in Ligonier Valley, Pennsylvania, where he became a large landowner.

At the outbreak of the Revolutionary War he became colonel of the 2nd Pennsylvania Battalion of militia and led them at the battle of Three Rivers in Canada in 1776. He was then commissioned a brigadier general in the Continental Army and took part in the battles of Trenton and Princeton in 1776–77. He was promoted to major general in February 1777, and took over command of the Northern Department. After he gave up Fort Ticonderoga to the British in July 1777, he was given no other important field commands for the rest of the war. He represented Pennsylvania in the Continental Con-

General Arthur St. Clair

gress in 1785–88, serving as its President from February 2, 1787, to January 22, 1788.

President Washington appointed him the first governor of the Northwest Territory 1789–1802, during which time, as major general of the new United States Army, he was defeated in a battle with the Miami Indians in 1791. After retiring as territorial governor, he returned to Pennsylvania, where he was one of the founders of the iron-making business in Pittsburgh. However, he was no more successful as a businessman than as a general, and he died in poverty near Youngstown, Pennsylvania, on August 31, 1818.

• DEBORAH SAMPSON   1760–1827

The only woman known to have fought in the Revolutionary War disguised as a man, Deborah Sampson was born in Plympton, Massachusetts, on December 17, 1760. While she was a small child, the community removed her from the care of her parents because of their abuse and neglect. She was placed in the care of a farm family as an indentured servant to work for her keep until she was eighteen and as a result received no formal education. Determined to better herself, when she was released from her period of indenture in 1778, she supported herself by working part time for a farm family and the other half of the time attended the local school. Because of her intense desire to learn, she quickly absorbed everything the local teacher had to offer, and the community then employed her to be in charge of the school. Becoming inspired to help her country in its struggle for independence, perhaps by using her newly acquired education to read a copy of Tom Paine's widely distributed *Common Sense*, she secretly sewed herself a suit of men's clothing, walked to the town of Medway, Massachusetts, where she was not known, and enlisted in the army as "Robert Shirtliffe."

Captain Nathan Thayer, who was enlisting the company in which "Robert" enrolled, invited the new recruit to live with his family until his roster was full and the company was ready to leave for war. During this time, having been supplied with a uniform that did not fit, she was surprised by Mrs. Thayer in the act of using needle and scissors to alter the clothes. But "Robert" explained away this non-masculine activity by saying that, since he had no sister, his mother had taught him how to sew. An acquaintance who knew Deborah Sampson about this time, later described her in these words: "Although not beautiful, her features were animated and pleasing, and her figure, tall for a woman, was finely proportioned. As a man, she might have been called handsome; her general appearance was extremely prepossessing, and her manner calculated to inspire confidence."

Authorities differ as to the details of her length of service and the actions in which she was engaged, but most agree that

Deborah Sampson

she was wounded twice. First she received a sword slash on the right side of her head during a skirmish with Loyalists near Tarrytown, New York. A few months later she was ambushed and shot through the shoulder with a musket ball. The fact that the secret of her sex was not discovered in either instance speaks for itself as to the general quality of medical treatment provided for soldiers at that time.

Having been transferred to Philadelphia, where she worked as an orderly in the home of Colonel Patterson, she became ill with a high fever. Placed in a military hospital, her secret finally was discovered by a Dr. Binney, who sympathetically told no one of the matter, but removed the girl to his own home so she could receive better care. There the doctor's attractive young niece became infatuated with "Robert," making him promise that he would come back to her when the war was over.

Upon her recovery she reported back for duty, and there her commanding officer gave her a letter to deliver to General Washington. At this point let's pick up her story as told by Elizabeth F. Ellet who had it firsthand from Deborah Sampson's friends and relatives:

"Her worst fears were now confirmed. From the time of her removal into the doctor's family, she had cherished a misgiving, which sometimes amounted almost to a certainty, that he had discovered her deception. In conversation with him she anxiously watched his countenance, but not a word or look indicated suspicion, and she had again flattered herself that she was safe from detection. When the order came for her to deliver a letter into the hands of the commander-in-chief, she could no longer deceive herself.

"There remained no course but simple obedience. When she presented herself for admission at the headquarters of Washington, she trembled as she had never done before the enemy's fire. Her heart sank within her; she strove in vain to collect and compose herself, and overpowered with dread and uncertainty, was ushered into the presence of the Chief. He noticed her extreme agitation, and supposing it to proceed from diffidence, kindly endeavored to reassure her. He then bade her retire with an attendant, who was directed to offer her some refreshment, while he read the communication of which she had been the bearer.

"Within a short time she was again summoned into the presence of Washington. He said not a word, but handed her in silence a discharge from the service, putting into her hand at the same time a note containing a few brief words of advice, and a sum of money sufficient to bear her expenses to some place where she might find a home. The delicacy and forbearance thus observed affected her sensibly.

"'How thankful' she has often said, 'was I to that great and good man who so kindly spared my feelings! He saw me ready to sink with shame; one word from him at that moment would

Children's toys

have crushed me to the earth. But he spoke no word—and I blessed him for it.'"

After the war she married Benjamin Gannet, a farmer of Sharon, Massachusetts, and they had three children. As her story became known, the state of Massachusetts awarded her a veteran's bonus, and Congress voted her a small pension as a disabled soldier. In 1820, when in her sixties, Deborah Sampson appeared in court in Dedham, Massachusetts, to renew her pension claims as a Revolutionary War soldier. Seven years later she died in Sharon on April 29, 1827.

• ALEXANDER SCAMMELL 1747—1781

A Continental Army officer who served as General Washington's adjutant general and later was killed at the battle of Yorktown, Alexander Scammell was born in Mendon (now Milford), Massachusetts, on March 24, 1747. After graduation from Harvard in 1769, he taught school for a short time and then began studying law in the office of John Sullivan in Durham, New Hampshire. When Sullivan was appointed a brigadier general in the Continental Army in June 1775, Scammell went with him to the siege of Boston, where he was commissioned as a major in Sullivan's brigade. At the battle of Long Island, New York, he served as an aide to General Washington, and in November 1776 was appointed colonel in command of the 3rd New Hampshire Regiment. In 1777 he was wounded while leading his regiment in the battles of Saratoga. From 1778 to 1781 Scammell was adjutant general of the army. In 1781 he was placed in command of the 1st New Hampshire Regiment, marching with them to Virginia. On September 30, 1781, as Washington's forces were closing in on Cornwallis at Yorktown, Scammell went forward to investigate reports that the British had evacuated a fortified position. Unexpectedly running into a British patrol, he was captured. Having been wounded in the incident, he was paroled and released back to American custody, but died six days later in Williamsburg, Virginia, on October 6, 1781.

• JAMES SCHUREMAN 1756—1824

A delegate to the Continental Congress from New Jersey, James Schureman was born in New Brunswick, New Jersey, on February 12, 1756. After graduation from Rutgers College in 1775, he served in the Revolutionary War. He was elected to the New Jersey general assembly 1783–85 and 1788, and was a delegate to the Continental Congress in 1786–87. Schureman was elected as a Federalist to the First U.S. Congress 1789–91, to the Fifth U.S. Congress 1797–99 and to the U.S. Senate 1799–1801. He served as mayor of New Brunswick 1801–13, was again elected to the Thirteenth U.S. Congress 1813–15, and again was elected mayor from 1821 until his death in New Brunswick on January 22, 1824.

• PHILIP JOHN SCHUYLER   1733–1804

A Revolutionary War general and a delegate to the Continental Congress, Philip John Schuyler was born in Albany, New York, on November 20, 1733. At twenty-one he was commissioned a captain in the British Army in the French and Indian War. He fought at the battle of Lake George in September 1755, and then spent most of the rest of the war as commissary with the rank of major, provisioning the army. In 1761 he went to England with General Bradstreet to settle claims and accounts. Having inherited a fortune from his father and grandfather, he was one of New York's largest landholders by the time of the Revolutionary War. In June 1775 the Continental Congress appointed him as a major general, the third ranking officer under General Washington, and he was placed in charge of the Northern Department. He was replaced in this command by Gen. Horatio Gates in 1777, and was charged with incompetence for having given up Fort Ticonderoga to the British. Although acquitted by a court martial in 1778, Schuyler resigned in 1779. He was chosen as a member of New York's delegation to the Continental Congress 1775–

General Philip John Schuyler

1781, but was absent much of the time because of his military duties. He was elected to the New York state senate as a Federalist in 1780–84 and 1786–90, and then to the U.S. Senate in 1797–98. He died November 18, 1804 in Albany.

• CHARLES SCOTT   1733–1820

A general in the Continental Army and later governor of Kentucky, Charles Scott was born in Cumberland County, Virginia, in 1733. He served under George Washington in the French and Indian War as a Virginia militia corporal at the defeat of General Edward Braddock at Fort Duquesne (Pittsburgh) in 1755. At the beginning of the Revolutionary War in 1775 he raised and commanded the first company of militia to be organized south of the James River in Virginia. As colonel of the 3rd Virginia Regiment he played a major role in Washington's victories at Trenton and Princeton, New Jersey, in the winter of 1776–1777. As a result, at Washington's request, Congress promoted him to brigadier general in April 1777. Later that year he fought in the battles of Brandywine and Germantown, and in the battle of Monmouth in 1778. Scott later told of the dressing-down Washington gave General Charles Lee on the battlefield at Monmouth, saying that Washington "swore that day till the leaves shook on the trees." Having taken his troops to the Southern States to operate under General Benjamin Lincoln, Scott was taken prisoner by the British at the surrender of Charleston, South Carolina, in May 1780. He saw no further service during the war because he was paroled but not exchanged. He was brevetted as a major general at the end of the war in 1783.

Moving to Kentucky after the war, he fought in several battles against the Indians in succeeding years, most prominently leading more than a thousand volunteers in the battle of Fallen Timbers in 1794. He was elected governor of Kentucky 1808–12, and then retired from public life. He died in Kentucky on October 22, 1820.

• GUSTAVUS SCOTT   1753–1800

A delegate to the Continental Congress and one of the commissioners who superintended the construction of Washington, D.C., Gustavus Scott was born at "Westwood" in Prince William County, Virginia, in 1753. After graduation from King's College in Aberdeen, Scotland, Scott studied law at the Middle Temple in London, England, and began practice in Somerset County, Maryland, in 1771. He was elected to the Maryland house of delegates in 1780 and represented Maryland in the Continental Congress in 1784–85. He served as one of the commissioners to superintend the erection of the public buildings in Washington, D.C., from 1794 until his death in Washington on December 25, 1800.

• JOHN MORIN SCOTT   1730–1784

A delegate to the Continental Congress, John Morin Scott was born in New York City in 1730. After graduation from Yale College at sixteen, he studied law and began practice in New York City in 1752. Elected as an alderman 1756–61, he was one of the founders of the Sons of Liberty. He was elected a member of the New York Revolutionary congress 1775–77, and was a brigadier general in the militia. Scott was elected to state senate 1777–82, and was secretary of state of New York 1778–84. He represented New York in the Continental Congress 1780–83. Scott died in New York City on September 14, 1784.

• THOMAS SCOTT   1739–1796

One of Pennsylvania's first U.S. Congressmen, Thomas Scott was born in Chester County, Pennsylvania, in 1739. After studying law, Scott moved to Westmoreland County in 1770 and settled on Dunlaps Creek near the Monongahela River. From 1776 he was elected to the Pennsylvania legislature, and won election to the First U.S. Congress 1789–91. He was again elected to the Third U.S. Congress 1793–95. Scott died in Washington, Pennsylvania, on March 2, 1796.

• NATHANIEL SCUDDER   1733–1781

A delegate to the Continental Congress who died fighting during the Revolutionary War, Nathaniel Scudder was born at Monmouth Court House, New Jersey, on May 10, 1733. After graduation from the College of New Jersey in 1751, he studied medicine and commenced practice in Monmouth County, New Jersey. Scudder was speaker of the New Jersey general assembly in 1776 and represented New Jersey in the Continental Congress 1777–79 where he signed the Articles of Confederation. As a colonel of militia, he was killed on October 17, 1781, while resisting a British invading party at Blacks Point, near Shrewsbury, New Jersey.

• JAMES SEARLE   1730–1797

A Pennsylvania delegate to the Continental Congress, James Searle was born in New York City in 1730. A merchant, he moved to Philadelphia in 1762. He represented Pennsylvania in the Continental Congress 1778–80. He was sent by Pennsylvania in 1780–82 as commissioner to France and Holland in an unsuccessful effort to negotiate a loan for the state. Searle died in Philadelphia on August 7, 1797.

York, Pennsylvania was the seat of government from September 30, 1777 to June 27, 1778 when the Second Continental Congress sought sanctuary there in the darkest days of the Revolution while the British occupied Philadelphia and General Washington was encamped at Valley Forge. This Court House in the city square served as the meeting place during historic days. Unfortunately since it occupied a place that blocked the central intersection in the growing city, it was torn down in 1849.
—From a sketch of a model by Kay Smith

• ISAAC SEARS   1729–1786

The leader of the rebellion in New York City at the beginning of the Revolutionary War, Isaac Sears was born in Norwalk, Connecticut, in 1729. He became a seaman and then a shipmaster. During the French and Indian War, he fought as a privateer in the West Indies. He then settled in New York, where he became a successful merchant with ships trading with Europe and the West Indies. When the acts of the British parliament began to interfere with his business, he became the outspoken leader of the patriotic movement in New York City. As leader of the waterfront and of the Sons of Liberty, he became known as "King" Sears. He was thoroughly hated by the royal government and its supporters and was constantly abused and ridiculed in the Loyalist press, as, for example, this newspaper verse published when the Loyalists won control of the New York legislature just before the Revolutionary War:

> *And so my good masters, I find it no joke,*
> *For York has stepped forward and thrown off the yoke*
> *Of Congress, committees, and even King Sears,*
> *Who shows you good nature by showing his ears*

On April 15, 1775, just four days before the battles of Lexington and Concord, Sears called a meeting in New York City at which he exhorted the people to arm themselves and prevent any further shipment of supplies to the British troops quartered in Boston. At the end of the meeting he was arrested and taken before the mayor. Refusing to give bail, he was about to be taken off to prison when a group of Sons of Liberty rescued him and paraded him through town preceded by a band. When news reached New York on April 24 of the battles of Lexington and Concord, Sears and John Lamb led the Sons of Liberty in seizing the city hall and the customs house. They then took into custody all the merchants who had been trading with the British in Boston, and formed a "committee of one hundred" to govern New York City. After British troops captured New York City in 1776, Sears went to Boston where he directed the operation of privateers against the British. After the war, while on a trading trip to China, he died in Canton on October 28, 1786.

- ## THEODORE SEDGEWICK 1746−1813

A delegate to the Continental Congress and one of Massachusetts' first U.S. Congressmen, Theodore Sedgewick was born in West Hartford, Connecticut, on May 9, 1746. After attending Yale College, he studied law and at the age of twenty began practice in Great Barrington, Massachusetts. During the Revolutionary War he served in the expedition against Canada in 1776. Sedgewick was elected to the state legislature 1780−85, and then represented Massachusetts in the Continental Congress 1785−88. After serving as speaker of the state house of representatives in 1787−88, he was elected as a Federalist to the first and three succeeding U.S. Congresses 1789−96. The state legislature elected Sedgewick to the U.S. Senate 1796−99, where he served as president pro tempore of the Senate 1798−99. Elected to the Sixth U.S. Congress 1799−1801, Sedgewick served as Speaker of the U.S. House of Representatives. After retiring from Congress in 1801, Sedgewick was appointed to the supreme court of Massachusetts, serving on that tribunal for eleven years until his death in Boston on January 24, 1813.

- ## JOSHUA SENEY 1756−1798

A delegate to the Continental Congress and one of Maryland's first U.S. Congressmen, Joshua Seney was born near Church Hill, Maryland, on March 4, 1756. After graduation from the College of Philadelphia at seventeen, he studied law and began practice in Queen Annes County. Seney was elected to the state house of delegates 1785−87, and then represented Maryland in the Continental Congress in 1787−88. He won election to the First and Second U.S. Congresses, serving from

1789 until his resignation in 1792 to accept appointment as chief justice of the 3rd U.S. district court of Maryland. Seney retired from the bench in 1796, and died near Church Hill on October 20, 1798.

- **JONATHAN DICKINSON SERGEANT**   **1746–1793**

A delegate to the Continental Congress from New Jersey and attorney general of Pennsylvania during the Revolutionary War, Jonathan Dickinson Sergeant was born in Newark, New Jersey, in 1746. After graduation from the College of New Jersey in 1762 and from the College of Philadelphia in 1763, he studied law and began practice in Princeton, New Jersey, in 1767. Sergeant was very active in the Revolutionary political activities in New Jersey, serving as secretary and treasurer of the New Jersey Revolutionary congress in 1775–76, and as a member of the committee of safety in 1775–76. He was a member of the committee that drafted the first constitution of New Jersey in 1776, and represented New Jersey in the Continental Congress 1776–77. He resigned from Congress to accept appointment as attorney general of Pennsylvania 1777–80. He died in Philadelphia on October 8, 1793.

- **JOHN SEVIER**   **1745–1815**

A frontiersman who fought as a colonel in the Revolutionary War and later helped found the state of Tennessee, John Sevier was born in Rockingham County, Virginia, on September 23, 1745. In 1769 he went on an exploring expedition to what is now eastern Tennessee, helping build Fort Watauga near the Holston River. A few years later he moved his family to the area. In 1780 as a militia colonel he led more than 200 "over the mountain men" to South Carolina to help win the American victory at the battle of Kings Mountain on October 7. After the war, he helped found the independent state of Franklin and served as its governor during its brief existence from 1785 to 1788. When North Carolina established its control over the area, Sevier won election to the First U.S. Congress as one of North Carolina's Representatives 1789–91. Upon Tennessee's admission to the Union in 1796, he served as the state's first governor until 1801 and was again elected governor 1803–1809. He again won election to Congress, this time as a Representative of Tennessee, from 1811 to 1815. While serving as a member of a commission to determine the boundary between Tennessee and the Creek nation, he died in Fort Decatur, Alabama, on September 24, 1815.

John Sevier

- **WILLIAM SHARPE**   **1742–1818**

A delegate to the Continental Congress from North Carolina, William Sharpe was born near Rock Church, Maryland, on

367

December 13, 1742. After studying law, Sharpe commenced practice in Mecklenburg County, North Carolina, in 1763. He was elected to the North Carolina Revolutionary congress in 1775. The next year he served as an aide to Gen. Griffith Rutherford in the campaign against the Cherokee Indians. In 1777 he was one of four commissioners appointed by Governor Caswell to negotiate a treaty with the Indians. Sharpe represented North Carolina in the Continental Congress 1779–82. He died near Statesville, North Carolina, on July 1, 1818.

The storming of Fort Ticonderoga —From *Harper's Encyclopedia of U.S. History*

• DANIEL SHAYS   c.1747–1825

An officer in the Continental Army and a leader of Shays' Rebellion in Massachusetts in 1786–87, Daniel Shays was born in Hopkinton, Massachusetts, about 1747. A farmer, he was one of the Minutemen who hurried to answer the alarm sounded by the battles of Lexington and Concord. He then was commissioned a lieutenant in the militia and fought bravely at the battles of Bunker Hill and Ticonderoga. In January 1777 he was promoted to captain of the 5th Massachusetts Continental Regiment, and with them fought in the battles of Saratoga and Stony Point. In recognition of his bravery, the

Marquis de Lafayette presented him with a sword (which Shays later had to sell for needed cash). When the war moved to the South, Shays resigned from the army to take care of his farm and his family.

After the war Shays and other farmers in Massachusetts became increasingly discontented with the way the state government was being managed. The legislature imposed higher and higher taxes on property owners and demanded that the taxes be paid in hard money rather than paper. Foreclosures of mortgages and auctions of private possessions became an everyday matter. Mobs began to attack courthouses to prevent any more foreclosures. On September 26, 1786, Shays led five hundred or more men to Springfield and forced the state supreme court from holding a session there. To protect the federal arsenal at Springfield, Congress voted that federal troops be raised to protect it. On January 25, 1787, Shays and his men attacked the arsenal, but were unable to take it. General Benjamin Lincoln at the head of a hastily raised federal army caught up with Shays' forces a few days later, taking many prisoner, and dispersing the others. Shays and other leaders of the rebellion were tried and sentenced to death, but a year later were pardoned and set free.

The net effect of the rebellion was to emphasize the need for a stronger federal government, causing such leaders as George Washington and Benjamin Franklin to press for the Constitutional Convention which met later that same year and drafted the United States Constitution.

Shays moved to Sparta, New York, where he died on September 29, 1825.

A minuteman

- **ISAAC SHELBY   1750–1826**

A frontier militia colonel and first governor of Kentucky, Isaac Shelby was born in North Mountain, Maryland, on December 11, 1750. As a lieutenant in the company commanded by his father, Evan Shelby (1720–1794), young Shelby fought at the battle of Point Pleasant (now in West Virginia) in Lord Dunmore's War. He then remained there until 1775 as second in command of the fort. Promoted to captain in the militia, he acted for several years as commissary, providing supplies for various frontier expeditions. In 1780 he was commissioned colonel of militia and led his "over the mountain men" to South Carolina, where they captured the Loyalist garrison at Thicketty Fort in July, destroyed a Loyalist force of about 200 at Musgrove's Mill in August, and took part in the victory at King's Mountain in October. Shelby was credited with planning the tactics that were successful in the latter battle. He was elected to the North Carolina legislature in 1781–82. After the war he moved to Kentucky where he was elected as the state's first governor 1792–96 and served in that office again in 1812–16. In the War of 1812 he led an

369

army of 4,000 on an invasion of Canada, helping win the battle of the Thames in October 1813. He died near Stanford, Kentucky, on July 18, 1826.

• WILLIAM SHEPARD   1737–1817

An officer in the Revolutionary War and later a U.S. Congressman, William Shepard was born in Westfield, Massachusetts, on December 1, 1737. During the French and Indian War, he enlisted at seventeen and served for six years, advancing to the rank of captain. In 1775 he joined the patriotic army at Boston as a lieutenant colonel of Minutemen. He was wounded at the battles of Long Island and Pell's Point, New York, in 1776. Commissioned as a colonel in the Continental Army, he took command of the 4th Massachusetts Regiment in 1777, leading his men in fighting around Saratoga, New York. Shepard was elected to the Massachusetts house of representatives in 1785–86. As a major general of militia, he successfully defended the Springfield Arsenal during Shays' Rebellion in 1787. Shepard was a member of the governor's council of Massachusetts 1792–96. He was elected and re-elected to the U.S. Congress 1797–1803. Shepard died in Westfield, Massachusetts, on November 16, 1817.

• ROGER SHERMAN   1721–1793

A signer of the Declaration of Independence, the Articles of Confederation, and the United States Constitution, Roger Sherman was born in Newton, Massachusetts, on April 19, 1721. After learning the trade of shoe-making, Sherman set up a cobbler's shop at the age of twenty-two in New Milford, Connecticut. While making shoes, he studied law. At the age of thirty-two he was admitted to the bar and began practice. By the beginning of the Revolutionary War he had served twenty years in public office as a judge and as a member of the Connecticut legislature. While continuing in the state senate and as a judge of the superior court, Sherman represented Connecticut in the Continental Congress 1774–81 and 1783–84.

Sherman was a member of the committee that drafted the Declaration of Independence, a member of the committee that prepared the Articles of Confederation, and the only member of the Continental Congress who signed all four of the great state papers: the Articles of Association of 1774, the Declaration of Independence of 1776, the Articles of Confederation of 1778, and the United States Constitution of 1787. At the federal Constitutional Convention in Philadelphia in 1787, Sherman was an important figure in achieving compromise between the large and small states. Sherman was elected to the First U.S. Congress 1789–91, and then to the U.S. Senate from 1791 until his death in New Haven, Connecticut, on July 23, 1793.

Roger Sherman

- **WILLIAM SHIPPEN**   **1712–1801**

A physician and delegate to the Continental Congress, William Shippen was born in Philadelphia on October 1, 1712. After studying medicine, he developed a large medical practice in Philadelphia. He was one of the founders of the College of Philadelphia (later the University of Pennsylvania), serving as a trustee 1749–79. He also was one of the founders of the College of New Jersey (later Princeton University), serving as a trustee 1765–96. Shippen represented Pennsylvania in the Continental Congress 1778–80. He died in Germantown, Pennsylvania, on November 4, 1801. His son, William Shippen (1736–1808), was chief physician and director of hospitals for the Continental Army from 1777 to 1781.

- **PETER SILVESTER**   **1734–1808**

One of New York's first U.S. Congressmen, Peter Silvester was born at Shelter Island, Long Island, New York, in 1734. After being admitted to the bar in 1763, he began practice in Albany, New York. He was a member of the Albany committee of safety in 1774, and served in the New York Revolutionary congresses in 1775–76. Silvester was elected to the First and Second U.S. Congresses 1789–93, to the state senate 1796–1800, and to the state assembly 1803–06. He died in Kinderhook, New York on October 15, 1808.

- **THOMAS SINNICKSON**   **1744–1817**

One of New Jersey's first U.S. Congressmen, Thomas Sinnickson was born near Salem, New Jersey, on December 21, 1744. A merchant, he served as captain in the militia during the Revolutionary War. He was elected to the New Jersey general assembly for six years between 1777 and 1788. Sinnickson won election to the First and Fifth U.S. Congresses in 1789–91 and 1797–99. He died in Salem on May 15, 1817.

- **JOHN SITGREAVES**   **1757–1802**

A delegate to the Continental Congress from North Carolina, John Sitgreaves was born in England in 1757. After attending Eton College, he immigrated to North Carolina. He settled in New Bern, North Carolina, where he studied law and commenced practice. During the Revolutionary War he was a lieutenant in the militia, and served as military aide to General Caswell. He represented North Carolina in the Continental Congress in 1784–85, and was speaker of the state house of representatives in 1787–88. Appointed U.S. district judge for North Carolina in 1789, he served on the bench thirteen years until his death in Halifax, North Carolina, on March 4, 1802.

• WILLIAM SMALLWOOD   1732–1792

A Continental Army general, William Smallwood was born in Kent County, Maryland, in 1732, the son of a wealthy planter. In 1776 Smallwood mustered an elite regiment of men from Maryland's aristocracy and became its colonel. At the battle of Long Island, New York, in August his men fought with great courage and many of them died, but Smallwood himself was absent during most of the battle on other duties, arriving only in time to help some escape from a British trap. Two months later he was promoted to brigadier general and a few days later led his brigade with distinction at the battle of White Plains, New York, where he was badly wounded. Sent to raise militia for the defense of Philadelphia, he and his new troops arrived too late to take part in the battle of Germantown in October 1777. Assigned to the Southern theater of operations in 1780, his troops were held in reserve at the battle of Camden, South Carolina, and did not take part in the fighting. Promoted to major general, Smallwood refused to serve as a subordinate to Baron von Steuben, who had been placed over him, so he was sent back to Maryland to recruit more troops. He took no further part in the fighting. After the war Smallwood was elected governor of Maryland in 1785–88. He died in Prince Georges County, Maryland, on February 14, 1792.

William Smallwood

• JAMES SMITH   c. 1719–1806

A signer of the Declaration of Independence, James Smith was born in Ireland about 1719. His father brought him to Pennsylvania in 1727. After attending the College of Philadelphia, he studied law and was admitted to the bar in 1745.

James Smith and his wife

Smith settled in York, Pennsylvania, where he began an iron manufacturing business. In 1774 he raised the first company of militia for the defense of Pennsylvania, and the next year expanded the company to a battalion. Smith held the honorary title of colonel, but did not take an active command. He represented Pennsylvania in the Continental Congress 1776–78, where he signed the Declaration of Independence. Smith was commissioned a brigadier general of militia in 1782. After the war he practiced law in York until his death there on July 11, 1806.

• JONATHAN BAYARD SMITH   1742–1812

A Pennsylvania delegate to the Continental Congress, Jonathan Bayard Smith was born in Philadelphia on February 21, 1742. He was graduated from the College of New Jersey in 1760. Smith was secretary of the Philadelphia committee of safety 1775–77, and represented Pennsylvania in the Continental Congress in 1777–78, where he signed the Articles of Confederation. Smith served on the board of aldermen of Philadelphia 1792–94, and was auditor general of Pennsylvania in 1794. He died in Philadelphia on June 16, 1812.

• MELANCTHON SMITH   1744–1798

A delegate to the Continental Congress, Melancthon Smith was born in Jamaica, Long Island, New York, on May 7, 1744. At the beginning of the Revolutionary War, Smith was clerking in a store at Poughkeepsie, New York. He was a delegate to the New York patriotic congress in 1775, and then joined the Continental Line Regiment that was organized on June 30, 1775. Later, he helped organize and became captain of the Dutchess County Minutemen, and was secret service commissioner and sheriff of Dutchess County in 1777–78. He was chosen as one of New York's delegates to the Continental Congress 1785–88. Smith died in New York City on July 29, 1798.

• MERIWETHER SMITH   1730–1790

A delegate to the Continental Congress, Meriwether Smith was born at "Bathurst" on Piscataway Creek near Dunnsville, Virginia, in 1730. Smith was elected to the Virginia house of burgesses in 1774–75, to the Virginia Revolutionary conventions of 1775–76, and to the Virginia house of delegates 1776–78. He was chosen as one of Virginia's delegates to the Continental Congress 1778–82. Smith again was elected to the state house of delegates in 1781–82, 1785, and 1788. He also was a delegate to the Virginia convention that ratified the United States Constitution on June 26, 1788. He died at "Marigold," near Oceana, Virginia, on January 25, 1790.

• RICHARD SMITH   1735–1803

A delegate to the Continental Congress, Richard Smith was born in Burlington, New Jersey, on March 22, 1735. After studying law, he was admitted to the bar in 1762 and practiced in Burlington, New Jersey. He was chosen as one of New Jersey's delegates to the Continental Congress in 1774–76. He then served as treasurer of New Jersey 1776–77. He later moved to Mississippi where he died near Natchez on September 17, 1803.

• THOMAS SMITH   1745–1809

Thomas Smith
—From the only known portrait,
a miniature owned by W.J.DeRenne

A delegate to the Continental Congress, Thomas Smith was born near Cruden, Aberdeenshire, Scotland, in 1745. After attending the University of Edinburgh in Scotland, he immigrated to Pennsylvania in 1769. He studied law and began practice in 1772. With the coming of the Revolutionary War, he served in the militia as a deputy colonel. Smith was elected to the Pennsylvania house of representatives 1776–80, and represented Pennsylvania in the Continental Congress 1780–82. He served as a justice of the Pennsylvania supreme court from 1794 until his death in Philadelphia on March 31, 1809.

• WILLIAM SMITH   1728–1814

A member of the Continental Congress and one of Maryland's first U.S. Congressmen, William Smith was born in Donegal Township, Lancaster County, Pennsylvania, on April 12, 1728. At the age of thirty-three, Smith moved to Baltimore, Maryland, in 1761. He was a member of the local committee of correspondence in 1774. He was chosen as one of Maryland's delegates to the Continental Congress in 1777–78. Smith was elected as a Federalist to the First U.S. Congress 1789–91. He died in Baltimore on March 27, 1814.

• WILLIAM LOUGHTON SMITH   1758–1812

One of South Carolina's first U.S. Congressmen, William Loughton Smith was born in Charleston, South Carolina, in 1758. At twelve he was sent to England, where he went to preparatory school, and then studied law in the Middle Temple in London. He next continued his studies in Geneva, Switzerland, finally returning to Charleston in 1783. He was elected to the South Carolina house of representatives 1784–88, and to the first and four succeeding U.S. Congresses 1789–97. He then served as ambassador to Portugal and Spain in 1797–1801. Returning to Charleston, he ran unsuccessfully as a Federalist candidate for Congress in 1804, 1806, and 1808. He died in Charleston on December 19, 1812.

• RICHARD DOBBS SPAIGHT   1758–1802

A signer of the United States Constitution and governor of North Carolina who died as the result of a duel with a political rival, Richard Dobbs Spaight was born in New Bern, North Carolina, on March 25, 1758. After attending the University of Glasgow in Scotland, he returned home in 1778 and became military aide-de-camp to Gov. Richard Caswell. Spaight fought in the battle of Camden in 1780 and later was promoted to lieutenant colonel. He was elected to the North Carolina house of commons 1781–83, and represented North Carolina in the Continental Congress 1782–85. At the age of twenty-nine he was chosen as a delegate to the federal Constitutional Convention in Philadelphia, where he signed the new United States Constitution in 1787. Spaight was elected governor of North Carolina 1792–95, and then was elected as a Democrat to the U.S. Congress 1798–1801. Spaight and his Federalist successor in Congress, John Stanly, began a name-calling debate that ended in a duel in which Spaight was fatally wounded, dying on September 6, 1802, in New Bern.

Richard Dobbs Spaight
—Courtesy of Eastern National Park
and Monument Association

• JOSEPH SPENCER   1714–1789

A general in the Revolutionary War and a delegate to the Continental Congress, Joseph Spencer was born in East Haddam, Connecticut, on October 3, 1714. A lawyer by profession, he served in the French and Indian War as a lieutenant colonel of militia. He was sixty and a brigadier general of militia when the Revolutionary War began in 1775, and he hurried with his troops to take part in the siege of Boston. He was made a brigadier general in the Continental Army when it was formed in June 1775, and was promoted to major general the following year. He took part in the fighting in New York, and then was placed in charge of troops in New England. In September 1777 he aborted a planned attack on the British in Rhode Island. When Congress complained, Spencer asked for and received a court of inquiry that exonerated him. But he resigned his commission in January 1778. He was then chosen by the Connecticut legislature as a delegate to the Continental Congress 1778–79. He then served nine years on the Connecticut executive council, from 1780 to his death in East Haddam on January 13, 1789.

• JOHN STARK   1728–1822

A Continental Army general who won the battle of Bennington because he had refused to obey orders, John Stark was born in Londonderry, New Hampshire, on August 28, 1728. While he was a small boy, his family moved to Derryfield (now Manchester) on the New Hampshire frontier. Growing up he became an excellent hunter and woodsman. He once

375

was kidnaped by Indians and ransomed. Later he was adopted as a member of the tribe. He served during the French and Indian War in Rogers' Rangers, rising from lieutenant to captain 1755–59.

In April 1775, hearing of the battles of Lexington and Concord, Stark mustered a regiment of 800 men in one day and marched at their head as colonel to aid Massachusetts. At the battle of Bunker Hill in June 1775, Stark's regiment held the left side of the line. As he and his men were moving into position across a stretch of land under fire from British warships, he was urged by a fellow officer to move faster so as to get out of the line of fire. Stark, without quickening his pace, replied: "One fresh man in action is worth ten fatigued men." The excellent marksmanship of Stark's troops accounted for many of the British casualties in the ensuing fight. In 1776 he was commissioned as a colonel in the Continental Army, and in December he led the vanguard of Washington's army in the victory at Trenton, New Jersey. He also fought at the battle of Princeton in January 1777, but when Congress failed to promote him while handing out generals' commissions to others Stark resigned in March.

Returning to New Hampshire, he was placed in command of the state's militia that had been raised to oppose General John Burgoyne's invasion from Canada. When Continental Army Major General Benjamin Lincoln ordered Stark to march to the Hudson River to join the main army, Stark refused, pointing out that he had only agreed to take command of the militia on the condition he would be responsible only to the New Hampshire legislature and not to Congress. When Congress heard of the matter they fired off a reprimand to New Hampshire.

General John Stark

General Stark at the Battle of Bennington
—From an engraving by J. Godfrey after J. R. Chapin

On August 16, 1777, Stark led his brigade of about two thousand militia in an attack on part of Burgoyne's army that was attempting to make a raid on Bennington, Vermont. As Stark began the main attack he shouted to his men: "We'll beat them before night, or Molly Stark will be a widow." In the fight that followed more than two hundred of the enemy were killed and seven hundred captured, while the Americans lost only fourteen killed and about forty wounded. In addition Stark captured a huge amount of ammunition and weapons. The victory greatly weakened Burgoyne's forces and skyrocketed the morale of Americans. As a reward Congress appointed Stark as a brigadier general in October 1777.

Stark served through the rest of the war, but had no further opportunities for spectacular victories. He was brevetted a major general at the end of the war. Unlike most of the Continental Army generals, Stark stayed out of politics after the war. He worked his farm and enjoyed his family of eleven children, living to the age of ninety-three before his death on May 8, 1822.

- **JOHN STEELE   1764–1815**

One of North Carolina's first U.S. Congressmen, John Steele was born in Salisbury, North Carolina, on November 1, 1764. A farmer, he served two years in the state legislature before being elected to the First and Second U.S. Congresses in 1789–93. President Washington appointed Steele as Comptroller of the Treasury in 1796, and he was reappointed by both President John Adams and President Jefferson, serving until 1802. He then was appointed member of the board of commissioners to determine the boundary line between North Carolina and Georgia 1805–14. He died August 14, 1815, in Salisbury, North Carolina.

- **ADAM STEPHEN   c.1730–1791**

A Continental Army major general blamed for the American failure to win the battle of Germantown and dismissed from the service, Adam Stephen was born in Virginia about 1730. During the French and Indian War he served as a captain of militia under George Washington in the opening phases of that war and at its end nine years later had risen to the rank of brigadier general in command of the Virginia frontier. At the start of the Revolutionary War he was a colonel in command of the 4th Virginia Regiment. He was promoted to brigadier general in September 1776. A few months later at the battle of Trenton, New Jersey, he became the object of Washington's wrath when without authorization he sent out a patrol the day before the battle, jeopardizing the secrecy of the planned attack. Washington is said to have turned on him in anger, shouting: "You, sir, may have ruined all my plans by having put them on guard." Nevertheless, because of Stephen's past military experience he was advanced to major general in February 1777. Eight months later at the battle of Germantown, when Washington's army was on the point of winning a great victory, Stephen's division collided with that of General Anthony Wayne, and Stephen was said to have ordered a retreat that rapidly turned into a panicky rout of the entire American army. Court-martialed after the battle, he was found guilty of drunkenness and dismissed from the army. He died in Virginia in November 1791.

General Friedrich von Steuben

• BARON VON STEUBEN   1730–1794

The inspector general of the Continental Army who helped teach Washington's troops the techniques of warfare developed in Prussia, Friedrich von Steuben was born in Magdeburg, Prussia, on November 15, 1730, the son of a Prussian army officer. At fourteen young Steuben served as a volunteer under command of his father at the siege of Prague. By the time he was seventeen, he had been commissioned as an officer. In 1762 he became a member of the general staff of Frederick the Great. Two years later he became grand-marshal and general of the guard for the Prince Hohenzollern-Hechingen, who gave him the title of baron. When the prince ran into financial difficulties, the Baron had to seek employment elsewhere. He offered his services to Benjamin Franklin in Paris, and the American envoy gave him letters of introduction to George Washington.

When the Baron came to America and offered his services as an unpaid volunteer, the Congressional delegates gladly accepted. After reporting to George Washington at Valley Forge in February 1778, he was immediately put to work teaching the half-frozen, half-starved American troops the rudiments of Prussian military drill. That he achieved quick results is evidenced by Washington's recommendation two months later that the Baron be given a major general's commission and be named inspector general of the army. Congress rapidly acquiesced.

During 1778–79 the Baron wrote the first manual of regulations for the army, developed a training system, and in many other ways drew on his experience with the Prussian general staff to turn an amateur army into a professional one. In 1780–81 he served as second in command to General Nathanael Greene in the Southern States and at the battle of Yorktown commanded one of Washington's three divisions.

After the war he was showered with gifts to show America's appreciation for his services. He was voted American citizenship by the legislatures of Pennsylvania and New York. New York gave him a 16,000-acre estate, New Jersey gave him a farm, and Congress voted him a $2,500-a-year pension. He died at his estate, "Steubenville," in New York on November 28, 1794.

• JOHN STEVENS   1715–1792

A member of the Continental Congress, John Stevens was born in Perth Amboy, New Jersey, in 1715. A merchant and shipowner, he helped raise troops in the French and Indian War and served as paymaster for Colonel Schuyler's regiment 1756–60. He was vice president of the council of New Jersey 1770–82, and represented New Jersey in the Continental Congress in 1783–84. Stevens presided over the state constitutional convention in 1787. He died in Hoboken, New Jersey, on May 10, 1792.

• CHARLES STEWART   1729–1800

A militia officer in the Revolutionary War and a delegate to the Continental Congress, Charles Stewart was born in Gortlea, County Donegal, Ireland, in 1729. At twenty-one he immigrated to New Jersey in 1750, where he became a farmer. Active in the pre-Revolutionary movement, he was commissioned colonel of a militia battalion in 1776. Stewart was appointed commissary general by the Continental Congress in 1777. He represented New Jersey in the Continental Congress 1784–85. Stewart died in Flemington, New Jersey, on June 24, 1800.

The residence of Richard Stockton in Princeton, New Jersey

Richard Stockton

• RICHARD STOCKTON   1730–1781

A signer of the Declaration of Independence who died before the Revolutionary War was won, Richard Stockton was born at "Morven," near Princeton, New Jersey, on October 1, 1730. At seventeen he graduated in the first class from the College of New Jersey in 1748. He then studied law, was admitted to the bar in 1754, and developed a successful practice in Princeton. From 1768 to 1776 he was a member of the executive council of the royal governor of New Jersey, and an associate justice of the colony's supreme court from 1774 to 1776. After the patriots arrested the governor, William Franklin, Stockton resigned his two crown positions and was elected as a delegate to the Continental Congress where he voted for and signed the Declaration of Independence. While in Congress he served as chairman of a committee that inspected the northern army at Ticonderoga. Upon his return he was taken prisoner by the Tories near Freehold, New Jersey, on November 30, 1776, and imprisoned as a common criminal in New York City. By the time Stockton was released his health was ruined, and he found that his estate had been pillaged and his library burned. He died at "Morven," near Princeton on February 28, 1781.

- **MICHAEL JENIFER STONE   1747–1812**

One of Maryland's first U.S. Congressmen, Michael Jenifer Stone was born at "Equality," near Port Tobacco, Maryland, in 1747, a younger brother of Thomas Stone. He was elected to the Maryland house of delegates 1781–83, and to the state convention that ratified the United States Constitution in 1788. He then won election to the First U.S. Congress 1789–91. Appointed judge of the 1st U.S. district court of Maryland in 1791, he served in that position until his death on his estate "Equality," near Port Tobacco, Maryland, in 1812.

- **THOMAS STONE   1743–1787**

A signer of the Declaration of Independence, Thomas Stone was born at "Poynton Manor" in Charles County, Maryland in 1743, an older brother of Michael Jenifer Stone. He studied law, and at twenty-one was admitted to the bar, commencing practice in Frederick, Maryland. He was chosen as one of Maryland's delegates to the Continental Congress 1775–79, where he voted for and signed the Declaration of Independence and served on the committee that drafted the Articles of Confederation. Stone then was elected to the state senate 1779–83. He again represented Maryland in Congress 1783–84, serving for a short time as acting president of that body. While on a trip, he died in Alexandria, Virginia, on October 5, 1787.

- **CALEB STRONG   1745–1819**

One of Massachusetts' first U.S. Senators, Caleb Strong was born in Northampton, Massachusetts, on January 9, 1745. After graduation from Harvard College at nineteen, he studied law and commenced practice in 1772. He was a member of the committee of correspondence and safety in 1774–75. Strong was elected to the state house of representatives 1776–78, and then to the state senate 1780–88. He was chosen as a delegate to the federal Constitutional Convention but illness in his family compelled his absence before the convention ended. He was elected and re-elected as a Federalist to the U.S. Senate in 1789–96. Strong completed his public career with election as governor of Massachusetts 1800–07 and 1812–16. He died in Northampton on November 7, 1819.

Thomas Stone

- **JEDEDIAH STRONG   1738–1802**

A delegate to the Continental Congress, Jedidiah Strong was born in Litchfield, Connecticut, on November 7, 1738. After graduation from Yale College in 1761, he studied law, and commenced practice in Litchfield in 1764. Beginning in 1771, he was regularly elected to the Connecticut house of representatives for thirty years. He represented Connecticut in the

Continental Congress 1782–84. Strong also served as associate judge of the Litchfield County court 1780–91. He died in Litchfield on August 21, 1802.

- JONATHAN STURGES   1740–1819

A delegate to the Continental Congress for thirteen years and then one of Connecticut's first U.S. Congressmen, Jonathan Sturges was born in Fairfield, Connecticut, on August 23, 1740. After graduation from Yale College at nineteen, he studied law and commenced practice in Farifield in 1772. He immediately won election to the Connecticut house of representatives, serving in that body for the next twelve years. He represented Connecticut in the Continental Congress 1774–87, and then was elected to the First and Second U.S. Congresses 1789–93. For the next twelve years Sturges served as associate justice of the state supreme court 1793–1805. He died in Fairfield on October 4, 1819.

- JAMES SULLIVAN   1744–1808

A delegate to the Continental Congress and governor of Massachusetts, James Sullivan was born in Berwick, Maine (then part of Massachusetts), on April 22, 1744, a younger brother of John Sullivan. After studying law, he became a successful attorney in Biddeford. Active in the pre-Revolutionary movement, he was elected to the Revolutionary congress of Massachusetts in 1774–75. He was appointed justice of the Massachusetts superior court 1776–82, and also represented the state in the Continental Congress in 1782. He then served seventeen years as Massachusetts' attorney general 1790–1807. He was elected governor of Massachusetts in 1807 and 1808, dying while holding that office on December 10, 1808, in Boston.

- JOHN SULLIVAN   1740–1795

A major general in the Continental Army, a delegate to the Continental Congress, and chief executive of New Hampshire after the war, John Sullivan was born in Somersworth, New Hampshire, on February 17, 1740, an older brother of James Sullivan. After studying law, he commenced practice at the age of twenty in Durham, New Hampshire. An ardent patriot, Sullivan played a leading role in one of the incidents that led to the Revolutionary War when he and John Langdon led a band that captured Fort William and Mary from the British in the harbor of Portsmouth, New Hampshire, seizing 100 barrels of gunpowder that later were used in the battles of Lexington and Concord.

Sullivan represented New Hampshire in the Continental Congress 1774–75. When the Continental Army was formed,

General John Sullivan

he was appointed as a brigadier general in June 1775 and commanded a brigade in the siege of Boston. He led a relief column to the American army in Canada in June 1776, and then joined Washington's army in New York, where he was promoted to major general. He was captured in the battle of Long Island in August 1776, but was released a month later. He took an important part in the American victory at Trenton in December 1776, and in the following year fought in the battles of Princeton, Brandywine, and Germantown. In 1778 he was in command of the unsuccessful attempt to recapture Newport, Rhode Island. In 1779 he led a 4,000-man army against the Iroquois Indians on the Pennsylvania frontier, destroying 40 Indian towns and all their crops.

In November 1779 Sullivan resigned from the army on account of ill health. He again was sent as a delegate to the Continental Congress in 1780–81. He then served as attorney general of New Hampshire 1782–86, and as president of New Hampshire in 1786–89. In 1789 President Washington appointed Sullivan as judge of the U.S. district court of New Hampshire, a post he held until his death in Durham on January 23, 1795.

General Thomas Sumter

• THOMAS SUMTER   1734–1832

A fighting militia general in the Revolutionary War and one of South Carolina's first U.S. Congressmen, Thomas Sumter was born in Hanover County, Virginia, on August 14, 1734. He fought in the French and Indian War as a sergeant of Virginia militia, and then settled in South Carolina in 1765. As a lieutenant colonel early in the Revolutionary War he fought against the Indians, took part in a few skirmishes, and then resigned in September 1778. But when the British Legion under Lt. Col. Banastre Tarleton invaded the South in 1780, Sumter again took up arms. He was appointed senior brigadier general of militia and gathered an army of partisans, whose pay was the loot they plundered from the estates of Loyalists.

In November 1780 he was badly wounded in a battle with Tarleton at Blackstocks.

Throughout the spring and summer of 1781 Sumter and his guerrillas battled and plundered, until Gov. John Rutledge declared an end to "Sumter's law" and forbade plundering. Sumter resigned his commission and took up politics, winning election to the South Carolina legislature. He opposed ratification of the United States Constitution, and was elected as an anti-Federalist to the U.S. Congress, serving 1789–93 and 1797–1801. He then was elected as a U.S. Senator in 1801–10. Retiring from public life, he lived his last years on his plantation "South Mount," near Statesburg, South Carolina, where he died on June 1, 1832.

• **JOHN SWAN** 1760–1793

A delegate to the Continental Congress, John Swan was born in Pasquotank County, North Carolina, in 1760. After attending William and Mary College, he became a planter. He represented North Carolina in the Continental Congress in 1788, and then returned to private life. Swan died in 1793 on his plantation, "The Elms," in Pasquotank County.

• **JAMES SYKES** 1725–1792

A delegate to the Continental Congress, James Sykes was born in Delaware in 1725. An attorney, he served as a lieutenant in Capt. Caesar Rodney's company of Dover militia in the French and Indian War in 1756. Early in the Revolutionary War, Sykes was a member of the council of safety and a delegate to the state constitutional convention in 1776. He represented Maryland in the Continental Congress in 1777–78. He later served in the state legislature and as judge of Delaware's high court of errors and appeals. He died in Dover, Delaware, on April 4, 1792.

• **JOHN CLEVES SYMMES** 1742–1814

A delegate to the Continental Congress from New Jersey, John Cleves Symmes was born in Riverhead, Long Island, New York, on July 21, 1742. Before the Revolutionary War, Symmes moved to New Jersey. He was chairman of the committee of safety of Sussex County in 1774, and served in the militia in the early years of the war. Symmes was appointed chief justice of the New Jersey supreme court 1777–87. He represented New Jersey in the Continental Congress in 1785–86. He was appointed one of the three federal judges of the Northwest Territory in 1788 and held the position until Ohio was admitted to the Union in 1803. Symmes died in Cincinnati, Ohio, on February 26, 1814.

Lieutenant Benjamin Tallmadge

• BENJAMIN TALLMADGE   1754–1835

An officer in the Continental Army and head of the secret service during the Revolutionary War, Benjamin Tallmadge was born in Brookhaven, Long Island, New York, on February 25, 1754. After graduation from Yale College at nineteen, he became superintendent of Wethersfield (Conn.) high school 1773–76. He joined the Continental Army as a lieutenant in June 1776. After fighting in the battles of Long Island and White Plains, he was promoted to captain in December 1776 and to major in April 1777.

His investigation of the capture of British Maj. John André led to the exposure of Benedict Arnold's treason in September 1780. Two months later Tallmadge led the expedition that captured Fort George and destroyed the magazines of the British army at Oyster Bay, Long Island, New York, for which he received the public tribute of the Continental Congress and General Washington. For most of the time during the rest of the war, Tallmadge supervised secret intelligence operations for General Washington. He was brevetted as lieutenant colonel in 1783. After the war he became a business-

George Taylor

man in Litchfield, Connecticut, where he was appointed postmaster in 1792. Beginning in 1801, he was elected and reelected to the U.S. Congress as a Federalist, serving 1801–1817. Tallmadge died in Litchfield on March 7, 1835.

• **GEORGE TAYLOR   1716–1781**

A former indentured servant who proudly signed the Declaration of Independence, George Taylor was born in Ireland in 1716. At the age of twenty he immigrated to Pennsylvania as a bound servant, where he worked for an iron-maker in Chester County. When his master died, Taylor married the widow and became owner of the ironworks. He was elected to the Pennsylvania legislature 1764–69, where he became an early advocate of overthrowing British rule. Although he was a colonel of militia, he took no part in the fighting in the Revolutionary War. Again elected to the Pennsylvania legislature in 1775, he was chosen as one of Pennsylvania's pro-Independence delegation to the Continental Congress in 1776–77, where he signed the Declaration of Independence. Taylor died in Easton, Pennsylvania, on February 23, 1781.

• **EDWARD TELFAIR   1735–1807**

A delegate to the Continental Congress and governor of Georgia, Edward Telfair was born in "Town Head," Scotland, in 1735. At twenty-three he immigrated to America, where he worked in Virginia and North Carolina before establishing a commission house in Savannah, Georgia, in 1766. Active in the pre-Revolutionary movement, he was a member of the council of safety in 1775–76 and a delegate to the Georgia Revolutionary congress at Savannah in 1776. Telfair represented Georgia in the Continental Congress in 1778–82, 1784–85, and 1788–89. He was one of the signers of the Articles of Confederation in 1778. Telfair was elected governor of Georgia in 1786 and 1790–93. He died in Savannah on September 17, 1807.

• GEORGE THACHER   1754–1824

A delegate to the Continental Congress and one of Massachusetts' first U.S. Congressmen, George Thacher was born in Yarmouth, Massachusetts, on April 12, 1754. After graduation from Harvard College in 1776, he studied law and in 1778 began practice in York (now in Maine). He was chosen as a member of the Massachusetts delegation to the Continental Congress in 1787. Thacher won election as a Federalist to the first and five succeeding U.S. Congresses 1789–1801. For the next twenty years he served as an associate judge of the supreme court of Massachusetts 1800–1820. After Maine was admitted to the Union in 1820, Thacher was appointed judge of the supreme court of Maine, serving on that tribunal until his death in Biddeford, Maine, on April 6, 1824.

• CHARLES THOMSON   1729–1824

As secretary of the Continental Congress, Charles Thomson was the only person to serve with that body throughout the entire fifteen-year period of its existence from 1774 to 1789. Born in Maghera, Ireland, on November 29, 1729, Thomson at the age of eleven came to America with his three older brothers in 1741. He became a teacher in a Quaker school in New Castle, Delaware, from 1757 to 1760, and then helped negotiate treaties with the Indians. He was adopted as a member of the Delaware tribe, who gave him an Indian name meaning "one who always speaks the truth." In the years before the Revolution he became a prosperous merchant in Philadelphia, where he was a friend of Benjamin Franklin. A leader in the patriotic movement, he was called "the Sam Adams of Philadelphia" by John Adams.

When the first Continental Congress was being organized in 1774, a messenger brought him word: "They want you at Carpenters' Hall to keep the minutes of their proceedings, as you are very expert at that business." On July 4, 1776, he and John Hancock were the only two men to sign the original Declaration of Independence, the other delegates signing later.

When the U.S. Congress took over from the Continental Congress in 1789, the fifty-nine-year-old Thomson was disappointed at not being given a position in the new government.

Charles Thomson

He had gathered much material for a history of the Revolution, but to the dismay of later historians destroyed it. Retiring from public life, he devoted his time to a translation of the Bible from the Greek, which was completed in 1808, and then wrote a religious work published in 1815. Thomson died in Merion, Pennsylvania, on August 16, 1824.

Matthew Thornton

- **MATTHEW THORNTON**   c. 1714–1803

A physician and signer of the Declaration of Independence, Matthew Thornton was born in Ireland about 1714. While still a baby, Thornton was brought to America by his parents in 1716. After studying medicine, he commenced practice in Londonderry, New Hampshire, in 1740. In 1745 he served as a surgeon of New Hampshire troops in the first battle of Louisbourg in Nova Scotia. He was elected a member of the New Hampshire assembly when it was organized in 1758. At the outbreak of the Revolutionary War in 1775, Thornton was elected chief executive of New Hampshire as president of its provincial congress and chairman of the committee of safety. He was chosen speaker of the New Hampshire general assembly in 1776. He represented New Hampshire in the Continental Congress in 1776–78. Although he was not present when the Declaration of Independence was adopted, Thornton was allowed to sign the document in November 1776. He then served as judge of the superior court of New Hampshire 1776–82. At the age of eighty-nine he died while visiting a daughter in Newburyport, Massachusetts, on June 24, 1803.

- **MATTHEW TILGHMAN**   1718–1790

First head of the Revolutionary government of Maryland and a delegate to the Continental Congress, Matthew Tilghman was born at the "Hermitage," near Centerville, Maryland, on February 17, 1718. Known as "the patriarch of Maryland," he served more than a quarter of a century in the Maryland legislature before the Revolutionary War, and was speaker of the house in 1773–75. He was elected president of the Revolutionary convention that directed the affairs of the colony 1774–77. He represented Maryland in the Continental Congress 1774–77, but was summoned from his seat in Congress to preside at the Revolutionary convention at Annapolis, Maryland, convening June 21, 1776, and consequently missed voting for or signing the Declaration of Independence, which he supported. After chairing the committee that wrote Maryland's first state constitution, he retired to his plantation "Rich Neck," near Claiborne, Maryland, where he died on May 4, 1790. His nephew, Tench Tilghman (1744–1786), was aide-de-camp to General Washington 1776–81, and was given the honor of carrying news of the victory at Yorktown to the Continental Congress.

• **JAMES TILTON** 1745–1822

A military surgeon in the Revolutionary War and a delegate to the Continental Congress, James Tilton was born in Kent County, Delaware, on June 1, 1745. After receiving a medical degree from the College of Philadelphia in 1771, he began practice in Dover, Delaware. He served in the Revolutionary War as a surgeon, and was head of the military hospital at Princeton, New Jersey. He represented Delaware in the Continental Congress 1783–85. Tilton was elected several times as a member of the state house of representatives. In the War of 1812 he was appointed Surgeon General of the United States Army 1813–15. Tilton died at his home near Wilmington, Delaware, on May 14, 1822.

• **PAUL TRAPIER** 1749–1778

A delegate to the Continental Congress, Paul Trapier was born in Prince George's Parish near Georgetown, South Carolina, in 1749. After graduation from Eton College and Cambridge University in England, Trapier studied law at the Middle Temple in London. Returning to South Carolina at the beginning of the Revolutionary War, he was elected to the South Carolina general assembly in 1776, and was commissioned as a captain of militia artillery. He represented South Carolina in the Continental Congress in 1777–78. At the age of twenty-nine, Trapier died at his home near Georgetown on July 8, 1778.

• **JOHN TREADWELL** 1745–1823

A delegate to the Continental Congress and governor of Connecticut, John Treadwell was born in Farmington, Connecticut, on November 23, 1745. After graduation from Yale College in 1767, he studied law and commenced practice in Farmington. Beginning in 1776 Treadwell was regularly elected to the state legislature for twenty-one years, serving in the house 1776–85, and in the upper house 1785–97. He represented Connecticut in the Continental Congress 1785–86. He also served as judge of probate and the supreme court of errors of Connecticut 1789–1809. Treadwell won election as lieutenant governor of Connecticut 1798–1809, and as governor 1809–11. He died in Farmington on August 18, 1823.

• **JOHN TRUMBULL** 1751–1831

A poet of the Revolutionary War, John Trumbull was born in Westbury (now Watertown), Connecticut, on April 24, 1751. A genius, he learned Latin and Greek before he was six years old. At the age of seven he passed the entrance examination for Yale College, but because of frail health he did not enter

that school until he was thirteen. Graduating from Yale at sixteen in 1767, he became a tutor for several years and then took up the study of law. Upon being admitted to the bar in 1773, he entered the law office of John Adams in Boston. The following year he began a law practice in New Haven, Connecticut. In 1775 he wrote and published the first canto of what was to be his most celebrated poem, *M'Fingal*, which told in satiric style the story of the unfolding Revolution. Following is a sample from the poem:

> When Yankees, skill'd in martial rule,
> First put the British troops to school;
> Instructed them in warlike trade,
> And new maneuvers of parade;
> The true war-dance of Yankee reels,
> And *manual exercise* of heels;
> Made them give up, like saints complete,
> The *arm* of flesh and trust the *feet*,
> And work, like Christians undissembling,
> Salvation out with fear and trembling.

After publishing the final third canto of the poem in 1782, Trumbull lost interest in poetry and devoted his full attention to law. He served as judge of Massachusetts' superior court 1801–19 and judge of the court of errors 1808–19. At the age of seventy-four he moved to Detroit, Michigan, where he died six years later on May 10, 1831.

John Trumbull

- **JOHN TRUMBULL**   1756–1843

An officer in the Revolutionary War whose paintings recorded the major events of the period, John Trumbull was born in Lebanon, Connecticut, on June 6, 1756, the son of Jonathan Trumbull, who was governor of Connecticut during the Revolution. After graduating from Harvard College at seventeen in 1773, he taught school in Lebanon. Having taught himself to draw, he attracted the attention of George Washington, who made him one of his aides-de-camp in July 1775. Preferring to fight than to make military sketches, he accepted a commission as a brigade major in August 1775, seeing action during the siege of Boston. He accompanied Washington's army to New York, and in June 1776 became deputy adjutant general to General Gates with the rank of colonel. During the winter of 1776–77 he served under Benedict Arnold in Rhode Island, and then resigned from the army in February 1777 in a dispute over the date of his commission. In 1778 he returned to military duty as a volunteer aide-de-camp to General John Sullivan during the battle of Rhode Island.

Finally, determined to become a serious painter, he sailed for Europe in 1780 to study art. With the help of Benjamin Franklin he became a student of the artist, Benjamin West, in London. But upon going to England, he was arrested on

The Battle of Bunker Hill —From a painting by John Trumbull

charges of treason and imprisoned for eight months. Remaining in London after the war, Trumbull began his remarkable series of historic paintings under the guidance of West. In 1786 he completed his "Battle of Bunker Hill." Returning to the United States in 1789 he painted scores of portraits from life of the famous men of the time for use later in his historic series. In 1817 Congress commissioned Trumbull to execute the four huge paintings that hang in the Capitol rotunda: Surrender of General Burgoyne at Saratoga, Surrender of Lord Cornwallis at Yorktown, The Declaration of Independence, and Resignation of Washington at Annapolis. During his lifetime he told the story of the Revolutionary War in about three hundred paintings. He died in New York City on November 10, 1843.

• JONATHAN TRUMBULL   1710–1785

Governor of Connecticut throughout the revolutionary period, Jonathan Trumbull was born in Lebanon, Connecticut, on October 12, 1710. After graduation from Harvard College in 1727, he preached for a few years, studied law, and then joined his father's firm as a merchant. He began his political career by election to the Connecticut legislature at the age of twenty-three. In 1766 he was chosen lieutenant-governor and chief justice of the superior court. An ardent patriot, he refused in 1768 to take an oath of loyalty to the crown. The following year the legislature elected him governor, an office he held for fifteen years from 1769 to 1784. During the Revolutionary War he was a bulwark of strength to the American cause. Connecticut provided much of the supplies needed by the Continental Army, and George Washington constantly consulted with Trumbull on important matters. The British began to call all Americans "Brother Jonathan" during the revolutionary period, supposedly because while trying to solve a problem General Washington indicated that it should be referred to Governor Trumbull by remarking: "We must consult Brother Jonathan." Accused by his opponents of trading with the British in secret, Governor Trumbull called for an investi-

Jonathan Trumbull

gation by the legislature, which found that the accusations had been inspired by the British themselves in an effort to discredit him. Retiring from public life after the war, Trumbull died in Lebanon on August 17, 1785.

• **JONATHAN TRUMBULL   1740–1809**

An officer in the Revolutionary War and later a Congressman, U.S. Senator, and governor of Connecticut, Jonathan Trumbull was born in Lebanon, Connecticut, on March 26, 1740, a son of the wartime governor of the same name. After graduation from Harvard College at nineteen, he remained there in graduate school, receiving an M.A. degree in 1762. He won election to the Connecticut legislature and by the beginning of the Revolutionary War, while his father was governor, he became speaker of the house. From 1775 to 1778 he was paymaster of the Continental Army in the Northern theater of operations. From 1778 to 1779 he was comptroller of the treasury for the Continental Congress. When Alexander Hamilton resigned as General Washington's chief aide-de-camp in 1781, Trumbull was chosen by Washington to replace him with the rank of lieutenant colonel. He served in that capacity until Washington retired from the army in 1783. Trumbull was elected as a Federalist to the first and two succeeding U.S. Congresses in 1789–1795, serving as Speaker of the House 1791–93. Elected to the U.S. Senate in 1795, he resigned the following year to become lieutenant governor of Connecticut. When Governor Oliver Wolcott died in 1797, Trumbull succeeded him and won re-election to eleven consecutive terms, holding the office of governor from 1797 until his death in Lebanon on August 7, 1809.

• **JOSEPH TRUMBULL   1737–1778**

A member of the Continental Congress and the first commissary general of the Continental Army, Joseph Trumbull was born in Lebanon, Connecticut, on March 11, 1737, the eldest son of the wartime governor. After graduation from Harvard College in 1756, he joined his father's business as a merchant. He was elected as one of Connecticut's delegates to the Continental Congress in 1774–75. General Washington observed Trumbull's efficiency in meeting the supply needs of Connecticut troops at the siege of Boston, and at his urging Congress appointed Trumbull as commissary general of the Continental Army with the rank of colonel. Coping as well as possible with the difficulties of keeping the new army fed, clothed, and supplied, Trumbull served in the thankless job until the spring of 1777. At that time Congress split the job into two positions and Trumbull resigned rather than accept what he regarded as a demotion. Later that year he was appointed by Congress to the newly created Board of War, but resigned in 1778 because of ill health brought on by overwork during the period that he was commissary general. He died in Lebanon on July 23, 1778.

• THOMAS TUDOR TUCKER   1745–1828

A military surgeon in the Revolutionary War and one of South Carolina's first U.S. Congressmen, Thomas Tudor Tucker was born in Port Royal, Bermuda, on June 25, 1745. After studying medicine at the University of Edinburgh, Scotland, he immigrated to South Carolina where he practiced medicine. He served as a military surgeon in the Revolutionary War. Tucker represented South Carolina in the Continental Congress in 1787–88. Then he was elected as a Federalist to the First and Second U.S. Congresses 1789–93. Tucker was appointed United States Treasurer in 1801 by President Jefferson and served in that office until his death in Washington, D.C., on May 2, 1828.

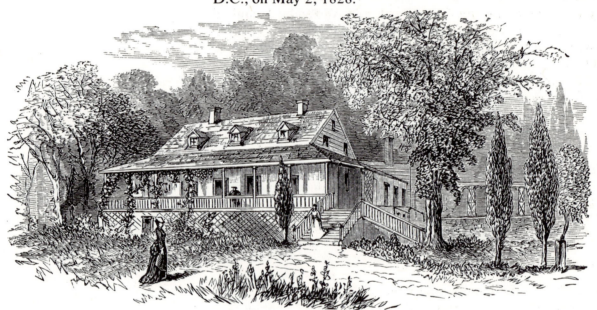

The Van Cortlandt Manor House, Cortlandt Manor, Tarrytown, New York

• PHILIP VAN CORTLANDT   1749–1831

An officer in the Continental Army throughout the Revolutionary War and later a U.S. Congressman from New York, Philip Van Cortlandt was born in New York City on August 21, 1749. After graduation at eighteen from King's College (later Columbia University), he became a civil engineer. He began active duty in the Revolutionary War as a lieutenant colonel of militia in June 1775. In 1776 he served on the headquarters staff of General Washington and then was commissioned colonel in charge of a Continental Army regiment. He led his men in the battles at Saratoga, New York, in 1777 and on Gen. John Sullivan's expedition against the Iroquois Indians in 1779. He was cited for bravery in the battle of York-town in 1781, and was promoted to brigadier general. After serving in the state assembly 1788–90 and the state senate 1791–93, Van Cortlandt was elected as a Democratic-Republican to the third and seven succeeding U.S. Congresses 1793–1809. He died at Van Cortlandt Manor, Croton on Hudson, New York, on November 1, 1831.

• NICHOLAS VAN DYKE   1738–1789

A delegate to the Continental Congress and president of Delaware, Nicholas Van Dyke was born in New Castle County, Delaware, on September 25, 1738. After studying law, he was admitted to the bar in 1765. A member of the Delaware legislature, he was a delegate to the Continental Congress 1777–82, where he signed the Articles of Confederation. Van Dyke then was elected president of Delaware 1783–86. He died at his home in New Castle County on February 19, 1789.

• JEREMIAH VAN RENSSELAER   1738–1810

One of New York's first U.S. Congressmen, Jeremiah Van Rensselaer was born at the manor house, "Rensselaerswyck," near Albany, New York, on August 27, 1738. He graduated from the College of New Jersey in 1758. In the Revolutionary War he was a member of the Albany committee of safety. He was elected to the First U.S. Congress 1789–91, but was an unsuccessful candidate for re-election. He was a member of the first board of directors of the Bank of Albany in 1792 and president of that bank 1798–1806. As a Democratic-Republican, he was elected lieutenant governor of New York 1801–04. He died in Albany on February 19, 1810.

• JAMES MITCHELL VARNUM   1748–1789

A general in the Revolutionary War and a delegate to the Continental Congress, James Mitchell Varnum was born in Dracut, Massachusetts, on December 17, 1748. After graduation from the first class from the College of Rhode Island in 1769, he studied law and commenced practice in East Greenwich, Rhode Island, in 1771. As a militia colonel of the "Kentish Guards," he marched his regiment to take part in the siege of Boston after learning of the battles of Lexington and Concord in 1775. He was commissioned colonel of the 9th Continental Infantry in 1776, and was promoted to brigadier general in the Continental Army in February 1777. Although he served actively for four years, he played no significant part in any battles or campaigns. He resigned from the Continental Army in 1779, and was appointed major general of Rhode Island militia a few months later. Varnum represented Rhode Island in the Continental Congress 1780–82 and 1786–87. He was appointed in 1787 as one of the federal judges for the Northwest Territory, and moved to Marietta, Ohio, where he died on January 10, 1789.

• JOHN VINING   1758–1802

A delegate to the Continental Congress and one of Delaware's first U.S. Congressmen, John Vining was born in Dover, Delaware, on December 23, 1758. After studying law, he commenced practice in New Castle County in 1782. At twenty-five he was chosen to represent Delaware in the Continental Congress 1784–86. He then was elected to the First and Second U.S. Congresses 1789–1793, and to the U.S. Senate 1793–98. Vining died in Dover in February 1802.

• JAMES WADSWORTH   1730–1817

A militia general in the Revolutionary War and delegate to the Continental Congress, James Wadsworth was born in Durham, Connecticut, on July 8, 1730. After graduation from Yale College at seventeen, in 1748, he studied law and began to practice. He became a member of the committee of safety at the beginning of the Revolutionary War. He was appointed brigadier general of Connecticut militia in 1776, and promoted to major general in 1777 when he was assigned to defend Connecticut's coastal towns. After the war he represented Delaware in the Continental Congress 1783–86. He violently opposed ratification of the United States Constitution. Underscoring his opposition, he refused to take the oath of allegiance to the United States required of public officials, and as a consequence withdrew from public life. He died in Durham on September 22, 1817.

• JEREMIAH WADSWORTH   1743–1804

Commissary general of the Continental Army, delegate to the Continental Congress, and one of Connecticut's first U.S. Congressmen, Jeremiah Wadsworth was born in Hartford, Connecticut, on July 12, 1743. He went to sea as a sailor at seventeen, and worked his way up to first mate and subsequently master. From the beginning of the Revolutionary War he served as deputy and commissary general of the Continental Army in 1775–79, during which time he was permitted to make a profit on the supplies he purchased for the troops. After resigning in 1779, he served as commissary for the French army in America to the end of the Revolutionary War. He represented Connecticut in the Continental Congress 1787–88, and then was elected as a Federalist to the U.S. Congress in 1789–95. After serving in the state executive council 1795–1801, he retired. He died in Hartford on April 30, 1804.

• JOHN WALKER   1744–1809

An aide to General Washington in the Revolutionary War and a delegate to the Continental Congress, John Walker was born at "Castle Hill," near Cobham, Virginia, on February 13, 1744. After graduation from William and Mary College in 1764, he became a planter in Albemarle County, Virginia. He served as an aide with the rank of colonel to General Washington in the early years of the Revolutionary War. In 1777 Washington commended him to Gov. Patrick Henry of Virginia for confidential service. In 1780 he was chosen to represent Virginia in the Continental Congress, and in 1790 he served eight months as a U.S. Senator to fill a vacancy. He died near Madison Mills, Virginia, on December 2, 1809. His father, Thomas Walker (1715–1794), is believed to have been the first colonist to explore Kentucky in 1750. He served as commissary general under George Washington in the French and Indian War. The Walker Mountains in southwestern Virginia were named for him.

George Walton

• GEORGE WALTON   1741–1804

A signer of the Declaration of Independence and one of the leading political figures of Georgia, George Walton was born near Farmville, Virginia, in 1741. Apprenticed to a carpenter while he was a boy, young Walton educated himself by reading at night. He persuaded a lawyer to help him study law, and at the age of thirty-three Walton was admitted to the bar in Savannah, Georgia, in 1774. He became a member of Georgia's first committee of correspondence and was secretary of Georgia's revolutionary congress in 1775. He represented Georgia in the Continental Congress in 1776–77, during which time he voted for and signed the Declaration of Independence, and served in Congress in 1780–81. Commissioned as a colonel in the militia in 1778, he took part in the battle of Savannah in December, in which he was badly wounded and captured. After being held prisoner for nine months he was released in September 1779. A month later he was elected governor of Georgia, serving in that office two months before resuming his seat in Congress. From 1783 to 1789 he was chief justice of Georgia, resigning from that position to accept election as governor again in 1789–90. In 1790 he became a judge of the state supreme court, a post he held until his death on February 2, 1804, at his home "Meadow Garden" in Augusta, Georgia.

• JOHN WALTON   1738–1783

A delegate to the Continental Congress, John Walton was born in Virginia in 1738, an older brother of George Walton. Before the Revolutionary War he became a successful planter near Augusta, Georgia. He was a delegate to the Revolutionary congress at Savannah, Georgia, in 1775. He represented Georgia in the Continental Congress in 1778, where he signed the Articles of Confederation. He died at New Savannah, Georgia, in 1783.

• ARTEMAS WARD   1727–1800

A major general of the Continental Army second in command only to George Washington at the beginning of the Revolutionary War, Artemas Ward was born in Shrewsbury, Massachusetts, on November 27, 1727. After graduation from Harvard College in 1748, he became active in politics, winning election to the colonial legislature. During the French and Indian War he served as a militia lieutenant colonel, taking part in the attack on Fort Ticonderoga in 1758. As the patriots of Massachusetts prepared for war, Ward was appointed brigadier general of militia in October 1774. When word of the battles of Lexington and Concord reached him in April 1775, Ward was at home sick in bed, but he leaped up and hurried to the scene to take command of the initial phase of the siege of Boston. The battle of Bunker Hill took place while the army was under his command, but he did not take part in the fighting, remaining at his headquarters behind the battle lines. When Congress appointed Washington as commander-in-chief of the Continental Army and made Ward his second in com-

General Artemas Ward

mand, the Massachusetts general was resentful, and during the siege of Boston they worked together with mutual mistrust. After the British left Boston in the spring of 1776, Ward resigned from the army. He was president of the Massachusetts executive council in 1777–79, and then was elected to the state legislature in 1779–85. He represented Massachusetts in the Continental Congress in 1780–82, and was elected as a Federalist to the Second and Third U.S. Congresses in 1791–95. He died at his home in Shrewsbury on October 28, 1800.

- **SAMUEL WARD   1725–1776**

A former royal colonial governor who was a delegate to the Continental Congress, Samuel Ward was born in Newport, Rhode Island, May 27, 1725. A farmer who lived near Westerly, Rhode Island, he first was elected to the Rhode Island general assembly in 1756. That same year he was one of the founders of Rhode Island College (now Brown University). He was appointed chief justice of Rhode Island 1761–62, and then became governor under the royal charter in 1762–1763 and 1765–1767. An active patriot and a friend and correspondent of Washington and Franklin, he was a delegate to the Continental Congress 1774–76, but died of smallpox in Philadelphia on March 26, 1776, before the Declaration of Independence was written.

- **SETH WARNER   1743–1784**

A leader of Vermont's Green Mountain Boys in the Revolutionary War, Seth Warner was born in Woodbury (now Roxbury), Connecticut, on May 17, 1743. He and his family moved to Bennington, Vermont, in 1765. There he became noted for his marksmanship as a hunter. He and Ethan Allen became leaders of the Green Mountain Boys, who used strong-arm tactics to keep settlers from New York out of the area. In 1774 the state of New York declared Warner an outlaw and offered a reward for his arrest. Upon the outbreak of the Revolutionary War, he and Allen hurried north with their men and on May 10, 1775, captured strategic Fort Ticonderoga in the first American victory of the war. When the Green Mountain Boys were incorporated into the Continental Army, Warner was named lieutenant colonel. He and his men then took part in the invasion of Canada. On the retreat from Canada in 1776, Warner commanded the rear guard in several actions. At the battle of Bennington in August 1777, Warner and his woodsmen arrived at a critical moment after a hurried march of twenty miles and helped win the victory. In 1778 he was promoted to brigadier general of militia, but took no further part in any fighting because of sickness. He died in Roxbury on December 26, 1784.

• JOSEPH WARREN 1741–1775

A hero of the Battle of Bunker Hill who died during the fighting, Joseph Warren was born in Roxbury, Massachusetts, on June 11, 1741. After graduation from Harvard College at eighteen in 1759, he studied medicine and became one of the leading physicians of Boston. With James Otis, Sam Adams, and John Hancock, Warren was one of the leading figures in organizing the patriotic movement in Massachusetts. He was a member of the committee of correspondence from its inception, and delivered annual orations on the anniversary of the Boston Massacre. In 1775 he headed the rebel government of Massachusetts as president of the provincial revolutionary congress and as head of the committee of safety. As such, he gathered the intelligence about British movements and sent Paul Revere and William Dawes speeding on their way to spread the alarm to Lexington and Concord. He then picked up his musket and took part in the fighting that drove the British back to Boston on April 19, 1775. He was elected major general in command of the Massachusetts militia on June 14,

Dr. Joseph Warren

Birthplace of Joseph Warren

1775, but he declined to take command of the battle of Bunker Hill, which already had been planned with Israel Putnam and William Prescott in charge. Instead, he took his place as a private volunteer in the redoubt under command of Prescott. When on their third charge the British overran the redoubt at the height of the battle on June 17, Warren was one of the thirty Americans who were killed. When the British discovered Warren's body, British General William Howe exclaimed that Warren's death was worth that of five hundred American privates. Abigail Adams wrote to her husband John, who was in Philadelphia attending the Continental Congress: "Not all the havoc and devastation they have made has wounded me like the death of Warren. We want him in the Senate; we want him in his profession; we want him in the field. We mourn for the citizen, the senator, the physician, and the warrior."

• MERCY OTIS WARREN   1728−1814

A woman who influenced more Americans with her pen than the British did with their swords, Mercy Otis was born in Barnstable, Massachusetts, on September 25, 1728, the sister of James Otis, the first major pre-Revolutionary movement leader. She was as brilliant and as dedicated to the American cause as her brother, but, because she was a woman at a time when women were not supposed to meddle in politics, her influence was more limited than if she had been a man. Her early years were like those of many other girls of well-to-do families, spent at home reading, drawing, and doing needlework. At the age of twenty-six in 1754 she married James Warren, a young merchant of Plymouth, Massachusetts (who was not a relation of Joseph Warren, the patriot leader killed at Bunker Hill, but who, by a strange coincidence of names,

Mercy Warren

succeeded Joseph Warren as president of the Massachusetts revolutionary congress upon the latter's death).

As her brother became the leader of the opposition to the writs of assistance in 1760, she became his counselor and confidante, and that of his friends, such as Samuel Adams and John Hancock. It was at a meeting with her in 1765 that her brother became convinced that he should introduce resolutions in the Massachusetts legislature that led to the convening of the Stamp Act Congress in New York—the first rallying of the colonies to oppose British oppression. And at another meeting at her house with Sam Adams that same year, the idea of the committees of correspondence among the colonies was born.

During this period she began to write patriotic poetry, largely for her own amusement and that of her friends. Her "Massachusetts Song of Liberty," sold at the Boston bookstore run by Henry Knox who later was the general in charge of Washington's artillery, became the most popular patriotic song of the times, spreading the idea of liberty with the printed word while Tom Paine was still grubbing as a tax collector in England. Here are the first few verses of that song published in 1770:

Come swallow your bumpers ye Tories, *and roar,*
That the Sons of fair Freedom are hamper'd once more;
But know that no Cut-throats *our spirits can tame,*
Nor a host of Oppressors *shall smother the flame.*

In Freedom we're born, and, like Sons of the brave,
Will never surrender,
But swear to defend her,
And scorn to survive, if unable to save.

Our grandsires, bless'd heroes, we'll give them a tear,
Nor sully their honors by stooping to fear;
Through deaths and through dangers their Trophies
they won,
We dare be their Rivals, *nor will be outdone.*

In Freedom we're born, &c.

Let tyrants and minions presume to despise,
Encroach on our RIGHTS, and make FREEDOM
their prize;
The fruits of their rapine they never shall keep,
Though vengeance may nod, yet how short is her sleep.

In Freedom we're born, &c.

. . . Then join hand in hand, brave AMERICANS all,
To be free is to live, to be slaves is to fall;
Has the land such a dastard as scorns not a LORD,
Who dreads not a fetter much more than a sword!

In Freedom we're born, &c."

She began to write political satires in the form of plays, such as "The Adulateur" in 1773 and "The Group" in 1775. In the latter she described the royal governor of Massachusetts Thomas Hutchinson in these words:

> But mark the traitor—his high crime glossed o'er
> Conceals the tender feelings of the man,
> The social ties that bind the human heart;
> He strikes a bargain with his country's foes,
> And joins to wrap America in flames.
> Yet with feigned pity, and satanic grin,
> As if more deep to fix the keen insult,
> Or make his life a farce still more complete,
> He sends a groan across the broad Atlantic,
> And with a phiz of crocodilian stamp,
> Can weep, and wreathe, still hoping to deceive;
> He cries—the gathering clouds hang thick about her,
> But laughs within; then sobs—
> Alas, my country!

George Washington, John Adams, Alexander Hamilton, and other great men of the day were guests at her home, and she maintained a steady flow of correspondence with them and their wives. Hamilton wrote to her in 1791 concerning one of her newly published poems: "It is certain that in the *Ladies of Castile*, the sex will find a new occasion of triumph. Not being a poet myself, I am in the less danger of feeling mortification at the idea that in the career of dramatic composition at least, female genius in the United States has outstripped the male."

After the war her complete poetic works were published in 1790, with a dedication to George Washington. In 1805 she completed and published a three-volume *History of the Revolutionary War*. Living to the age of eighty-six, she lost her sight in her latter years, but continued her voluminous correspondence by dictating to a secretary. She died in Plymouth on October 19, 1814.

• GEORGE WASHINGTON   1732–1799

The "Father of Our Country" who won independence and established a constitutional democracy, George Washington was born on February 22, 1732, on Pope's Creek Farm in Westmoreland County, Virginia. His father, a well-to-do planter, died when George was eleven, and four years later the boy dropped out of school to become a frontier surveyor. When he was nineteen he accompanied his older half-brother Lawrence Washington on a trip to the Barbados Islands in the West Indies, the only trip he ever made outside the United States. In the West Indies he became ill with smallpox and his fortunate recovery made him immune to this dread disease for the rest of his life.

Washington's tea caddy
—Sketch by Kay Smith

Washington's portable camp chest
—Sketch by Kay Smith

At the age of twenty Washington began his military career, receiving a commission as major in the militia. The following year, in November 1753, he set out on a dangerous mission for Virginia's royal governor, Robert Dinwiddie. The governor had heard that the French had established a fort near present-day Erie, Pennsylvania, and he asked Washington to carry a message to them, telling them to leave because the territory belonged to the British crown. Washington's round trip on foot and on horseback through the winter snows in the wilderness took two months. He brought back word from the French that they had no intention of obeying Dinwiddie's order to get out of the Ohio River Valley.

In 1754 the Virginia governor promoted the twenty-two-year-old Washington to lieutenant colonel and sent him back to the Ohio Valley with a company of two hundred militia to protect from the French a fort that was being built at the site of present-day Pittsburgh. En route Washington learned that the French already had taken the fort, and in May he and his men ran into a French scouting party, firing the first shots of what was to be the long French and Indian War of 1754–63. Washington won the first skirmish, killing ten Frenchmen and capturing twenty-one. A few weeks later, on July 4, 1754, Washington suffered his first defeat, when he was forced to surrender a hastily-built stockade fort, called Fort Necessity, to a superior French force.

In 1775 Washington served as a volunteer aide with the rank of colonel to British General Edward Braddock in an ill-fated expedition to try to wrest Fort Duquesne from the French, at the site of present-day Pittsburgh. Braddock and many of his men were killed when the French and Indians attacked from ambush. Washington escaped, and never forgot what he had witnessed—that a well-equipped British army could be beaten by a surprise attack.

At twenty-three Washington was placed in command of all Virginia militia with the rank of colonel. In 1755–58 he secured the Virginia frontier from French and Indian attacks, and served in an expedition led by British General John Forbes that captured Fort Duquesne and renamed it Fort Pitt.

With the end of fighting in Virginia, Washington retired from military service and in January 1759 married Martha Dandridge Custis, a young widow with two children that Washington adopted as his own. Washington also began his political career that year, taking his seat in the Virginia house of burgesses to which he had been elected while serving on the frontier—a seat he was to occupy for the next fifteen years until he was called to military duty again by the Revolutionary War.

Active in the pre-Revolutionary movement in Virginia, Washington was a member of Virginia's delegation to the First and Second Continental Congresses in 1774–75. After the battles of Lexington and Concord, Congress established a Continental Army and on June 15, 1775, chose Washington as

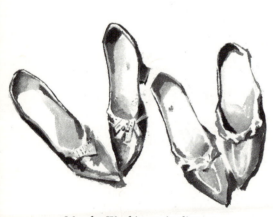

Martha Washington's slippers
—Sketch by Kay Smith

General George Washington

405

Washington taking command of the American Army at Cambridge, Massachusetts. —From a painting by F. T. Merrill

its commander-in-chief. Washington accepted, but on condition that he receive no pay, only his expenses.

During the eight years that the Revolutionary War lasted, it was largely Washington's unbending determination to surmount every obstacle that brought victory and independence for the United States. He lost most battles, but he won the war. After the peace treaty had been signed ending the war in 1783, Washington resigned his commission on December 23 and retired to private life at his estate "Mount Vernon" on the bank of the Potomac River in Virginia. He hoped that his days of public service were through.

However, in the years that followed it became increasingly clear to Washington that the national government needed strengthening. Shays' Rebellion in Massachusetts was symptomatic of the troubles facing the nation because of the imperfect Articles of Confederation that bound the states together too loosely. At the urging of his friends, the fifty-five-year-old Washington came out of retirement in 1787 to accept election by Virginia's legislature to head the state's delegation to the Constitutional Convention in Philadelphia. On the day the convention opened, May 25, 1787, Washington was unanimously elected as presiding officer. In the four months of debate that followed, it again was largely Washington's determination that a new, stronger government must be formed that held the disputing delegates together and resulted in the drafting of the new United States Constitution.

Washington's state coach

After the states had ratified the Constitution, Washington again bowed to public opinion and accepted his unanimous election as the first President of the United States. During the eight years of his administration from 1789 to 1797, Washington surrounded himself with outstanding men to aid him in the formation of the new government, including: John Adams as Vice President, Thomas Jefferson as Secretary of State, Alexander Hamilton as Secretary of the Treasury, Henry Knox as Secretary of War, Edmund Randolph as Attorney General, and John Jay as Chief Justice. As these men left the government in the years that followed, he replaced them with other leaders. He exercised the great powers of the Presidency with discretion, endeavoring to cause all parts of the government to act with initiative and responsibility. In his *Farewell Address* to the American people published on September 17, 1796, he cautioned against foreign alliances and warned against the "ill founded jealousies and false alarms" of political parties.

Washington's retirement again was interrupted when President John Adams prevailed upon him to accept appointment on July 3, 1798, as lieutenant general and commander of the new United States Army being formed because of a war threat with France. He was still serving in that capacity at his death at the age of sixty-seven on December 14, 1799, in Mount Vernon.

• WILLIAM WASHINGTON   1752–1810

A daring cavalry officer in the Continental Army, William Washington was born in Stafford County, Virginia, on February 28, 1752, a second cousin of George Washington. Joining the 3rd Virginia Continental Regiment in February 1776 as a captain, he first fought in the battle of Long Island, New York, in August, where he was badly wounded. Having recovered, he took part in the battle of Trenton, New Jersey, in December, where he was wounded in the hand while leading the attack against the enemy's artillery. Although not re-

Colonel William Washington

407

covered from his wounds, he again fought in the battle of Princeton, New Jersey, in January 1777. In 1777 he was promoted to major in the cavalry, and the following year was advanced to lieutenant colonel. Washington led his cavalry to the South in 1779–81, where he took part in many skirmishes and battles with the hated British cavalry leader, Banastre "Bloody" Tarleton. At the battle of Cowpens in January 1781 Washington distinguished himself in aiding in the American victory, and in the final stages of the battle wounded Tarleton in a sabre duel before the British officer escaped. Congress voted him a silver medal for his valor at Cowpens. Eight months later Washington was wounded and captured at the battle of Eutaw Springs. Held prisoner in Charleston, South Carolina, he fell in love with one of the local girls, married her, and settled there after the war. He was elected to the state legislature, but declined to run for governor, saying that he had no talent for making speeches. He died in Charleston on March 6, 1810.

The ancient Powder Magazine dating back to about 1713, in Charleston, South Carolina, is one of the oldest structures in the colonial states, with walls more than thirty inches thick made of brick and oyster shell mortar—now serving as a museum, shown here with St. Philip's Church in the background.
—Sketch by Kay Smith

General Anthony Wayne

• ANTHONY "MAD ANTHONY" WAYNE 1745—1796

One of the most daring and successful generals of the Revolutionary War, Anthony Wayne was born in East Town, Pennsylvania, on January 1, 1745. Before the Revolutionary War, he followed his father's trade in becoming a well-to-do tanner. He was elected to the Pennsylvania house of representatives in 1774–75. In January 1776 he was commissioned as a colonel in the Continental Army in command of the 4th Pennsylvania Battalion. He led his men in their first battle at Three Rivers, Canada, in June 1776. He carried out a successful attack against a superior force, but the remainder of American troops were forced to retreat and Wayne had to give up the ground he had won. He then commanded Fort Ticonderoga, where he put down a mutiny.

Promoted to brigadier general in February 1777, Wayne commanded Pennsylvania troops in the battles of Brandywine, Paoli, and Germantown. At the battle of Monmouth in 1778 he helped prevent a total rout by holding the center of the defensive line. At Stony Point, New York, he planned and carried out a victorious raid in July 1779, which won him a gold medal and the thanks of Congress. At the end of the war in 1783, Wayne was brevetted major general. He was elected to the Pennsylvania assembly in 1784. Then he moved to Georgia and settled on a tract of 800 acres granted him by that state for his military service. He was elected to the Second U.S. Congress by Georgia, but he was refused the seat when the election was disputed on grounds he had not met residence requirements.

In March 1792 President Washington commissioned him as major general in command of the American army. In 1794 Wayne led his 2,600 troops in an attack on the frontier Indians in the Northwest Territory, achieving a major victory at the battle of Fallen Timbers in August 1794. He then concluded a treaty on August 3, 1795, with the hostile Indians northwest of the Ohio River. Wayne died in Presque Isle (now Erie), Pennsylvania, on December 15, 1796.

—Sketch by Kay Smith

• GEORGE WEEDON   c.1730–1793

A tavern-keeper who became a brigadier general in the Continental Army, George Weedon was born in Fredericksburg, Virginia, about 1730. Active in the pre-Revolutionary movement, he was a great admirer of George Washington, who was a patron of the tavern he ran. As colonel in command of the 3rd Virginia Continental Regiment, he took part in the battles in New York and New Jersey in 1776. In February 1777 he was appointed brigadier general and for a time he served as Washington's deputy adjutant general. He fought as part of General Nathanael Greene's division in the battles of Brandywine and Germantown in the fall of 1777. Angry because he was not promoted to major general in 1778, he left the army to return home. But when the British invaded Virginia in 1780–81, Weedon, who was known to his men as "Joe Gourd," left his tavern to help organize the militia for resistance. He commanded militia troops near Gloucester during the siege of Yorktown. He died in Fredericksburg in November 1793.

• JOHN WENTWORTH, JR.   1745–1787

A New Hampshire delegate to the Continental Congress, John Wentworth, Jr. was born at Salmon Falls, New Hampshire, on July 17, 1745. After graduation from Harvard College in 1768, he studied law and commenced practice in Dover, New Hampshire, in 1771. A member of the New Hampshire house of representatives 1776–80, he was chosen as a delegate to the Continental Congress in 1778–79, where he signed the Articles of Confederation. He then was a member of the state council 1780–84, and of the state senate 1784–86. He died in Dover on January 10, 1787.

• SAMUEL WHARTON   1732–1800

A delegate to the Continental Congress from Delaware, Samuel Wharton was born in Philadelphia on May 3, 1732. During Pontiac's War in 1763, the Indians had destroyed a large amount of goods owned by Wharton's Indiana Company. In 1768 Wharton and his partners got the Indians to agree to give the company 1.8 million acres along the Ohio River in what is now West Virginia as indemnification for the destroyed property. Wharton was in England trying to get permission to develop this land when the Revolutionary War began. He returned to America in 1780, and two years later was chosen to represent Delaware in the Continental Congress 1782–83. He died at his country home near Philadelphia in March 1800.

• ABRAHAM WHIPPLE   1733–1819

The third ranking captain of the Continental Navy, Abraham Whipple was born in Providence, Rhode Island, on September 16, 1733. Going to sea as a boy, he soon rose to command ships in the West Indies trade. During the French and Indian War, he captained the privateer *Game Cock*, capturing twenty-six French ships in a single cruise in 1759–60. In one of the most celebrated pre-Revolutionary incidents in June 1772, Whipple led a band of armed men in attacking and burning the British revenue schooner *Gaspée* in Narragansett Bay, as a protest against the vessel being stationed there to catch smugglers avoiding British taxes. At the beginning of the Revolutionary War Whipple was commissioned in June 1775 as commander of the Rhode Island Navy, which consisted of two armed vessels. Whipple immediately used the ships to drive the British frigate *Rose* out of Narragansett Bay and captured the *Rose*'s tender. When the Continental Navy was formed in October, Whipple was appointed as the third ranking captain under commodore Esek Hopkins, who was Whipple's brother-in-law. In July 1779 Whipple captured eight British merchantmen from a convoy surprised off Newfoundland and brought them into Boston harbor for perhaps the richest single haul of the war. While in command of the naval defense of Charleston, South Carolina, in 1780, he scuttled his ships rather than surrender them when the British captured the city. Whipple was paroled but not exchanged, so took no further part in the war. When the Ohio Company was formed after the war, he moved to Marietta, Ohio, about 1786. He died there on May 29, 1819.

Captain Abraham Whipple

• WILLIAM WHIPPLE   1730–1785

A signer of the Declaration of Independence and a fighting militia general in the Revolutionary War, William Whipple was born in Kittery, Massachusetts (now Maine), on January 14,

William Whipple

1730. He went to sea as a boy and was a ship's captain by the age of twenty. He sailed in the slave trade and saved enough money to retire from the sea by the age of twenty-nine. He settled in Portsmouth, New Hampshire, in 1760. He was sent as one of New Hampshire's delegates to the Continental Congress in 1776–79, where he signed the Declaration of Independence; but he was absent much of the time on military duty, having been commissioned a brigadier general of militia in 1777. Whipple led New Hampshire troops in the battles of Saratoga in 1777, and took part in the unsuccessful effort to recapture Rhode Island in 1778. He was elected to the state assembly 1780–84. For the last three years of his life he served as an associate justice of the state supreme court. He died in Portsmouth on November 28, 1785.

• **ALEXANDER WHITE**   **1738–1804**

One of Virginia's first U.S. Congressmen, Alexander White was born in Frederick County, Virginia, in 1738. After studying law at the Inner Temple in London, England, he returned to Virginia and began the practice of law. He was elected to the Virginia house of delegates in 1782–86 and 1788. He then won election as a Federalist to the First and Second U.S. Congresses 1789–1793. White was appointed by President Washington in 1795, as one of three commissioners to lay out the city of Washington, D.C., and supervise the construction of public buildings, serving until 1802 when the board was abolished. He died on his estate, "Woodville," in Frederick County on September 19, 1804.

• JAMES WHITE   1749–1809

A delegate to the Continental Congress, James White was born in Philadelphia on June 16, 1749. After attending a Jesuit College in St. Omer, France, White studied medicine at the University of Pennsylvania, and then studied law. He settled in Davidson County, North Carolina, and was elected to the state general assembly in 1785. He then was chosen as a delegate to the Continental Congress 1786–88. When Davidson County became part of the new Territory South of the River Ohio (later Tennessee) in 1790, White was elected to the first Territorial legislature. He then was elected as the territorial delegate to the U.S. Congress in 1794–96. White moved west again in 1799, this time to Louisiana. There he was appointed judge of Attakapas district and of St. Martin Parish. He died in Attakapas, Louisiana, in October 1809.

• PHILLIPS WHITE   1729–1811

A delegate to the Continental Congress from New Hampshire, Phillips White was born in Haverhill, Massachusetts, on October 28, 1729. After attending Harvard College, he served in the French and Indian War as an officer in the colonial army at the battle of Lake George in 1755. He later settled in New Hampshire. White was elected to the New Hampshire house of representatives 1775–82, serving as speaker in 1775 and 1782. He represented New Hampshire in the Continental Congress in 1782–83. White died at his farm near South Hampton, New Hampshire, on June 24, 1811.

• LAMBERT WICKES   c.1735–1777

A Continental Navy captain who went down with his ship, Lambert Wickes was born about 1735 in Maryland. Little is known of his early life other than that he became a merchant ship captain. He was commissioned a captain in the Continental Navy in 1776 and was given command of the 46-gun *Reprisal*. In a cruise to the West Indies in the summer of 1776 he captured several prizes, fought off the British warship *Shark*, and returned to Philadelphia with a valuable cargo of guns and gunpowder. He next took Benjamin Franklin to France in the *Reprisal*, arriving in November 1776. The next summer Wickes in the *Reprisal* with two other ships, the *Lexington* and *Dolphin*, sailed completely around Ireland, capturing and destroying fourteen ships in five days, in a bold display of American disdain for the British Navy. On his voyage home in the fall of 1777, the British ship *Alert* captured the *Lexington*, and the *Reprisal* was driven aground on rocks off Newfoundland with the loss of Wickes and his crew.

• JOHN WILLIAMS   1731–1799

A delegate to the Continental Congress, John Williams was born in Hanover County, Virginia, on March 14, 1731. He moved to North Carolina in 1745 with his parents, who donated the land and laid out the town of Williamsboro, North Carolina. After studying law, he commenced practice in Williamsboro. Before the Revolutionary War Williams served as deputy attorney general of the colony. In 1775 he was elected a delegate to the provincial Revolutionary congress. He then won election to the state house of commons in 1777–78, where he served as speaker. He represented North Carolina in the Continental Congress in 1778–79. Williams was appointed a judge of the supreme court of North Carolina in 1779, and served on the court for twenty years until his death at "Montpelier," near Williamsboro on October 10, 1799.

• WILLIAM WILLIAMS   1731–1811

A signer of the Declaration of Independence and a devoted public servant who was elected to office for more than fifty years, William Williams was born in Lebanon, Connecticut, on April 28, 1731. After graduation from Harvard College in 1751, he studied theology for a year, and then became a businessman. At twenty-two he was elected town clerk of Lebanon, an office he held for the next forty-three years. In 1755 he fought at the battle of Lake George in the French and Indian War. At the age of twenty-six in 1757, he was elected to the Connecticut legislature, where he continued to serve for the next forty-seven years, first in the house and then in the council. He represented Connecticut in the Continental Congress in 1776–78 and 1783–84, signed the Declaration of Independence and helped draft the Articles of Confederation. In addition to these positions, Williams also served most of the last forty years of his life as probate judge and county judge for Windham County, Connecticut. At the age of eighty he died in Lebanon, Connecticut, on August 2, 1811.

William Williams

• HUGH WILLIAMSON   1735–1819

A military surgeon in the Revolutionary War, a signer of the United States Constitution, and one of North Carolina's first U.S. Congressmen, Hugh Williamson was born on Oterara Creek in West Nottingham Township, Pennsylvania, on December 5, 1735. After graduation from the College of Philadelphia in 1757, he studied theology and was licensed as a Presbyterian minister in 1759. The next year he returned to the College of Philadelphia, where he obtained an M.A. degree, and then taught mathematics until 1763. He then went to study medicine in Edinburgh, Scotland, and in Utrecht, Holland, where he received an M.D. Degree in 1768. He returned to Philadelphia and practiced medicine there until 1773 when he decided to make another trip abroad. He was in Boston awaiting his ship at the time of the "Boston Tea Party," and when he got to England he was closely examined by the privy council about the incident. While returning to America in 1777 his ship was captured by a British warship, but he and another passenger escaped in a row boat. Because Philadelphia was in the hands of the British, Williamson went to Edenton, North Carolina, where he established a medical practice. During the Revolutionary War, he was surgeon general of North Carolina troops 1779–82. Williamson was elected to the state house of commons in 1782 and then represented North Carolina in the Continental Congress 1782–85 and 1787–1788. He was chosen as a delegate to the federal Constitutional Convention where he helped draft and signed the new United States Constitution, suggesting among other things the six-year term for U.S. Senators. Williamson was elected as a Federalist to the First and Second U.S. Congresses 1789–93. He remained in New York City after retiring from Congress, devoting the rest of his life to science, medicine, and writing. He died in New York City on May 22, 1819.

• THOMAS WILLING   1731–1821

A Pennsylvania delegate to the Continental Congress who opposed the Declaration of Independence, Thomas Willing was born in Philadelphia on December 19, 1731. After studying law at the Inner Temple in London, England, he returned to Philadelphia and became a business partner of Robert Morris, who was to become "the financier of the Revolution." Willing was elected mayor of Philadelphia in 1763, and then became associate justice of the supreme court of Pennsylvania 1767–77. He was a member of the committee of correspondence in 1774 and of the committee of safety in 1775. A member of Pennsylvania's delegation to the Continental Congress in 1775–76, he voted against the Declaration of Independence, hoping that some accommodation might be reached with England. After that he was suspected of Loyalist sympathies and held no more elective offices. After the war, when the Bank of the United States was created in 1791, President Washington appointed Willing as its first president, a position he held for the next twenty years, until 1811. Willing died at the age of eighty-nine in Philadelphia on January 19, 1821.

• JAMES WILSON   1742–1798

A signer of both the Declaration of Independence and the United States Constitution, James Wilson was born in Carskerdo, near St. Andrews, Scotland, on September 14, 1742. After attending the Universities of St. Andrews, Glasgow, and

James Wilson

Edinburgh, he immigrated to America. He settled in Philadelphia in 1766, obtaining a job teaching Latin at the College of Philadelphia (now the University of Pennsylvania). He then studied law in the offices of John Dickinson, "The Penman of the Revolution," and was admitted to the bar in 1767. He developed a law practice in Carlisle, Pennsylvania, and began to take an active part in the pre-Revolutionary movement. He represented Pennsylvania in the Continental Congress in 1775–76, 1782–83, and 1785–87. In the Congress he voted for and signed the Declaration of Independence, and served on the board of war as well as on many other important committees. At the same time Wilson developed his legal practice and became known as one of the best lawyers in the nation.

As a delegate to the federal Constitutional Convention of 1787, Wilson worked hard to ensure that the basic power of the government would rest with the people. "Can we forget for whom we are forming a government?" he asked. "Is it for *men*, or for the imaginary beings called *States?*" President Washington appointed Wilson as one of the first associate justices of the Supreme Court of the United States in 1789, a position Wilson held for the rest of his life. Wilson also became the first professor of law in the College of Philadelphia in 1790 and in the University of Pennsylvania when they were united in 1791. He died in Edenton, North Carolina, on August 28, 1798.

- **PAINE WINGATE** **1739–1838**

A Congregational clergyman, delegate to the Continental Congress, U.S. Senator, and U.S. Congressman, Paine Wingate was born in Amesbury, Massachusetts, on May 14, 1739. After graduation from Harvard College in 1759, he studied theology and was ordained a minister of the Congregational Church at Hampton Falls, New Hampshire, in 1763. He held the pastorate in that town thirteen years until 1776. He then moved to Stratham, New Hampshire, where he took up farming. He was elected to the state house of representatives in 1783, and then represented New Hampshire in the Continental Congress in 1787–88. As a Federalist he won election to the first U.S. Senate, serving 1789–93. He next was elected to the Third U.S. Congress 1793–95. His final public service was eleven years as judge of the supreme court of New Hampshire 1798–1809. Retiring from the bench at the age of seventy, he lived twenty-eight more years, dying at the age of ninety-eight in Stratham on March 7, 1838.

- **HENRY WISNER** **1720–1790**

A New York delegate to the Continental Congress who voted for but missed signing the Declaration of Independence, Henry Wisner was born near Florida, New York, in 1720. A landowner and miller who lived near Goshen, New York, Wisner was elected to the New York colonial assembly 1759–69. He was a delegate to the New York provincial Revolutionary congresses in 1775–77, and to the Continental Congress 1774–76. He voted for the Declaration of Independence, but was absent at the time the engrossed copy was signed in August, attending the provincial Revolutionary congress in New York. Wisner built three gunpowder mills in the vicinity of Goshen, and supplied powder to the Continental Army during the Revolution. He was a member of the committee that framed the first constitution of New York in 1777, and of the commission for fortifying the Hudson River, which constructed forts at West Point and placed the chain across the river in 1777–78. Wisner was elected to the state senate 1777–82, established an academy at Goshen in 1784, was a member of the first board of regents of the University of the State of New York 1784–87, and served as a member of the state convention that ratified the United States Constitution in 1788. He died in Goshen on March 4, 1790.

- **JOHN WITHERSPOON** **1723–1794**

The only clergyman and college president to sign the Declaration of Independence, John Witherspoon was born in Gifford, Haddingtonshire, Scotland, on February 5, 1723. After graduation from Edinburgh University in 1739, he studied theology

John Witherspoon

and was licensed as a Presbyterian minister in 1743. By the 1760s he was widely known for his sermons and writing dealing with controversial religious subjects. Richard Stockton and Benjamin Rush, both of whom later also signed the Declaration of Independence, persuaded Witherspoon to come to America. He and his family arrived in 1768, and he was installed as president of the College of New Jersey (now Princeton University). Among his new students at the school were many men who played important roles in the later founding of the United States, including James Madison. the "Father of the Constitution."

Witherspoon was active in the pre-Revolutionary movement. He was elected to the New Jersey provincial Revolutionary congress in 1776 and represented New Jersey in the Continental Congress 1776–82. In Congress, when a reluctant delegate remarked the time was "not ripe" for a declaration of independence, Witherspoon is said to have replied: "In my judgement, sir, we are not only ripe, but rotting." He voted for and signed the Declaration of Independence, was a member of the secret committee of the Congress on the conduct of the war, a member of the board of war and signed the Articles of Confederation in 1778.

A prolific writer, Witherspoon coined the term "Americanism" in an article in 1781 discussing differences between the American and English language. As leader of the Presbyterian Church in America, he presided over the first general assembly of Presbyterians in 1789. After the death of his first wife, the sixty-eight-year-old Witherspoon married a twenty-three-year-old widow. Blind for the last two years of his life, Witherspoon died at his farm, "Tusculum," near Princeton, New Jersey, on November 15, 1794.

• OLIVER WOLCOTT   1726–1797

An active major general of militia in the Revolutionary War, a signer of the Declaration of Independence, and a governor of Connecticut, Oliver Wolcott was born in Windsor, Connecticut, on December 1, 1726, the youngest son of Roger Wolcott, who was colonial governor of Connecticut in 1751–54. After graduation from Yale College in 1747, Oliver Wolcott was commissioned a captain by the governor of New York in 1747, raised a company of volunteers, and served on the northwestern frontier in King George's War. After returning to Connecticut in 1748, he studied medicine but did not practice. He was elected sheriff of the newly organized county of Litchfield, Connecticut, in 1751. He was elected to the state council 1774–86 and at the same time was judge of the county court of common pleas and judge of probate for Litchfield. Wolcott was chosen as a delegate to the Continental Congress in 1775–78 and 1780–84, but was absent much of the time on military duty as major general in charge of Connecticut's militia. He was absent during the debates on the Declaration of Independence, but signed it in September 1776. Wolcott led fourteen Connecticut regiments to the defense of New York in 1776, and commanded a brigade of militia that took part in the defeat of General Burgoyne at Saratoga in 1777.

After the war, Wolcott served ten years as lieutenant governor of Connecticut 1786–96, and then was elected governor, serving in that office from 1796 until his death in Litchfield on December 1, 1797. His older brother, Erastus Wolcott (1722–1793), served as a militia brigadier general in the Revolutionary War and later was a justice of the Connecticut

Oliver Wolcott

Carpenters' Hall,
meeting place of the first Continental Congress,
September 1774

supreme court. His son, Oliver Wolcott, Jr. (1760–1833), was Secretary of the Treasury of the United States in 1795–1800 and governor of Connecticut 1817–27.

• JOSEPH WOOD   1712–1791

An officer in the Revolutionary War and a delegate to the Continental Congress, Joseph Wood was born in Pennsylvania in 1712. When in his sixties, Wood moved to Sunbury, St. John's Parish (afterward Liberty County), Georgia. At the outbreak of the Revolutionary War he returned to Pennsylvania to serve as a major, lieutenant colonel, and colonel of the 2nd Pennsylvania Battalion, which later became the 3rd Pennsylvania Regiment fighting in Canada in 1776. Upon his return to Georgia, he was chosen as a delegate to the Continental Congress 1777–78. Wood died on his plantation near Sunbury in September 1791.

• WILLIAM WOODFORD   1734–1780

A Continental Army general who died while imprisoned by the British, William Woodford was born in Carolina County, Virginia in 1735. While in his twenties he served as a militia officer in the French and Indian War. He and Patrick Henry were colonels in command of Virginia's two militia regiments at the beginning of the Revolutionary War, and as such he had a leading part in the various skirmishes and confrontations that drove the royal British governor, Lord Dunmore, out of Virginia. In 1777 he was commissioned a brigadier general in the Continental Army commanding the 1st Virginia Brigade. He fought in the battles of Brandywine and Germantown in 1777 and in the battle of Monmouth in 1778. In 1780 he marched his brigade south to the relief of Charleston, South Carolina, traveling about five hundred miles in less than a month. When the British forced Charleston to surrender in May 1780, Woodford was taken prisoner. Taken to New York City for his imprisonment, he died there on November 13, 1780.

• TURBUTT WRIGHT   1741–1783

A Maryland delegate to the Continental Congress, Turbutt Wright was born at "White Marsh," near Chester Mills (now Centerville), Maryland, on February 5, 1741. A planter, he was a member of the general assembly of Maryland in 1773–74, and a signer of the Association of Freemen of Maryland on July 26, 1775. He was elected to the Maryland constitutional convention in 1776, and was a member of the Maryland council of safety in 1777. He represented Maryland in the Continental Congress 1781–82. Wright died on his estate, "White Marsh," in 1783.

• HENRY WYNKOOP   1737–1816

A delegate to the Continental Congress and one of Pennsylvania's first U.S. Congressmen, Henry Wynkoop was born in Northampton Township, Bucks County, Pennsylvania, on March 2, 1737. After studying law, he became at the age of twenty-seven a justice of the Bucks County court in 1764 and served on that court for most of the remaining fifty-two years of his life except for the two years he was a U.S. Congressman. Wynkoop was a delegate to the provincial Revolutionary conferences of 1774–75, and of the general committee of safety in 1776–77. He represented Pennsylvania in the Continental Congress from 1779 to 1783, and was elected to the First U.S. Congress 1789–91. He then resumed his seat on the Bucks County court until his death in that county on March 25, 1816.

Henry Wynkoop

421

At Jamestown when the settlers arrived, the most available material for constructing suitable cabins was the combination of timber and tall grasses.

• GEORGE WYTHE   1726–1806

The man who taught Thomas Jefferson his law and therefore took special pride in signing the Declaration of Independence, George Wythe was born near Back River, Virginia, in 1726. After attending the College of William and Mary, he studied law and commenced practice in Elizabeth City County in 1755. He was elected to the Virginia house of burgesses 1758–68, and then served as clerk of that legislative body 1768–75. He gained a reputation as the best lawyer in Virginia, and taught many young men their law, including Thomas Jefferson, John Marshall, James Monroe, and Henry Clay.

Wythe represented Virginia in the Continental Congress 1775–77. He was absent in Virginia writing a state constitution during the debates on the Declaration of Independence, but returned in August to sign the document. He became the first professor of law in the United States at the College of William and Mary, serving from 1779 to 1791, when he resigned and moved to Richmond, Virginia. He conducted a private law school in Richmond, where he continued teaching until his death. He was one of Virginia's delegates to the federal Constitutional Convention in 1787, where he prepared the rules for the convention, but returned to Virginia before the United States Constitution was completed and signed.

As a Democratic-Republican presidential elector in 1800 and 1804 he had the pleasure of helping twice elect his former student Jefferson as President. From 1786, Wythe served for twenty years as chancellor of the state of Virginia. He died at the age of eighty in Richmond on June 8, 1806, from drinking a cup of coffee believed to have been poisoned by his only heir, a grandnephew.

George Wythe

• ABRAHAM YATES   1724–1796

The first chief executive of the state of New York and a delegate to the Continental Congress, Abraham Yates was born in Albany, New York, on August 23, 1724. He was sheriff of Albany County 1755–59. As president of the New York provincial Revolutionary congresses 1775–77, he was the first chief executive of New York during the Revolutionary War. He then was elected to the new New York state senate 1778–90. He was appointed by Congress as the first postmaster of Albany in 1783. Yates represented New York in the Continental Congress in 1787–88, and then was elected mayor of Albany in 1790, an office he held until his death on June 30, 1796, in Albany.

• PETER WALDRON YATES   1747–1826

A New York delegate to the Continental Congress, Peter Waldron Yates was born in Albany, New York, on August 23, 1747, a nephew of Abraham Yates. After studying law, he commenced practice in Albany. He was a member of the Albany committee on correspondence in 1775. He was elected to the state assembly in 1784–85, and represented New York in the Continental Congress 1785–87. Yates died in Caughnawaga, New York, on March 9, 1826.

• JOHN JOACHIM ZUBLY   1724–1781

A Georgia clergyman and delegate to the Continental Congress who turned traitor, John Joachim Zubly was born in St. Gall, Switzerland, on August 27, 1724. He immigrated to America as a boy, becoming a clerk in Wando Neck, South Carolina. At the age of twenty he was ordained to the ministry in 1744. He became the first pastor of the Presbyterian Church in Savannah in 1760. Zubly took a prominent part in the early Revolutionary movement. He served in the Revolutionary provincial congress of Georgia in 1775, and was sent as a representative to the Continental Congress. In November 1775, Samuel Chase, the firebrand delegate of Maryland, discovered that Zubly was sending secret reports to the royal governor of Georgia Sir James Wright. Chase denounced Zubly as a traitor on the floor of Congress, but the clergyman escaped before he could be arrested for treason, and sought protection by the British. The patriots of Georgia ordered Zubly banished from the state and confiscated half his property. In 1779 Zubly returned to Georgia and resumed pastoral duties in British-occupied Savannah, where he died on July 23, 1781.

By the UNITED STATES of America, in Congress assembled.

A PROCLAMATION,

Declaring the Cessation of Arms, as well by Sea as by Land, agreed upon between the United States of America and His Britannic Majesty; and enjoining the Observance thereof.

WHEREAS Provisional Articles were signed at Paris, on the Thirtieth Day of November last, between the Ministers Plenipotentiary of the United States of America, for treating of Peace, and the Minister Plenipotentiary of His Britannic Majesty, to be inserted in and to constitute the Treaty of Peace, proposed to be concluded between the United States of America and His Britannic Majesty, when Terms of Peace should be agreed upon between their Most Christian and Britannic Majesties: And whereas Preliminaries, for restoring Peace between their Most Christian and Britannic Majesties, were signed at Versailles, on the Twentieth Day of January last, by the Ministers of their Most Christian and Britannic Majesties: And whereas Preliminaries, for restoring Peace between the said King of Great-Britain and the King of Spain, were also signed at Versailles, on the same Twentieth Day of January last.

By which said Preliminary Articles it hath been agreed, That as soon as the same were ratified, Hostilities between the said Kings, their Kingdoms, States and Subjects, should cease in all Parts of the World; and it was farther agreed, That all Vessels and Effects that might be taken in the Channel and in the North Seas, after the Space of Twelve Days from the Ratification of the said Preliminary Articles, should be restored; that the Term should be One Month from the Channel and North Seas as far as the Canary Islands inclusively, whether in the Ocean or the Mediterranean; Two Months from the said Canary Islands as far as the Equinoctial Line or Equator; and lastly, Five Months in all other Parts of the World, without any Exception, or more particular Description of Time or Place: And whereas it was declared, by the Minister Plenipotentiary of the King of Great-Britain, in the Name and by the express Order of the King his Master, on the said Twentieth Day of January last, that the said United States of America, their Subjects and their Possessions, shall be comprised in the above mentioned Suspension of Arms, at the same Epochs, and in the same Manner, as the Three Crowns above mentioned, their Subjects and Possessions respectively; upon Condition that, on the Part and in the Name of the United States of America, a similar Declaration shall be delivered, expressly declaring their Assent to the said Suspension of Arms, and containing an Assurance of the most perfect Reciprocity on their Part: And whereas the Ministers Plenipotentiary of these United States did, on the same Twentieth Day of January, in the Name and by the Authority of the said United States, accept the said Declaration, and declare, that the said States should cause all Hostilities to cease against His Britannic Majesty, his Subjects and his Possessions, at the Terms and Epochs agreed upon between His said Majesty the King of Great-Britain, His Majesty the King of France, and His Majesty the King of Spain, so and in the same Manner as had been agreed upon between those Three Crowns, and to produce the same Effects: And whereas the Ratifications of the said Preliminary Articles between their Most Christian and Britannic Majesties were exchanged by their Ministers on the Third Day of February last, and between His Britannic Majesty and the King of Spain on the Ninth Day of February last: And whereas it is Our Will and Pleasure, that the Cessation of Hostilities between the United States of America and His Britannic Majesty should be conformable to the Epochs fixed between their Most Christian and Britannic Majesties:

We have thought fit to make known the same to the Citizens of these States, and We hereby strictly charge and command all Our Officers, both by Sea and Land, and others, Subjects of these United States, to forbear all Acts of Hostility, either by Sea or Land, against His Britannic Majesty or his Subjects, from and after the respective Times agreed upon between their Most Christian and Britannic Majesties as aforesaid.

And We do further require all Governors and others, the Executive Powers of these United States respectively, to cause this Our Proclamation to be made public, to the End that the same may be duly observed within their several Jurisdictions.

DONE in Congress, at Philadelphia, this Eleventh Day of April, in the Year of Our Lord One Thousand Seven Hundred and Eighty-three, and of Our Sovereignty and Independence the Seventh.

ELIAS BOUDINOT, President.

Attest. CHARLES THOMSON, Sec'ry.

State of RHODE-ISLAND and PROVIDENCE PLANTATIONS.

Providence, April 22, 1783.

THE preceding is a true Copy of the Original, lodged upon File in my Office, which is published and transmitted to the several Town Clerks by Order of his Excellency the Governor, that the same may be made known to the Inhabitants.

WITNESS, *Henry Ward, Sec'ry*

PROVIDENCE: Printed by JOHN CARTER.

Kay Smith